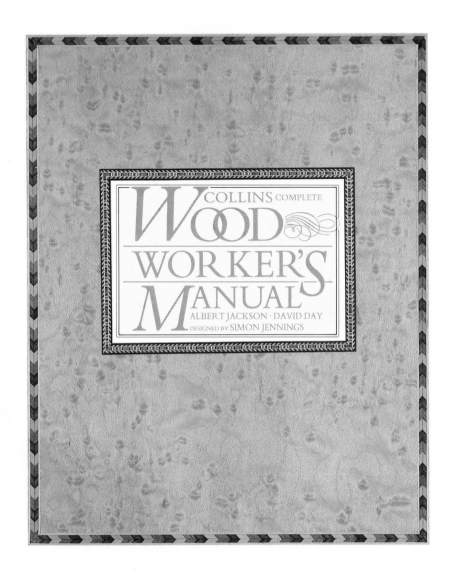

COLLINS COMPLETE

WOOD
WORKER'S
MANUAL

ALBERT JACKSON · DAVID DAY

DESIGNED BY SIMON JENNINGS

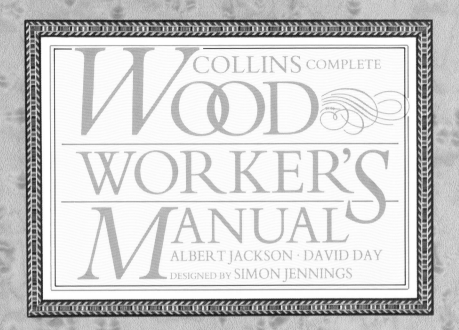

COLLINS COMPLETE

WOOD

WORKER'S

MANUAL

ALBERT JACKSON · DAVID DAY

DESIGNED BY SIMON JENNINGS

HarperCollins*Publishers*

TITLE PAGE & CHAPTER-OPENER PANELS MADE OF
SYCAMORE (OUTER BORDER) & BIRD'S-EYE MAPLE (CENTRE PANEL)
TEXT SET IN 8½ ON 9PT TIMES NEW ROMAN
HEADLINES SET IN 28PT GOUDY HANDTOOLED
DISPLAY SETTING IN 48PT, 42PT & 12PT BEMBO ROMAN & ITALICS
CONCEIVED, EDITED & DESIGNED BY INKLINK

THE COLLINS COMPLETE WOODWORKER'S MANUAL
WAS CREATED EXCLUSIVELY FOR WILLIAM COLLINS SONS &
CO. LTD BY INKLINK AND PRODUCED AT 1-3 HIGHBRIDGE
WHARF GREENWICH LONDON SE10 9PS ENGLAND. THE TEXT
WAS WRITTEN BY ALBERT JACKSON & DAVID DAY
AND EDITED BY PETER LEEK. THE BOOK WAS DESIGNED
AND ART DIRECTED BY SIMON JENNINGS. THE PAGE
LAYOUTS WERE DESIGNED AND ASSEMBLED BY ALAN
MARSHALL. ORIGINAL COLOUR PHOTOGRAPHY NEIL
WAVING. LINE ILLUSTRATIONS BY ROBIN HARRIS &
DAVID DAY. DESIGN-SKETCH-BOOK DRAWINGS BY ALBERT
JACKSON. WOODS & WOOD-FINISH EXAMPLES PREPARED BY
DAVID DAY. JOINT-MAKING EXAMPLES BY WILLIAM
BROOKER. TITLE PANELS VENEER & INLAY WORK BY
DESMOND RYAN. SPECIAL WOODCARVING EXAMPLES
BY MARCUS CORNISH AND DAVID DAY. TYPESETTING BY
VICTOR CHAMBERS AND ANTONY WALLACE. COLOUR
ORIGINATION BY BRIGHT ARTS HONGKONG. PRINTED &
BOUND BY WILLIAM COLLINS SONS & COMPANY LTD GLASGOW.

FIRST PUBLISHED IN 1989 BY
WILLIAM COLLINS SONS & CO. LTD
LONDON · TORONTO · SYDNEY · AUCKLAND · JOHANNESBURG
COPYRIGHT © 1989 WILLIAM COLLINS SONS & CO. LTD
EXECUTIVE EDITOR FOR COLLINS ROBIN WOOD

COLLINS COMPLETE WOODWORKER'S MANUAL IS
PUBLISHED IN ASSOCIATION WITH BOSCH POWER TOOLS

FIRST PUBLISHED IN 1989
REPRINTED IN 1989, 1990 (TWICE), 1991 (TWICE)
BRITISH LIBRARY CATALOGUING IN PUBLICATION DATA
JACKSON, ALBERT, 1943–
COLLINS COMPLETE WOODWORKER'S MANUAL
1. WOODWORKING MANUALS
I. TITLE. II. DAY, DAVID, 1944–
648'.08
ISBN 0-00-411565-1

INTRODUCTION

In our everyday lives we are all surrounded by timber structures and wooden commodities. Our homes and workplaces are partially or even wholly constructed from timber; we frequently eat, sleep and work with wooden furniture and utensils; our children are raised with wooden playthings; and even as adults wood supplies our recreational needs in the form of sports equipment or games boards and pieces. In short, wood is so commonplace we invariably take it for granted. And yet once its special beauty has been revealed to anyone working it with blade or cutter, wood is anything but ordinary. Wood has lasting qualities like no other material – it is both warm and pleasing to the touch and its wealth of colour and texture is a delight to the eye. Indeed, the nature of wood is such that it imparts a uniqueness to every single workpiece – something that cannot be said of even precious metals. Together with other concerned woodworkers around the world, we are acutely aware that certain woods are now a diminishing resource. Responsible action must be taken to preserve what remains of the world's rainforests and to replant native hardwood trees that are becoming rarer year by year. It is imperative that we take steps to protect and replace the sources of our precious raw material if future generations of woodworkers are to inherit the same privileges we enjoy today. We fully support those individuals and agencies dedicated to that end.

Albert Jackson   David J. Day

CONTENTS

CONTENTS

INKLINK ARE ALSO GRATEFUL TO THE FOLLOWING INDIVIDUALS AND
ORGANIZATIONS FOR THEIR CONTRIBUTIONS & ASSISTANCE:- FOR THE SUPPLY OF
WOOD SAMPLES: C. F. ANDERSON & SON LTD., ANNANDALE TIMBER &
MOULDING CO. PTY. LTD., THE ART VENEER CO. LTD., JOHN BODDY'S FINE WOOD
& TOOL STORE LTD., EGGER LTD., FIDOR, GENERAL WOODWORKING SUPPLIES,
HIGHLAND FOREST PRODUCTS PLC, E. JONES & SON, LIMEHOUSE TIMBER, RAVENS-
BOURNE COLLEGE OF DESIGN AND COMMUNICATION, SEABOARD INTER-
NATIONAL LTD., F. R. SHADBOLT & SONS LTD. HANDTOOLS: THE ART
VENEER CO. LTD., JOHN BODDY'S FINE WOOD & TOOL COMPANY LTD., BURTON
McCALL LTD., E. C. EMMERICH, GARRETT WADE CO. LTD., GEORGE HIGGINS LTD.,
RECORD MARPLES LTD., SKARSTEN MANUFACTURING CO. LTD., ALEC TIRANTI
LTD., TOOLMAIL LTD. POWER TOOLS: THE BLACK & DECKER CORPORATION,
BLACK & DECKER PROFESSIONAL PRODUCTS DIVISION, ROBERT BOSCH LTD., LEROY
SOMER ELECTRIC MOTORS LTD., M & M DISTRIBUTORS LTD. MACHINE TOOLS:
BLACK & DECKER PROFESSIONAL PRODUCTS DIVISION, CORONET LATHE AND TOOL
CO., HEGNER LTD., RECORD MARPLES LTD., ROBERT SORBY LTD., STARTRITE
MACHINE TOOL CO. LTD., TYME MACHINES LTD., WARREN MACHINE TOOLS LTD.
BENCHES & ACCESSORIES: EMMERICH (BERLON) LTD. WOOD FINISHES:
ENGLISH ABRASIVES & CHEMICALS LTD., GRACO LTD., RUSTINS LTD., JOHN
MYLAND LTD. FIXINGS & FITTINGS: EUROPEAN INDUSTRIAL SERVICES LTD.,
JOHN MYLAND LTD., WOODFIT LTD. ILLUSTRATION P. 10 MICHAEL WOODS.
DRAWING EQUIPMENT P. 74 GELLIOT WHITMAN. ADDITIONAL REFERENCE
SUPPLIED BY: ADVANCED MACHINERY IMPORTS LTD., AMERICAN PLYWOOD
ASSOCIATION, AUSTRALIAN PARTICLEBOARD RESEARCH INSTITUTE INC., P & J DUST
EXTRACTION LTD., BORDEN LTD., CIBA-GEIGY PLASTICS, CLICO TOOLING LTD.,
COUNCIL OF FOREST INDUSTRIES OF BRITISH COLUMBIA, DUNLOP ADHESIVES,
EURO MODELS, EVODE LTD., FELDER WOODWORKING MACHINES, FINNISH
PLYWOOD INTERNATIONAL, WALTER FISCHER, FURNITURE INDUSTRY RESEARCH
ASSOCIATION, LOUISIANA-PACIFIC, LUNA TOOLS AND MACHINERY LTD.,
MICROFLAME LTD., THEODOR NAGEL (G.M.B.H. & CO.), IAN & BETTY NORBURY –
THE WHITE KNIGHT GALLERY, PLYWOOD ASSOCIATION OF AUSTRALIA LTD., RYOBI
LTD., TIMBER DEVELOPMENT ASSOCIATION (N.S.W.) LTD., TIMBER RESEARCH
AND DEVELOPMENT ASSOCIATION, TIMBER TRADE FEDERATION, JOHN TIRANTI,
U.S. FOREST PRODUCTS LABORATORY, VEREIN DEUTSCHER HOLZEINFUHRHÄUSER
e.V., WOODWORKING MACHINES OF SWITZERLAND LTD., CARL ZEISS JENA LTD.
SPECIAL CONSULTANTS: FREDERICK SPALDING – MACHINE TOOLS. LES REED –
VENEERING & MARQUETRY. JOHN PERKINS – OTHER MATERIALS. JIM CUMMINS,
U.S. CONSULTANT. INDEX COMPILED BY JILL FORD. PROOFREAD BY PHILIP HIND.
DESIGNER-MAKERS: ASHLEY CARTWRIGHT PAGES 43BL; 45TR. CHRIS AUGER
PAGE 44TR. DAVID COLWELL PAGE 49BR. DAVID FIELD PAGE 48TL, TR. DAVID PYE
PAGE 45C. DEREK PEARCE PAGE 48B. DESMOND RYAN PAGES 44B; 45BL. GORDON
RUSSELL PAGE 46TR. HUGH SCRIVEN PAGES 45TL; 47CR; 49TL, TR. HUW DAVIES PAGE
46CR. IAN NORBURY PAGES 275; 281TL. JANE CLEAL PAGE 42BL, BC. MATTHEW
MORRIS PAGE 49CR. MIKE SCOTT PAGE 47B. NICHOLAS DYSON PAGES 47TL, TR; 49CL.
PAUL PHILLIPS PAGE 49BL. RICHARD LA TROBE-BATEMAN PAGE 42BR. ROBERT
WILLIAMS PAGES 41B; 46BR. ROD WALES PAGES 45BR; 46TL, BL. STEPHEN HOUNSLOW
PAGE 47CL. STEWART LINFORD PAGE 41T. STUART GROVES PAGE 44TL. ALL
PHOTOGRAPHS BY INKLINK EXCEPT: BLACK & DECKER PROFESSIONAL
PRODUCTS DIVISION PAGE 187. BUCKINGHAMSHIRE COLLEGE OF HIGHER
EDUCATION PAGES 42BL, BC; 46TR; 49CR, BL. CARTWRIGHT DESIGNS PAGES 43BL;
45TR. DAVID FIELD PAGE 48TL, TR. GEORG OTT WERKZEUG-UND MASCHINEN-
FABRIK GMBH & CO. PAGE 212BR. HUGH SCRIVEN PAGES 45TL; 47CR; 49TL, TR.
KODAMA WOODWORK PAGE 46CR. NICHOLAS DYSON FURNITURE LTD. PAGES 47TL,
TR; 49CL. PEARL DOT LTD. PAGES 41B; 46BR. RICHARD LA TROBE-BATEMAN PAGE
42BR. ROBERT BOSCH LTD: PAGE 149TR. ROD WALES PAGE 46TL. THEO BERGSTROM
PAGE 41T. TRANNON FURNITURE PAGE 49BR. WARREN MACHINE TOOLS LTD. PAGES
186, 188, 190, 191. WOODWORKER MAGAZINE PAGE 44TR.

KEY TO PHOTOGRAPHIC CREDITS: L = LEFT, R = RIGHT, T = TOP, TL = TOP LEFT, TR =
TOP RIGHT, C = CENTRE, UC = UPPER CENTRE, LC = LOWER CENTRE, CL = CENTRE
LEFT, CR = CENTRE RIGHT, B = BOTTOM, BL = BOTTOM LEFT, BR = BOTTOM RIGHT,
BC = BOTTOM CENTRE.

WOOD

The diversity of colour and texture and the physical properties of stiffness or bendability and of strength in proportion to weight give each species of timber a character of its own, offering both a challenge and a source of inspiration to the creative woodworker. The antiquity of woodworking techniques is reflected in the design and construction of buildings and furniture over the centuries, yet despite its traditional links with the past wood is also very much a modern material. It is being used at a greater rate today than ever before and, thanks to modern manufacturing methods, new composite wood-based materials are constantly being developed, further expanding its versatility and range of applications. A selection

THE RAW MATERIAL

of softwoods and hardwoods from all over the world and manufactured materials in the form of veneers and man-made boards are illustrated in the following pages and their characteristics described.

HOW TREES GROW

Trees are undeniably a valuable source of wealth, but they are not valuable in the same way gold is. Although it could be argued that wood is as beautiful and desirable as any precious metal, the great value
of trees lies in their being a renewable resource. Nor, historically, has any other material been so adaptable and of such immeasurable benefit to mankind as wood with its infinite variety of types and uses.

THE LIVING TREE

In order to appreciate the properties of wood and how it is worked and finished, it is worthwhile understanding something of the way trees grow.

Trees form an important division of the plant kingdom known as the Spermatophyta (seed bearing plants). This division is subdivided into Gymnospermae and Angiospermae. Gymnosperms are needle-leaved coniferous trees commonly referred to as softwoods. Angiosperms are broadleaved trees known as hardwoods and may be either deciduous or evergreen.

The structure of a tree
A typical tree has a main stem, known as the bole or trunk, which carries a crown of leaf-bearing branches. A root system anchors the tree in the ground and absorbs water and minerals to sustain the tree. The trunk carries the sap from the roots via the cell system to the leaves.

The structure of wood
Wood is a mass of cellulose tubular cells bonded together with an organic chemical called lignin. The cells vary in size and shape, but are generally long and thin and run longitudinally with the main axis of the tree's trunk or branches. It is this orientation of the cells that produces the direction of the grain.

Cells provide support for the tree, circulation of sap and food storage. Softwoods or conifers have a simple cell structure composed mainly of tracheid (fibrelike) cells which provide initial sap conduction and physical support. They form regular radiating rows and make up the main body of the tree.

Hardwoods or deciduous trees have fewer tracheids than softwoods and have vessels or pores that conduct sap and fibres which provide support. It is this cell specialization that enables cut wood to be identified as a softwood or hardwood. The size and distribution of the cells vary from species to species, producing fine-textured or coarse-textured wood.

A tree grows by an annual deposition of cells formed by the cambium layer. This is the thin layer of active living cells between the bark and the wood. During the growing period the cells subdivide to form new wood on the inner side and phloem or bast (tissue that conducts synthesized food to all parts of the plant) on the outside.

As the girth of the tree increases, the old bark splits and new bark is formed. The new wood cells develop into specialized cells to form sapwood. Sapwood is made up partly of living food-storage cells and partly of non-living cells which are capable of conducting sap up the tree and do not store food.

Leaf-bearing branches
The leaves produce nutrients to feed the tree by photosynthesis.

Angiosperms
Broadleaved trees.

Gymnosperms
Needle-leaved trees.

Trunk
The trunk supports the leaf-bearing branches and is the main source of wood.

Root system
The roots that anchor the tree also absorb water and minerals from the ground.

Food storage
Evaporation from the leaves draws the sap through minute cells which form the structure of the tree. Carbon dioxide in the air is taken in by the tree through pores in the leaves known as stomata. The food produced by the leaves is dispersed to the growing parts of the tree as well as being stored by some of the cells.

Photosynthesis
Photosynthesis (a reaction of organic compounds from carbon dioxide and water) takes place when energy in the form of light is absorbed by chlorophyll, the green pigment present in leaves, to produce the nutrients on which a tree lives. As a by-product of this process, oxygen is given off to the atmosphere.

In addition to cells following the axis of the trunk, there are ray cells radiating from the centre of the tree. These carry and store nutrients horizontally through the sapwood. Ray cells form flat vertical bands which are hardly visible in softwoods but plainly obvious in some hardwoods, such as oak, when they are quarter-sawn.

As the tree grows, a new ring of sapwood is built up around the previous year's growth. The oldest sapwood is now no longer used to conduct water, and gradual chemical changes convert it into heartwood to form the structural spine of the tree. In this way the heartwood increases in area, while the thickness of the sapwood remains relatively constant throughout the tree's life.

Sapwood and heartwood

Sapwood is light in colour and is usually recognizable by its contrast with the darker heartwood. The colour difference is not so marked on light-coloured woods, particularly the softwoods. Sapwood is inferior to heartwood and is usually cut to waste by furniture-makers. It is not so resistant to fungal decay, and it is also prone to beetle attack because of the carbohydrates stored in some of the cells. The relatively thin-walled cells are porous and give up moisture quickly. As a result, sapwood shrinks more than the denser heartwood. However, its porosity allows stains and preservatives to be readily absorbed.

Since heartwood is the inner part of the maturing tree and is formed from old sapwood, it plays no active part in the growth of the tree. Hence the dead cells can become blocked with organic material, causing the cell walls to change colour through the presence of chemical substances called extractives. The extractives are responsible for the rich colours found in many hardwoods. They also impart a measure of resistance to fungus and insect attack.

Earlywood and latewood

As with many plants, the way trees grow depends on climatic conditions. In a temperate climate there is generally rapid growth in the spring, less in summer and no new growth in winter.

Earlywood or springwood is, as the name implies, the part of the annual growth ring laid down in the early part of the growing season. Thin-walled tracheid cells in softwoods and open tube-like vessels in hardwoods form the bulk of the earlywood to facilitate the rapid conduction of sap. Earlywood can usually be recognized as the wider band of paler-coloured wood in each annual growth ring.

Latewood or summerwood is the part of the annual ring that develops in the latter part of the growing season and produces thicker-walled cells, creating denser and usually darker wood which is less able to conduct sap but adds support to the tree.

This distinct banding corresponds to one season's growth, so reveals the age of the felled tree and the kind of climatic conditions in which it has grown. Wide annual rings indicate good growing conditions, narrow ones poor or drought conditions.

The difference in texture between earlywood and latewood is of importance to the woodworker since it can render a wood more or less difficult to work. The lighter-weight earlywood is easier to cut than the denser latewood. This is not a particular problem for most hand and machine processes, providing the tools' cutting edges are sharp.

However, the difference in hardness can show where latewood is left proud of earlywood after finishing with a sander. Generally, woods with even-textured growth rings are the easiest to work and finish.

The distribution of hardwood cells has a marked effect on the texture of the wood. 'Ring-porous' hardwoods such as oak or ash have clearly defined rings of large vessels in the earlywood, and dense fibres and cell tissue in the latewood. These woods are more difficult to finish than 'diffuse-porous' woods, such as beech, which have vessels and fibres distributed relatively evenly. Although woods like mahogany are often diffuse-porous, their larger cells can make them coarse-textured.

Earlywood and latewood

Ring-porous wood

Diffuse-porous wood

● **Cambium layer**
A thin layer of living cell tissue that forms the new wood and bark.

● **Sapwood**
The new wood, the cells of which conduct or store nutrients.

● **Heartwood**
The mature wood that forms the spine of the tree.

● **Pith**
The central core of cells. Often weak and suffers from fungus attack.

● **Growth ring**
The layer of wood which is formed in one growing period. Large earlywood and smaller latewood cells make up the annual growth ring.

● **Ray cells**
Radiating sheets of cells that conduct nutrients horizontally, also known as 'medullary rays'.

● **Phloem or bast**
The inner bark tissue that conducts synthesized food.

● **Bark**
The outer protective layer of dead cells. The term can also include the living inner tissue.

CONVERTING WOOD

It takes many years, hundreds in the case of some species, for a tree to grow to a commercially viable size. Yet with modern forestry methods straight-growing trees such as pine can be cut down, topped and debarked in a matter of minutes. Since conifers are relatively fast-growing, with careful husbandry it *is possible to control supply and demand of softwoods. It is a sad fact, however, that the forests of the world are being depleted – particularly of the slow-growing hardwoods, which are becoming increasingly scarce, though most specialist suppliers stock small pieces of exotic woods.*

THE CONVERSION PROCESS

Most commercial wood is cut from the trunk of the tree. Some larger limbs may also be cut into logs, but branch material usually has asymmetric growth rings that produce unstable 'reaction' wood, which warps and splits easily. Reaction wood is formed in limbs or trunks which do not grow upright. In softwoods the growth is mainly on the underside and produces 'compression wood'; in hardwoods it forms on the upper side and is known as 'tension wood'.

Felled trees are cut into logs or butts and transported to local sawmills for conversion into rough-sawn timber; the *trimmings are usually made into paper products and manufactured boards. Exporters of timber may deal in whole or sawn logs, or both. But the producers of some exotic hardwoods, in Peninsular Malaysia, Indonesia, the Philippines and Brazil, for example, now trade in sawn wood only. This is in a quest to protect their trees from overcutting and also to provide employment for their people and an increase in revenue. The top-quality logs with large even boles command high prices and are usually converted into veneer.*

Planes of reference
The terms refer to the direction of the cut in relation to the growth rings.

Types of cut
1 Plain-sawn
2 Rift-sawn
3 Quarter-sawn

Milling

Today most logs are converted into sawn timber by band-saw or circular-saw machines. Before the machine age this task was achieved by hand, using the pitsaw technique. A large two-man saw was used, with one sawyer in a pit below the log and the other standing on top of it. Pushing and pulling the saw between them, they would gradually convert the log into boards or beams.

The main types of cut produced by modern methods are known as 'plain-sawn' and 'quarter-sawn'. Plain-sawn boards are broadly those where the growth rings meet the face of the board at an angle of less than 45 degrees. Quarter-sawn is broadly defined as timber which has the growth rings at not less than 45 degrees to the face of the board.

Within both these categories other terms may be used. Plain-sawn timber can be known as flat-sawn, flat-grain or slash-sawn; and quarter-sawn as rift-sawn, comb-grain, edge-grain and vertical-grain.

In America, plain-sawn boards are those where the growth rings meet the face at an angle of less than 30 degrees. Those where the rings meet at more than 30 degrees but at less than 60 degrees are known as rift-sawn boards.

True quarter-sawn boards are cut radially with the annual rings perpendicular to the board's face, but in practice all boards with rings at an angle of not less than 60 degrees are classified as quarter-sawn.

Plain-sawn boards are cut on a tangent to the annual-growth rings and display a decorative and distinctive elliptical figure.

Rift-sawn boards display a straight figure with some ray-cell patterning, and are sometimes referred to as comb-grain.

Quarter-sawing reveals a straight figure crossed with the ribbon-like or 'flake' figure found in hardwoods such as oak.

Converting a log

The stability and figure of the wood are determined by the plane of the saw in relation to the annual growth rings. The most economical method for converting a log is to cut it 'through and through' (1). This process makes parallel cuts through the length of the log and produces plain-sawn, rift-sawn and a small percentage of quarter-sawn boards. Plain-sawn logs are cut partly through and through, and produce a mixture of plain-sawn and rift-sawn boards (2).

Converting a log to produce quarter-sawn boards can be done in a number of ways. The ideal is to cut each board parallel with the rays, like the radiating spokes of a wheel, but this method is wasteful and not used commercially. The conventional method, albeit a compromise, is to cut the log into quarters and then cut each quadrant into boards (3). Commercial quarter-sawing first cuts the log into thick slices, which are then converted into quartered boards (4).

To select quarter-sawn wood, look at the end grain. Choose boards which have the growth rings at about 90 degrees to the surface. Not all merchants will allow you to select random boards. In any case, expect selected boards to be more expensive.

1 Through and through

2 Plain-sawn

3 Quarter-sawn

4 Quarter-sawn

DRYING WOOD

Green wood newly cut from a log contains a very high percentage of moisture. The cell walls are saturated and free water is held by the cell cavities. Drying or 'seasoning' wood is the process of removing the free water and much of the bound moisture from the cell walls. As the wood dries, free water is lost from the cell cavities until only the cell walls contain moisture. This is known as the fibre-saturation point and occurs at about 30 per cent moisture content, depending on species. It is when moisture starts to be lost from the cell walls that shrinkage begins. The loss of water will stop when it is in balance with the relative humidity of its surroundings. This is known as the equilibrium moisture content (EMC).

It is most important that the seasoning process is carried out properly, in order to prevent stresses being created within the wood and to ensure that the EMC is at the appropriate level to avoid problems with swelling and shrinkage.

BUILDING-BLOCK WEIGHTS
STICKERS
COVER (MAN-MADE BOARD)
BUILDING-BLOCK SUPPORTS
WOODEN BEAMS
BOARDS

Air-drying at home
Construct an even stack of 'stickered' boards for air to pass through.

Air-drying
Air-drying is the traditional method for seasoning wood. The boards are stacked evenly on spacer battens, or 'stickers', which are 25mm (1in) square and are spaced 450mm (18in) apart. The stacks are usually built well clear of the ground in a sheltered position and are protected from rain and direct sunlight. The natural airflow through the stack gradually dries the wood. As a rough guide, it takes about one year to dry every 25mm (1in) thickness for hardwoods and about half that time for softwoods.

This method is inexpensive but can only reduce the moisture content to about 14 to 16 per cent, depending on the relative humidity. For interior use, the wood needs further drying in a kiln or is left to dry naturally in the environment in which it is to be used.

Kiln-drying
Wood for interior use needs a moisture content of about 8 to 10 per cent, or possibly lower, depending on the humidity of the location.

Kiln-drying is used commercially to reduce the moisture content of the wood below air-dry level, and only takes a matter of days. The boards are loaded onto trolleys in stickered stacks and rolled into the kiln, where a carefully controlled mixture of hot air and steam is pumped through the piled wood and the humidity is gradually reduced to a specified moisture content according to the species of wood being dried. Wood dried below air-dry level will try to take up moisture if left exposed – so, where possible, keep kiln-dried wood in the environment in which it is to be used.

Stability
When wood dries, it shrinks. The shape of the board can change or 'move' as shrinkage takes place. In general, the shrinkage along the line of the annual rings amounts to approximately twice the shrinkage across them. Tangentially cut plain-sawn boards therefore shrink more in their width. Quarter-sawn boards shrink only slightly in their width and very little in their thickness.

Shrinkage movement can also cause some distortion. The concentric growth rings of a tangentially cut plain-sawn board run approxi-mately edge to edge and differ in length. The longer outer rings shrink more than the inner rings, resulting in a tendency for the board to bend, or 'cup', across its width. Square sections of wood are liable to become parallelograms, and round sections to become oval.

The growth rings of a quartered board run from face to face and, being virtually the same length, suffer little or no distortion. This stability, coupled with an even-wearing surface, makes quartered boards the preferred type for flooring and furniture-making.

Shrinkage movement
Sections of wood will distort differently depending on orientation of the growth rings.

Commercial air-drying
Sawn boards, spaced apart with stickers, are placed on pallets and set in huge stacks at the mill (below).

Checking moisture content
The moisture content of wood is given as a percentage of its oven-dry weight. This is calculated by comparing the original weight of a sample block (preferably taken from the centre of the board rather than the end) with the weight of the sample after it has been fully dried in an oven. The dry weight is subtracted from the original weight to determine the weight loss, and the following equation used to calculate the moisture-content percentage:

$$\frac{\text{Weight of water lost from sample}}{\text{Oven-dry weight of sample}} \times 100$$

Moisture meters with two-pin electrodes are a simple and convenient way to check the moisture content. The meter measures the resistance of the moist wood and gives an instant reading of the moisture-content percentage.

Insert the electrodes into the wood at various points along the board to check the average level, as not all parts of the board dry at the same rate.

SELECTING WOOD

Timber suppliers usually stock spruce, fir and pine, the softwoods most commonly used for carpentry and joinery. These woods are generally sold as 'dimension' or 'dressed' stock – that is, as sawn or surface-planed sections cut to standard sizes. One or more of the faces may be surfaced. Note that the planing process can remove at least 3mm ($\frac{1}{8}$in) from each face of the wood, making the actual width and thickness less than the 'sawn size' quoted by the timber

merchant. The length, on the other hand, is always as quoted. Although the majority of hardwoods are generally sold as boards of random width and length, certain types of mahogany, teak, oak and ramin can be bought as dimension stock. Dimension timber is sold by the foot or in 300mm units. Check which system your supplier uses, as the metric unit is about 5mm ($\frac{3}{16}$in) shorter than an imperial foot. Always allow extra on the length for waste.

Grading

Softwoods are graded for evenness of grain and amount of allowable defects such as knots. The better-quality 'appearance grades' and 'non-stress grades' are probably of most interest to the general woodworker. Stress-graded softwoods are rated for structural use where strength is important. The term 'clear timber' is often used for knot-free or defect-free wood, but this kind of timber is not usually available from suppliers unless specified.

The grading of hardwoods is determined by the area of defect-free wood. The greater the area, the higher the grade. The best grades are 'firsts' and 'firsts and seconds' (FAS).

Many specialist firms will supply wood by mail order – but whenever possible, select the wood yourself. When you go to buy wood, take a block plane with you so you can plane a small sample if the colour and grain are obscured by dirt or by sawing.

WOOD DEFECTS

Unless wood is dried carefully, stresses can be introduced which mar it or make it difficult to work. Insufficient drying can lead to shrinkage of dimensioned parts, joints opening, and warping and splitting.

Before buying wood, check the surface for splits, knots and uneven grain. Look at the end-section to identify the cut from the log and any distortion. Sight along the length to check for twisting or bowing.

Honeycomb checks occur inside the board when the outside stabilizes before the inside is dry. The inside shrinks more than the outside, which usually results in torn internal fibres.

Shakes are splits that occur in the structure of the wood due to growth defects or shrinkage stresses. Cup or ring shakes are splits that open between the annual-growth rings.

Bow

Twist or wind

Spring

Ingrown bark can mar the appearance and weaken the structure of the wood.

Surface checking usually occurs along the rays, and is usually caused by rapid drying of the surface.

End splits are common and are caused by rapid drying of the exposed end. Sealing the ends with waterproof paint can prevent splitting.

Bowing or warping is caused by stacking boards badly and introduces stresses which make the wood difficult to cut. 'Reaction' wood is also prone to cast when dried or cut.

Dead or encased knots are the remains of dead branches, the stumps of which are overgrown by new growth rings. Dead knots tend to fall out when the wood dries. The grain of the wood surrounding a knot is irregular, which makes it hard to work.

THE PROPERTIES OF WOOD

Since wood is a product of nature, each piece is unique. Each section of wood taken from a tree, or even from the same board, will be different. It may have the same strength or colour, but not the same grain pattern. It is this diversity of character, strength, colour, workability and even scent that makes wood so appealing to woodworkers. Working wood is a learning process, and each piece of wood is a challenge to the worker's skills. Only by handling wood and experiencing the way it behaves can a full appreciation of its properties be gained. The natural characteristics of wood are briefly set out below, and different kinds of wood from all over the world are illustrated on the following pages.

NATURAL CHARACTERISTICS

The appearance of wood – the grain pattern, colour and texture – is the prime consideration when choosing wood for a project. Its working or strength characteristics are usually a secondary consideration, but they are no less important and the wood must also be selected for fitness of purpose. If you are not familiar with a particular wood which appeals to you, discuss its properties with your supplier to make sure it will suit your requirements.

Selecting wood is a process of balancing appearance with strength, workability, pliability, weight, cost and availability. The appearance and characteristics of wood are determined by the nature of its cell structure.

Grain

The mass of the wood's cell structure constitutes the 'grain' of the wood, which follows the main axis of the tree's trunk, and the nature of the grain is determined by the disposition and degree of orientation of these longitudinal cells.

Trees which grow straight and even produce 'straight-grained' wood. 'Cross-grained' wood is formed where the cells deviate from the main axis of the tree. Some trees twist as they grow and produce 'spiral grain'. In some instances the spiral growth veers from one angle to another, with each change taking place over a few growth rings; this results in 'interlocked grain'. 'Wavy grain' and 'curly grain' occur in trees that have an undulating cell structure; the former has short even waves, the latter is irregular.

Irregular-grained woods can be difficult to work and finish, as the cells constantly change direction, creating 'wild grain'.

Boards with random or undulating grain display various patterns according to the angle to the surface and light-reflectivity of the cell structure. These effects are exploited in the production of veneers.

The term grain is also used in referring to the way wood is cut or worked. Sawing 'with the grain' refers to cuts made along the length of the wood, that is with the longitudinal cells.

Planing a surface 'with the grain' follows the direction of the grain where the fibres are parallel or slope up and away from the direction of the cutting action. This results in a smooth trouble-free cut.

Planing 'against the grain' refers to cuts made where the fibres slope up and towards the direction of the planing action, producing a rough cut.

Sawing or planing 'across the grain' refers to cuts made more or less perpendicular to the grain.

Figure

The term grain is commonly used to describe the appearance of wood, but what is really being referred to is a combination of natural growth features collectively known as the 'figure'.

The difference in growth between the earlywood and latewood, the density of the annual growth rings, the concentricity or eccentricity of the rings, the distribution of colour, the effect of disease or physical damage and the method used to convert the wood into boards all contribute to the figure.

Most trees produce conically shaped trunks which when cut tangentially produce typical plain-sawn boards displaying a U-shaped pattern where the layers of annual growth rings are exposed by the plane of the cut. When a log is cut radially or quarter-sawn the annual rings are perpendicular to the plane of cut and the figure is less distinctive, showing a series of parallel lines. Some woods, however, have distinctive ray cells which are exposed by quarter-sawing and produce an attractive 'ray-fleck' figure.

The form of the figure is not restricted to wood from straight trunks. The fork formed by a branch and the main stem of the tree produces 'curl' or 'crotch' figure much prized as veneer, as is burr wood which is an abnormal growth caused by some injury. Stumpwood also yields interesting random-grain figure which, like burr, can be used for turning work.

Texture

The term 'texture' refers to the relative size of the wood's cells. Fine-textured woods have small closely spaced cells, whilst coarse-textured woods have relatively large cells. 'Texture' is also used to describe the distribution of the cells in relation to the annual growth rings. Where the difference between earlywood and latewood is slight the wood is even-textured, whereas wood with marked contrast in the growth rings has an uneven texture.

IDENTIFYING WOOD

Some common woods can be readily identified by their grain, colour, texture and smell. However, unfamiliar woods can be extremely difficult to identify – and even experts sometimes have to resort to microscopic analysis of the cell structure.

The following pages illustrate in colour a selection of commercial woods from around the world. Each wood is referred to by its standard name and, where appropriate, its commercial or local names are included.

The genus and species are given in italics. These are all important, since the botanical name is the only universal classification that can be relied on to identify a species of wood accurately. In reference books and suppliers' catalogues the term 'sp.' or 'spp.' is commonly used to indicate that a wood may be one of a variety of species within a genus, or 'family',of trees.

The main source of supply is specified for each wood. However, although the predominant woods in any country are usually the indigenous species, imported woods – particularly exotic hardwoods – can be found in most countries, their availability being limited only by supply and demand.

SOFTWOODS OF THE WORLD

The term softwood refers to the botanical grouping of the wood rather than its physical properties. Softwoods come from coniferous trees, which belong to the botanical group Gymnospermae (plants that bear exposed seeds). Most cone-bearing trees are evergreen and have narrow, needle-shaped leaves. The standing tree is commonly depicted as having a tall, pointed outline – but not all conifers are this shape. When converted into boards, softwoods are readily identified by their relatively light colour range, from pale yellow to reddish brown, and by the grain pattern created by the contrast in colour and density between the earlywood and latewood in the annual growth rings.

Distribution of softwoods
■ Coniferous forest
■ Coniferous and broadleaved deciduous mixed forest

The scale of the map permits the areas of tree distribution to be shown in broad terms only.

The softwood regions of the world
The prime source of the world's supply of commercial softwoods is the northern hemisphere, which extends across the arctic and subarctic regions of Europe and North America down to the southeastern United States.

Conifers are relatively fast-growing, producing straight trunks which can be economically cultivated and harvested in man-made forests. They are cheaper than hardwoods and widely used for building construction and joinery and in the manufacture of fibreboard and paper.

Softwood boards
Whole boards of home-grown timber, complete with waney edge and bark, can be bought from local sawmills. The 'waney edge' is the uncut edge of the board. Imported boards are usually supplied debarked or square-edged. The larch example shows the bark, sapwood and mature heartwood. The sapwood is the light-coloured wood which is less resistant to fungal and insect attack than the heartwood.

Colour changes
The colour of wood can vary considerably, not only in the same species but also in the same tree. Most woods darken with exposure to light, though some lighten or even change colour. Applied finishes, no matter how clear, tend to darken the colour of the wood. The small square samples show the wood, actual size, before and after the application of a clear finish.

A simple test to see the effect of a clear finish on the colour of a wood is to lick your finger and wet the surface of the wood.

CEDAR OF LEBANON
Cedrus libani
Other names: True cedar.
Sources: Middle East.
Characteristics: An aromatic wood, with light-brown heartwood. Clearly marked grain produced by contrasting earlywood and latewood. Can be knotty.
Workability: Good.
Average dried weight: 560kg/m³ (35lb/ft³).
Common uses: Interior and garden furniture, construction, joinery.
Finishing: Good.

CEDAR, WESTERN RED
Thuja plicata
Other names: Giant arbor vitae (USA); red cedar (Canada); British Columbia red cedar (UK).
Sources: Canada, USA, UK, New Zealand.
Characteristics: Relatively soft aromatic timber. Reddish brown in colour, fading to silver-grey after long exposure to weathering.
Workability: Good.
Average dried weight: 370kg/m³ (23lb/ft³).
Common uses: Shingles, exterior boarding and cladding, greenhouses and sheds.
Finishing: Good.

● **Colour change**
The small square samples show the actual grain-size of each species and the effect when a clear finish is applied.

Cedar of Lebanon   Cedar, Western red

CEDAR, YELLOW

Chamaecyparis nootkatensis

Other names: Alaska yellow cedar, Pacific coast yellow cedar.
Sources: Pacific coast of North America.
Characteristics: A pale-yellow even-textured wood, with fine straight grain. It is relatively light, stiff and stable when dry.
Workability: Good.
Average dried weight: 500kg/m³ (31lb/ft³).
Common uses: Furniture, boatbuilding, joinery, veneer.
Finishing: Good.

FIR, DOUGLAS

Pseudotsuga menziesii

Other names: British Columbian pine, Oregon pine.
Sources: Canada, Western USA, UK.
Characteristics: A straight-grained reddish-brown timber, with pronounced grain. Obtainable in large knot-free sizes.
Workability: Good.
Average dried weight: 530kg/m³ (33lb/ft³).
Common uses: Plywood, joinery. Widely used in North America for building work.
Finishing: Fair.

FIR, SILVER

Abies alba

Other names: Whitewood.
Sources: Central and Southern Europe.
Characteristics: A pale-cream non-resinous and almost colourless wood, with straight grain and fine texture. Similar to and often marketed together with Norway spruce (*Picea abies*).
Workability: Good.
Average dried weight: 480kg/m³ (30lb/ft³).
Common uses: Joinery, construction, boxes, plywood, poles.
Finishing: Good.

HEMLOCK, WESTERN

Tsuga heterophylla

Other names: Pacific hemlock, British Columbia hemlock.
Sources: Canada, USA, UK.
Characteristics: A pale-brown semi-lustrous wood, with relatively distinct growth rings. It is even-textured, has straight grain and is non-resinous.
Workability: Good.
Average dried weight: 500kg/m³ (31lb/ft³).
Common uses: Construction work, joinery, plywood.
Finishing: Good.

KAURI, QUEENSLAND

Agathis spp.

Other names: North Queensland kauri, South Queensland kauri.
Sources: Australia.
Characteristics: A straight-grained wood, with fine even texture. Colour varies from pale cream-brown to pinkish-brown.
Workability: Good.
Average dried weight: 480kg/m³ (30lb/ft³).
Common uses: Joinery, furniture.
Finishing: Good.

LARCH

Larix decidua

Other names: None.
Sources: Europe, particularly mountainous areas.
Characteristics: Tougher than most conifers, it is a straight-grained timber of uniform texture. Pale to rich-red heartwood, light-coloured sapwood. Larches shed their needles in winter.
Workability: Medium.
Average dried weight: 590kg/m³ (37lb/ft³).
Common uses: Joinery, pit props, boat planking.
Finishing: Fair.

Larch

Cedar, Yellow   Fir, Douglas   Fir, Silver   Hemlock, Western   Kauri, Queensland

●PINE, HOOP
Araucaria cunninghamii
Other names:
Queensland pine
(though not a true pine).
Sources: Australia,
Papua New Guinea.
Characteristics:
A straight-grained fine-
textured wood. Similar
to Parana pine in
appearance, it has wide
light-brown sapwood
with yellow-brown
heartwood.
Workability: Good.
Average dried weight:
560kg/m³ (35lb/ft³).
Common uses:
Joinery, furniture,
turnery, construction.
Finishing: Good.

●PINE, PARANA
Araucaria angustifolia
Other names:
Brazilian pine (USA).
Sources: Argentina,
Brazil and Paraguay.
Characteristics:
Even-textured straight-
grained timber, with
inconspicuous growth
rings. Light-brown
heartwood, with dark-
brown core. Often has
bright-red streaks.
Workability: Good.
Average dried weight:
540kg/m³ (33lb/ft³).
Common uses: Joinery,
furniture, turnery.
Finishing: Good.

●PINE, PONDEROSA
Pinus ponderosa
Other names: Western
yellow pine, Californian
white pine (USA);
British Columbia soft
pine (Canada).
Sources: Western
Canada and USA.
Characteristics:
The wide pale-yellow
sapwood is soft, non-
resinous and even-
textured. The heavier
heartwood is deep
yellow to reddish
brown, and resinous.
Workability: Good/fair.
Average dried weight:
480kg/m³ (30lb/ft³).
Common uses:
Pattern-making, doors,
furniture (sapwood);
joinery, construction
(heartwood).
Finishing: Fair.

●PINE, SUGAR
Pinus lambertiana
Other names:
Californian sugar pine.
Sources: USA.
Characteristics:
Moderately soft, with
medium-coarse texture
and even grain. It has
white sapwood and
pale to reddish-brown
heartwood.
Workability: Good.
Average dried weight:
430kg/m³ (26lb/ft³).
Common uses: Joinery,
light construction.
Finishing: Fair.

**●PINE,
WESTERN WHITE**
Pinus monticola
Other names:
Idaho white pine.
Sources: Canada, USA.
Characteristics:
A straight-grained even-
textured wood. Pale
yellow to reddish brown,
with little variation in
colour between early-
wood and latewood.
Workability: Good.
Average dried weight:
450kg/m³ (28lb/ft³).
Common uses: Joinery,
construction, furniture,
boatbuilding, plywood.
Finishing: Good.

●PINE, YELLOW
Pinus strobus
Other names: Eastern
white pine, Northern
white pine (USA);
Quebec pine, Weymouth
pine (UK).
Sources: USA,
Eastern Canada.
Characteristics:
A soft pine with straight
grain, fine even texture
and inconspicuous annual
growth rings. It is pale
yellow to pale brown in
colour, with fine resin-
duct marks.
Workability: Good.
Average dried weight:
420kg/m³ (26lb/ft³).
Common uses:
Pattern-making,
joinery, musical
instruments, furniture,
construction work.
Finishing: Good.

● Colour change
The small square
samples show the actual
grain-size of each
species and the effect
when a clear finish is
applied.

Pine, Hoop   Pine, Parana   Pine, Ponderosa   Pine, Sugar   Pine, Western white   Pine, Yellow

RIMU
Dacrydium cupressinum
Other names: Red pine.
Sources: New Zealand.
Characteristics:
A fine even-textured straight-grained timber. Heartwood is reddish brown, turning to lighter shades of brown through to the yellowish sapwood.
Workability: Good.
Average dried weight: 530kg/m³ (33lb/ft³).
Common uses: Furniture, joinery, plywood, veneers.
Finishing: Good.

REDWOOD, EUROPEAN
Pinus sylvestris
Other names: Scots pine, Scandinavian redwood, Russian redwood.
Sources: Europe, Northern Asia.
Characteristics:
A light-coloured resinous wood, with yellow-brown to reddish-brown heartwood and light white-yellow sapwood. Distinct figure, with light earlywood and reddish latewood.
Workability: Medium.
Average dried weight: 510kg/m³ (32lb/ft³).
Common uses: Furniture, joinery, construction work.
Finishing: Good.

SEQUOIA
Sequoia sempervirens
Other names: Californian redwood.
Sources: USA.
Characteristics:
A straight-grained reddish-brown timber, with marked contrast between earlywood and latewood. The texture can vary from fine and even to relatively coarse. It is non-resinous.
Workability: Fair.
Average dried weight: 420kg/m³ (26lb/ft³).
Common uses: Shingles, exterior cladding, interior joinery, coffins, posts, plywood.
Finishing: Good.

SPRUCE, NORWAY
Picea abies
Other names: European whitewood, European spruce.
Sources: Europe.
Characteristics:
A lustrous straight-grained even-textured wood, with almost white earlywood and pale yellow-brown latewood.
Workability: Good.
Average dried weight: 470kg/m³ (29lb/ft³).
Common uses: Construction, joinery, boxes, plywood, piano soundboards and violin bellies.
Finishing: Good.

SPRUCE, SITKA
Picea sitchensis
Other names: Silver spruce.
Sources: Canada, USA, UK.
Characteristics: A non-resinous creamy-white wood, with slightly pink heartwood. Usually straight-grained with even texture, depending on rate of growth.
Workability: Good.
Average dried weight: 450kg/m³ (28lb/ft³).
Common uses: Boatbuilding, interior joinery, construction, musical instruments, gliders, oars, racing sculls, plywood.
Finishing: Good.

YEW
Taxus baccata
Other names: Common yew, European yew.
Sources:
Europe, Asia Minor, North Africa, Burma and the Himalayas.
Characteristics:
A tough, hard softwood. It has an orange-red heartwood, with distinct light-coloured sapwood. The growth pattern makes the wood very decorative.
Workability: Difficult.
Average dried weight: 670kg/m³ (42lb/ft³).
Common uses: Furniture, turnery, joinery.
Finishing: Good.

Rimu

Redwood, European

Sequoia   Spruce, Norway   Spruce, Sitka   Yew

HARDWOODS OF THE WORLD

The term hardwood (like softwood) refers to the botanical grouping of the wood rather than its physical properties. It is, however, a useful label since the majority of hardwoods are in fact harder than woods from the softwood group. The outstanding exception is balsawood – which, although botanically a hardwood, is the softest wood in the two groups. Hardwoods come from broadleaved trees, which belong to the botanical group Angiospermae (flowering plants). Angiosperms produce seed-bearing ovaries that develop after fertilization into fruits or nuts. This group is regarded as a higher evolutionary order than the older and more primitive coniferous Gymnosperms, which have a simpler cell structure. Most broadleaved trees grown in temperate zones are deciduous and lose their leaves in winter – but not all, for some have developed into evergreens. Broadleaved trees grown in tropical forests are mainly evergreen. Hardwoods are generally more durable than softwoods and offer a wider choice of colour, texture and figure. They are also more expensive and many of them, particularly the highly prized exotic woods, are converted into veneer.

Distribution of hardwoods
Broadleaved evergreen forest
Broadleaved deciduous forest
Broadleaved evergreen and deciduous hardwood forest
Broadleaved deciduous and coniferous mixed forest

The scale of the map permits the areas of tree distribution to be shown in broad terms only.

Hardwood regions of the world
There are thousands of species of hardwood trees distributed throughout the world, hundreds of which are harvested for commercial use. Climate is the most important factor governing which species grows where. In general, deciduous broadleaved trees are native to the temperate northern hemisphere and broadleaved evergreens to the tropics and southern hemisphere.

Hardwoods grow relatively slowly, and, although programmes for replanting help maintain the forests, the new trees are not always of such good quality as the older stock.

The map shows the distribution of broadleaved evergreens and broadleaved deciduous trees, evergreen and deciduous hardwoods, and broadleaved and coniferous mixed forests.

Endangered species
The indiscriminate destruction of the world's rainforests is leading to a severe shortage of tropical hardwoods. To conserve valuable resources, use only those woods grown on plantations or managed forests. The species most at risk are marked with a felled-tree symbol.

● **Colour change**
The small square samples show the actual grain-size of each species and the effect when a clear finish is applied.

● **AFRORMOSIA**
Pericopsis elata
Other names: Assemela (Ivory Coast, France); kokrodua (Ghana, Ivory Coast); ayin, egbi (Nigeria).
Sources: West Africa.
Characteristics: A durable wood, with straight to interlocked grain. The yellow-brown heartwood darkens to the colour of teak, which it resembles, though it is finer textured and not so oily as teak.
Workability: Good.
Average dried weight: 710kg/m³ (44lb/ft³).
Common uses: Veneer, interior and exterior joinery, interior and exterior furniture, construction.
Finishing: Good.

● **ALDER, RED**
Alnus rubra
Other names: Western alder, Oregon alder.
Sources: Pacific coast of North America.
Characteristics: A soft relatively straight-grained even-textured wood, pale yellow to reddish brown in colour.
Workability: Good.
Average dried weight: 530kg/m³ (33lb/ft³).
Common uses: Furniture, turnery, carving, plywood, veneer.
Finishing: Good.

Afrormosia

Alder, Red

●ASH, AMERICAN WHITE

Fraxinus americana

Other names: Canadian ash (UK); white ash (USA).

Sources: Canada and USA.

Characteristics: A coarse but generally straight-grained wood; with almost white sapwood, and pale-brown heartwood similar to European ash.

Workability: Medium.

Average dried weight: 670kg/m³ (42lb/ft³).

Common uses: Sports equipment and tool handles, boatbuilding, joinery.

Finishing: Good.

●ASH, EUROPEAN

Fraxinus excelsior

Other names: English, French, Polish ash etc. (according to origin).

Sources: Europe.

Characteristics: A tough coarse-textured straight-grained wood, whitish to pale brown in colour. Logs with dark stained heartwood are known as 'olive ash'.

Workability: Good.

Average dried weight: 710kg/m³ (44lb/ft³).

Common uses: Sports equipment and tool handles, bentwood furniture, cabinet-making, plywood, veneer.

Finishing: Good.

●BALSA

Ochroma lagopus

Other names: Guano (Puerto Rico, Honduras); lanero (Cuba); polak (Belize, Nicaragua); topa (Peru); tami (Bolivia).

Sources: South America.

Characteristics: The softest and lightest commercial hardwood. An open straight-grained wood, with lustrous very pale beige to pinkish colour.

Workability: Good.

Average dried weight: 160kg/m³ (10lb/ft³).

Common uses: Insulation, buoyancy aids, model-making, packaging

Finishing: Fair.

●BASSWOOD

Tilia americana

Other names: American lime.

Sources: Canada, USA.

Characteristics: A fine straight-grained even-textured wood. Creamy-white colour, turning to pale brown on exposure.

Workability: Good.

Average dried weight: 416kg/m³ (26lb/ft³).

Common uses: Carving and turnery, pattern-making, veneer, joinery.

Finishing: Good.

●BEECH, AMERICAN

Fagus grandifolia

Other names: None.

Sources: Canada, USA.

Characteristics: Straight-grained wood, with fine even texture. Light brown to reddish brown in colour, slightly coarser than European beech.

Workability: Medium.

Average dried weight: 740kg/m³ (46lb/ft³).

Common uses: Cabinet-making, bentwood furniture, interior joinery, turnery.

Finishing: Good.

●BEECH, EUROPEAN

Fagus sylvatica

Other names: English, Danish, French beech etc. (according to origin).

Sources: Europe.

Characteristics: Straight-grained wood, with fine even texture. Whitish brown, turning to yellowish brown on exposure. 'Steamed beech' is reddish brown.

Workability: Medium.

Average dried weight: 720kg/m³ (45lb/ft³).

Common uses: Cabinet-making, bentwood furniture, interior joinery, veneer, turnery, plywood.

Finishing: Good.

Ash, American white   Ash, European   Balsa   Basswood   Beech, American   Beech, European

21

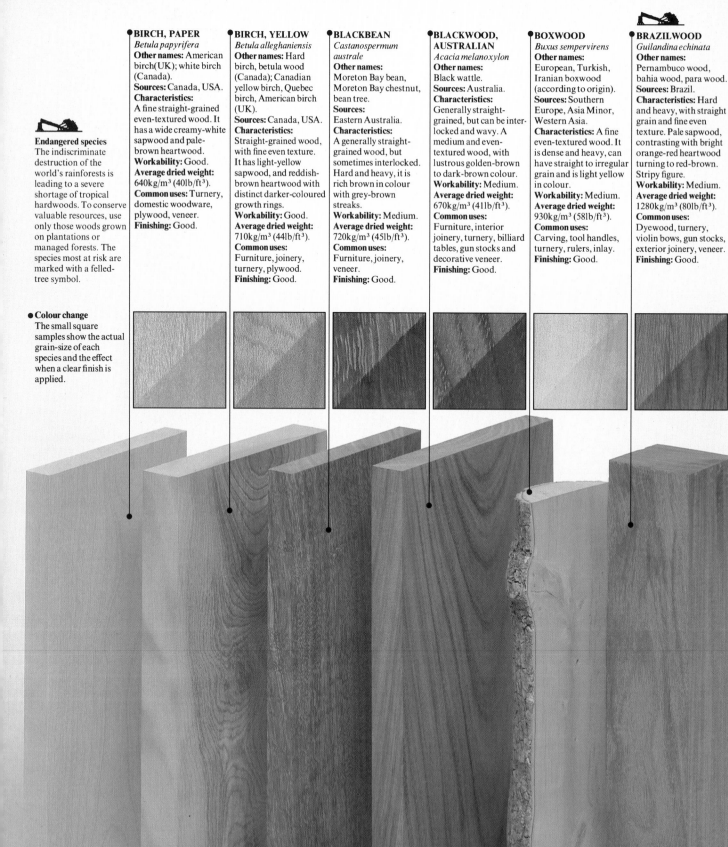

Endangered species
The indiscriminate destruction of the world's rainforests is leading to a severe shortage of tropical hardwoods. To conserve valuable resources, use only those woods grown on plantations or managed forests. The species most at risk are marked with a felled-tree symbol.

● **Colour change**
The small square samples show the actual grain-size of each species and the effect when a clear finish is applied.

● **BIRCH, PAPER**
Betula papyrifera
Other names: American birch (UK); white birch (Canada).
Sources: Canada, USA.
Characteristics: A fine straight-grained even-textured wood. It has a wide creamy-white sapwood and pale-brown heartwood.
Workability: Good.
Average dried weight: 640kg/m³ (40lb/ft³).
Common uses: Turnery, domestic woodware, plywood, veneer.
Finishing: Good.

● **BIRCH, YELLOW**
Betula alleghaniensis
Other names: Hard birch, betula wood (Canada); Canadian yellow birch, Quebec birch, American birch (UK).
Sources: Canada, USA.
Characteristics: Straight-grained wood, with fine even texture. It has light-yellow sapwood, and reddish-brown heartwood with distinct darker-coloured growth rings.
Workability: Good.
Average dried weight: 710kg/m³ (44lb/ft³).
Common uses: Furniture, joinery, turnery, plywood.
Finishing: Good.

● **BLACKBEAN**
Castanospermum australe
Other names: Moreton Bay bean, Moreton Bay chestnut, bean tree.
Sources: Eastern Australia.
Characteristics: A generally straight-grained wood, but sometimes interlocked. Hard and heavy, it is rich brown in colour with grey-brown streaks.
Workability: Medium.
Average dried weight: 720kg/m³ (45lb/ft³).
Common uses: Furniture, joinery, veneer.
Finishing: Good.

● **BLACKWOOD, AUSTRALIAN**
Acacia melanoxylon
Other names: Black wattle.
Sources: Australia.
Characteristics: Generally straight-grained, but can be interlocked and wavy. A medium and even-textured wood, with lustrous golden-brown to dark-brown colour.
Workability: Medium.
Average dried weight: 670kg/m³ (41lb/ft³).
Common uses: Furniture, interior joinery, turnery, billiard tables, gun stocks and decorative veneer.
Finishing: Good.

● **BOXWOOD**
Buxus sempervirens
Other names: European, Turkish, Iranian boxwood (according to origin).
Sources: Southern Europe, Asia Minor, Western Asia.
Characteristics: A fine even-textured wood. It is dense and heavy, can have straight to irregular grain and is light yellow in colour.
Workability: Medium.
Average dried weight: 930kg/m³ (58lb/ft³).
Common uses: Carving, tool handles, turnery, rulers, inlay.
Finishing: Good.

● **BRAZILWOOD**
Guilandina echinata
Other names: Pernambuco wood, bahia wood, para wood.
Sources: Brazil.
Characteristics: Hard and heavy, with straight grain and fine even texture. Pale sapwood, contrasting with bright orange-red heartwood turning to red-brown. Stripy figure.
Workability: Medium.
Average dried weight: 1280kg/m³ (80lb/ft³).
Common uses: Dyewood, turnery, violin bows, gun stocks, exterior joinery, veneer.
Finishing: Good.

Birch, Paper   Birch, Yellow   Blackbean   Blackwood, Australian   Boxwood   Brazilwood

BUBINGA
Guibourtia demeusei
Other names: African rosewood; kevazingo (Gabon); essingang (Cameroons).
Sources: Cameroons, Gabon.
Characteristics: Moderately coarse even-textured wood. It can have straight or inter-locked and irregular grain. Red-brown in colour, with purple veining.
Workability: Good.
Average dried weight: 880kg/m³ (55lb/ft³).
Common uses: Furniture, veneer, woodware.
Finishing: Good.

BUTTERNUT
Juglans cinerea
Other names: White walnut.
Sources: Canada, USA.
Characteristics: A straight-grained coarse-textured wood, with medium-brown heartwood.
Workability: Good.
Average dried weight: 450kg/m³ (28lb/ft³).
Common uses: Furniture, carving, interior joinery, veneer.
Finishing: Good.

CHERRY, AMERICAN
Prunus serotina
Other names: Black cherry (Canada, USA); cabinet cherry (USA).
Sources: Canada, USA.
Characteristics: A hard straight-grained wood, with fine texture. Heart-wood is reddish brown to deep red, with brown flecks and some gum pockets.
Workability: Good.
Average dried weight: 580kg/m³ (36lb/ft³).
Common uses: Furniture, pattern-making, joinery, musical instruments, tobacco pipes.
Finishing: Good.

CHESTNUT, AMERICAN
Castanea dentata
Other names: Wormy chestnut.
Sources: Canada, USA.
Characteristics: Coarse-textured, with wide growth rings. Similar to oak in appear-ance, but lacks broad rays. Insect attack causes 'wormy chestnut'.
Workability: Good.
Average dried weight: 480kg/m³ (30lb/ft³).
Common uses: Furniture, coffins, poles, stakes.
Finishing: Good.

CHESTNUT, SWEET
Castanea sativa
Other names: Spanish chestnut, European chestnut.
Sources: Europe, Asia Minor.
Characteristics: Coarse-textured, with straight or spiralled grain. Colour and texture similar to oak, but lacks oak ray figure. Reacts to ferrous metals.
Workability: Good.
Average dried weight: 560kg/m³ (35lb/ft³).
Common uses: Furniture, turnery, coffins, poles, stakes.
Finishing: Good.

COCOBOLO
Dalbergia retusa
Other names: Granadillo (Mexico).
Sources: West coast of Central America.
Characteristics: Hard, heavy, tough wood with irregular grain and medium texture. Attractive variegated colour, from purple to yellow, with black markings turning to deep orange-red on exposure.
Workability: Good.
Average dried weight: 1100kg/m³ (68lb/ft³).
Common uses: Turnery, cutlery handles, brush backs, veneer.
Finishing: Good.

Bubinga   Butternut   Chestnut, Sweet   Cocobolo

Cherry, American   Chestnut, American

Endangered species
The indiscriminate destruction of the world's rainforests is leading to a severe shortage of tropical hardwoods. To conserve valuable resources, use only those woods grown on plantations or managed forests. The species most at risk are marked with a felled-tree symbol.

● **Colour change**
The small square samples show the actual grain-size of each species and the effect when a clear finish is applied.

● **EBONY**
Diospyros ebenum
Other names:
Tendu, tuki, ebans.
Sources:
Sri Lanka, India.
Characteristics: A hard, dense and heavy wood with fine even texture and straight, irregular or wavy grain. The sapwood is yellowish, the heartwood dark brown to black.
Workability: Difficult.
Average dried weight: 1190kg/m³ (74lb/ft³).
Common uses: Turnery, musical instruments, cutlery handles, inlay.
Finishing: Good.

ELM, AMERICAN WHITE
Ulmus americana
Other names: Water elm, swamp elm, soft elm (USA); orhamwood (Canada).
Sources: Canada, USA.
Characteristics: A coarse-textured, strong, tough, medium-density wood; usually straight-grained, but can be interlocked. Has good bending properties. The heartwood is a pale reddish brown.
Workability: Good.
Average dried weight: 580kg/m³ (36lb/ft³).
Common uses: Boat-building, cooperage, furniture, agricultural implements.
Finishing: Good.

ELM, DUTCH & ENGLISH
Ulmus hollandica
Ulmus procera
Other names:
Dutch: Cork bark elm.
English: Red elm.
Sources: Europe.
Characteristics: Coarse-textured wood, with distinct irregular growth rings giving attractive figure. The heartwood is beige-brown in colour. Sometimes in short supply because of Dutch elm disease.
Workability: Medium.
Average dried weight: 560kg/m³ (35lb/ft³).
Common uses: Furniture, bentwood furniture, turnery, boatbuilding.
Finishing: Good.

● **GONÇALO ALVES**
Astronium fraxinifolium
Other names:
Zebrawood (UK); tigerwood (USA).
Sources: Brazil.
Characteristics: Hard, medium-textured wood with irregular, interlocked grain and hard and soft layers of material. Reddish-brown with dark streaks, similar in appearance to rosewood.
Workability: Difficult.
Average dried weight: 950kg/m³ (59lb/ft³).
Common uses: Furniture, turnery, veneer.
Finishing: Good.

● **HICKORY, PECAN**
Carya illinoensis
Other names:
Sweet pecan.
Sources: USA.
Characteristics: A coarse-textured wood, generally straight-grained but can be irregular or wavy. The sapwood is white, heartwood reddish brown.
Workability: Difficult.
Average dried weight: 750kg/m³ (46lb/ft³).
Common uses: Striking-tool handles, sports equipment, chairs and bentwood furniture.
Finishing: Good.

● **JELUTONG**
Dyera costulata
Other names:
Jelutong bukit, jelutong paya (Sarawak).
Sources:
Southeast Asia.
Characteristics: A soft, lustrous, fine, even-textured wood with straight grain. Creamy pale brown in colour. Latex ducts may be present.
Workability: Good.
Average dried weight: 470kg/m³ (29lb/ft³).
Common uses: Pattern-making, drawing boards, interior joinery, carving.
Finishing: Good.

Ebony

Elm, American

Elm, Dutch & English

Gonçalo Alves

Hickory, Pecan

Jelutong

KAUVULA
Endospermum medullosun
Other names: Sasa, New Guinea basswood.
Sources: Papua New Guinea, Solomon Islands.
Characteristics: An even-textured wood, pale yellow-brown in colour, with a rather plain appearance.
Workability: Good.
Average dried weight: 480kg/m³ (30lb/ft³).
Common uses: Interior joinery and furniture.
Finishing: Good.

KINGWOOD
Dalbergia cearensis
Other names: Violet wood, violetta (USA).
Sources: South America.
Characteristics: A fine even-textured lustrous wood. The heartwood has attractive variegated striped figure of violet-brown, black, and golden yellow.
Workability: Good.
Average dried weight: 1200kg/m³ (75lb/ft³).
Common uses: Inlay, turnery, marquetry.
Finishing: Good.

LAUAN, RED
Shorea negrosensis
Other names: None.
Sources: Philippines.
Characteristics: A relatively coarse-textured wood, with interlocked grain. The heartwood is medium to dark red in colour.
Workability: Good.
Average dried weight: 630kg/m³ (39lb/ft³).
Common uses: Interior joinery, boat-building, furniture, veneer.
Finishing: Good.

LIME
Tilia vulgaris
Other names: Linden (Germany).
Sources: Europe.
Characteristics: A soft straight-grained wood, with fine uniform texture. Colour white to pale yellow, darkening to light brown on exposure.
Workability: Good.
Average dried weight: 560kg/m³ (35lb/ft³).
Common uses: Broom handles, hat blocks, sounding boards, piano keys, harps, toys, clogs, carving.
Finishing: Good.

MAHOGANY, BRAZILIAN
Swietenia macrophylla
Other names: Central American, Honduran, Costa Rican Peruvian mahogany etc. (according to country of origin).
Sources: Central and South America.
Characteristics: A medium-textured wood with straight and even or interlocked grain. Heartwood is reddish brown to deep red.
Workability: Good.
Average dried weight: 560kg/m³ (35lb/ft³).
Common uses: Interior panelling and joinery, boat planking, carving, furniture, pianos, veneers.
Finishing: Good.

LIGNUM VITAE
Guaiacum officinale
Other names: Guayacan (Spain); bois de gaiac (France); guayacan negro, palo santo (Cuba); ironwood (USA).
Sources: West Indies and tropical America.
Characteristics: Very hard, heavy wood; has fine texture and closely interlocked grain. Heartwood is dark greenish brown to black. Naturally oily.
Workability: Difficult.
Average dried weight: 1250kg/m³ (78lb/ft³).
Common uses: Bearings, pulleys, mallets, turnery.
Finishing: Good.

Kauvula

Kingwood

Lauan, Red

Lime

Mahogany, Brazilian

Lignum Vitae

Endangered species
The indiscriminate destruction of the world's rainforests is leading to a severe shortage of tropical hardwoods. To conserve valuable resources, use only those woods grown on plantations or managed forests. The species most at risk are marked with a felled-tree symbol.

● **Colour change**
The small square samples show the actual grain-size of each species and the effect when a clear finish is applied.

MAPLE, HARD
Acer saccharum
Other names: Rock maple, sugar maple.
Sources: Canada, USA.
Characteristics: Hard, heavy, straight-grained wood with fine texture. White sapwood, with light reddish-brown heartwood.
Workability: Difficult.
Average dried weight: 740kg/m³ (46lb/ft³).
Common uses: Furniture, turnery, musical instruments, butcher's blocks, flooring, veneer.
Finishing: Fair.

MAPLE, SOFT
Acer rubrum
Other names: Red maple.
Sources: Canada, USA.
Characteristics: Straight-grained fine-textured wood, not as strong as hard maple. Light creamy-brown in colour.
Workability: Medium.
Average dried weight: 630kg/m³ (39lb/ft³).
Common uses: Furniture, interior joinery, turnery, veneers, musical instruments, flooring, plywood.
Finishing: Good.

OAK, AMERICAN RED
Quercus rubra
Other names: Northern red oak.
Sources: Canada, USA.
Characteristics: Straight-grained, with coarse texture and less attractive figure than white oak. Pinkish red in colour.
Workability: Good.
Average dried weight: 790kg/m³ (49lb/ft³).
Common uses: Furniture, interior joinery, flooring, veneer.
Finishing: Good.

OAK, AMERICAN WHITE
Quercus alba
Other names: White oak (USA).
Sources: USA, Canada.
Characteristics: Straight-grained, with medium-coarse to coarse texture. Similar in appearance to European oak, but more variable in colour.
Workability: Good.
Average dried weight: 770kg/m³ (48lb/ft³).
Common uses: Construction, flooring, furniture, interior joinery, plywood, veneers.
Finishing: Good.

OAK, JAPANESE
Quercus mongolica
Other names: Ohnara.
Sources: Japan.
Characteristics: Straight-grained and coarse-textured wood, milder than European and American white oak. Light yellowish brown in colour.
Workability: Good.
Average dried weight: 670kg/m³ (41lb/ft³).
Common uses: Furniture, panelling, flooring, boatbuilding, joinery, veneer.
Finishing: Good.

OAK, EUROPEAN
Quercus robur
Quercus petraea
Other names: English, French, Polish oak etc. (according to country of origin).
Sources: Europe, Asia Minor, North Africa.
Characteristics: A coarse-textured and straight-grained wood, with distinct growth rings and broad rays when quarter-sawn. Pale brown in colour.
Workability: Good.
Average dried weight: 720kg/m³ (45lb/ft³).
Common uses: Furniture, joinery, external woodwork, flooring, carving, boatbuilding.
Finishing: Good.

Maple, Hard

Maple, Soft

Oak, American red

Oak, American white

Oak, Japanese

Oak, European

OBECHE
Triplochiton scleroxylon
Other names: Obechi, arere (Nigeria); wawa (Ghana); samba, wawa (Ivory Coast); ayous (Cameroons).
Sources: West Africa.
Characteristics: A light-weight rather featureless wood, with fine even texture. The grain can be interlocked. Creamy white to pale yellow in colour.
Workability: Good.
Average dried weight: 390kg/m³ (24lb/ft³).
Common uses: Interior joinery, drawer linings, furniture, plywood, model-making.
Finishing: Good.

PADAUK, AFRICAN
Pterocarpus soyauxii
Other names: Camwood, barwood.
Sources: West Africa.
Characteristics: A hard, heavy wood with straight to interlocked grain and moderately coarse texture. Rich red to purple-brown colour, with red streaks.
Workability: Good.
Average dried weight: 710kg/m³ (44lb/ft³).
Common uses: Interior joinery, furniture, turnery, handles, flooring; known as a dyewood.
Finishing: Good.

PLANE, EUROPEAN
Platanus acerifolia
Other names: London plane; English, French plane etc. (according to origin).
Sources: Europe.
Characteristics: Straight-grained wood, with fine to medium texture. Light reddish-brown heartwood, with distinct darker rays producing attractive fleck figure known as 'lacewood' when quarter-sawn. Similar to but darker than American sycamore (*Platanus occidentalis*).
Workability: Good.
Average dried weight: 640kg/m³ (40lb/ft³).
Common uses: Furniture, joinery, turnery, veneer.
Finishing: Good.

PURPLEHEART
Peltogyne spp.
Other names: Amaranth (USA); koroboreli, saka, sakavalli (Guyana); purplehart (Surinam); pau roxo, amarante (Brazil).
Sources: Central and South America.
Characteristics: Uniform fine to medium texture. Usually straight-grained. Attractive purple colour, darkening to rich brown due to oxidation.
Workability: Medium.
Average dried weight: 880kg/m³ (55lb/ft³).
Common uses: Construction work, boatbuilding, veneer, turnery, furniture.
Finishing: Good.

RAMIN
Gonystylus macrophyllum
Other names: Melawis (Malaysia); ramin lelur (Sarawak).
Sources: Southeast Asia.
Characteristics: Moderately fine even texture, usually straight-grained. Pale creamy-brown colour.
Workability: Good.
Average dried weight: 670kg/m³ (41lb/ft³).
Common uses: Furniture, interior joinery, turnery, toys, carving, flooring, veneer.
Finishing: Good.

ROSEWOOD, BRAZILIAN
Dalbergia nigra
Other names: Rio rosewood, Bahia rose-wood (UK); jacaranda da Bahia, jacaranda preto (Brazil); palis-sander, palissandre du Brazil (France).
Sources: Brazil.
Characteristics: Hard and heavy; medium texture, with straight grain. Highly figured, with brown, violet-brown to black colour.
Workability: Medium.
Average dried weight: 870kg/m³ (54lb/ft³).
Common uses: Veneer, furniture, joinery, turnery, carving.
Finishing: Good.

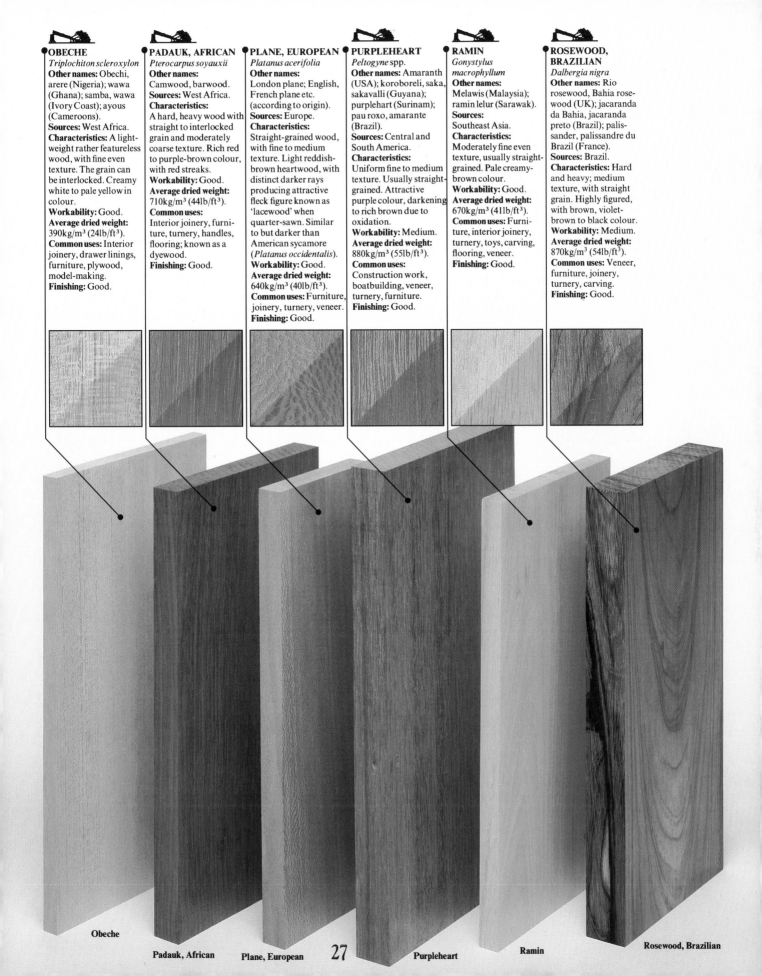

Obeche

Padauk, African

Plane, European

Purpleheart

Ramin

Rosewood, Brazilian

ROSEWOOD, INDIAN
Dalbergia latifolia
Other names: East Indian rosewood; Bombay rosewood (UK); Bombay blackwood (India).
Sources: India.
Characteristics: Heavy, moderately coarse and uniform texture. Interlocked grain, producing narrow bands. Golden brown to purple-brown with streaks of dark purple or black.
Workability: Medium.
Average dried weight: 870kg/m³ (54lb/ft³).
Common uses: Furniture, shop fittings, musical instruments, boatbuilding, veneer, turnery, flooring.
Finishing: Good.

SATINWOOD
Chloroxylon swietenia
Other names: East Indian satinwood.
Sources: Central and Southern India, Sri Lanka.
Characteristics: Heavy lustrous wood, with fine even texture and interlocked grain producing striped figure. Golden brown, with darker streaks.
Workability: Medium.
Average dried weight: 990kg/m³ (61lb/ft³).
Common uses: Furniture, interior joinery, turnery, veneer.
Finishing: Good.

SILKY OAK
Cardwellia sublimis
Other names: Bull oak, Northern silky oak (Australia); Australian silky oak (UK).
Sources: Australia.
Characteristics: Coarse even-textured wood, usually straight-grained with large rays. Reddish-brown colour similar to American red oak, though not a true oak.
Workability: Good.
Average dried weight: 550kg/m³ (34lb/ft³).
Common uses: Furniture, veneer, interior joinery.
Finishing: Good.

SYCAMORE, AMERICAN
Platanus occidentalis
Other names: American plane (UK); buttonwood (USA).
Sources: USA.
Characteristics: Fine even texture usually with straight grain. Botanically a plane tree, but lighter than European plane. Pale brown, with distinct darker rays producing lacewood when quarter-sawn.
Workability: Good.
Average dried weight: 560kg/m³ (35lb/ft³).
Common uses: Joinery, furniture, butcher's blocks, veneer.
Finishing: Good.

SYCAMORE, EUROPEAN
Acer pseudoplatanus
Other names: Sycamore plane, great maple (UK); plane (Scotland).
Sources: Europe, Western Asia.
Characteristics: Fine even texture. Usually straight-grained – but can be wavy, producing fiddleback figure when quarter-sawn. White to yellowish-white colour.
Workability: Good.
Average dried weight: 630kg/m³ (39lb/ft³).
Common uses: Turnery, furniture, kitchen utensils, flooring. Fiddleback sycamore is used for violin backs.
Finishing: Good.

TEAK
Tectona grandis
Other names: Kyun, sagwan, teku, teka.
Sources: South and Southeast Asia, Africa, Caribbean.
Characteristics: Coarse uneven texture with oily feel. Straight or wavy-grained, according to origin. Burma teak is a uniform golden brown; others are darker and more marked.
Workability: Good.
Average dried weight: 660kg/m³ (41lb/ft³).
Common uses: Interior and exterior joinery, boatbuilding, exterior and garden furniture, plywood, turnery, veneer.
Finishing: Good.

Rosewood, Indian   Satinwood   Silky Oak   Sycamore, American   Sycamore, European   Teak

● **TULIPWOOD**
Dalbergia frutescens
Other names: Pinkwood (USA); bois de rose (France); pau rosa, jacaranda rosa, pau de fuso (Brazil).
Sources: Brazil.
Characteristics: Dense, hard wood with medium to fine texture; usually has irregular grain. Attractive pinkish-yellow colour, with pink to violet-red stripes.
Workability: Difficult.
Average dried weight: 960kg/m³ (60lb/ft³).
Common uses: Turnery, woodware, boxes, inlay, veneer.
Finishing: Good.

● **UTILE**
Entandrophragma utile
Other names: Sipo (Ivory Coast); assie (Cameroons).
Sources: Africa.
Characteristics: A medium-textured wood; usually with interlocked grain, producing striped figure when quarter-sawn. Pinkish-brown colour, turning to red-brown.
Workability: Good.
Average dried weight: 660kg/m³ (41lb/ft³).
Common uses: Furniture, interior and exterior joinery, boat-building, flooring, plywood, veneer.
Finishing: Good.

● **WALNUT, AMERICAN**
Juglans nigra
Other names: Black American walnut, Virginia walnut (UK); black walnut (UK, USA).
Sources: USA, Canada.
Characteristics: A tough wood, with rather coarse texture; usually straight-grained, but can be wavy. Rich dark brown to purplish black.
Workability: Good.
Average dried weight: 660kg/m³ (41lb/ft³).
Common uses: Furniture, gun stocks, interior joinery, musical instruments, turnery, carving, plywood, veneer.
Finishing: Good.

● **WALNUT, EUROPEAN**
Juglans regia
Other names: English, French, Italian walnut etc. (according to origin).
Sources: Europe, Asia Minor, Southwest Asia.
Characteristics: Rather coarse texture, with straight to wavy grain. Grey-brown with darker streaks, though colour and markings vary according to origin.
Workability: Good.
Average dried weight: 670kg/m³ (42lb/ft³).
Common uses: Furniture, interior joinery, gun stocks, turnery, carving, veneer.
Finishing: Good.

● **WALNUT, QUEENSLAND**
Endiandra palmerstonii
Other names: Australian walnut, walnut bean, oriental wood.
Sources: Australia.
Characteristics: Similar to European walnut in appearance, but not a true walnut. Usually has interlocked and wavy grain. Wide colour variation, from light to dark brown.
Workability: Difficult.
Average dried weight: 690kg/m³ (43lb/ft³).
Common uses: Furniture, interior joinery, shop fittings, flooring, veneer.
Finishing: Good.

● **WHITEWOOD, AMERICAN**
Liriodendron tulipifera
Other names: Yellow poplar, tulip poplar (USA); tulip tree (UK and USA); canary whitewood (UK).
Sources: Eastern USA, Canada.
Characteristics: A moderately soft and lightweight wood, with straight grain and fine texture. White sapwood; pale olive-green to brown heartwood, with coloured streaks.
Workability: Good.
Average dried weight: 510kg/m³ (31lb/ft³).
Common uses: Joinery, furniture, carving, light construction, interiors, boats, toys, plywood.
Finishing: Good.

Tulipwood   Utile   Walnut, American   Walnut, European   Walnut, Queensland   Whitewood, American

VENEERS

Veneers are very thin sheets or 'leaves' of wood which are cut from a log for constructional or decorative purposes. It is ironic that even though veneers of the rarest woods have been used in making some of the finest furniture ever produced, some people still regard veneering as inferior to solid wood. However, few would disagree that veneer, whether selected for its natural colour and figure or worked into floral or formal patterns, brings a unique quality to furniture and woodware. Today, with the widespread use of modern adhesives and stable man-made backing boards, veneered products are superior to solid wood in certain applications. With our natural resources of fine woods gradually disappearing, veneer enables us to use wood economically so we can continue to enjoy it.

VENEER PRODUCTION

The manufacture of veneer requires specialist knowledge. The production starts with the log buyer, who must have the skill to interpret the quality of a log for conversion into commercially viable veneer. Using his judgement and experience, he has to assess the condition of the wood within the log solely on the basis of an external examination.

By looking at the end of the log, the buyer has to determine the quality of the wood, the potential figure of the veneer, the colour, and the ratio of sapwood to heartwood. Other factors that will affect the value of the log must also be noted, including the presence and extent of any staining and any weaknesses or defects such as shakes, ingrown bark or excessive knots and resin ducts or pockets. Much of this information will be revealed by the first cut through the length of the log – but the buyer has, of course, to purchase the log before it is cut.

Once the log has been purchased and delivered to the sawmill, it is the expertise of the veneer cutter that counts, since it is the veneer cutter who has to decide the best way to convert the wood to yield the maximum number of high-quality veneers.

Grading

As decorative veneers are cut, they are taken from the slicer and stacked in sequence. The veneers then pass through a drying process before being graded. Most species are 'clipped' on a guillotine to trim them into regular shapes and sizes. Others, such as yew or burr veneer, are left as they are cut from the log.

Veneers are priced according to their size and quality. They are checked for natural or milling defects, thickness, type of figure and colour, for example, and graded accordingly. A particular log may yield veneers of various value. The better veneers are graded as 'face quality' and have a greater value than the narrower or poorer 'backing grade'.

The veneers are kept in multiples of four for matching purposes and bound into 'bundles' of 16, 24, 28 or 32 leaves. The bundles are restacked in consecutive order and the reassembled log is stored in a cool warehouse ready for sale.

CUTTING VENEER

Veneer logs are cut from the main stem of the tree between the root butt and the first branch. The bark is removed and the log checked for foreign matter such as nails.

Before the log is converted into veneer it is softened by immersion in hot water or by steaming. The whole log may be treated, or it may first be cut by a huge bandsaw into 'flitches' to suit the veneer-cutting method. The duration of this conditioning is controlled according to the type and hardness of the wood and the thickness of the veneer to be cut. It may be a matter of days or weeks. Pale woods such as maple are not pre-treated, as the process would discolour the veneer.

There are basically three methods for cutting veneer: saw cutting, rotary cutting and flat slicing.

Saw cutting

Until the early eighteenth century, when veneer-slicing machines were developed, all veneers were cut using first handsaws and then power saws. These veneers were relatively thick, some being about 3mm ($\frac{1}{8}$in).

Sawn veneers, although wasteful of material, are still cut by huge circular saws, but only for special or difficult-to-work irregular-grained woods such as curls or where it proves the most economical method. They are usually about 1 to 1.2mm ($\frac{1}{25}$ to $\frac{1}{21}$in) thick.

You can use your workshop bandsaw or table saw to produce strips of veneer for laminating purposes, particularly if this proves to be more economical or will provide you with material better suited to your needs than the veneers that are commercially available.

Rotary cutting

Constructional veneers of softwood and some hardwoods are cut by the rotary peeling method. The whole log is set in a huge lathe which peels off a continuous sheet of veneer.

The log is rotated against a pressure bar and knife which run the full length of the machine. The knife is set just below the bar and forward of it by the thickness of the veneer. The setting of the bar and knife in relation to the log is critical, to prevent surface failures known as 'checks'. For each revolution of the log, the knife is automatically advanced by the thickness of the veneer.

Veneer produced in this way can be recognised by a distinctive watery-patterned figure where the continuous tangential cut has sliced through the growth rings.

Rotary cutting is a particularly efficient way to produce veneers suitable for the manufacture of man-made boards, as they can be cut to any width.

Although primarily used for the manufacture of constructional veneers, the method is also used to produce decorative veneers such as bird's-eye maple.

Off-centre cutting

The rotary lathe can also be used to produce wide decorative veneers with sapwood on each edge in order to give a figure something like that of typical flat-sliced crown-cut veneer. This is done by offsetting the log in the lathe chucks to produce an eccentric cutting action.

A 'stay-log' is a mounting positioned between the lathe centres to hold a full or half-round log. A veneer cut on a stay-log is cut at a shallower angle than one taken from an eccentrically mounted log but is not so wide. The figure is closer to that of flat-sliced crown-cut veneer.

Half-round logs can be mounted on a stay-log with the heartwood facing outwards. This is known as 'back cutting' and is used for cutting decoratively figured butts and curls.

Flat slicing

Flat slicing is used for producing decorative hardwood veneers. How the log is sliced depends on the natural characteristics of the wood. A log is first cut in two lengthways and the grain assessed for figure. It may then be further cut into flitches, according to the type of figure required. It is the way the log is cut and mounted for slicing which determines the character of the figure. The width of flat-sliced veneer is limited by the size of the flitch.

A half or quartered log or flitch is mounted on a sliding frame which can move up and down. The pressure bar and knife are set horizontally in front of the wood, and a slice of veneer is removed with every downstroke of the frame. After each cut the knife or flitch is advanced by the required thickness of the veneer.

A flat-sliced half-round log produces the crown-cut veneers commonly used in cabinet work. They have the same attractive figure as tangentially cut flat-sawn boards.

Woods that display striking and attractive figure when radially cut are converted into quarter-cut or near quarter-cut flitches. These are mounted with the rays of the wood following the direction of the cut as closely as possible, to produce the maximum number of radially cut veneers.

Quartered flitches can also be mounted to produce tangentially cut flat-sliced veneer. These are narrower than crown-cut veneers cut from half-round logs but can display attractive figure.

KNIFE CHECKS

Veneer-slicing machines are like giant planes, with the veneer representing the shaving. In this case it is important that the 'shaving' is produced to a fine tolerance and with a clean cut. The quality of the cut is controlled by the pressure bar and knife setting (1).

Fine cracks known as 'knife checks' can occur on the back face of the veneer, particularly when rotary-peeled. The back face of the veneer is called the 'open' or 'loose' face; and the other, the 'closed' or 'tight' face. You can identify the faces by flexing the veneer, which will bend to a greater degree when the open face is convex (2).

Always try to lay veneer with the open face down, since the slightly coarser surface does not finish quite so well as the closed face. This is not always possible, however, for when laying book-matched veneers it is necessary to turn alternate veneers over.

1 Knife checks on back face

2 Bend the veneer as a test

Saw cutting
This is not a common method today but is still used for some thick-cut veneers.

Rotary cutting
Widely used for constructional and some decorative veneers, such as bird's-eye maple.

Off-centre cutting
A rotary-cutting method that produces a figure similar to flat-sliced veneer.

Half-round cutting
This is similar to off-centre cutting, and also produces figure like flat-sliced veneer.

Back cutting
A rotary method used for cutting decorative butt and curl veneers.

Flat slicing
A common method for producing traditional crown-cut veneers.

Quarter-cut slicing
Used to produce veneers displaying attractive quarter-cut figure.

Flat-sliced quartered
Quartered logs are sometimes cut tangentially to make flat-sliced veneers.

TYPES OF VENEER

The veneer-manufacturing process makes available a wide choice of hardwoods, many of which are uneconomic or unsuitable for use in 'solid' form. A tree can be converted into various types of decorative veneer. The figure depends not only on the natural features of the wood, such as colour, grain and texture, but also on which part of the tree is used and how it is cut into veneer. Most veneer is cut from the main trunk, which gives the longest and usually the widest-figured veneers. The variety of types is obtained by slicing the log in different ways. The type description may refer to the method of cutting – as in 'crown-cut walnut' – or to the part of the tree from which the veneer is cut, as in 'burr' or 'burl' veneer. Most sliced veneer is cut about 0.6mm ($\frac{1}{42}$in) thick. Thicker veneer for furniture restoration is also produced in some woods.

BUYING VENEER

You can buy single leaves or full bundles of veneer from specialist suppliers and from some timber merchants, either by mail order or directly. Because it is important to keep the veneers in consecutive order for matching purposes, you will be supplied with veneer from the top of the stack. The merchant will not usually pull out selected leaves, as that would reduce the value of the veneer flitch.

Before buying veneer, calculate the area you need and make an allowance for wastage. Err on the generous side – since each veneer is unique and if you have to order more you are unlikely to obtain a match. Full leaves are customarily priced by the square foot, and some merchants will supply pre-cut lengths at a set price per piece. Selected small pieces of veneer are available in specialist packs for marquetry.

Small orders of full veneers supplied through the mail are usually rolled for dispatch. Small pieces of veneer, such as burrs or curls, are generally packed flat – but they can also be sent with a package of rolled veneer, in which case they may be dampened to allow them to bend without breaking. Since veneers are fragile, open a rolled package carefully, so that it doesn't spring open and cause damage. End splits are not uncommon in veneer. Repair them promptly with gummed paper tape (particularly light-coloured woods) to prevent dirt entering.

If the veneer remains curled after unpacking, dampen it with steam from a kettle or pass it through a tray of water, then press it flat between sheets of chipboard. Do not leave it between boards in a damp condition, or mildew may develop. Store veneers flat and protect them from dust and strong light, as wood is light-sensitive and can lighten or darken according to the species.

Parts of the tree used for veneers
1 Crotch
2 Trunk
3 Burr or burl
4 Stump or butt

Examples of commercially available veneers

1 Thuya burr	8 Masur birch
2 American walnut butt veneer	9 Bird's-eye maple
3 Chemically coloured 'harewood'	10 Quilted willow
4 Colour-dyed veneer	11 Quarter-cut 'lacewood'
5 Crown-cut American walnut	12 Quarter-cut 'ray-fleck' oak
6 Curly-figured 'fiddleback' veneer	13 Stripe-figured zebrano
7 Mahogany curl	14 Ribbon-figured ayan

● **Burr or burl veneer**
Burrs or burls are abnormal growths on the trunk of a tree. Burr veneers display an attractive pattern of tightly packed bud formations that appear as rings and dots. They are the most expensive type of veneer and are highly prized for furniture and small woodware. Burr veneers are supplied in irregular shapes and various sizes, from 150 × 100mm (6 × 4in) to about 1m (3ft 3in) long by 450mm (1ft 6in) wide.

● **Butt veneer**
Butt veneers are cut from the stump, or 'butt', of certain trees. Highly figured veneers, caused by the distorted grain, occur by back-cutting on a rotary lathe.

● **Coloured veneer**
Artificially coloured veneers are available from specialist suppliers. Light-coloured woods, such as sycamore, are used. 'Harewood' is chemically treated sycamore which turns silver-grey to dark-grey. Dyes are used to produce other colours, the veneer being pressure-treated for maximum penetration.

1

2

4

● **Crown-cut veneer**
Tangentially cut flat-sliced veneer is known as 'crown-cut'. It displays an attractive figure of bold sweeping curves and ovals along the centre of the leaf, with striped grain nearer the edges. Crown-cut veneer is produced in lengths of 2.4m (8ft) or more and in various widths, ranging from about 225mm (9in) to 600mm (2ft), depending on species. It is used for furniture-making and wall panelling.

● **Curly-figured veneer**
Wavy-grained woods produce veneers with bands of light and dark grain running across the width of the leaf. 'Fiddleback' sycamore is a typical example. The wood gets its name from its use for violin backs.

● **Curl veneer**
Curl veneer is cut from the 'crotch' or 'fork' of a tree where the trunk divides. When the crotch is sliced perpendicularly an attractive figure is revealed. The distorted diverging grain produces a lustrous upward-sweeping plume pattern known as 'feather figure'. It is available in sizes from 300mm to 1m (1ft to 3ft 3in) long and 200 to 450mm (8in to 1ft 6in) wide.

● **Freak-figured veneer**
Hardwood logs with irregular growth may be rotary-cut to produce veneer displaying various patterns. Bird's-eye maple and masur birch are examples. Irregular-grained woods can also produce veneer with 'blistered figure' and 'quilted figure'.

● **Ray-figured veneer**
Woods such as oak and plane have striking figure when quarter-cut. The distinct ray cells in oak produce 'ray-fleck' or 'splash' figure. Quarter-cut plane veneer is known as 'lacewood'.

● **Striped veneer**
Quarter-cut veneers usually display a striped figure where the radial cut is taken across the width of the growth rings. Striped or 'ribbon' veneer also occurs on woods which grow with interlocked reverse-spiral grain. The stripes of ribbon veneer appear to change from light to dark, depending on the angle they are viewed from.

MAN-MADE BOARDS

Man-made boards are relatively new and have been taken up enthusiastically by industry and the home woodworker alike. Board manufacturers are constantly developing their products with a view to improving quality, economy of raw materials and ease of working. Consequently, there is a wide range of boards available today. These fall into roughly three categories: laminated boards, particle boards and fibreboards. As new products are introduced, some kinds of laminated boards, such as solid-core blockboard, may be replaced by cheaper particle-board and fibreboard types.

PLYWOOD BOARDS

Plywood is a laminated material made from thin sheets of wood known as construction veneers, plies or laminates, which are bonded in layers to form a strong stable board. Laminating wood was a technique known to craftsmen in ancient times, but plywood is a relatively modern material first produced commercially around the mid-nineteenth century. Its panel size, stability and ease of working made it a useful material for interior joinery and carcass construction, but it was not until the development of waterproof adhesives in the 1930s that it found a place in the construction industry.

Plywood construction
A board of solid wood is relatively unstable and will shrink or swell to a greater degree across the fibres than it will along them. In so doing it is also likely to distort, depending on how it is cut from the tree. The tensile strength of wood is greatest following the direction of the fibres, but it will also readily split with the grain.

Plywood is constructed with the fibres or grain of alternate plies set at right angles to one another to counter movement of the wood. This produces a stable warp-resisting board which has no natural direction of cleavage. The greatest strength of a panel is usually parallel to the face grain.

Most plywood is made with an odd number of plies to give a balanced construction, three being the minimum. The number varies according to the thickness of the plies and the finished board. Whatever the number, the construction must be symmetrical about the centre ply or the centre line of the panel thickness.

The surface veneers of a typical plywood board are known as 'face plies'. Where the quality of one of the outer plies is better than the other, the better ply is called 'the face' and the other 'the back'. The grade of the face plies is usually specified by a letter code. The perpendicularly laid plies immediately beneath the face plies are known as 'cross-bandings'. The centre ply (or plies) is known as 'the core'.

Sizes
Plywood is made in a wide range of sizes. The thickness of commercially available plywood generally ranges from 3mm ($\frac{1}{8}$in) to 30mm ($1\frac{3}{16}$in), in approximately 3mm ($\frac{1}{8}$in) increments. Thinner 'aircraft plywood' is available from specialist suppliers.

The typical width of a board is 1.22m (4ft), but 1.52m (5ft) boards are also available. The most common length is 2.44m (8ft), although boards up to 3.66m (12ft) are made. The dimensions are expressed in imperial or metric measurements depending on the source of manufacture or supply.

The grain of the face ply usually follows the longest dimension of the board, but not always. Normally, it runs parallel to the first dimension quoted by the manufacturer. Thus a 1.22 × 2.44m (4 × 8ft) board will have the grain running across the width.

BONDING

The performance of plywood is determined not only by the quality of the plies but also by the type of adhesive used in its manufacture. Plywoods can be grouped according to usage.

Interior plywood (INT)
Plywoods of this grade should be used only for non-structural interior applications. They are generally produced with an appearance-grade face ply and a poorer quality for the back.

INT plywoods are manufactured with urea-formaldehyde adhesive, which is light in colour. Most boards are suitable for use in dry conditions, such as furniture or wall panelling. Modified adhesive employed in the manufacture of certain types of board affords them some degree of moisture resistance, enabling them to be used in areas of high humidity. Never use interior-grade plywood for exterior applications.

Exterior plywood
Exterior-grade plywoods can be used for fully or semi-exposed conditions (depending on the quality of the adhesive), where structural performance is not required.

Boards suitable for fully exposed conditions are bonded with dark-coloured phenol-formaldehyde (phenolic) adhesive. This type produces 'weather and boil proof' (WBP) plywood. WBP adhesives comply with an established standard, and systematic tests, as well as their record in service over many years, have proved them to be highly resistant to weather, micro-organisms, cold and boiling water, steam and dry heat.

Exterior-grade plywoods are also produced using melamine urea-formaldehyde adhesive. This type of board is semi-durable under exposed conditions.

Exterior-grade plywood is a good material for kitchen fitments and for applications around showers or bathrooms.

Marine plywood
Marine plywood is a high-quality face-graded structural plywood primarily produced for marine use. It is constructed from selected plies from a limited range of mahogany-type woods. Marine ply has no 'voids', or gaps, and is bonded with a durable phenolic (WBP) adhesive. It can also be used for interior fitments.

Structural plywood
Structural or engineering-grade plywood is manufactured for applications where strength and durability are the prime consideration. It is bonded with phenolic resin adhesive. An appearance-grade face ply of a lower quality is used, and the boards may not be sanded.

TYPES OF PLYWOOD

Different types of plywood are produced for such diverse applications as agricultural installations, aircraft and marine construction, structural building work, interior fitments, toys and furniture. Performance and suitability of application depend on species of wood, type of bond and grade of veneer.

Plywood boards are manufactured in many parts of the world and the species of wood used varies according to place of origin. The face veneers and core may be made from different species or the boards may be constructed from the same species throughout.

Softwood boards are commonly made from Douglas fir or various species of pine, common hardwood types from light-coloured temperate woods such as birch, beech and basswood. Tropical woods used for plywood construction include lauan, meranti and gaboon, all of which are red in colour.

APPEARANCE GRADING

Plywood producers employ a coding system to grade the quality of the plies used in the manufacture of their boards.

A typical system uses the letters A, B, C, C-plugged and D. The A grade is the best quality, being smooth-cut with virtually no defects. The D grade is the poorest, having the maximum amount of permitted defects such as knots, holes, splits and discoloration.

The letters quoted or stamped on the board refer to the appearance of the face plies only and do not indicate the structural performance of the board. An A-A grade plywood has two good faces, while a B-C board has poorer-grade outer plies (the better B grade being the face and the C grade the back). Decorative plywoods are faced with selected matched veneers, and are referred to by the face veneer.

Decorative plywood is faced with selected flat-sliced or quarter-cut matched veneers, usually of hardwoods such as afrormosia, beech, cherry or oak, and is mainly used for panelling. A balancing veneer of lesser quality is applied to the back of the board.

Three-ply board has the face veneers bonded to a single core veneer. Their thickness may be the same, or the core may be thicker to improve the balance of the construction. This type is sometimes called 'balanced' or 'solid core' plywood. Thin three-ply boards are used for drawer bottoms and cabinet backs.

Drawerside plywood is the exception to the cross-banding construction method. This type has the grain of all the plies running in the same direction. It is made of hardwood to a nominal thickness of 12mm ($\frac{1}{2}$in) and is used for drawer sides in place of solid wood.

Multi-ply has a core consisting of an odd number of plies. The thickness of each ply may be the same, or the cross-banded ones may be thicker. This helps give the board equal stiffness in its length and width. It is a good material for use in making veneered furniture.

Four-ply and six-ply Four-ply has two thick-cut plies bonded together, with their grain in the same direction and perpendicular to the face plies. This type is stiffer in one direction and is usually used for structural work. Six-ply (shown here) is similar to four-ply in construction but has the core parallel to the face, with cross-banded ply in between.

BLOCKBOARD AND LAMINBOARD

Blockboard is a form of plywood, being of laminated construction. It differs from conventional plywood in that the core is constructed from strips of solid wood cut approximately square in section and edge-butted, but not glued. The core is faced with one or two layers of ply on each side.

Laminboard is similar to blockboard but the core is constructed from narrow strips approximately 5mm ($\frac{3}{16}$ in) wide, which are usually edge-glued.

● **Laminboard**
is superior to blockboard for veneer work, as the core is less likely to show through. It is also more expensive. Boards of three-ply and five-ply construction are produced. The plies of the five-ply type may either be perpendicular to the core or cross-banded.

● **Blockboard**
is a stiff material suitable for furniture applications, particularly shelving and worktops. It makes a good substrate for veneer work, but the core strips can 'telegraph' (i.e. show through). It is made in panel sizes similar to plywood, in thicknesses ranging from 12mm ($\frac{1}{2}$in) to 25mm (1in). Thicker boards of three-ply are made up to 44mm (1$\frac{3}{4}$in).

PARTICLE BOARDS

Wood-particle boards are made from small chips or flakes of wood bonded together under pressure. Various types are produced according to the shape and size of the particles, their distribution through the thickness of the board and the type of adhesive used to bind them together. Softwoods are generally used, although a proportion of hardwood material is sometimes included.

Types of board
Particle boards are stable and uniformly consistent materials. Those constructed with fine particles have featureless surfaces and are highly suitable as groundwork for veneer. A wide range of pre-veneered decorative boards using wood, paper foil or plastic laminates are available. Most particle boards are relatively brittle and have a lower tensile strength than plywood.

Chipboard
Most types of particle board of interest to the woodworker are of interior quality, commonly known as chipboard. Chipboard, like other wood products, is adversely affected by excess moisture – the board swells in its thickness and on drying does not recover. However, moisture-resistant types suitable for flooring or wet conditions are made.

STORING AND FIXING BOARDS

Storing boards
To save space, store boards on edge. Make a rack to keep the edges clear of the floor and support the boards evenly at a slight angle. When storing thin boards, support the full area of each board with a thicker board underneath.

Fixing boards
Screw-fixings in the edges of man-made boards are not as strong or secure as those made in the face.
Drill pilot holes in the edge of plywood to prevent splitting. The diameter of the screws used should not exceed 25 per cent of the board's thickness.
Blockboard and laminboard will hold screws well in the side edges, but not in the end grain.
Screw-holding in chipboard depends on the density of the board. It is usually relatively weak, but special chipboard screws hold better than standard wood screws. Always drill pilot holes, both for face-fixing and edge-fixing. Use special fastenings or inserts for improved holdings.

● **Single-layer chipboard**
is made from a mat of
similar-sized particles
evenly distributed
throughout. It has a
relatively coarse surface.
This type is suitable for
wood veneer or plastic
laminate, although not
for painting.

● **Three-layer chipboard**
has a core layer of coarse
particles sandwiched
between two outside
layers of fine high-
density particles. The
outer layers contain a
higher proportion of
resin, which produces a
smooth surface suitable
for most finishes.

● **Graded-
density chipboard**
has surfaces of very fine
particles and a core of
coarser particles. Unlike
layered types, there is a
gradual transition from
the coarse particles
to the fine surface.

● **Decorative chipboard**
is manufactured with a
facing of selected wood
veneer, plastic laminate
or a thin melamine foil.
The wood-veneered
boards are sanded ready
for polishing, the foil-
faced and plastic-
laminated boards need
no finishing. Some
plastic-laminated boards
for worktops are made
with finished profiled
edges, while matching
edging strips are
available for lipping
melamine-faced and
wood- veneered boards.

● **Oriented-strand board**
is a three layered
material made from long
strands of pine. The
strands in each layer are
laid in one direction,
and each layer is per-
pendicular to the next
in the same manner
as plywood.

● **Flakeboard or waferboard**
uses large shavings of
wood which are laid
horizontally and overlap
one another. These
boards have greater
tensile strength than
standard chipboard.

FIBREBOARDS

Fibreboards are made from wood that has been reduced to its basic fibre elements and reconstituted to make a stable homogeneous material. Boards of various density are produced, according to the pressure applied and the adhesive used in their manufacture.

SEE ALSO

Cabinet
construction   63,65,70

Hardboards

Hardboard is a high-density fibreboard produced from wet fibres pressed at high pressure and temperature. The natural resins in the fibres are used to bond them together.

Tempered hardboard is a standard-density board which has been impregnated with resin and oil to produce a stronger material that is water-and-abrasion-resistant.
Standard hardboard has only one smooth face. It is made in a wide range of thicknesses from 1.5 to 12mm ($\frac{1}{16}$ to $\frac{1}{2}$in). A cheap material, it is commonly used for drawer bottoms and cabinet backs.
Duo-faced hardboard is similar to standard hardboard but has two smooth faces.
Decorative hardboard is produced in the form of perforated, moulded or lacquered boards.

Medium boards

Medium boards are made in a similar way to hardboard. They are produced in two grades. Low-density (LM) board, 6 to 12mm ($\frac{1}{4}$ to $\frac{1}{2}$ in) thick, is used for pinboard or wall panelling. High-density (HM) board is stronger and is used for interior panelling.

Medium-density fibreboard (MDF) is a fibreboard with two smooth faces manufactured by a dry process. The fibres are bonded together with a synthetic resin adhesive. It has a uniform structure and a fine texture which allows the edges and faces to be cleanly profile-machined.
  This type of fibreboard can be worked like wood and can be used as a substitute for solid wood in some applications. It makes an excellent substrate for veneer and takes paint finishes well. MDF boards are made in thicknesses of 6 to 32mm ($\frac{1}{4}$ to $1\frac{1}{4}$in) and a wide range of panel sizes.

Medium boards
1 High-density (HM) board
2 Low-density (LM) board
3 Medium-density fibreboard (MDF)
4 Oak-veneered MDF board

Hardboards
5 Standard hardboard
6 Tempered hardboard
7 Embossed hardboard
8 Decorative-faced hardboard
9 Perforated hardboard

CHAPTER TWO

DESIGNING

Designing in three dimensions requires the ability to visualize how an object will eventually look before you actually make it. The design process is never easy and if you are working with unfamiliar forms or materials it becomes even more complex than usual. Indeed, you may find it is often necessary to construct a series of prototypes in order to evaluate every design decision and to make sure the object you are designing will function satisfactorily. However, even if you are a beginner, you can draw on the experience and expertise accumulated by generations of craftsmen-designers. This chapter looks at the various questions a designer needs to consider, including structure, safety and intended **IN WOOD** use, as well as aesthetic and decorative considerations. Also included are sketches illustrating the basic principles of chair, table and storage-unit construction, which you can use as a source of ideas and as a guide to the various practical aspects of furniture design, such as choice of joints and order of assembly.

THE DESIGN PROCESS

New forms or concepts are rarely dreamed up out of thin air. If you look back over the history of furniture design, for example, you will detect a gradually evolving pattern as woodworkers learned to deal with the inevitable movement of solid timber responding to humidity. You will see how techniques were modified as a result of changing technology, and how the appearance of furniture was influenced by contemporary taste. But the rate of change was slow. The majority of woodworkers were artisans, rather than designers in the modern sense. They would continue to make familiar objects, using the same tools, methods and materials as their fathers and grandfathers, knowing exactly what the results would be. Only the most fashionable workshops were producing innovative designs, for clients wealthy enough to pay what we today call development costs. These innovations had to be tried and tested before they became part of the average workman's repertoire. A modern-day woodworker could do a lot worse than follow this example while acquiring the basic skills of designing in wood. No one wants to stifle originality nor discourage woodworkers from developing their creative talents, but it would be perverse to ignore that wealth of experience simply to avoid copying what's been done previously. Before attempting to break new ground a designer should endeavour to understand how his or her chosen material behaves, appreciate how the finished item is to function and avoid visual gimmickry.

FUNCTION

Much is said about designing for function, but to understand what that means one has to examine the concept from several angles. A solid block of wood can function as a stool, but a well-designed stool is something else. A bar stool supports a seated human being and so does a milking stool – yet they have completely different functions and, consequently, different dimensions. Should a stool be light enough to be portable – or should it, in a public building, be bolted to the ground to prevent it being toppled, blocking a fire-escape route? Should a stool be adjustable in height? Should it fold for storage? And will it tip easily when someone shifts their weight? A designer has to pose questions of this nature in order to define how an object is to function, then provide a design solution based on real requirements, as opposed to preconceptions. But even then, the solution will almost certainly to some extent be a compromise. An elegant solution is one that comes close to answering all the questions – it will seldom, if ever, be perfect.

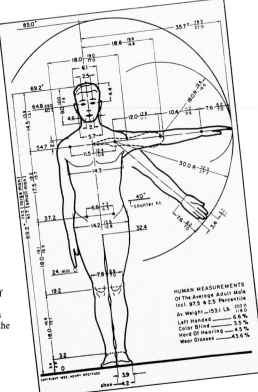

The average human
The American designer Henry Dreyfuss pioneered the study of anthropometrics. His book 'Designing for People' provides us with detailed dimensions of the average male and female.

Designing for people
In order to be functional, most items of woodwork have to relate in some way to the human body. As a species we differ widely in size, shape and weight – so when designing a chair for an individual, you need to take careful measurements of that person's anatomy before you can be sure the chair will be comfortable. However, anthropometry and ergonomics – the statistical sciences concerned with the comparative study of the human body and how it relates to its environment – provide designers with the optimum dimensions for furniture and work stations that suit people of average height and build. Most people are reasonably comfortable using furniture based on these dimensions, but if you are making something for a specific group of people, such as children or the elderly, you may have to create custom-built artefacts tailored to their needs. Specific anthropometric data is given where appropriate throughout this chapter.

Adaptability
Designing something to be adaptable increases its usefulness. Bunk beds that convert to two full-size beds – especially welcome in a family with growing children – are a good example of built-in adaptability. An ergonomic typist's chair is designed to be comfortable for people of any stature; and a draw-leaf table is an example of compactness coupled with flexibility. In a bookcase adjustable shelves are more useful than fixed ones; and in a cupboard simple drawers, sliding trays or baskets may give a greater degree of versatility than rigid compartments.

Structural requirements
Nothing functions well or lasts long unless it is properly constructed. A table that rocks when you are cutting your steak is annoying; a desk top that vibrates while you're typing is distracting; and a chair that suddenly collapses is positively dangerous, as well as being a nuisance.

A wooden structure can support considerable weight without noticeable distortion, providing it is designed to counteract the stresses and strains of normal use.

The leg frame of a traditional stick chair illustrates the principle perfectly. The four legs are plugged into the underside of a solid seat. Horizontal stretcher rails not only prevent the legs bending under load, but also stop them sliding apart. The angles at which the components meet are such that they reinforce one another against shifting forces, mainly because a straight pull is never exerted on any of the joints. And if the chair is tipped onto its splayed back legs, they are ideally placed to support the additional weight at that angle. The structure is, in fact, superbly suited to its intended purpose.

An overloaded shelf sags and may eventually break because of the combination of compression and tension. But if you cut off a 50mm (2in) strip, turn it through 90 degrees and glue it to the underside of the shelf, it will be able to support more weight without bending – by turning the strip on edge you have constructed an effective beam. The rails supporting a table top or chair seat perform a similar function.

The load on a beam is transferred to whatever is supporting it at each end – the legs of a table or chair, for example. The joints between the rails and legs must be capable of resisting shear forces (the downward pressure of the load being opposed by the rigid supports). Shear forces are increased considerably when sideways pressure is applied to a structure, exerting leverage on the joints. A strong dowel joint or the tongue of a mortise and tenon is able to cope with this leverage, especially if the rail is deep enough to provide decent shoulders for the joints and if glued corner blocks are used to reinforce the structure on the inside of the rails.

The joints of a cabinet or a box are especially vulnerable to sideways pressure, which causes the frame to 'rack', forming a parallelogram. However, a rigid back panel, vertical pilasters or corner plates will prevent movement in the joints and create a rigid structure. A built-in plinth or shelf-support rails will achieve the same purpose, while metal-strip cross-bracing prevents racking by tying opposite diagonal corners together.

The effects of load on a shelf

A strip on edge provides support

Legs oppose the load on a rail

Sideways pressure exerts leverage on the joints

Strong joints and corner blocks hold the frame rigid

The traditional stick chair
The underframe components are ideally placed to counteract the stresses and strains imposed by normal use.

The near-perfect back rest
An ergonomic back rest is both beautiful and comfortable.

An unsupported box will collapse

Making a box rigid
To create a rigid structure the joints of a box or cabinet must be reinforced using one of the following methods.

Rigid back panel

Vertical pilasters

Corner plates

Plinth and shelf rails

Cross-bracing

DESIGNING FOR SAFETY

If it is possible to misuse something, you can be sure someone will eventually do so. People often stand on the flimsiest of chairs or use the stretcher rails as a ladder to reach the top shelf of a bookcase, while tipping a chair onto its back legs after dinner is a common abuse. Even though a chair is not built for such purposes, you should take them into consideration as part of the design process and, if possible, modify your design to minimize the risk of an accident occurring.

The effects of leverage

People often sit on tables. Providing the rails and joints are strong enough, the table rarely suffers anything more than scuffs and scratches caused by back-pocket studs or buttons. But if the top is cantilevered – like a fall flap on a bureau, for example – the leverage created at the hinges is considerable, even when someone merely rests their weight on the flap. Suspending the flap from folding metal stays alleviates the risk of tearing out the hinges, or you can use lopers (rails that slide out of the bureau to support the flap from below). Both methods move the effective pivot point forward, away from the hinge line towards the front of the flap, thus decreasing the leverage.

If the door of a sideboard or kitchen unit is allowed to swing towards a tier of drawers next to it, it is only a matter of time before the corner of a drawer that has not been pushed home acts as a fulcrum to pull the door off its hinges. If you cannot alter the position of the door or drawers, use stays to stop the door opening further than 90 degrees.

The effect of leverage
Levering a door against a drawer can pull it off its hinges.

Oak bureau
Pull-out lopers housed in the underframe (below) support a leather-lined fall flap (centre).

An unsupported flap strains hinges

Folding stays decrease leverage

Lopers have a similar effect

Stability

A piece of furniture may be stable under normal circumstances, but ask yourself whether it can be easily toppled. A dining chair will be stable providing its centre of gravity remains within the area defined by the four points where the legs meet the floor (1) – but if leaning against the back rest moves the centre of gravity outside that area (2), the chair becomes unstable and will topple. For this reason, the back legs of a chair are often made to slope (3) so that it will remain safely balanced even when tipped slightly backwards (4).

A chest of drawers can become dangerously unstable if all the drawers are open at the same time. However, a short cabinet with a wide base has a relatively low centre of gravity and will maintain its equilibrium unless it is toppled deliberately. A taller cabinet may have to be screwed to the wall or floor. Similarly, large heavy doors that would cause a freestanding wardrobe to topple are usually made to slide, instead of being hinged.

1 Stable chair

2 Unstable chair

3 A sloping back leg widens a chair base

4 Centre of gravity acts within base area

Splayed-leg chair
The wide base of this robust armchair prevents it being toppled accidentally.

DESIGNING WITH WOOD IN MIND

Avoiding hazardous details
Even small details can cause serious injuries. Think twice about leaving sharp edges or corners, especially if they are at a level where children may fall against them. Glass table tops are especially dangerous in this respect. A round top is relatively safe providing that all the sharp edges are removed by polishing, but it is advisable to enclose a rectangular glass top within a rebated frame.

Sharp edges are even worse if they close with a scissor action. Trapping your fingers between a heavy inset lid and the side of a box is painful, to say the least; but the consequences of a similar accident with a folding chair collapsing under your weight can be far more serious.

A swivelling desk chair with arms constitutes a less obvious risk. There should be sufficient clearance for your knuckles between the underside of the desk top and the chair arms if you are to avoid an unpleasant surprise as you swivel the chair in order to stand up.

Sharp projecting handles can tear clothing, even though they may not cause actual physical harm, so choose smooth rounded knobs and handgrips or fit flush or drop handles.

Safe detailing
Integral drawer handles can be a safe yet striking feature.

In principle, most factors relating to function and safety are applicable no matter what material you are using, but when designing with wood in mind you need to take into consideration the fact that timber continues to absorb and exude moisture according to the humidity of its immediate surroundings, regardless of when it was cut from the tree. If you take a 100-year-old chest of drawers from an unheated room and stand it next to a radiator, it will still dry out; and if you return it to its original environment, it will absorb moisture from the air. The problem for the woodworker is the dimensional changes that accompany these exchanges of moisture – wood shrinks as it loses water and expands when it takes it up again. If this movement is restricted in any way, the wood will split or warp. Allowing for this movement to occur without detriment to the work is another aspect of the designer's activity.

Allowing for movement
The differential movement that occurs even within a single piece of timber often causes problems.

Due to the grain structure of wood, a solid board will shrink or expand to a greater extent across its width than along its length (1). If you make a box from four pieces of similar wood, joining them at the corners so that all four pieces have their grain running in the same direction, they will move together by exactly the same amount and no damage or distortion will occur (2).

If you attach other components rigidly with their grain running contrary to the wood grain of the box's sides, they restrict the natural movement across the box until the resulting stresses are relieved by splits opening along the grain (3). The solution is to devise a way of attaching the components with fixings such as slotted screws that allow for an element of movement.

A common safeguard against movement in thin solid-wood panels is to locate them in grooved components – they should never be glued in place. This is the principle employed in traditional frame-and-panel construction.

1 Shrinkage is greater across grain

2 Box sides move together

3 Cross battens restrict movement until splits relieve the stresses.

Fixings that allow for movement

SLOTTED SCREW FIXING

FRAME-AND-PANEL CONSTRUCTION

Disguising the effects of movement
An experienced designer uses some form of visual distraction whenever he or she anticipates that movement in the timber will affect the detailing of a workpiece. An inset drawer front may fit like a glove when it leaves the bench, but an unsightly gap can open up all round after only a few months. A narrow moulding attached to or cut around the edges of the drawer front or surrounding frame is enough to disguise the gap (1).

Alternatively, you can make a feature of a gap from the outset, knowing that it is going to occur in any case. For example, the movement between the components of tongue and groove panelling is imperceptible due to the strong linear pattern created deliberately by the open joints (2).

The edge of a table top planed flush with the underframe may look beautifully crisp at first, but the effect is spoiled as soon as the top shrinks (3). A rebate cut in the top or rail creates a strong shadow-line so the movement is indiscernible (4). Alternatively, let the top overhang the rail (5) or mould and set back the edge from the face of the rail (6).

Avoiding the problem
It is perfectly acceptable for a designer to select stable man-made boards for table tops or cabinet construction to avoid the problem of shrinkage that occurs in solid-timber panels.

1 Disguising a gap

2 A deliberate feature

3 Shrinkage spoils the effect of a flush top

4 Rebated table top

5 Overhanging top

6 Set-back table top

DESIGNING FOR APPEARANCE

It might seem reasonable to suppose that the appearance of a piece you are designing should be largely determined by selection of optimum dimensions and by those features or mechanical devices that combine to make the end product function as well as possible. Indeed, the overused maxim 'Form follows function' is based on that premise. In reality, it is too simplistic a view. Designers go to great lengths in order to get something to look its best. They will tinker with its proportions, take time to select the piece of wood that will enhance its appearance and incorporate mouldings, carvings, inlays or shaped components, all to increase its visual appeal. In short, the appearance of a piece of work is just as important as its pure function, but it is virtually impossible to be objective about the aesthetic merits of any design. The only solution is to develop your own sense of what is pleasing and what is most likely to be acceptable.

1 Padauk box
A deliberately simple design that features square-knuckle hinges cut from solid wood.

2 Hexagonal boxes
They are machined from solid Indian rosewood with burr-veneered lids.

3 Dominoes
African-blackwood dominoes inlaid with sycamore 'spots'.

4 One-piece box
A small decorative box cut from yew.

Antique-style Pembroke table
Copying genuine antiques is one way to ensure your work fits a period interior perfectly.

Traditional oak tool cabinet
A beautifully-proportioned tool cabinet that seems almost too good for the workshop.

Suitability

How is it we can appreciate the quality of a simple undecorated stick or Windsor chair yet find a fine carved Sheraton-style dining chair equally appealing? They could hardly be more different in appearance. One possible reason is the way we envisage them in totally different settings – in the rooms for which they were originally designed. Stick chairs would look ridiculous beside a highly polished table in an elegantly decorated dining room, whilst a Sheraton-style chair would look equally out of place in a cottage kitchen. Swap them around, and each fits naturally into its intended environment.

It is necessary to anticipate how and where an object is to be used – then design it accordingly, selecting the appropriate timbers, shapes, proportions and finish to achieve the desired result. Although some people have a talent for combining furniture and fittings of all styles and periods, it is certainly easier if you reflect the style and decor of the intended location. This doesn't mean you have to reproduce period furniture or fittings: if you use similar materials and detail, your design will at least be in harmony with its surroundings.

Veneered cabinet
A simple yet decorative cabinet for a modern interior. It is made from stained and painted sycamore.

Caned dining chair
Narrow edges to legs and seat rails add delicacy to a sturdy dining chair.

Carved wooden bowls
Cut and carved from solid cherry, rosewood and walnut, these bowls are decorated with precise fluting.

5

6

5 Nine men's morris
A games board made from burr-elm veneer inlaid with rosewood and brass. The pieces are turned from boxwood and cocobolo.

6 Desk tidy and bowl
Both items are made from thin birch plywood held with padauk buttons.

Folding screen
Constructed largely
from bent-plywood
panels, this folding
screen is an attractive
combination of black
lacquer, ash and stain-
less steel.

London-plane cheval mirror
A stylish full-length pivoting
mirror is surrounded by pigeon-
hole storage compartments.

Decorative detailing
Padauk-veneer inserts
interrupt the line of a
laminated cherry
lipping.

Table-column joints
Even simple joints can
be enhanced by the
careful selection of
coloured timbers.

Deceiving the eye
This sideboard appears to levitate
on its deeply curved base.

Refined simplicity
An ash tripod table that reflects
the classic tradition for elegant
drawing-room furniture.

SIMPLICITY & DECORATION

Aiming for simplicity
If there is no designated
location for a piece you are
making, it is best to aim for
simplicity so it will look right
in virtually any setting. But
don't be misled into think-
ing this is an easy option.
Professional designers spend
years honing their skills in
order to achieve the subtlety
required to reduce a piece of
work to its bare essentials
and to arrive at precise proportions upon which the
aesthetic qualities of the
design will stand or fall.
Moreover, making a simple
workpiece requires crafts-
manship of a high standard
– since, when there is not the
slightest embellishment to
distract the eye, defects
such as a less-than-perfect
finish, imprecise joints
or clumsy detailing may
well become noticeable
at a glance.

Including decoration
As previously described,
mouldings are often used
to disguise the effects of
shrinkage, and carving can
be used to texture a surface
which would otherwise have
to be finished immaculately.
This was a common ploy in
the days when all woodwork
was produced by hand; but
now that machines are available to alleviate the chore
of planing and sanding flat
surfaces, designers tend to
employ decoration purely
for richness of effect. Exotic
veneers, for example, are
used exclusively for their
decorative qualities, as are
marquetry, parquetry and
wood or metal inlays.
   With imagination, you can
exploit virtually any aspect
of woodworking for visual
impact. Indeed, skilled
craftsmen sometimes design
pieces specifically to focus
attention on exquisitely
made finger joints or decorative dovetails – deliberately
creating features for fellow
woodworkers to admire.

The bare essentials
Stacked pivoting drawers and a
rectangular top constitute a desk
devoid of superfluous detail.

COLOUR, TEXTURE & ILLUSION

Colour and texture

Selecting the right timber may be all that is needed to upgrade a mundane workpiece, but combining wood with other materials provides further opportunities to delight the eye. The cool smooth texture of glass or marble can make a pleasing contrast to a rich grain pattern, and the gleam of polished brass fittings or inlay may add to the appeal of a dark-coloured timber.

The choice of surface finish can transform the appearance of a piece significantly. Stains and clear finishes enhance any timber's depth of colour, and then there is the difference between the reflective qualities of a matt polish and a gloss varnish. There are also endless possibilities for the application of pure colour in the form of sprayed or brushed paint.

Creating optical illusions

If you are not satisfied with the exact proportions of a piece or want to make it appear lighter or heavier than it really is, you can use detailing to create the desired effect.

Adding a deep lipping to a shelf or the edge of a panel suggests solidity and mass without significantly increasing its weight. Conversely, applying a linear moulding or inlay to a deep rail has a slimming effect.

You can lend elegance to a thick table top by cutting wide shallow bevels on the underside so that a thin edge only is visible all round. Tapering the legs of a table will make it look taller and lighter, and a deep curve cut in the underside of a plinth rail gives a lift to a heavy-looking sideboard or chest of drawers.

Even the texture and tone of the wood used for a piece can affect the way we perceive it. A large expanse of dark wood may dominate a room, whereas a paler tone is less obtrusive. A wild grain pattern can introduce a sense of vigour, while the striped nature of radial-cut veneer is more tranquil.

Richly decorated occasional table
Marquetry combines colour and texture for a table top (right) on turned pear and wenge legs.

Decorative joint
This original laminated-oak leg joint is both strong and distinctive.

Eye-catching colour
This freely painted table is an example of how colour can be used to make a unique workpiece.

Turned bowl
Flaming the workpiece part way through the turning process accentuates the natural colour and texture of an elm burr.

Freestanding cabinet
Derived from an original concept, this 'tower' cabinet is accessible from two sides.

Duck-pond table
Dipping ducks support a glass table top that represents the surface of water.

DEVELOPING YOUR OWN STYLE

Developing a visual style that stamps their work with their own individuality is surely the ultimate goal of most serious woodworkers. In order to be distinctive, your style does not have to be flamboyant or eccentric. For instance, you may draw your inspiration from a recognized historical style – not copying pieces faithfully in every detail, but using the essence of that style as a starting point or spring-board for your own ideas. On the other hand, it may be that a particular method of production holds a special fascination for you and has a strong influence on the forms and shapes you create. Designing for the woodturning lathe, for example, or using only curved components made from laminated veneers are both ways of channelling your thoughts and energies in a definite direction.

Perhaps the most difficult approach of all is deliberately setting out to break the rules. Challenging pre-conceived notions of what something is supposed to look like takes imagination and skill, as well as the courage to pull it off success-fully. We take it for granted that storage units usually stand against a wall, but it is perfectly possible to make a freestanding unit with access from all sides. By convention, most tables have four legs, but a three-legged table would look arresting and, incidentally, be more stable on an uneven floor. And why take up valuable floor space with a bed when it may be possible to suspend it from the ceiling? Addressing such questions will not always elicit original answers. You may be drawn back to the accepted ways of making things again and again simply because they happen to work best – but just occasionally you may hit upon the germ of an idea that will lead to a truly original piece of work.

Nesting stools
Stained-ash stools that
are designed to form an
attractive group.

Laminated stools
A matching pair of stools with
bowed side panels of laminated ply
bolted to solid cherry seats.

Walnut desk and chair
Made from solid walnut
this furniture is a
comfortable blend of
traditional and modern
styles.

Veneered sideboard
A striking ash and rosewood
cabinet with Art-Deco influences.

Chippendale-style chair
A carved mahogany dining chair.

Recliner and footstool
Flowing curves are
inevitable with steam-
bent components.

PRINCIPLES OF CHAIR CONSTRUCTION

The familiar upright dining chair has been with us for centuries in one form or another and yet the basic design requirements remain unchanged. A chair must support the user in such a position that he or she can eat or work at a table comfortably and, if it has arms, sit down and get up without difficulty. It must be strong enough to bear the weight of the person yet light

enough to be moved without effort. At first sight it would appear to be a tall order but there are traditional 'themes' that solve the problem admirably to which every designer and craftsman returns. There are endless combinations, but the examples of chair construction that follow provide useful starting points from which to develop your own designs.

DESIGNING A COMFORTABLE CHAIR

To construct chairs that will be reasonably comfortable for the majority of the population designers base their work on standard recommended dimensions, but to confirm the precise

height, shape and angle of a chair's components it may be necessary to make a mock-up of the critical elements or to test and modify certain details as the work progresses.

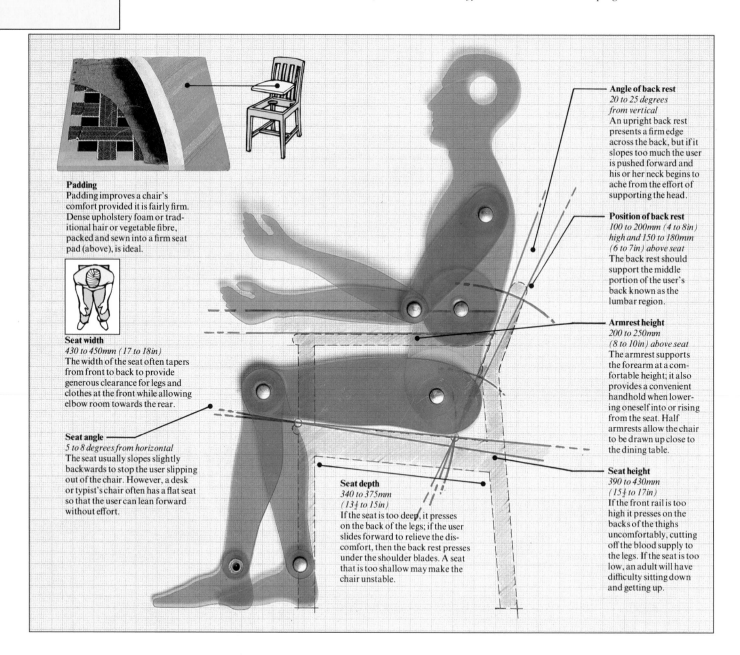

Padding
Padding improves a chair's comfort provided it is fairly firm. Dense upholstery foam or traditional hair or vegetable fibre, packed and sewn into a firm seat pad (above), is ideal.

Seat width
430 to 450mm (17 to 18in)
The width of the seat often tapers from front to back to provide generous clearance for legs and clothes at the front while allowing elbow room towards the rear.

Seat angle
5 to 8 degrees from horizontal
The seat usually slopes slightly backwards to stop the user slipping out of the chair. However, a desk or typist's chair often has a flat seat so that the user can lean forward without effort.

Seat depth
340 to 375mm
(13¼ to 15in)
If the seat is too deep, it presses on the back of the legs; if the user slides forward to relieve the discomfort, then the back rest presses under the shoulder blades. A seat that is too shallow may make the chair unstable.

Angle of back rest
20 to 25 degrees from vertical
An upright back rest presents a firm edge across the back, but if it slopes too much the user is pushed forward and his or her neck begins to ache from the effort of supporting the head.

Position of back rest
100 to 200mm (4 to 8in) high and 150 to 180mm (6 to 7in) above seat
The back rest should support the middle portion of the user's back known as the lumbar region.

Armrest height
200 to 250mm (8 to 10in) above seat
The armrest supports the forearm at a comfortable height; it also provides a convenient handhold when lowering oneself into or rising from the seat. Half armrests allow the chair to be drawn up close to the dining table.

Seat height
390 to 430mm (15¼ to 17in)
If the front rail is too high it presses on the backs of the thighs uncomfortably, cutting off the blood supply to the legs. If the seat is too low, an adult will have difficulty sitting down and getting up.

FRAME CHAIRS

The frame chair is the most versatile form of dining chair. The four rails of the seat frame are jointed into a leg at each corner of the structure, while the back legs extend upwards to form the main support of the back rest. The seat itself may be upholstered, caned, rush-covered or made from solid wood.

- **BACK REST** stub-tenoned together & into back legs
- **DROP-IN PAD**
- **UPHOLSTERY** Drop-in pad improves comfort
- **Corner blocks** screwed to rails reinforce seat frame
- CREST RAIL
- BACK REST
- CORNER BLOCK
- USE HAUNCHED JOINT FOR FRONT
- **SEAT RAILS** are joined to the legs with mortise & tenons

- **BACK LEG** stub-tenoned into crest rail
- STUB TENON
- SEAT-PAD REBATE
- **SEAT PAD REBATES** on inside of rail support drop-in seat pad

- **CENTRAL SPLAT** is tenoned into the underside of the crest rail
- SPLAT
- **Seat pad rests on BATTENS** screwed to seat rails
- STUB TENON
- SEAT PAD
- BATTEN
- CREST RAIL
- **UPHOLSTERED SEAT PAD** overhangs curved front rail
- SEAT RAIL
- **TAPERED FRAME** provides plenty of clearance between arms
- **DOWEL JOINTS** Are nearly as strong as mortise & tenon joints
- BACK LEG
- SEAT-RAIL JOINTS

ORDER OF CONSTRUCTION
Frame chair

- Assemble back rest.
- Plug back legs onto back rest and seat rail.
- Plug crest rail onto back legs.
- Attach legs to front seat rail.
- Join front and back frames with side rails.
- Make and upholster seat pad.

- **FOLDING SEAT** jointed to front legs with pivots
- HINGES
- SCREWED SLATS
- METAL PEGS in seat rails slide in grooves

- **TURN BUTTON** Holds down seat
- **LEG FRAME** stops against seat rail
- **DIAGONAL RAIL** keeps frame rigid
- **SLATTED SEAT** screwed to frame
- CANVAS SEAT
- **FOLDING STAY** provides security

FOLDING CHAIRS & STOOLS
The classic space-saving folding chair is in effect an A-frame chair. Folding stools have an X-shaped frame with a rigid slatted seat or a seat platform of stretched canvas.

ARM CONSTRUCTION
An armrest is usually housed into the back leg and fixed with a dowel or screw. The support is housed into the side rail in a similar way. The joint between armrest and support can be a stub tenon or, for extra strength, a wedged through tenon.

- **ARMREST JOINT** is usually housed & dowelled or screwed
- JOINTS DOWELLED OR SCREWED
- **FLAT ARMRESTS** are glued & screwed
- MORTISE & TENON JOINTS
- GLUED & SCREWED
- **MORTISE & TENON JOINTS** are used for arms in line with seat rails & back legs

STACKING CHAIRS

The narrow seat frames provide clearance for the back legs when stacking chairs are piled one on top of another for storage.

• LAMINATED BACK REST (SEE BOX)

• SEAT RAILS
side rails tenoned into front & back rails

• CREST RAIL is finger jointed to top of back legs

• WEDGES

FRONT RAIL

SIDE RAIL

Wedged through tenon (twin)

FINGER JOINT

SEE ALSO

Designing a comfortable chair	50
Finger joints	163
Scarf joint	218
Mortise & tenons	226-234
Dowel joints	236-237
Steam bending	251-253
Laminated bending	254-256
Woodscrews	304-305

ORDER OF CONSTRUCTION
Stacking chair

● Join back legs to back rail, then fit crest rail.
● Attach front legs to front seat rail.
● Join front and back frames with side rails.
● Glue back rest to crest rail, and plywood seat panel to chair frame.

• Corner reinforcing blocks

• WEDGED THROUGH TENON (SINGLE)
Wedges make an extra strong seat-rail joint

• LEG JOINTS
Legs jointed to front rail with wedged through tenon (single)

• LAMINATED SEAT PANEL glued to rails or fixed with counterbored screws

• ANGLED BACK LEGS make chair less likely to tip over

• BACK LEG secured to seat frame with dowel

• CURVED CREST RAIL
Cut from solid timber & then tenoned or dowelled onto ends of back legs

• BACK LEG

ALTERNATIVE BACK RESTS
Three common back rests that can be adapted for frame and stacking chairs.

• LAMINATED BACK REST is glued to the back rail

BALLOON-BACK CHAIR

This type of chair takes its name from the distinctively curved back-support rails.

MID RAIL tenoned between legs

• CANE SEAT for lighter weight

• WIDE CREST RAIL
Back legs can be dovetail-housed

ORDER OF CONSTRUCTION
Balloon-back chair

● Assemble back frame, including back stretcher rails.
● Assemble seat frame.
● Assemble remaining stretcher rails and front legs.
● Plug seat frame onto front legs, then fit it into the notched back legs and fix with through dowels.
● Apply a finish to the chair before caning the seat.

• SEAT FRAME notched into back legs

• STRETCHER RAIL essential to reinforce leg & frame joints

• UPHOLSTERED BACK REST
Hardwood frame covered with foam & fabric & screw fixed

Shaped horizontal rails of seat frame dowelled together

• FRONT LEGS are turned and plug into seat rail

BENTWOOD CHAIRS

Bentwood chairs are constructed by bolting and screwing together steam-bent beech components. This type of chair is extremely tough and resilient providing the fixings are not allowed to work loose.

Classic side-chair and armchair configurations

one-piece stretcher rail

• SIDECHAIR

Hooped stretcher rail

• ARMCHAIR

BACKLEG

SEAT HOOP

•PLYWOOD SEAT PANEL glued in rebated seat hoop

BOLT

Back legs are bolted to the seat hoop

ORDER OF CONSTRUCTION
Bentwood chair

● Steam-bend and shape all components separately.
● Bolt back-rest assembly to seat hoop.
● Plug front legs into seat hoop.
● Screw stretcher hoop to all four legs.
● Fit arms, if required.

BACK REST & LEGS bent from one piece of wood

BOLT

Hooped STRETCHER RAIL is screwed to the legs

LAMINATED CHAIRS

Structurally-weak short grain is avoided by making chair frames from thick laminated veneers. This type of structure is strong and resilient.

Use tongue & groove joints for side frame

• SIDE FRAME

•BACK REST tongues fit in grooved side frames

• Laminated seat and back rest

• FILLERBLOCK

side frames constructed from three laminations

• FILLER BLOCK could be stained for decorative infill

ORDER OF CONSTRUCTION
Laminated chair

● Laminate side-frame components, seat and back rest separately.
● Glue together laminated components to make side frames, and insert filler blocks with glue.
● Rout grooves in side frames and tongues on seat and back rest.
● Glue seat, back rest and rail between side frames.

• ARMS are screwed onto back rest and seat hoop

KNEELING CHAIR
Many preconceptions regarding chair design have been challenged recently. With a 'kneeling chair', the weight of the body is thrown forward onto the knees in order to improve posture and relieve pressure on the lower back.

• SEAT PANEL

• BLOCK

• SEAT HOOP

•FRONT LEGS are plugged into the seat hoop, fixed with glue & screwed from the inside

• FRONT LEG

• SCARF JOINT

• SEAT HOOP made from continuous square section of wood that is scarf-jointed.

STICK CHAIRS

The stick chair in its countless variations is a beautifully proportioned and functional piece of furniture that has evolved under the trained eye and experienced hands of craftsmen from all over Europe and America. It relies for its strength and rigidity on the fact that the large number of components share the load in such a way that the forces applied to the structure do not attempt to pull it apart. Stick chairs have always been made from tough dense native timbers such as beech, oak, ash and elm, which can be softened with steam before being bent for the bow-back versions of the chair.

LADDER-BACK STICK CHAIR
All the back-rest crossrails are stub-tenoned into the turned legs.

CROSS-RAILS

WOVEN RUSH SEAT

STUB TENON

RAIL

TURNED LEGS

STRETCHER RAILS plugged into tapered holes

SPINDLE

SEAT BOARD

WEDGE

CREST RAIL

BACK SPINDLES

MAIN BACK SPINDLE

• WEDGED JOINT main back spindles pass through the seat board and are then expanded with wooden wedges

STRETCHER RAILS

ARMRESTS are cut from solid timber

CRESTRAILS are plugged onto the back spindles

SHAPED SOLID SEAT BOARD

CONTINUOUS ARM

MAIN SPINDLE

ORDER OF CONSTRUCTION
Stick chair

- Assemble legs and stretcher rails.
- Lay seat board face down on a bench, then hammer legs into holes in the underside of the seat.
- Tap back spindles into seat board, then fit crest rail.
- Fit armrests and supports.

KITCHEN CHAIR
This type of kitchen chair has a stick-chair underframe. The back rest and supports are cut from solid timber.

SEAT BOARDS are made from solid timber and are often carved into a saddle shape

PLUGGED & WEDGED JOINTS

SADDLE SHAPE

SOLID SEAT BOARD

CREST RAIL

CROSSRAIL

• BACKREST ASSEMBLY is fixed to the solid seat board with wedged through tenons

WEDGES

LEG

PLUGGED & WEDGED JOINTS

STRETCHER

STRETCHER

• STICK-CHAIR JOINTS all turned components are plugged into tapered holes

• STRETCHER RAILS are essential to tie the legs together

54

PRINCIPLES OF TABLE CONSTRUCTION

A table need be no more than a flat surface supported at a height that is convenient for dining, studying, typing or serving coffee, and yet designers have expended considerable creative energy on this seemingly simple category of furniture. They have experimented with table tops to see what is the best shape and size to accommodate the average dinner party; underframes range from straightforward structures designed to provide maximum leg room to exercises in functional sculpture; and perhaps most ingenuity has been invested in finding easy ways of increasing the size of compact tables when it is necessary to seat a large group of people. The examples that follow illustrate traditional methods and are applicable both to large and small tables. Basic folding and extending mechanisms are also described.

DESIGNING A FUNCTIONAL TABLE

Eating at a dining table can be either an enjoyable social occasion or a nightmare of cramped knees and colliding elbows, depending on the amount of room provided by the designer. Most people are able to write or draw comfortably at dining-table height, but before designing a table for someone to work at find out whether he or she will be using a typewriter or a word processor because at least part of the table top must be lowered to present a keyboard at the optimum level.

DINING TABLES

Moving a chair
700mm (2ft 4in)
A diner needs a space of this size in order to stand up from the table.

Dining-table height
700mm (2ft 4in)
This is a comfortable height for a dining table, though eating from a bowl with chopsticks is easier either at a table closer to the height of a kitchen worktop or sitting cross-legged at a low table little more than 300mm (1ft) from the ground.

Elbow room
600mm (2ft)
This is sufficient space for an adult to wield a knife and fork without obstructing his or her neighbour.

Leg room
600mm (2ft)
Allow at least this dimension between the table rail and the floor.

Knee clearance
250mm (10in)
This is the minimum distance from the edge of the top to a table leg in order to provide clearance for your knees when your chair is drawn up to the table.

Rectangular dining table
To seat six people comfortably, a rectangular dining table should be a minimum of 1.5 × 1m (5ft × 3ft 3in).

Circular dining table
A circular dining table of only 1m (3ft 3in) diameter will seat up to four persons.

Increase the diameter to 1.2m (4ft) for six diners and to about 1.5m (5ft) to accommodate eight people.

WORKTABLES

Desk height
700mm (2ft 4in)
A desk should be the same height as a dining table.

Typing and word processing
650mm (2ft 2in)
A worktable should be 50mm (2in) lower than the average desk to accommodate typing or word processing.

Maximum reach
475mm (1ft 7in)
A seated person can reach a bookshelf at this height above a desk.

OCCASIONAL TABLES

300 to 600mm (1 to 2ft)
Occasional or coffee-table height varies a great deal. The lowest ones often look very stylish, but are a little too low for comfort.

Dining-table seating arrangements

FRAME TABLES

A frame table has four legs, one at each corner. With strong mortise and tenon or dowel joints, the classic design can be adapted successfully for tables of practically any size. You can make the top from solid timber, but for stability the larger ones are often constructed from lipped and veneered blockboard.

• SOLID TOPS
• PLYWOOD TONGUE } FOR GREATER strength.
• BUTT JOINT

ORDER OF CONSTRUCTION
Frame table
● Glue legs to end rails and leave to set.
● Glue assembled end-frames to long rails.
● Fit top.

SOLID-WOOD STRIP EDGING
• BLOCKBOARD TOP

• Solid tops are made from strips of timber either butt-jointed or joined with plywood tongues

• SOLID TOP Fit top as described right
• END RAIL
• LONG RAIL

CORNER JOINTS can be either mortise & tenon or metal corner plates

• BLOCKBOARD TOPS solid-wood lippings are glued to edges to strengthen them & to hide core
HAUNCH

• MORTISE & TENON
HAUNCH
• MORTISE & TENON
• DOWEL JOINT

• Veneer applied over lipping
• Veneer applied before lipping
• Veneer applied before moulded lipping

LEG JOINTS conventional mortise & tenon or dowel joints

• GROOVE
• RAIL
• SCREW

• LEG

STANDARD FRAME CONSTRUCTION

• METAL CORNER PLATE fits into grooves cut in rails & fixed with screws. Metal bolt screwed into table leg passes through plate & is tightened with a wing nut.

HANGER BOLT
• WING NUT

ATTACHING TABLE TOPS
A table top made from stable man-made board can be fixed rigidly to an underframe. A solid-wood top must be attached using a method that allows it to shrink or swell.

• BUTTONS
• GROOVE
• TOP (UNDERSIDE)

BUTTONS ~ small hardwood blocks fit into grooves cut in rails

• SHRINKAGE PLATE
• TOP (UNDERSIDE)

METAL SHRINKAGE PLATE screwed to rail & top using slots running across the grain

• COUNTERBORED
• POCKET SCREWED

COUNTERBORE OR POCKET SCREW laminboard or blockboard tops

• DROP-IN TOP
• REBATE

REBATED RAIL for drop-in board or glass tops

• REINFORCING CORNER BLOCKS

STRETCHER
LEG

• REBATED
• CHAMFERED

• FINE FRAME CONSTRUCTION requires stretcher rails for strength

STUB-TENONED STRETCHER RAILS support the main-frame joints by holding the legs together near their ends

• OVERHANGING

TOP/RAIL JUNCTIONS Designed to minimize effects of shrinkage

DESK OR SIDE TABLE
To make a desk or side table, frame-table construction is modified to include drawers.

• SIDE DRAWER RUNNER
• BACK RAIL
• END RAIL
• KICKER
• TOP RAIL
• LOWER RAIL

• SCREW
• GUIDE
• DOVETAIL
• RUNNER

• **DRAWER RUNNER & GUIDE** ~ runner is dovetailed into back rail, guide is screwed to runner

• TOP RAIL
• END RAIL
• END RAIL
either or
• TOP RAIL
• LEG
• LEG

• **TOP RAIL** is dovetailed into leg & end rail

• END RAIL
• TOP RAIL

• **CENTRAL POST** is stub-tenoned into both front rails

• DRAWER CONSTRUCTION see page 71

• **DRAWER RUNNER** is tenoned into front rail

• LOWER RAIL
• LEG
• **LOWER RAIL** is stub-tenoned into leg & end rail.

ORDER OF CONSTRUCTION
Desk or side table

● Glue legs to end rails and leave to set.
● Join back rail and lower front rail to endframes, then fit central post to lower rail and fit top rail.
● Fit central drawer runner, clamp frame and leave glue to set.
● Fit side drawer runners.
● Fit top.
● Make and fit drawers.

ORDER OF CONSTRUCTION
Slab-sided desk

● Assemble frame and allow glue to set.
● Lip end panels.
● Bolt completed slab panels to frame and fit modesty board (if required), using knock-down fitting.
● Fit top.

• BOLTS
• MODESTY BOARD
• FRAME (FRONT)

• **CENTRE RAIL** is stub-tenoned into frame

• MODESTY BOARD is fitted to side panel with K-D fittings

SLAB-SIDED DESK
A slab-sided desk made by bolting chipboard or blockboard panels to a solid-wood frame is another variation on the frame-table theme. A deep modesty board prevents racking.

• BOLT
• SIDE PANEL
• FINGER JOINT
• FRAME (SIDE)
• FRAME (FRONT)

• **FRAME & PANEL CONSTRUCTION** the four corners of the frame are finger-jointed together, the complete frame is then bolted to the side panel.

FRAME TABLE WITH TURNED LEGS
Constructed like a standard frame table, this is particularly suitable as a round-top dining or coffee table.

• LEG
• RAIL
• **CORNER BLOCKS** for smaller tables ~ particularly suitable for three-legged tables

• **FIXING**
• Glue block to rails then cut shoulder on drill press. Fix leg with woodscrew.

• WOODSCREW
• BLOCK

• TABLE TOP
Fix top with buttons or shrinkage plates, see opposite

• DOWEL JOINTS
• TURNED LEGS

• RAILS
• **DOWEL JOINTS** for larger table
• TURNED LEG

REFECTORY TABLE

This type of underframe is suitable for dining and coffee tables. It is usually made to 'knock down' for transportation. Larger frames, especially, must be well made to prevent racking. Attach a solid top to the endframes, using shrinkage plates. A blockboard top can be attached with screws passed through the top rails of the endframes.

- TOP RAIL
- WEDGES
- ENDFRAME
- VERTICAL POST
- WEDGED THROUGH TENON
- CROSSRAIL
- FOOT
- **VERTICAL POST** is fixed to top rail & foot with wedged through tenons
- **TOP** solid-wood or blockboard.
- DEEP CROSSRAIL
- TENON
- **CROSSRAIL JOINT** is a loose-wedged through mortise & tenon.
- WEDGE
- FOOT
- **ENDFRAME CONSTRUCTION** using wedged through tenons
- **CROSSRAIL** is attached to endframes with a loose-wedged through mortise & tenon joint ~ no glue required.

ORDER OF CONSTRUCTION
Refectory table
- Assemble endframes and allow glue to set.
- Fit crossrail.
- Fit top.

DROP-LEAF TABLES

Deep flaps hinged to a fixed top are one way of providing a table top of variable size. When raised, the flaps are supported on pivoting legs or brackets.

- **RULE JOINT** ~ helps support raised flaps, reduces strain on hinges.
- FLAP DOWN
- FLAP UP
- **RULE JOINT**
- SPECIAL ASYMMETRIC TABLE HINGES REQUIRED FOR RULE JOINT
- **MOULDED EDGE** is revealed when flap is down
- FIXED TOP
- RULE JOINT
- FLAP
- **DRAWER** often included in gate-leg table
- DRAWER STOP
- HALVING JOINT
- DOWEL JOINT
- DRAWER RUNNER
- KICKER
- MAIN FRAME
- UPPER DRAWER RAIL
- SHORT CROSS-RAIL
- GATE
- **MAIN FRAME** is constructed like a standard frame table
- **PIVOT PEGS** pivot in holes drilled in table rails
- PIVOT PEG
- **GATE-LEG CONSTRUCTION**
- **HALVING JOINTS** allow gate to be folded flush against frame

ORDER OF CONSTRUCTION
Gate-leg table
- Assemble pivoting gates.
- Assemble both long side frames, fitting the gates between the rails at the same time. Allow glue to set.
- Join the long side frames with the shorter crossrails, fitting the upper drawer rail last.
- Fit drawer runners.
- Join flaps to central part of top.
- Fix central part of top to underframe.

- **GATE LEG** folded flush against frame
- **PIVOTING GATE**
- **GATE STOP** Gate stops against block of wood screwed to underside of flap

GATE-LEG TABLE
The gate-leg table takes its name from the pivoting leg frames that support the flaps on each side.

PEMBROKE TABLE

This is a small refined drop-leaf table. Its flaps are supported on hinged wooden brackets.

DRAWER RUNNER

DRAWER KICKER

CROSS RAIL

SIDE FRAME

UPPER DRAWER RAIL

KNUCKLE-JOINTED SUPPORT BRACKET

FIXED TOP

FLAP

DRAWER STOP

DRAWER *often included in pembroke table*

SIDE FRAME

KNUCKLE JOINTS *Large purpose-made hinges are best for joining the support brackets to the side frame.*

HINGES *deep metal hinges can be used but not as strong as knuckle joints.*

HINGE

SUPPORT BRACKET

SUPPORT BRACKET

KNUCKLE JOINT

ORDER OF CONSTRUCTION
Pembroke table

- Assemble both long side frames. Allow glue to set.
- Join side frames with crossrails, fitting upper drawer rail last.
- Screw and glue hinged brackets to side rails.
- Fit drawer runners.
- Make and fit drawer.
- Join flaps to central part of top.
- Fix central part of top to underframe.

DRAW-LEAF TABLES

Pull-out leaves mounted on sliding bearers are often used to extend the length of a dining table. One popular variety of draw-leaf table has a loose top that is dropped into place between the pulled-out leaves.

STAGGERED NOTCH

LEAF BEARER

DRAW LEAF

END RAIL

LEG

LOOSE TOP *A block screwed to underside of top locates into slot cut in crosspiece.*

TOP LOCATES INTO SLOT

LEAF BEARERS *run in notches cut in end rails. Notches are staggered so bearers can run side by side.*

STAGGERED NOTCH

DRAW LEAF

UNDERFRAME

CROSSPIECE

ORDER OF CONSTRUCTION
Draw-leaf table

- Assemble underframe as for a standard frame table.
- Screw bearer guides to crosspiece, then screw crosspiece to side rails.
- Screw and glue bearers to underside of each leaf.
- Locate bearers in notches cut in end rails.
- Screw and glue location block to underside of table top.
- Lower top onto table so that location block fits into slot cut in crosspiece.

VARIATIONS ON THE DRAW-LEAF THEME
A loose 'spare leaf' (sometimes hinged for storage) can be stored out of sight within the table frame, beneath the sliding leaves, when it is not in use.

LOOSE LEAF

HINGED LOOSE LEAF

BEARER

BEARER

SLIDING BEARERS *run in notches cut in end rails*

DRAW LEAF

UNDER FRAME

LEG

WOODEN BLOCKS *screwed to underside of crosspiece guide bearers*

FOLDING-TOP TABLES

One way to reduce the area of a table top when it is not in use is to split it down the middle and hinge it, so that one half can be folded over to lie on top of the other.

SIDE TABLE

A side table can be converted into a card table or small dining table by swivelling the two back legs on knuckle joints and opening the hinged top.

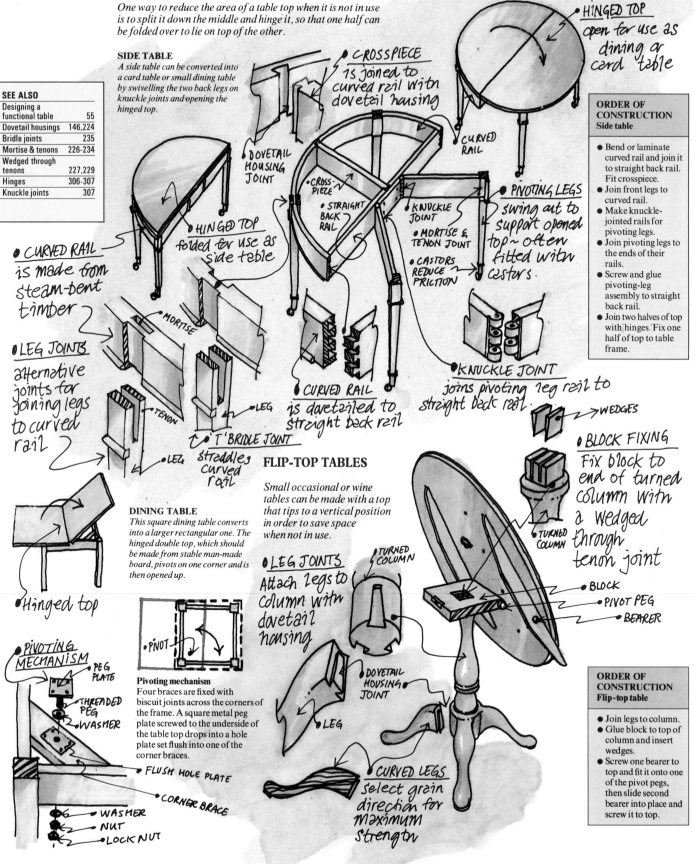

• HINGED TOP open for use as dining or card table

• CROSSPIECE is joined to curved rail with dovetail housing

CURVED RAIL

DOVETAIL HOUSING JOINT

• CROSS-PIECE
• STRAIGHT BACK RAIL

KNUCKLE JOINT

MORTISE & TENON JOINT

CASTORS REDUCE FRICTION

• PIVOTING LEGS swing out to support opened top~ often fitted with castors.

• HINGED TOP folded for use as side table

• CURVED RAIL is made from steam-bent timber

• LEG JOINTS alternative joints for joining legs to curved rail

MORTISE

TENON

LEG

• LEG

'T' BRIDLE JOINT straddles curved rail

• CURVED RAIL is dovetailed to straight back rail

• KNUCKLE JOINT joins pivoting leg rail to straight back rail

WEDGES

• BLOCK FIXING Fix block to end of turned column with a wedged through tenon joint

TURNED COLUMN

• BLOCK
• PIVOT PEG
• BEARER

ORDER OF CONSTRUCTION
Side table

• Bend or laminate curved rail and join it to straight back rail. Fit crosspiece.
• Join front legs to curved rail.
• Make knuckle-jointed rails for pivoting legs.
• Join pivoting legs to the ends of their rails.
• Screw and glue pivoting-leg assembly to straight back rail.
• Join two halves of top with hinges. Fix one half of top to table frame.

FLIP-TOP TABLES

Small occasional or wine tables can be made with a top that tips to a vertical position in order to save space when not in use.

Hinged top

DINING TABLE

This square dining table converts into a larger rectangular one. The hinged double top, which should be made from stable man-made board, pivots on one corner and is then opened up.

PIVOT

Pivoting mechanism
Four braces are fixed with biscuit joints across the corners of the frame. A square metal peg plate screwed to the underside of the table top drops into a hole plate set flush into one of the corner braces.

• LEG JOINTS Attach legs to column with dovetail housing

TURNED COLUMN

DOVETAIL HOUSING JOINT

• LEG

• CURVED LEGS select grain direction for maximum strength

• PIVOTING MECHANISM

PEG PLATE

THREADED PEG
WASHER

FLUSH HOLE PLATE

CORNER BRACE

WASHER
NUT
LOCK NUT

ORDER OF CONSTRUCTION
Flip-top table

• Join legs to column.
• Glue block to top of column and insert wedges.
• Screw one bearer to top and fit it onto one of the pivot pegs, then slide second bearer into place and screw it to top.

STORAGE-UNIT CONSTRUCTION

As a rule, people are fairly tidy by nature and require an immense range of storage to keep their belongings hidden from view. Even collections of books, records or cassettes kept on open shelves need to be stored systematically so you can lay hands on a particular one without a prolonged search. Customarily, when we talk about the various kinds of furniture used for storage we refer to them by specific names – such as wardrobe, bureau, bookcase or dresser – that indicate their function and also their place in the home. Nowadays, many designers regard these traditional classifications as limiting and prefer to employ shelves, drawers and cupboards in whatever combination provides the most convenient and effective use of space – whether for kitchen, bedroom, office or elsewhere. In the following pages some of the many ways of constructing cupboard, drawer and shelf units are illustrated and described, so you can use them, either individually or in combination, to design storage to meet your own needs.

DESIGNING ACCESSIBLE STORAGE

Plan storage systems using recommended dimensions that permit a person of average build to reach the top shelf or gain access to the back of a cupboard or drawer without stretching.

Maximum shelf height
1.8m to 2m (6ft to 6ft 6in)
An adult can reach a shelf this distance from the floor.

Eye-level shelf
1.5m to 1.7m (5ft to 5ft 8in)
Mount a shelf at this height for books, files, cassettes or other objects that you want to scan easily.

Maximum reach above worktop
1.05m (3ft 6in)
An adult can just reach a shelf at this height when leaning across a standard kitchen worktop.

Optimum reach above worktop
900mm (3ft)
Store frequently used objects at this height

Lowest shelf above worktop
450mm (1ft 6in)
Shelves and cupboards mounted lower than this begin to obscure your view of the back of the worktop and obstruct the use of food mixers and blenders.

Standard worktop height
900mm (3ft)
A standing adult can work comfortably at a counter top fitted at this height.

Worktop depth
600mm (2ft)
Major electrical appliances (washing machines, dishwashers etc.) are designed to fit beneath a worktop of this depth.

Wall-cabinet depth
300mm (1ft)
The optimum depth for a wall-hung cupboard mounted above a worktop.

Crouching at a cupboard
1m (3ft 3in)
Allow this space in front of a low cupboard.

Safe passing space
900mm (3ft)
Cramped kitchens and workshops cause accidents. Allow this width as a safe access corridor, plus an additional 450mm (1ft 6in) so there is room for someone standing at a worktop.

Access to drawers
1.25m (4ft 2in)
This amount of space is required for someone kneeling at an open drawer.

Hanging space
1.45 to 1.6m (4ft 10in to 5ft 4in)
Allow this space below a hanging rail to accommodate long coats and dresses.

850mm (2ft 10in)
Jackets and shirts will hang in this space.

600mm (2ft)
A storage unit of this depth will accommodate clothing hung on a rail.

Drawer size
425 to 500mm (1ft 5in to 1ft 8in)
Make drawers or trays this depth for folded shirts, sweaters and towels.

SHELF UNITS

Simple open shelf units constructed from solid timber or man-made boards are suitable for storing books or records and for displaying collections. Similar forms of construction are used when shelving is incorporated in more complex storage units.

SOLID-WOOD UNIT
Solid softwood and hardwood shelf units are stronger and more attractive than units constructed from man-made boards.

ORDER OF CONSTRUCTION
Solid-wood unit

- Fit fixed bottom shelf into housing in side panels.
- Tap dovetailed top into side panels, then square up and allow glue to set.
- Fix back in rebate with fillets.
- Fit adjustable shelves.

ADJUSTABLE SHELVES proprietary adjustable shelving can be used for intermediate shelves

FIXED TOP

SHELF STUDS

SHELF WIRES

SYSTEM SHELVING

ADJUSTABLE SHELF (see fixing details right)

FILLETS

BACK

SIDE PANEL

BOTTOM SHELF

MITRED DOVETAIL JOINT

DOVETAIL JOINTS FOR TOP

LAPPED DOVETAIL JOINT

FILLET
PLY BACK

FILLET
SOLID BACK

SOLID OR PLY BACK held in rebate with screwed fillet

DECORATIVE T&G BACK held in rebate by fillets pinned to side panel

HOUSING JOINTS FOR BOTTOM

TOP Dovetail-jointed

STOPPED HOUSING JOINT

either/or

BOTTOM Housing-jointed

DOVETAIL HOUSING JOINT

STRENGTHENING
Books & records etc. impose heavy loads strengthening is needed

BATTEN
SQUARE EDGE

BATTEN
ROUND NOSE

BATTEN
REBATED

FIXED SHELF

TALL UNIT
An intermediate fixed shelf is needed to hold sides together

INTERMEDIATE SUPPORT

STOPPED HOUSING JOINT

WIDE UNIT needs an intermediate vertical support

BACK spans width of cabinet & is screwed to vertical support

• ADJUSTABLE SHELF
for adjustable shelf drill holes for proprietary shelf fitting

• FIXED SHELF UNITS
Use knock-down fittings or one of these joints:~

BISCUIT

• BISCUIT JOINTS

• BISCUIT JOINT (MITRED)

• DOWEL JOINT

• BAREFACED HOUSING JOINT

• ASSEMBLED

CHIPBOARD UNIT
A shelf unit made from chipboard or from MDF is likely to be cheaper than one constructed from solid timber. Also, both materials are perfectly stable.

• FIXED TOP SHELF

• ADJUSTABLE SHELF

• BACK

GROOVE

• FIXED BOTTOM SHELF

PLINTH

• PLINTH is jointed into side panels and glued to bottom shelf

BISCUIT JOINT

DOWEL JOINT

• ALTERNATIVE PLINTH-RAIL JOINTS

WALL-HANGING UNIT
Screw unit to wall through a strongly jointed back rail, or (for lightweight loads) through a ply back fitted into an all-round groove.

• SIDE PANEL
• TOP SHELF
• PLY BACK

• LIGHTWEIGHT LOADS. 2 screw directly through ply back panel; for heavy loads fit a back rail ~(see right).

• BACK FIXING
the back is held in a groove cut in the side panels

• BACK SCREWED TO BOTTOM SHELF

SIDE PANEL

GROOVE

LET GROOVE RUN THROUGH, PAST THE BOTTOM SHELF

• ALTERNATIVELY LET BACK FIT INTO GROOVES ALL ROUND

SIDE PANEL
BACK
BOTTOM SHELF
GROOVE

• BACK-FIXING DETAILS (REAR VIEW)

• BAREFACED TONGUE & GROOVE JOINT
SIDE PANEL
BACK RAIL
• SCREW

• BACK RAIL
For heavy loads screw through strongly jointed back rail

• SIDE PANEL
Alternative side panel detail

ORDER OF CONSTRUCTION
Chipboard unit

● Glue plinth to bottom shelf.
● Join side panels with fixed shelves. Include back at same time or slide it into groove from below afterwards, then screw it to back edge of bottom shelf.
● Fit adjustable shelves.

CUPBOARDS

Traditional or modern methods of construction can be utilized to make free-standing cupboards and, with modifications, used as a basis for designing and building kitchen storage units.

TRADITIONAL CABINET CONSTRUCTION

Constructing a cabinet from solid timber requires considerable thought and careful making in order to allow for the movement of the wood.

BUTT JOINT

TONGUE & GROOVE JOINT

• SOLID TOP WITH MOULDED EDGE

• TOP & SIDES
Use solid boards joined with butt or T&G joints

SIDE

• CORNERS
Glue triangular blocks to rails for strong wide corner joints

• BACK
plywood back

• SLOTTED SCREWS FOR TOP-FIXING

SCREW SLOT.

• SHELF STUDS

• TOP-FIXING BLOCKS
Use slotted screws to allow for movement of top & sides

• FRONT TOP RAIL

• TWIN TENON
• FRONT VERTICAL POST

• SIDE PANEL

• PLYWOOD BACK IS HELD IN REBATE

• BOTTOM PANEL (BASE)

• FRONT VERTICAL
post is joined to front rail with twin tenons

• DOOR STOP IS GLUED TO POST

• DOOR
Frame & panel construction (see overleaf)

• SIDE PANEL

(BASE)

Joined with lapped dovetails
SIDE PANELS & BASE

• CROSS RAIL

REINFORCING BLOCKS

• PLINTH
corners joined with mitres reinforced with screwed & glued blocks

• SIDE PANEL
• BEAD
• DOOR

• DOOR LINE
Bead moulding cut in side panel to disguise door line

ALTERNATIVE DECORATIVE PLINTH RAIL

Cabinet sits in rebated plinth

• CABINET
• REBATE
• PLINTH

PLINTH CONSTRUCTION

ORDER OF CONSTRUCTION
Traditional unit

• Join both side panels to bottom panel.
• Insert front vertical post and fit top rails. Square up cabinet and allow all glue to set.
• Fit back panel and screw it to top rail.
• Fit top-fixing blocks, then fit door stops.
• Fit cupboard top.
• Assemble doors and let the glue set, then join them to cupboard with hinges.
• Assemble plinth.

- OVERHANGING TOP

- SET-BACK TOP

- REBATE

- TOP EDGES
Edge treatments for cupboard tops are designed to disguise movement.

- TWIN DOORS
Rebate ensures snug fit

- FITTING A SHELF
Turn a one-piece adjustable shelf at an angle to get it into cupboard

- CORNICE MOULDING

- BLOCK glued to top locates back of cornice

- HOUSING JOINT

- MITRE

- BACK
- SIDE
- CABINET TOP
- FRONT

- APPLIED MOULDING TO FRONT & SIDES

- CORNICE MOULDING
for the top of tall cupboard is constructed in a similar way to plinth.

MODERN CABINET CONSTRUCTION

Constructing a cabinet from man-made boards is relatively simple since the materials are stable. If you are planning to make several identical cupboards, consider using machine-made joints for speed, accuracy and strength.

- WARDROBE UNIT is identical in construction — simply alter proportions

- MITRED BISCUIT JOINTS

- LAY-ON DOORS

- TOP
- BACK
- DIVIDER
- SIDE PANEL
- BOTTOM PANEL

- PANEL CONSTRUCTION
use MDF or chipboard lipped on long edges & veneered

- PLINTH RAIL

- BACK
slides in groove and screwed to bottom panel

- GROOVE
- SIDE PANEL

- BISCUIT JOINT
- BOTTOM PANEL

- PLINTH RAIL is biscuit-jointed to bottom panel

- SHELVING
Fit adjustable shelves on each side of divider

ORDER OF CONSTRUCTION
Modern unit

- Fit plinth rail to bottom panel.
- Fit both side panels to bottom panel.
- Fit central panel (divider) and then the top. Allow glue to set.
- Fit back panel.
- Hang doors.

CUPBOARD DOORS

All sorts of doors and flaps can be fitted to cupboards, storage units and other kinds of furniture. The most common forms of door construction are described and illustrated here.

FRAME-AND-PANEL CONSTRUCTION
The traditional frame-and-panel door is constructed to accommodate the inevitable shrinkage and expansion of the thin solid-wood panel. Because of its visual appeal and stylistic associations, designers often select this type of construction for doors with plywood panels, too.

• FRAME & PANEL DOOR VARIATIONS

• REBATE
• MOULDED REBATE
• APPLIED MOULDINGS
• FIELDED PANELS

FRAME
FILLET
PANEL
MOULDED FRAME
FILLET
PANEL

SUITABLE FOR SOLID-WOOD, PLY OR GLAZED PANELS

SUITABLE FOR SOLID-WOOD PANELS ONLY

• PANEL is held in rebate by a screwed fillet. No glue is used

• FILLET
• FRAME
• PANEL

HAUNCHED MORTISE & TENON JOINTS

• FRAME & PANEL CONSTRUCTION
whatever type of moulding is used the frame is joined with haunched mortise & tenon joints

TALL PANELLED DOOR
Tall cupboard doors are divided by crossrails and upright muntins to reduce the size of solid-wood infill panels.

• CROSS RAIL
• PANEL
• STILE
• CROSSRAIL
• STILE
• MUNTIN
• PANEL
• PANEL
• CROSSRAIL
• CROSSRAIL
• HAUNCHED MORTISE & TENON
• STILE

• MORTISE & TENON JOINT
• MUNTIN
STILE
HAUNCHED MORTISE & TENON JOINT

• DOOR TREATMENTS
① Doors meet over vertical post ② separated by post ③ Rebated

• POST
① DOORS MEET
• STOP
② DOORS SEPARATED
③
• DOORS REBATED

STILE

• INSET DOOR
• SIDE PANEL
• DOOR FRAME

• LAY-ON DOOR
• PANEL

TWIN DOORS
A pair of doors that meet in the centre can be treated in several different ways.

• FLUSH DOOR VENEERING VARIATIONS

• SIMPLE LIPPING
• VENEER

• MITRED LIPPING
• VENEER 2

• INSET DOOR

• LAY-ON DOOR

FLUSH DOORS

This type of door is simple to make and neat in appearance. It is usually made by lipping and veneering a man-made board.

VENEER applied after lipping. Simple lipping for inset doors. Mitred lipping for lay-on doors.

VENEER applied before lipping used where it is necessary to protect the edge of the veneer.

DEEP UPPER GROOVES ALLOW DOORS TO BE LIFTED FOR REMOVAL

GLASS DOORS SLIDE MORE EASILY IN PLASTIC TRACKS

• ROLLER BOLT helps insertion & removal of door

• SUITABLE FOR LIGHTWEIGHT GLASS OR PLYWOOD DOORS

A NARROW GAP BETWEEN GIVES A MORE SUBSTANTIAL LOOK

PLASTIC TRACKS

SLIDING DOORS

Doors are made to slide if they are too heavy to be hung from hinges or when space is too restricted for hinged doors to be opened. Various methods are used, from grooves cut directly in the wood for thin-glass or plywood doors to proprietary sliding-door mechanisms for large heavy wardrobe doors. A small selection only is shown here.

GROOVES CUT IN TIMBER

REBATED DOORS

• DOOR GUIDE runs on track.

MECHANISMS FOR HEAVIER SLIDING DOORS

• BACKFLAP HINGES

• STAYS hold fall flap

• UPPER SHELF
• STOPPED HOUSING JOINTS

HINGED FALL FLAP

• BACK PANEL
• UPPER SHELF

• STAY

FALL FLAPS

Flaps that open to form a horizontal work surface are used for desks and drinks cabinets. They are supported by stays or pull-out lopers.

LOPER is inserted from rear before back of cabinet is fixed in place

• BACK STOP
• FRONT STOP

• LOPER pulls out to support the fall flap.

• LOPER.

• LOPER GUIDE

• UPPER-SHELF HOUSING
• LOWER-SHELF HOUSING

• LOWER SHELF fixed with stopped housing joint

• VERTICAL POST tenoned into both shelves

FRONT STOP

BACK STOP

• STOPS the front stop prevents the loper from being pulled out too far. The back stop is inserted after loper is slid in from rear.

67

CUPBOARD DOORS

• LIFT-UP DOOR

• LIFT DOOR TO UNLOCK STAY

• DOOR

• CABINET

• CABINET

• DOOR

LIFT-UP-DOOR STAYS
A stay or pair of stays for a lift-up door (or lid) locks automatically when the door is raised; and is released by lifting the door slightly before allowing it to fall. Friction stays that prevent doors or lids slamming shut are available, too.

• STAY locks in open, raised position

• DOOR CLOSED (REAR VIEW)

• DOOR OPEN

• CONCERTINA DOOR

• CONCEALED CABINET HINGE

• CABINET HINGE

• SOSS HINGES mounted in door edges are invisible when closed

CONCERTINA DOORS
Folding doors have to be mounted on a special roller-guide system. They are useful in a restricted space and have the advantage of providing access to the whole of the interior, whereas sliding doors close off at least half of the cupboard.

• OPENING pulling on door causes it to slide

• ROLLER GUIDES mount doors in special roller-guide systems

• SOSS HINGE

• FEED GROOVE fill in feed groove after sliding in tambour

• TAMBOUR GROOVE tambour runs in groove cut in side of cabinet

• DOWEL JOINT

• CABINET SIDE

• TOP is dowel-jointed to cabinet side

• OPEN TAMBOUR STORED AT BACK OF CABINET

• TAMBOUR

• TOP

• SIDE

• DESK TOP is screwed to cabinet from below

• INSERTING tambour is fed into groove from back

• LAPPED DOVETAIL JOINT

• CANVAS

• OVERLAPPING STRIPS OF WOOD GLUED TO CANVAS BACKING

• FILLET TRAPS CANVAS TO RAIL

• BOTTOM RAIL

• DESK TOP joined to cabinet sides with lapped dovetail joint

TAMBOUR
A tambour is an attractive if complicated alternative to a door. It is made from narrow overlapping strips of wood glued to a canvas backing. This method of construction allows the tambour to negotiate bends as it slides in grooves cut inside the two sides of a roll-top desk.

• TAMBOUR CONSTRUCTION

DRAWER UNITS

Constructing a drawer unit, especially one made from solid timber, is much more complicated than making a cupboard unit of similar size and construction. Also, greater accuracy is required in order to ensure that the drawers fit snugly and will continue to run smoothly.

SOLID-WOOD CONSTRUCTION

A solid-wood chest of drawers is constructed like a cupboard made from solid wood but includes drawer runners, rails and kickers assembled in such a way that they do not impede the natural movement of the carcass. Bottom-run drawers slide on runners fixed to the side panels.

• EDGE DETAIL
a moulded overhang is one way to disguise the effects of shrinkage

• DRAWER & RAIL CONSTRUCTION
(seen from side)

• FRONT DRAWER RAIL stub-tenoned into side of cabinet. Grooved to receive runner & dust panel.

• CROSS PIECE
unglued tenon with 'open' shoulders holds cross-piece to back rail

• SOLID TOP
fixed to rails with slotted screws

• DRAWER RUNNER
fits unglued into housing
• SIDE PANEL
• RUNNER

• SINGLE SCREW HOLDS RUNNER TO SIDE PANEL

• DUST PANEL

• PLYWOOD DUST PANEL protects drawer below from dust. Fits in grooves - slid in from rear - no glue required

• DRAWER FRONT comes to rest against plywood stop glued & pinned to rail

• SHORT POST
short dove-tailed post supports central drawer-runner assembly.

• BACK PANEL
• BACK RAIL
• DUST PANEL
• FRONT RAIL

• TENON ON FRONT OF RUNNER FITS INTO GROOVE CUT IN FRONT RAIL

• STOPS

• TOP FIXING
slotted batten holds top down & acts as top-drawer kicker

• DRAWER RAILS
• BOTTOM PANEL

• STOPS

• BACK PANEL
fits into rebated side & bottom panels and screwed to back rail

• SIDE PANEL

• LAPPED DOVETAIL JOINTS

• SIDE PANEL

• FRONT RAIL

• RAILS
Front & back rails dovetailed into side panels

• SIDE PANEL
is joined to bottom with lapped dovetail

• BOTTOM

• PLINTH

• BLOCKS ON UNDERSIDE OF CABINET LOCATE INSIDE PLINTH FRAME
Blocks on underside of cabinet locate inside plinth frame

• FRONT POST
Tenoned top & bottom. Fits between adjacent drawers

• FRONT POST
• DRAWER GUIDE SCREWED TO RUNNER

• GROOVES
Dust panel fits in grooves.

• PLINTH RAIL
• LEG

• PLINTH
This type of plinth is made like a table frame

• FRONT RAIL
• RUNNER
Single piece of wood acts as runner for top drawers. Tenon slots into front rail.

• REAR POST FITS DOVETAIL JOINT

ORDER OF CONSTRUCTION
Solid-wood unit

- Join side panels with the two long drawer rails, then fit dovetailed bottom panel.
- Fit short front post to drawer rail. Then, after joining the two top rails with the crosspiece, join their dovetail joints to the side panels and fit front rail onto tenoned end of front post. Check for square and let glue set.
- Fit drawer runners, including central runner (with guide), which hangs from short rear post.
- Fit top-fixing battens, then fit top.
- Slide dust panels in from rear.
- Fit back panel.
- Assemble plinth. Fit location blocks on underside of cabinet and lower cabinet onto plinth.
- Make and fit drawers (see overleaf).
- Fit drawer stops.

DRAWER UNITS

FRAME-AND-PANEL CONSTRUCTION

Relatively lightweight cabinets can be made by using frame-and-panel construction with a solid top and a ply back panel. This method of construction can be adapted to make a cupboard or drawer unit or a combination unit with cupboard and drawers.

• **TOP-FIXING**
Batten & kicker assembly

DOVETAIL
Kicker
SIDE RAIL
UPRIGHT

• **SIDE PANELS** held in grooves

FRONT RAIL is dovetailed to both frame members

DUST PANEL

FRONT RAIL

DRAWER RAIL

• **CENTRAL POST** is required if there are twin top drawers

• Side panels held in grooves, no glue required

• **GROOVE** to hold side panel

• **FRAME** solid wood construction with mortise & tenon joints

• **DRAWER RUNNER** grooved to accept dust panel. Tenon fits into front rail & fixed to rear frame with single screw

FRAME
STUB TENON
FRONT RAIL
TENON

• **DRAWER GUIDE** screwed to runner

SIDE RUNNER fitted at rear with single screw

BOTTOM RAIL

BOTTOM RAIL

UPRIGHT

• **TOP** SCREWED TO rails

• **BACK PANEL** fits in rebated side panels and screwed to bottom panel & top rail

ORDER OF CONSTRUCTION
Frame-and-panel unit

- Assemble end panels.
- When the glue has set, join end panels with drawer rail and bottom rails, then fit both top rails plus central post.
- Screw drawer guide to runners, then fit the runners to the frame.
- Fit dust panels.
- Fit back panel.
- Make and fit drawers and/or door(s).

ORDER OF CONSTRUCTION
Slab-sided unit

- Glue plinth to bottom panel.
- Join side panels to rails and bottom panel. Check for square and allow to set.
- Fit back panel.
- Fit top of cabinet.
- Fit drawer runners.
- Make and fit drawers (see opposite).

SLAB CONSTRUCTION

MDF or other man-made boards are used for making simple cabinets. Join the panels and rails with knock-down fittings or biscuit or dowel joints. This method of construction is ideal for side-run drawers, which have grooved sides that run on battens screwed and glued to the cabinet's side panels.

FALSE FRONT

• **SIDE-RUN DRAWER** (see opposite)

• **RUNNERS** hardwood runners screwed to side panels, or into housings for stronger fixing

• **PLINTH** glued to bottom panel

• **JOINTS** can be joined with knock-down fittings, biscuit or dowel joints

DRAWERS

Drawers are designed to slide in and out of a cabinet in order to improve access to the interior. The drawer front protects the contents by filling the opening. Shallow widely spaced drawers or trays are often used as an alternative to shelves behind cupboard doors, especially in wardrobes or built-in storage units. Tray construction is usually very simple, often comprising no more than a finger-jointed box with a plywood bottom.

Bottom-run drawers
The bottom edges of the drawer's sides run on strips of hardwood fixed to the cabinet's side panels. The strips also act as 'kickers', which prevent the drawer below tipping when it is pulled out.

● BOTTOM-RUN

Side-run drawers
A stopped groove cut in each side of the drawer fits onto a hardwood batten screwed and glued to the cabinet. For a stronger fixing, cut a shallow housing in the sides of the cabinet for each runner.

● SIDE-RUN

Drawer slides
You can buy ready-made drawer-slide systems for screwing to the sides of heavier drawers. The drawer front must overlap at each side to cover the space needed for these fittings.

● DRAWER SLIDE

Inset drawers
Drawers of this type fit flush with the face of the cabinet. They need to fit snugly.

● INSET

Overlapping drawers
Overlapping drawers are often made with a false front, which makes for much easier fitting.

● OVERLAPPED

False front
Screwed to drawer.

● FALSE FRONT

TRADITIONAL BOTTOM-RUN DRAWER
A traditional bottom-run drawer has thin hardwood sides jointed with finely cut lapped dovetails at the front and through dovetails at the back. The bottom panel is set in a groove at the front and has a grooved slip moulding at each side.

● BOTTOMS
often made of plywood. If solid wood is used, grain must run side to side.

● SLIP MOULDINGS glued to each drawer side. End is notched to allow it to run under drawer back.

● FITTING
Slide bottom into place from rear. Screw to drawer back (do not glue) if it shrinks, it can be moved forward.

● BACK CORNER ● chamfered to ease insertion of drawer

● BACK made of thin hardwood, set about 3mm (⅛in) below sides

● ROUNDED TOP EDGE

WIDER RUNNING SURFACE

● FRONT use better quality hardwood for fronts

● SIDE can be made from cheaper hardwood

● SLIP MOULDING see above

● BOTTOM groove is concealed by bottom dovetail

STIFFENING A WIDE DRAWER BOTTOM
A hardwood crosspiece known as a muntin is used to separate and support the two sections of a wide drawer bottom.

● MUNTIN

either

● MUNTIN ● or

● MUNTIN

● BACK

SCREW muntin to drawer back

FITTING A DRAWER

First plane the drawer front to fit snugly in its opening. Make the other components to match the front, then assemble. If the finished drawer is a tight fit, look for shiny spots along the sides that indicate areas of friction. Skim them lightly with a plane, then lubricate all sliding surfaces by rubbing them with a candle.

LAPPED-AND-HOUSED DRAWER
For cheaper-quality furniture, drawers can be made with simple lap joints at the front and housing joints at the back. The strength of the joints relies on the glue, but they can be reinforced with panel pins.

● HOUSING JOINTS variation using housing joints front & back

● EXTENDED SIDES ● Can be used as drawer pulls

● FRONT

● GROOVES Bottom fits in groove in front & sides

● BOTTOM made from plywood or hardboard

● FRONT

● PULL RAIL made from dowel or metal tube

● FIXING Screw bottom to back as on dovetailed drawer

SIDE-RUN VERSION

BUILT-IN STORAGE UNITS

Built-in units fitted from wall to wall are relatively cheap to make. An alternative method is to construct 'modules' which are bolted side by side. Always make sure you can transport the units from your workshop and through doorways or up stairs. If need be, assemble the components on site or construct sub-assemblies which can be joined with screws or bolts. If the units are to be painted, nails and screw-fixings can be disguised with filler.

• DECORATIVE MOULDING
pinned and glued to front edge

• DOOR STOP
battens on underside act as door-stop •

• TOP

• RAIL either/or
• TOP
• RAIL

STOPS SHORT OF CEILING

• TOP-FIXING DETAILS

• RAIL & POST screwed to wall

HINGES are attached to cover strip

• BOTTOM

• PLINTH RAILS glued to bottom

• COVER STRIP scribed to wall

• DOOR Frame & panel construction

ORDER OF CONSTRUCTION
Alcove unit

- Stand bottom panel in position, after gluing the plinth rails to it.
- Screw the rails and posts to the wall on each side of the cupboard.
- Screw the top to the rails directly, or screw a batten to each rail then screw the battens to the top.
- Scribe upright cover strips to the walls and fix them to the posts. Check they are plumb, using a spirit level.
- Pin and glue moulding along front edge of top.
- Assemble doors and attach with hinges to cover strips.
- Pin battens to underside of top to act as door stop.

ALCOVE UNIT
Make the most of the space available by hanging hinged doors from wall-mounted posts. To avoid damaging mouldings, stop short of the ceiling.

ORDER OF CONSTRUCTION
Modular unit

- Assemble frames in workshop, then bolt them between upright dividing panels on site, working from one end. Screw the last panel to its frames from inside if there isn't enough room to fit bolts. Anchor assembly to wall with screws passed through top frames.
- Pin plinth cover strip to front edge of every upright panel.
- Drop plywood lids into rebates cut in frames.
- Attach doors to upright panels with hinges.
- Make and fit trays and/or other interior fittings.

MODULAR UNIT
Sub-assembled frames are bolted between dividing panels. You can fit full-length doors (perhaps with trays or shelves behind some and hanging space only behind others) or have one or two short doors, too, with drawers below.

• LID plywood lid drops in

• REBATE

• CONCEALED HINGES

• FRAME

• REBATE

• TONGUE~REINFORCED MITRE JOINT

SIDE PANEL

• PLINTH COVER STRIP
pinned to front of panels. Floor covering can run up front of cover strip.

• FLOOR COVERING

• FRAME with rebate to accept plywood lid.

• UPRIGHT PANELS are bolted to frame

FITTED-FRAME UNIT

Assemble the frame on site and screw it to the wall at each end, then scribe a filling strip to the ceiling. Use sliding doors across wide cupboard openings.

• FILLING STRIP
scribed plywood strip screwed to frame

• FRAME JOINTS
top corners of frame are finger-jointed

• FINGER JOINT

• SHELF

• FILLING STRIP

• DIVIDING PANEL

• SLIDING DOORS

• ROLLER BOLTS

DOORS
Fit heavy sliding doors using roller bolts and door glides (see cupboard-door construction).

• DOOR GLIDE

• SCREW DIVIDING PANEL TO WALL

• HANGING RAIL

• FRAME SCREWED TO WALL AT EACH END

• SHELF/HANGING-RAIL SUPPORT SCREWED TO WALL

• DIVIDING PANEL

• METAL BRACKET

• BOTTOM RAIL

• PLINTH

DIVIDING PANEL
Screw dividing panel to bottom rail using a small metal bracket

BOTTOM RAIL
join bottom rail with twin tenons

• PLINTH
is glued to bottom rail

ORDER OF CONSTRUCTION
Fitted-frame unit

● Glue and assemble frame on site. Hoist it into position, then screw it to wall at each end.
● Screw scribed filling strip to back of top frame member.
● Manoeuvre dividing panel into position, then screw it to wall and frame.
● Screw hanging-rail and shelf supports to walls and dividing panel.
● Drop shelving into position.
● Make and fit sliding doors.

USING SCRIBED FILLETS

Instead of trying to make an exact fit to an uneven wall, it is often better to use a fillet to fill a gap between the storage-unit panel and wall at each end.

• SET-BACK FILLET
Creates a shadow line at the side of the cabinet

• SCRIBED FILLET
scribe fillet to wall to leave a deliberate gap next to cabinet

• MOULDED FILLET
is fixed to cabinet cover strip

MAKING PLANS

An exceptionally gifted woodworker may be able to convert an idea into reality on the bench, but most *people find it necessary to plan a design in detail on paper and perhaps try it out in three dimensions.*

Front elevation

Side elevation

Plan

Section

Drawing equipment
1 Drawing board
2 Compass
3 Set square
4 T-square
5 French curves
6 Protractor
7 Circle template
8 Scale rule

Sketch drawings

In order to conceive the shape and general construction of a new workpiece, a designer will normally put down his or her first thoughts on paper in the form of sketches. These are visual notes (similar to those shown on the preceding pages) used to explore the various possibilities until the designer arrives at a solution that appears to answer all the requirements. Unfortunately it is all too easy to fool oneself with a sketch, either by underestimating the overall size of the piece or by exaggerating the section of a component. A prudent designer will make a measured scale drawing to check the proportions and constructional detail.

Scale drawings

A professional designer uses scale drawings to communicate information to the workshop or factory where an item is to be manufactured. It is convenient to use a similar system to work up your own sketch ideas. By convention a designer normally adopts a scale of 1:5 (10mm represents 50mm) when using the metric system, and 1:4 ($\frac{1}{2}$in represents 2in) when using imperial measurements. You can use either system, but do not attempt to mix them. Smaller scales, typically 1:20 for metric and 1:24 for imperial, are more convenient when designing built-in furniture. Chairs and other relatively small workpieces are usually drawn full size.

Specific views of a workpiece are drawn side by side. They represent the front elevation (front view), side elevation (side view) and plan (top view); in addition, drawn sections (i.e. slices through the workpiece) show the internal structure. Areas that are unusually complex are often drawn full size to clarify their construction.

Professional draughtsman's equipment is expensive, but you cannot make accurate drawings without a drawing board (any square-cut flat board will do), a T-square for drawing horizontal lines and a large set square for the vertical ones. In addition, you will need a scale rule marked in increments representing all the common scale measurements and a protractor for measuring angles. Although not essential, it is worth investing in plastic guides known as French curves for drawing curved lines, a circle template for drawing small radii and a compass for larger circles. Make scale drawings on tracing paper (using a sharp, reasonably hard pencil) so you can overlay subsequent drawings as the design develops.

Scale models

Having made a scale drawing, use it to construct a model of the workpiece out of balsawood and card so you can see what your design looks like in three dimensions. Some designers like to make a fully detailed model using the actual materials specified for the full-size piece, but this is hardly ever necessary unless you want to impress a client.

Mock-ups

Making a full-size mock-up from workshop scraps and cheap materials can be extremely informative. It is the only way, for example, to make sure a chair is as comfortable or structurally sound as you imagine. Erecting a visual mock-up made from lightweight materials such as fibreboard or even corrugated cardboard is the ideal way to check the proportions of a large workpiece, especially if you can assemble it on site to see how it fits into its intended environment.

Cutting lists

Before ordering materials from a timber supplier, write a cutting list which specifies the length, width and thickness of every component in a workpiece. The list should also state the material from which each component is to be made and the quantity required. Make sure your supplier is aware that the list specifies finished sizes so that he or she knows how much to allow for wastage.

SURVEYING A ROOM

Measure the room carefully and make notes of all the important features before you start to design built-in furniture.

- Use a long tape measure to take the main dimensions of the room, including the diagonals, in order to check whether it is square on plan. Don't assume the walls are perpendicular – take measurements at different heights where a good fit may be crucial.
- Measure the size and height of architectural features, such as ceiling cornices, skirting boards, dadoes and picture rails.
- Measure windows and doors, and make a note or sketch of how they open.
- Note the position of fireplaces and radiators.
- Make a note of electrical sockets, switches and lighting fixtures that may have to be relocated to accommodate your design.

HAND

At a time when more and more woodworkers are turning to machine tools for convenience or greater accuracy, someone coming fresh to woodwork might assume handtools were merely relics left over from the leisurely days when craftsmen were paid for the quality of their products rather than for their labour. However, that simply isn't true. A competent woodworker can often finish a job by hand in the time it takes to set up a machine for the same purpose. Working by hand also gives a feel for materials that cannot be derived from operating a machine — the way different grains respond to the blade, for example, and how some woods are more forgiving while others show up the slightest error on the part of the woodworker. For these and other reasons, not least because of the pleasure of

TOOLS

using them, a comprehensive set of handtools will no doubt always figure among the equipment of even the most sophisticated workshop.

MEASURING & MARKING TOOLS

It is good woodworking practice always to mark one component from another whenever possible. The way one half of a dovetail joint is marked from the other is a perfect example. It is not only the most precise method, it also avoids the possibility of misreading a rule or tape.

Four-fold rule

A traditional carpenter's folding rule is made from boxwood with brass hinges and protective endcaps.

A well-made rule will stay rigid in its extended form until the hinges are folded deliberately. A 1m (3ft) rule, folding into four equal parts, is the most popular model. Whatever system of measurement you prefer, it makes sense to buy a rule with metric dimensions marked on one side and feet and inches on the other.

● Maintaining rules

Treat rules and other measuring and marking tools with respect or they will lose their accuracy. Never cut against a wooden or plastic rule – use a metal rule only. Metal rules will rust in a damp atmosphere – smear them with oil for long-term storage. If you fold and kink a retractable tape measure it will not support itself when deployed.

Steel rule

A steel rule is primarily a metalworker's tool but you should have at least one 300mm (1ft) rule for making very precise measurements. It is also useful as a short straightedge.

It is convenient if one side is marked as a centre-finding rule, calibrated with equal divisions from the centre point towards each end of the rule.

Straightedge

An unmarked strip of steel with one bevelled edge, this tool is used to check the flatness of a surface and as a guide for cutting straight lines with a marking knife. Being thick and relatively heavy, a straightedge is especially useful for holding down veneers when trimming them to size. Straightedges range from 500mm (1ft 8in) to 2m (6ft 6in).

Boxwood four-fold rule

Plastic four-fold rule

Steel rule

Steel straightedge

Try square

Mitre square

Sliding bevel

Marking knife

Dovetail template

Retractable tape measure

Retractable tape measure

A flexible steel tape measure, about 5m (16ft) long, is an essential tool for every workshop. Choose one which is calibrated with metric and imperial dimensions on opposite edges so you can readily convert one system to another.

The hook at the tip of the tape is intentionally loose on its rivets so that it can move fractionally to take internal and external measurements. This hook can become displaced if you allow the tape to snap back into its case. Buy a tape with a locking mechanism that prevents the tape retracting accidentally.

Try square

A try square has a parallel-sided blade fixed at right angles to a wooden, cast-iron or plastic stock. It is used to check the accuracy of a 90-degree corner or for marking lines at right angles to an edge. If the tool is made with the top inside corner of the stock cut to 45 degrees, it can be used to mark out mitre joints.

A square with a plastic or cast-iron stock will remain accurate because the materials are inert. A wooden stock can react to humidity and the rivets holding the blade can work loose if the tool is dropped. However, the square with a rosewood stock edged in brass remains a firm favourite with woodworkers because it is such a beautifully made tool.

A try square with a 300mm (1ft) long blade will prove to be the most useful.

Mitre square

A mitre square's blade passes through the stock at an angle of 45 degrees. It is used for marking out mitre joints and for checking the accuracy of each half of the cut joint.

Sliding bevel

A sliding bevel functions like a mitre square, but its blade can be adjusted to any angle and locked in place with a lever or slotted screw.

Dovetail template

Use a special template to mark out dovetail joints. One blade is for tails in softwood with a slope of 1–6. The other has a ratio of 1–8 for hardwood tails.

Marking knife

Use a pencil for the preliminary marking of joints, but always use a marking knife to sever the wood fibres to ensure a clean edge when you saw to the line. The blade is bevelled on one side only. Use the knife on the waste side of the line, running the flat face of the blade against a try square.

USING MEASURING AND MARKING TOOLS

Every woodworker requires several tools for the initial stages of measuring and marking timber. Use and store the tools with care. Rough or careless treatment can affect their accuracy.

Dividing a board equally

Mark a board into equal divisions using any rule. To divide it by five, for example, align the tip of the rule with one edge of the board and the fifth division with the other, then make a pencil mark against divisions one to four.

Dividing a board equally

Checking for winding

A badly warped board is obvious, but check for subtle 'winding', as it is called, by holding a steel rule across each end of the board. If the rules look parallel, the board is flat.

Checking for winding

Checking for flatness

Place a straightedge on a surface you want to check for flatness. If you can see chinks of light beneath the edge or it rocks on a bump, the surface is not flat. Turn the tool to various angles to check a wide surface.

Checking for flatness on a wide surface

Taking internal and external measurements

When taking external measurements, hook the tape over one edge of the work and read the tape against the opposite edge (1). For internal measurements, read the tape where it enters the case, then add the length of the case itself to arrive at the true dimension (2).

1 Taking external measurements

2 Taking internal measurements

Checking a try square

To check that a square is accurate, first use it to draw a line at right angles to a surface. Turn the blade over and align it with the marked line. The edge of the blade and the line should match exactly.

Checking a try square

Using a try square

Use a try square to make sure two parts of a joint meet at 90 degrees (1). To mark a right angle, hold the stock firmly against the work and draw a marking knife or pencil along the blade (2). To mark a mitre, place the angled face of the stock against the work to mark a line at 45 degrees. (3).

1 Checking a joint

2 Marking a right angle

3 Marking a mitre

Checking a mitre

Slide a mitre square over the external corner of a mitre-joint component. The blade should be in contact across the entire width of the joint.

Checking a mitre

MARKING & CUTTING GAUGES

● **Storing wooden gauges**
The wooden stock of a gauge is such a close fit on the beam that it can jam if the wood should swell. If your workshop is damp keep the tool in a plastic bag.

Marking gauge
Mark a line parallel to a planed edge using a marking gauge. A sharp steel pin is fixed at one end of a hardwood beam. A fence, or 'stock', slides on the beam and is locked the required distance from the pin with a thumbscrew. Brass strips are set flush with the working face of the stock to prevent wear. A standard beam is 200mm (8in) long, but you can get a 300mm (1ft) beam for marking wide boards.

Cutting gauge
A cutting gauge is similar in every respect to a marking gauge, but instead of a steel pin it has a small blade held in place with a brass wedge. It is designed for marking timber across the grain where the pin of a marking gauge would tear the surface of the wood. A rounded blade is fitted as standard, but this can be substituted with a pointed knife-like blade for cutting veneers.

Mortise gauge
A mortise gauge has two pins for scribing both sides of a mortise or tenon simultaneously. One pin is fixed, while the other is attached to a metal slide adjusted to fine tolerances by a thumbscrew at the end of the beam. Most mortise gauges are dual-purpose tools having a single fixed pin on the opposite side of the beam like that on a standard marking gauge.

Curved-edge gauge
It is difficult to scribe a line parallel to a curved edge with the flat stock of an ordinary marking gauge. The special brass fence on a curved-edge gauge rests on two points to prevent the tool rocking as it follows the edge of the work. It can also be used on straight edges.

THUMBSCREW   Marking gauge   BEAM

Cutting gauge

STOCK

BLADE

FIXED PIN   Mortise gauge   THUMBSCREW FOR ADJUSTMENT

Curved-edge gauge

FENCE

MOVABLE PIN

Japanese mortise gauge

MARKING BLADES

Japanese marking gauges
A traditional Japanese marking gauge is similar in appearance to a Western gauge, but the stock is held tight with a wooden wedge. It is fitted with a small blade instead of a pointed pin.
A mortise gauge has two beams with a blade in each one. The beams are adjusted to align one blade with each side of the mortise.

OTHER GAUGES

Profile gauge
A profile gauge has a row of metal pins or plastic blades which, when pressed against a moulding, slide back to reproduce its shape exactly. A centre spring holds the pins by friction.

Chalked line
It is not possible to gauge a straight line on a board with a waney edge, but you can use a length of string to mark a cut line. The string in a purpose-made tool is wound into a case containing coloured chalk with which it is coated each time it is withdrawn. With an assistant, stretch the string taut along the intended cut line, then pluck it like a bow string against the wood to deposit a chalked impression on its surface.

Profile gauge

Chalked line

USING MARKING AND CUTTING GAUGES

When using marking and cutting gauges, the intention is to leave a clear but fine line on the work. Scoring a deep line can tear the wood, leading to inaccuracy.

Adjusting a marking gauge
Adjust the stock using a rule (1) and lock it in place with its thumbscrew. Check the measurement and make fine adjustments by tapping the base of the beam on a bench to increase the distance between pin and stock (2). Decrease it by tapping the tip of the beam (3).

1 Set the stock using a rule

2 Tap to increase measurement

3 Tap to decrease measurement

Adjusting a mortise gauge
Set the pins to match the width of a mortise chisel, then adjust the stock to suit the thickness of the rail.

Set pins to match chisel

Scribing with a gauge
Press the stock of a gauge against the edge of the work, then push the tool away from you, allowing the pin to trail behind the beam with its point just marking the timber.

Finding a centre line
When marking out certain joints it is essential to be able to find the exact centre of a rail. Using a rule is not an accurate method. Adjust a marking gauge as closely as possible to half the thickness of the rail, then check it by holding the stock against one side of the rail and making a single pin prick. Make a similar mark from the other side of the rail. If the two marks correspond exactly, the gauge is accurately set to the centre of the rail. If they overshoot or fall short of the centre line, adjust the gauge until the marks do coincide.

Cutting veneer strips
Align the planed edges of veneers with a straightedged board. Hold the veneers flat with a stout batten and use a cutting gauge to slice off parallel-sided strips.

SQUARING UP TIMBER

To plane a piece of timber flat and with adjacent surfaces at right angles to each other is known as 'squaring up'.

Method of squaring up
Select what appears to be the best face in terms of colour, grain pattern and freedom from blemishes. Plane it flat and designate it 'face side' with a pencilled loop trailing off at one edge (1). Plane this edge square to the face side, check it with a try square and mark it with an arrowhead pointing to the face-side loop (2). This is now the 'face edge'.

All other measurements must be taken from either face side or face edge.

Set a marking gauge to the required thickness and mark a line on both edges from the face side (3). Plane the unfinished side down to these lines (4). Mark the width on both sides from face edge (5), then plane the wood to size (6).

IMPROVISING A GAUGE

When absolute accuracy is not important use the tip of your finger to guide a pencil point parallel to an edge (1).

For a slightly wider measure, rest the pencil point against the end of a rule held at right angles to the edge of the work. Use the finger holding the rule like the stock of a marking gauge (2).

1 Gauging with finger

2 Gauging with rule

1 Mark face side

2 Mark face edge

3 Gauge the thickness

4 Plane to lines

5 Gauge the width

6 Plane to size

HOW A SAW WORKS

Woodworking saws have a very ancient pedigree stretching back over 4000 years. Through the centuries advances in technology have improved the quality of materials used in their production and the ingenuity of successive generations of craftsmen has supplied us with a variety of solutions to the task of cutting wood – fast cutting, straight cutting, curved cutting, fine cutting and so on. Some saws are designed to cut on the push stroke, others on the pull stroke. Nevertheless, every saw severs wood in basically the same way. A saw blade has a continuous row of pointed teeth along its cutting edge or edges. Each tooth acts like a miniature chisel or knife blade, cutting tiny shavings or slivers of wood which fall to the floor as sawdust.

The set

The set of saw teeth
If the teeth were merely stacked one behind the other, the saw blade would jam in the cut after a few minutes' work. To solve the problem, all but the finest teeth are 'set'. Alternate teeth are bent to the right or left to cut a groove or 'kerf' which is wider than the saw blade itself.

The shape of saw teeth
Saw teeth are shaped differently depending on the job they are required to do.
Rip teeth (**1**) are for cutting with the grain, such as sawing a plank to width. These are large teeth with upright leading edges. Each tooth is filed square to the face of the blade and its sharp tip slices wood like a chisel.
Crosscut teeth (**2**) are designed for sawing across the grain without tearing the wood fibres. This is necessary when cutting most joints or for sawing a plank to length. The leading edge of a crosscut tooth leans back slightly and is filed at an angle to form a sharp cutting edge and tip. Each tooth acts like a knife, scoring the wood on each side of the kerf, leaving the waste to fall out as it is cleared by the passage of the blade.
Japanese crosscut teeth (**3**) are similar in design, but they are tall and narrow with another bevel filed on the top of each one.
Dual-purpose teeth (**4**) are symmetrical and filed on both edges for cutting with and across the grain. They are also known as 'fleam teeth'.

The size of saw teeth
A saw designed for fine work – such as cutting a dovetail joint – will have small finely set teeth. However, small teeth cut slowly. To be able to cut through timber quickly, especially resinous softwoods, a saw must have large teeth with deep 'gullets' – the spaces between the teeth – which are capable of clearing large amounts of sawdust from the kerf.

Tooth size is measured by the number that fit into 25mm (1in) of saw blade. Despite metrication, saws are still specified in TPI (teeth per inch) – measured from the base of one tooth to the base of another. Alternatively, teeth are measured from point to point, in PPI (points per inch). There is always one more point per inch than teeth.

Occasionally a saw will be specified as having rising-pitch teeth – that is with progressively larger teeth towards the handle. The cut is started with the small teeth until the kerf is established, when the full length of the blade can be used.

1 Rip teeth

2 Crosscut teeth

3 Japanese teeth

4 Dual-purpose teeth

Saw-tooth size

Hardened teeth
A lot of saws are made with electronically hardened teeth. They stay sharp longer than ordinary steel teeth, but they cannot be file-sharpened by hand.

HANDSAWS

All handsaws have long flexible blades, but because the blades are very deep they are capable of maintaining a straight cut. The best handsaw blades are taper-ground – that is reduced in thickness above the teeth to give a better clearance in the kerf. They are also skew-backed, with a slow 'S' bend tapering sharply towards the toe to improve the balance of the tool. Blades are sometimes covered with polytetrafluoroethylene (PTFE) to reduce friction.

A well-made handsaw
SKEW-BACKED
TAPER-GROUND
ANGLE OF THRUST

HANDSAW HANDLES

The handles should be set low behind the blade for maximum thrust midway along the row of teeth. Although a few handsaws are still made with the old-fashioned pistol-grip handle, most are fitted with a stronger closed handgrip in wood or plastic. The traditional horned wooden handle is both functional and comfortable, but many manufacturers prefer the more economical plastic grips which are often designed in such a way that the long straight back of the blade can be used as an extra-large try square.

Pistol-grip handle

Closed wooden handle

Closed plastic handle

Using a saw as a try or mitre square

Ripsaw

The ripsaw is the largest of the handsaws, with a blade length of 650mm (2ft 2in), having 5 PPI. It is a specialized tool suitable only for cutting solid timber with the grain.

Crosscut saw

The crosscut saw is 600 to 650mm (2 to 2ft 2in) long, with 6 to 8 PPI. It is the ideal saw for cutting solid planks to length, but it is rather coarse for man-made boards. Some Western-style handsaws are made with fast-cutting Japanese-pattern crosscut teeth.

Panel saw

A panel saw has relatively fine crosscut teeth – 10 to 12 PPI – for cutting man-made boards, but it is also used as a general-purpose crosscut saw. Blade lengths vary from 500 to 550mm (1ft 8in to 1ft 10in).

Ripsaw

Crosscut saw

Panel saw

Frame saw

The traditional-style frame saw (see right) has hardly changed since medieval times. The narrow blade is held under tension by tightening a twisted cord or wire cable running between the two end posts or 'cheeks'. The blade can be turned to swing the frame clear of the work when ripping long boards. Blades of 4, 5, 6 and 11 PPI can be fitted as required.

TWISTED-WIRE TOURNIQUET

CHEEK

BLADE

1 The correct grip

2 Starting a cut

3 Keep kerf open with wedge

4 Supporting an offcut

5 The reverse-action grip

USING AND CARING FOR HANDSAWS

Position the work so that you can saw at approximately 45 degrees to its surface and with the blade in line with your forearm.

Controlling a handsaw
Hold a handsaw with your forefinger extended towards the toe of the blade **(1)**. This will give you greater control over the blade and prevent the handgrip twisting in your hand. To begin the cut, work just to the waste side of the marked line, guiding the blade with the thumb of your free hand **(2)** while making short backward strokes with the saw.

Once the kerf is established, use the full length of the blade with slow steady strokes. Fast erratic saw strokes are both tiring and inaccurate. If the saw begins to wander off line, twist the blade slightly to bring it back on course. If the kerf begins to close up and jam the blade, keep it open with a small wedge **(3)**. Rub the blade with a candle for a smoother action.

Finishing the cut
As you finish sawing a plank to length, support the offcut with your free hand **(4)**. Work slowly and gently to sever the last few fibres without splitting the wood.

As you approach the end of a long plank or man-made board, either turn round and saw back towards the kerf you have just made or change your grip on the tool so that you can continue in the same direction but with the saw facing away from you **(5)**. You may have to position the work at bench height for this manoeuvre to avoid striking the floor with the toe of the saw.

Caring for handsaws
Slip a plastic guard over the saw teeth to protect them when the saw is not being used. For long-term storage, wipe an oily rag over the blade to keep it rust free. Remove rust spots with wire wool dipped in white spirit.

SUPPORTING THE WORK

Unless you support the work properly you cannot hope to saw efficiently or safely. Support planks of solid timber or man-made boards on 550mm (1ft 10in) high trestles known as sawhorses. Thin sheet material will whip and bounce unless you support it from below on each side of the line with stiff planks. Hold down the work with your knee. If you are more comfortable sawing at bench height, clamp the work to the top with G-cramps or between bench stops.

Crosscutting on sawhorses
You may be able to use a single sawhorse to cut short lengths, but support a long plank on two.

Ripsawing
As you ripsaw up to a sawhorse, move it to the far side of the blade and continue with the cut.

Supporting a thin board
Place planks beneath a thin man-made board.

Crosscutting with a frame saw
To crosscut with a frame saw, set the blade just out of line with the frame so that you can see down the line of cut. Support the offcut as you finish sawing by passing your free hand through the frame and behind the blade.

Ripsawing with a frame saw
Clamp the work so that it overhangs the bench top. Set the blade at 90 degrees to the frame and use two hands to control the saw.

BACKSAWS

Backsaws, with their relatively thin blades and small finely set teeth, are the saws to use for precise work. The distinguishing feature of this family of saws is a heavy strip of brass or steel wrapped over the top edge of the blade. It keeps the blade straight and its weight makes for easy cutting without having to force the saw into the work.

Accessories
A bench hook is used for cross-cutting short lengths of timber with a backsaw. A mitre box is a jig for cutting mitres. The saw blade locates in slots in each side. A mitre block is a cheaper version with one side.

Mitre block

Mitre box

Bench hook

TRADITIONAL CLOSED HANDLE

HEAVY BRASS STRIP

Tenon saw
The tenon saw is the largest of the backsaws, having a 250 to 350mm (10in to 1ft 2in) blade with 13 to 15 PPI. It is a good general-purpose saw for cutting stout battens and large joints. It has a closed handle similar to those used for handsaws.

Dovetail saw
A dovetail saw is a smaller version of the tenon saw with a 200mm (8in) blade and 16 to 22 PPI. The finer teeth are not set in the accepted sense, relying on the burr produced by file-sharpening to provide sufficient blade clearance. The dovetail saw is traditionally made with a closed or an open pistol-grip handle. An alternative design of dovetail saw has a longer blade with a straight handle. Both patterns are for cutting fine joints in hardwood.

Offset dovetail saw
An offset dovetail saw is intended for flush-cutting through tenons, dowels and so on. The reversible-handle version allows for right-hand or left-hand use.

Bead saw
The bead saw is a miniature backsaw with 26 PPI for cutting delicate work.

Blitz saw
The blitz saw is an extremely fine backsaw suitable for model-making. The teeth, at 33 PPI, are so small on the finest blitz-saw blades that they cannot be sharpened, so are replaceable.

E.T. ROBERTS & LEE

Tenon saw (Traditional pattern)

Dovetail saw (Traditional pattern)

HANDLE PIVOTS TO OTHER END OF SAW

Offset dovetail saw (Reversible)

Offset dovetail saw (Fixed)

Dovetail saw

Bead saw

FINGER GRIP

Blitz saw

Using a backsaw
Start with short backward strokes with the saw at a low angle. Gradually lower the blade as you extend the kerf until the saw is horizontal, then continue with the cut.

CURVE-CUTTING SAWS

A family of special-purpose saws is available for cutting out curved components. The saws are graded in size to cope with work of all thicknesses, from stout hardwood planks to thin veneers.

Bow saw

This small lightweight frame saw is fitted with narrow blades for making curved cuts. They are 200 to 300mm (8 to 12in) long with 9 to 17 PPI and are sturdy enough to saw quite thick sections of solid timber. Blades can be turned through 360 degrees to swing the frame out of the way.

Coping saw

A 150mm (6in) coping-saw blade is held under tension by the spring of the metal frame. It is for cutting curves in solid timber, and also in man-made boards. The blades, with 15 to 17 PPI, are too narrow to sharpen and are discarded when blunt or broken.

Fret saw

A fret saw, with its extra-deep bowed frame, is designed to make extremely tight curved cuts in thin man-made boards or veneers. With up to 32 PPI, the blades are very fragile.

Compass saw

It is not possible to use any of the bowed saws to make a cut in the middle of a large board. The narrow tapering blade of a compass saw is capable of making reasonably tight curves, but is also deep enough to keep on a straight course. The pistol-grip handle will take a variety of blades with 8 to 10 PPI.

A straight-handled version of the saw, known as a pad-saw or keyhole saw, is preferred by some woodworkers because it feels comfortable in the hand when sawing in any direction.

Padsaw
The retractable blade is clamped by the slotted screws in the ferrule.

TOGGLE

TOURNIQUET

Bow saw

DEEP BOWED FRAME

Fret saw

Coping saw

BLADE FIXINGS

Compass saw

CHANGING CURVE-CUTTING SAW BLADES

Curve-cutting saws have relatively narrow blades which will eventually break or bend. Always have spare blades in stock.

Fitting a bow-saw blade

Slacken the cord tourniquet across the top of the saw, then locate the new blade, with teeth facing away from you, in the slotted handle-rods at each end (1). Pass the tapered pins through the holes in the rods and blade. Tighten the tourniquet to tension the blade and park the toggle against the central stretcher rail. Turn the handle at each end of the saw (2) to straighten the blade.

1 Fitting a bow-saw blade

2 Straightening the blade

Replacing a tourniquet

Replace a broken tourniquet with a length of new string. With the blade in position, lightly clamp the cheeks of the saw between bench stops. Tie the string to one cheek, then make a cord by winding it end-to-end about four times. Bind the loose end around the cord near one cheek and tie a knot through the strings (1).

Pass the wooden toggle through the centre of the cord (2) and wind it up until the blade is taut.

1 Making a new cord

2 Wind up cord with toggle

Changing a coping-saw blade

A coping-saw blade fits into slots in large retaining pins at each end of the saw (1). To fit a new blade, first turn the handle anticlockwise to reduce the gap between the retaining pins. Fit the blade at the toe of the saw with the teeth facing away from you, then flex the frame against the bench (2) to locate the other end of the blade. Holding its retaining pin, tighten the handle to tension the blade. Align the retaining pins by eye.

1 Fitting a coping-saw blade

2 Flexing a coping-saw frame

Fitting a fret-saw blade

Each end is clamped by a thumbscrew. Compress the frame slightly as you fit the blade with the teeth facing the handle. A fret saw cuts on the pull stroke.

Fitting a fret-saw blade

Fitting a compass-saw blade

To change a compass-saw blade, slacken the clamping screws and slide the slotted end of the blade into the handle. Then retighten.

Fitting a compass-saw blade

USING CURVE-CUTTING SAWS

Except for the compass saw, which is used like a conventional handsaw, curve-cutting saws feel clumsy in the hands of an inexperienced woodworker. It is necessary to master specific techniques to compensate for the twisting force applied by their bowed frames.

Using a bow saw

A bow saw is unwieldy unless you use the proper two-handed grip to control the tool. Take hold of the handle with one hand, extending your index finger in line with the blade. Place your free hand alongside the other, with index and middle finger wrapped around the cheek on each side of the blade.

Holding a bow saw correctly

Cutting with a coping saw

The narrow blade is difficult to keep on course. It is easier if you use a double-handed grip on the saw (1) or, alternatively, place the first joint of your extended index finger on the frame when using one hand. To make a closed cut some way from an edge, first drill a hole within the waste. Pass the blade through the hole and reconnect it to the saw frame (2).

1 Using a double-handed grip

2 Making a closed cut

Using a fret saw

Sit on a low stool when using a fret saw and allow the work to overhang the edge of the bench top. The blade is so narrow it will make a tight curve without having to be swivelled in its frame.

If the work is flexing and bouncing, cut a V-shaped notch in a block of wood or scrap plywood to support the work on each side of the blade. Clamp or screw the block to the bench.

Using a fret saw

Cutting with a compass saw

Drill a small hole in the waste to accept the tip of the saw. Work slowly and steadily to avoid buckling the narrow blade.

Using a compass saw

JAPANESE SAWS

Japanese saws cut on the pull stroke, so the blades are much thinner than their Western equivalents and the teeth are very finely set. As a result, they cut a narrow kerf with virtually no tearing of the grain. The best blades are taper-ground to reduce friction. Handles are bound with split bamboo.

Using a hugihiki
Flex the blade against the work to cut a dowel flush with its surface.

Cutting with a dozuki
Saw with the blade parallel to the bench. Some woodworkers like to saw a kerf on four sides before cutting through the work.

Kataba

Ryoba

Dozuki

FLEXIBLE BLADE

STIFF BLADE

BLADE-FIXING RIVETS

DOUBLE-EDGED BLADE

Mawashibiki

Kataba
A kataba is made with either rip or crosscut teeth on one side only and can be used to cut thick sections of timber where a ryoba would bind in the kerf. An extra-flexible version of the saw, known as a hugihiki (dowel saw), is used to flush-cut through tenons or dowel joints. It has no set on the teeth and is flexed against the surface of the work like a spatula.

Ryoba
The ryoba is a combination saw with rip teeth along one edge and crosscut teeth on the other. A blade of 210 to 240mm (8¼ to 9½in) is common, with 6 to 15 PPI. The saw must be used at a low angle to the work to prevent the upper row of teeth entering the kerf. Consequently, a ryoba is normally used to cut planks, not thick baulks of timber.

Dozuki
The dozuki is a 240mm (9½in) backsaw designed for cutting joints, like the Western tenon and dovetail saws. The dovetail version with 23 PPI is capable of sawing an especially narrow kerf – a real advantage when cutting fine joints. The teeth are graded with smaller ones towards the heel of the saw for starting the cut.

Mawashibiki
The mawashibiki is the Japanese keyhole or compass saw. Even with its thin taper-ground blade, the pull-stroke action of the mawashibiki reduces the risk of buckling the blade – a constant problem with the Western version of the saw.

SHARPENING SAWS

A saw needs to be sharpened as soon as it requires any real effort to drive it through the timber. Most woodworkers are happy to put the 'edge' back on a saw, but might prefer to send it to a professional when it requires resetting. Resetting is necessary after four or five sharpenings or if you find the saw constantly runs off course due to uneven setting. Electronically hardened teeth cannot be sharpened by hand and fine disposable saw blades are always discarded when blunt.

SELECTING A SAW FILE

Saw	PPI	File length
Ripsaw	5 to 7	250mm (10in)
Crosscut saw	6 to 8	230mm (9in)
Panel saw	10 to 12	200mm (8in)
Tenon saw	13 to 15	180mm (7in)
Dovetail saw	16 to 22	150mm (6in)

Saw files
The cutting edge of each saw tooth is maintained with a triangular file. Each side of the file should be about twice the height of the tooth. Use the chart as a rough guide to selecting a saw file.

Japanese saw files
Knife-edge files are available for sharpening Japanese saws. However, resetting and sharpening these saws is an exacting task best left to a professional.

Saw-file guide
A saw-file guide guarantees uniformity of angle and depth when sharpening tenon and handsaws.

Saw set
A saw set bends the top of saw teeth precisely to the required angle. Squeezing the handles together operates a plunger which presses the tooth against an angled anvil. The anvil is numerically graduated to correspond to tooth sizes up to 12 PPI. Saws with smaller teeth should be sent to a professional for resetting.

Saw cramp
A saw must be clamped firmly while being sharpened or it will vibrate noisily, throwing the file out of the gullet. Make an improvised cramp from two hardwood battens cut to match the length of the blade and shaped to fit around the handle. Clamp the saw between the battens in a bench vice. If necessary, attach a small G-cramp at one end.

2 Topping a saw

3 Setting saw teeth

4 Checking the set

5 Sharpening rip teeth

6 Sharpening crosscut teeth

Topping a saw
Topping a saw by filing the tips of the teeth is absolutely necessary to bring all the teeth to the same height when the saw has been damaged or inexpertly filed. However, a light topping before sharpening puts a tiny bright point on every tooth which will prove to be an invaluable guide to even sharpening. Make a topping jig by fitting a smooth file into a grooved block of hardwood (1). Tapering the top of the groove will allow you to introduce a tightening wedge. Run the block against the face of the saw with the file resting on the toothed edge (2). Two or three light passes should be enough to top a saw in good condition ready for sharpening. If your saw requires heavy topping before all the teeth show a bright point, send it to a professional who will reshape all the teeth before setting and sharpening.

1 Topping jig

Setting the teeth
Reset the teeth if your saw has been binding in the kerf or wandering off line. Adjust a saw set by undoing the locking screw, and turn the anvil to bring the required PPI number on its edge in line with the indicator on the tool. Retighten the locking screw. Working from one end of the saw, set every tooth that bends away from you (3). Turn the saw around and set the other teeth. Hold the saw at eye level with the teeth facing away from you to see if you have skipped a tooth (4).

Sharpening with a file
Hold the saw in the vice with the clamping battens just below the teeth and with the handle to your right.
  Steadying the file tip with your free hand, start at the toe of the saw by resting the file on the first tooth bent away from you and against the leading edge of the tooth next to it, which is bent towards you.
  For a ripsaw, settle the file in the gullet, at right angles to the blade and perfectly horizontal. Make two or three strokes with the file, applying pressure on the forward pass only until about half the bright point on the tip of the tooth is removed. Moving towards the handle, file alternate gullets until you have sharpened half the number of teeth. Turn the saw round and work from toe to heel again, filing the remaining gullets so that the bright points just disappear, leaving a sharp tip to each tooth (5).
  Sharpen a crosscut saw in the same way, but turn the file at an angle of about 65 degrees to the blade with the tip of the file towards the saw handle (6). Parallel lines drawn at 65 degrees across the top of the clamping battens will help to keep the file at a constant angle.

Saw-file guide
This jig fits onto the saw to guide the saw file at the required angle.

BENCH PLANES

Bench planes are everyday 'workhorses', used to smooth wooden surfaces while gradually reducing work to its finished dimensions. Wooden planes are lighter than their metal equivalents and skim smoothly across the work, but some of the more basic patterns are difficult to adjust when compared with a standard metal plane. Because they are mass-produced, metal planes are usually cheaper.

Wooden try plane

Scrub plane
A scrub plane is a specialized tool for quickly roughing timber to size. It is used diagonally across the grain in two directions before the wood is smoothed with a jack plane. The blade, with its convex cutting edge, is held in the body of the plane with a wooden wedge.

EXTRA-LONG SOLES FOR PLANING STRAIGHT EDGES

Traditional jack plane
Even though its wedged blade is difficult to adjust, this type of bench plane is popular with old-tool enthusiasts. Brand-new models are still available from specialist suppliers.

BLADE-FIXING WEDGE

STANLEY

Scrub plane

Scrub-plane blade

Metal try plane

Try or jointer plane
A try or jointer plane has a
sole up to 600mm (2ft) long
which bridges undulations in
the surface of the work.
Consequently, it planes a
perfectly straight edge where
a shorter plane might follow
the contours. A try plane is
especially useful for making
long butt joints between
planks used to construct a
wide panel.

Jack plane
The jack plane, between
350 and 387mm (1ft 2in and
1ft 3½in) long, is a general-
purpose tool used to plane
timber square and flat. In
common with other metal
bench planes, a jack plane
is made with a smooth sole
or one which is corrugated to
reduce friction when working on resinous timbers.

Corrugated sole

Smoothing plane
A smoothing plane is used
with a finely adjusted blade
to skim the surface to put a
final planed finish on the
work. A modern wooden
smoothing plane has a distinctive ergonomic handle at
its toe. The best planes have
self-lubricating lignum vitae
soles. Smoothing planes are
about 225mm (9in) long.

MEDIUM-LENGTH SOLES
FOR GENERAL-PURPOSE
WOODWORK

Metal jack plane

Wooden jack plane

Wooden smoothing plane

SHORT SOLES FOR
SKIMMING A WORKPIECE

Metal smoothing plane

All-metal bench plane

1 Handle	10 Frog
2 Lateral-adjustment lever	11 Frog locking screws
3 Blade	12 Lever-cap screw
4 Cap iron	13 Depth-adjustment lever
5 Lever	14 Depth-adjustment nut
6 Lever cap	15 Frog adjusting screw
7 Cap-iron locking screw	16 Sole
8 Knob	
9 Mouth	

Adjustable wooden plane

1 Depth-adjustment screw	
2 Cap-iron locking screw	8 Mouth-width adjustment screw
3 Blade	9 Crossbar
4 Cap iron	10 Tension screw
5 Regulator	11 Coil spring
6 Regulator locking screw	12 Tension-screw nut
7 Toe horn	13 Sole

THE CARE AND USE OF BENCH PLANES

Modern bench planes are precision-made tools but, as with all mass-produced items, a little judicious tinkering can make all the difference to their performance. In any case, all planes need to be serviced and adjusted from time to time to keep them functioning at their best.

Dismantling a metal plane
To remove the blade or cutting iron, first lift the lever on the lever cap and slide it from beneath its locking screw. Lift the blade with its cap iron out of the plane. Use a large screwdriver to loosen the cap-iron locking screw and slide the cap iron towards the cutting edge to pass the screw head through the hole in the blade, separating the two components.

Adjusting the frog
Removing the blade assembly exposes the frog. This is a wedge-shaped casting which incorporates both the blade-depth and the lateral-adjustment controls.

The frog itself slides backwards or forwards to regulate the size of the mouth – the opening in the plane sole through which the blade projects. For coarse planing the mouth is opened to provide adequate clearance for thick shavings. When the blade is set to take a fine cut, the mouth is closed to encourage the thin shavings to break and curl against the cap iron.

To adjust the frog, release the two locking screws and turn the adjusting screw with a screwdriver. Tighten the locking screws.

Assembling and adjusting the plane
Having sharpened the blade, hold it bevel downwards and lay the cap iron across it (**1**) to drop the screw head through the hole. Slide the cap iron away from the cutting edge and turn it to align with the blade (**2**). Slide the cap iron to within 1mm ($\frac{1}{16}$in) of the cutting edge (**3**) – or even closer for very fine shavings – and tighten the locking screw. Lower the blade assembly into the plane, cap iron uppermost, fitting it over the lever-cap screw and onto the depth-adjustment lever. Replace the lever cap. Turn the depth-adjustment nut until the blade protrudes from the sole. Inspect the cutting edge from the toe of the plane while moving the lateral-adjustment lever to bring the edge parallel to the sole. Back off depth adjustment to the required setting.

Dismantling a wooden plane
Back off the depth-adjustment screw by about 10mm ($\frac{1}{2}$in) and loosen the tension-screw nut at the heel of the plane. Turn the crossbar at the front of the tension screw through 90 degrees so that the blade assembly can be lifted out of the plane. Remove the two screws at the back of the blade to release the cap iron and regulator.

Assembling the plane
Having sharpened the blade, replace the cap iron and lower the assembly into the plane. Pass the tension-screw crossbar through the slot in the assembly and turn it to locate it in its seat in the cap iron. Slightly tighten the tension-screw nut and adjust the depth-adjustment screw until the blade protrudes. Use the regulator to make sure the cutting edge is parallel with the sole. Back off the depth-adjustment screw and finally tighten the tension-screw nut.

Set the mouth width by adjusting the screw behind the toe horn.

Replacing a cap iron

1 Lay cap iron across blade

2 Align cap iron with blade

3 Slide cap iron up to cutting edge

SERVICING A BENCH PLANE

More than likely your plane will function perfectly adequately direct from the supplier. However, if you are having problems achieving the desired results, check that there are none of the more obvious defects in its manufacture.

Warped sole
If you cannot get the plane to take a fine shaving, lay a straightedge across the sole to see if it is warped. You can flatten a metal sole on emery cloth held down to a sheet of glass with double-sided tape. This is a slow laborious process, however, and you might prefer to have the sole reground by a professional (or return the plane to the supplier).

Flattening a wooden plane on abrasive paper is easier. Withdraw the blade, hold the plane near its centre and rub it back and forth across the abrasive. Check the sole regularly with the straightedge.

Blade chatter
A loose blade will vibrate and skid across the work. Tighten the lever-cap screw or tension-screw nut.

If the fault persists, make sure there are no foreign bodies trapped behind the blade and, in the case of a metal plane, under the frog.

Shavings jamming under the cap iron
Unless the cap iron beds down perfectly on the blade, shavings will jam under its leading edge.

If the blade is bent, lay it on a flat board and strike it firmly with a hammer.

Hone the meeting edge of the cap iron on an oilstone until it is flat.

General care of planes
Wooden soles will become 'slick' with use and should not be treated in any way. Rubbing a candle across a metal sole can help relieve a 'sticky' plane. Withdraw the blades and store bench planes on their sides.

Using a metal bench plane

USING BENCH PLANES

The pattern of a tree's growth rings appears as dark lines or grain on the work. Clamp the work in a vice or lay it on the bench against bench stops so that these grain lines 'lean' away from you. Planing with the grain in this way permits the blade to cut smoothly. Planing in the other direction, against the grain, tears the wood's fibres.

Handling and controlling a bench plane
Grasp the handle of a metal bench plane with your fore-finger extended against the edge of the blade or frog. This will ensure control over the direction of the plane. Your free hand provides downward pressure on the plane, using the round knob on its toe.

To use a wooden smoothing plane, slip the crotch between thumb and fore-finger around the shaped rest below the depth-adjustment screw. Grasp the body with fingers and thumb. Your free hand will fit naturally around the toe horn.

Stand beside the bench with your feet apart. Your rearward foot points towards the bench, the other is parallel with it. Keeping your feet firmly planted, move the upper part of your body to propel the plane.

As you start the stroke, put pressure on the toe of the plane, relieving it only as you finish the stroke to prevent rounding-off at both ends of the work.

Holding the plane flat on the work but at a slight angle to the direction of travel produces a slicing action with the cutting edge which helps to shear through difficult grain.

Planing an edge square
To prevent the plane rocking while planing a narrow edge, maintain downward pressure with your thumb and curl your fingers under the sole to act as a fence against the work. Use a similar grip to hold the plane at an angle when planing a chamfer along the edge.

Planing a surface flat
To plane a surface flat, choose a try or jack plane, depending on the length of the work.

Plane in the general direction of the grain but at an angle across the work in two directions. Check for flatness with a straightedge (a try plane tilted onto one long edge is ideal), then plane parallel with the work's edges using a finely set blade for a final finish.

If the work is very convex, remove the majority of waste with a scrub plane before taking up another plane.

Using a wooden smoothing plane

Maintaining a square edge

Planing a chamfer

Making a straight edge
Start with pressure on the toe of the plane, but transfer it to the heel at the end of the stroke.

Planing a surface flat
Plane in two directions across the board, then plane along it.

Checking for flatness

REBATE PLANES

A rebate is a rectangular-section recess along the edge of a piece of timber. It is often used to receive a square-edged panel at right angles to the rebated wood – as when a plywood back panel is fitted into a cabinet, for example. Special planes are required to cut rebates.

Using a fence
Pin or clamp a fence to the work when using a bench rebate plane.

Using a rebate and filister plane
Start at the far end of a workpiece and work gradually backwards.

Bench rebate plane

Large rebates can be cut with a bench rebate plane – a specialized version of the standard jack plane – with a blade extending across the entire width of the sole. It has no fence or depth stop and must be used against a straight batten nailed or clamped to the work until the rebate itself is deep enough to guide the plane.

With the tool held firmly against the guide batten, plane down to a line marking the rebate depth.

Rebate and filister plane

This is a sophisticated rebate plane with an adjustable guide fence and depth stop. The cutter can be mounted in two positions – one for normal use and one near the toe for planing to the end of a stopped rebate. This type of plane is also fitted with a spur that scores ahead of the blade when rebating across the grain.

To cut a through rebate, set the guides and start planing at the far end of the work with short strokes. Keeping the fence pressed against the work, move backwards gradually lengthening the strokes. Plane the full length of the work until the depth stop prevents the plane from biting any further.

Bull-nose plane

A short snub-nose version of the shoulder plane, this small lightweight plane is used to trim stopped rebates or small joints. There are many versions of this plane in both wood and metal.

FULL-WIDTH BLADE

Bench rebate plane

CUTTER-DEPTH ADJUSTMENT LEVER

DEPTH GAUGE

NORMAL CUTTER POSITION

FORWARD CUTTER POSITION

GUIDE FENCE

BLADE-DEPTH ADJUSTMENT SCREW

Rebate and filister plane

LEVER CAP

BLADE   WEDGE

Metal shoulder plane

BLADES

Side rebate plane

THROAT-ADJUSTMENT CRAMP

BLADE
Wooden shoulder plane

LEVER CAP

BLADE-DEPTH ADJUSTMENT SCREW

WEDGE

BLADE
Metal bull-nose plane

BLADE

Wooden bull-nose plane

BLOCK PLANES

Shoulder plane
The shoulder plane has an accurately machined body with both sides perfectly square to the sole. It can be used like a bench rebate plane, but is most useful as a means of trimming the square shoulders of large joints (1). The blade is set at a low angle so that it will shave end grain.

There are metal and wooden planes with one-piece bodies, while others have detachable front ends to convert them into small chisel planes to work into a square stopped rebate.

Side rebate plane
This miniature plane is for shaving rebates or easing the sides of narrow grooves (2). It is used on edge, with the blade skimming the vertical wall. Having two opposing blades, the plane can be used to trim both sides of a groove from one direction – always working with the grain. Each nose is detachable for planing stopped grooves. The depth gauge riding on the top edge of the work helps to control the orientation of the blade.

The block plane is a lightweight general-purpose plane. It is used one-handed although extra pressure can be exerted on the toe with the fingertips of your free hand.

Block-plane blades
The wooden version has a large depth-adjustment knob for precise setting.

On the more sophisticated metal version, the blade is set at an angle of 20 degrees specifically for trimming end grain. A low-angle plane is also available in which the blade is set at 12 degrees. Both planes have control over the depth and lateral movement of the blade, and an adjustable mouth. The blade is removed for sharpening by detaching the cast-metal lever cap, which is locked in place by a small lever. When replacing a block-plane blade, ensure it is fitted bevel uppermost.

DEPTH-ADJUSTMENT KNOB

BLADE

LEVER CAP

DEPTH-ADJUSTMENT SCREW

LEVER CAP

Wooden block plane

THROAT-ADJUSTMENT LEVER

Metal block plane

1 Trimming a large shoulder

2 Easing a groove

PLANING END GRAIN

It is convenient to skim end grain with a lightweight block plane but, for a precise right angle or mitre, use a bench plane on a shooting board.

Using a block plane
When trimming end grain with a block plane, make sure the blade is razor sharp and put plenty of pressure on the toe (1). Plane from both ends towards the middle to avoid splitting wood from the edge of the work. Alternatively, plane a chamfer at one end down to the marked finished line (2) and plane towards that end only, or clamp a block of scrap wood against the work to support the edge (3).

Using a shooting board
Trim end grain with a bench plane on a special jig called a shooting board. The work is held against a stop mounted across the top of the jig. The plane is run on its side, and guided past the work by a wide rebate. With the work just projecting from the stop, trim the end grain with a finely set sharp blade.

A shooting board with angled stops is used to trim mitre joints.

2 Plane towards chamfer

3 Support edge with block

1 Apply pressure to toe

Shooting board

Using a shooting board

Mitre shooting board

JAPANESE PLANES

A traditional Japanese woodworking plane is very simply constructed, having a rectangular-section hardwood body, a blade and cap iron. A steel cross-pin keeps the cap iron pressed against the blade.

Almost legendary qualities are claimed for these planes. They cut on the pull stroke, with the work resting on a heavy beam supported on a triangular trestle at one end, the other end butted against a wall.

A hollowed sole
The sole of a kanna is hollowed to leave three points of contact with a workpiece.

Using a Kirimen-kanna
This type of plane sits on the corner of the work.

Kanna (Bench planes)

Japanese-oak bench planes range from 162 to 356mm (6½ to 14¼in) in length. The blades are laminated with a thin layer of high-carbon steel forming the cutting edge, backed by a thick strip of soft low-carbon steel to absorb the shock when planing knotty timber with irregular grain. The back of the blade is hollowed, which makes it easier to flatten on a stone and make a good fit with the cap iron.

Tap the top edge of the blade with a soft hammer or mallet to increase the depth of cut. Back off the blade by tapping the end of the plane body behind the blade. Give the plane a sharp blow in the same place to shock the blade out of its groove ready for sharpening.

In order to reduce friction on the work, the larger bench planes have hollowed soles produced with a special scraper plane (Dai-nishi-kanna), leaving a point of contact at the toe, just in front of the mouth and at the back of the sole.

Sakuri-kanna (Rebate plane)

This wooden plane is used like a European shoulder plane. The blade, from 12 to 24mm (½ to 1in) wide, is fitted into an oak body 275mm (11in) long.

Kirimen-kanna (Chamfer plane)

This very specialized plane has screw-adjusted fences which open up to plane chamfers up to 20mm (¾in) wide. The small plane 'body', with a skewed blade, slides sideways into the fences.

BLADE

CAP IRON

Kanna (Bench plane)

BLADE

CAP IRON

Sakuri-kanna (Rebate plane)

BLADE

CAP IRON

PLANE BODY

CHAMFER SCALE

FENCES

WIDTH-ADJUSTMENT SCREWS

Kirimen-kanna (Chamfer plane)

Japanese planes cut on the pull stroke

SPECIALIZED PLANES

There are other ways to achieve the results obtained with specialized planes, but these tools enable the discerning woodworker to complete the job quickly and with a greater degree of accuracy.

Compass plane

A compass plane is fitted with a standard bench-plane blade, cap iron and lever cap, but the sole is made from a strip of flexible steel. It is adjusted by means of a large knurled nut to form a concave or convex curve.

The compass plane is especially useful for trimming slow curves such as the edge of a round table where a spokeshave is likely to follow bumps and hollows.

Saw the wood roughly to shape and either set the sole of the plane to match the cut edge or draw the intended curve on a board as a guide to setting the sole exactly.

As you work, you must reposition the work periodically to be able to plane with the grain at all times.

Router plane

The router plane, once the preferred tool for levelling the bottoms of housings, has been largely replaced by the electric router.

However, due to its relative cheapness and simplicity, it is still to be found in many workshops, especially for making small recesses for locks and hinges. A very basic wooden router plane is available from European suppliers, but the metal version is far more adaptable.

Special cutters are screw-adjustable to fine tolerances. Chisel-like cutters are used to level square-sided recesses and there is a pointed cutter for working the undercut sides of a dovetail housing or into tight corners. The plane will level a through housing with a cutter mounted in the forward position of the cutter clamp. With a cutter mounted to the rear of the clamp, the plane is used in reverse to work up to the end of a stopped housing.

A small fence screwed to the sole guides a cutter at a set distance from a straight or curved edge. A depth gauge fitted with a small flat shoe closes the open throat at the front of the plane when the tool is used on a narrow edge where the bifurcated sole is ineffectual.

BLADE

SOLE-ADJUSTMENT NUT

FLEXIBLE STEEL SOLE

Compass plane

BLADE

Wooden router plane

Using a compass plane

FENCE

BLADE-DEPTH ADJUSTMENT NUT

STANDARD CUTTER

POINTED CUTTER

DEPTH GAUGE

Metal router plane

Cutting a housing
Saw down the line to the depth of the housing on both sides. Adjust the depth of the cutter little by little to remove the waste in stages down to the required depth of the housing.

Sharpening cutters
Sharpen a router-plane cutter on an oil-stone, like a chisel, but place the stone near the edge of a bench to provide clearance for the cutter shaft.

PLOUGH & COMBINATION PLANES

At the turn of the century the average woodworker would have had a tool chest half full of wooden moulding planes, plough planes and matching tongue and groove planes – every one of them designed for a specific purpose and with its purpose- *made cutter. Not surprisingly, a single tool that would combine all these functions was bound to be a success and, despite competition from the electric router, the combination plane is still popular, as much as anything for its ingenuity.*

Plough plane
This is a specialized plane designed to cut grooves, though it can also be used to cut narrow rebates. Square-edged cutters, from 3 to 12mm ($\frac{1}{8}$ to $\frac{1}{2}$in) wide, are held in the plane by a sliding clamp, and adjusted up and down by a knurled screw. The plane is fitted with a guide fence and depth gauge. Wooden planes are still made for old-tool enthusiasts.

Combination plane
A combination plane is a plough plane with extra features to make tongue and groove joints, including the rounded beading often used to decorate the shoulder line and disguise shrinkage.

A special tonguing cutter with an adjustable depth stop is matched to one of the grooving cutters. Beading cutters range in width from 3 to 12mm ($\frac{1}{8}$ to $\frac{1}{2}$in).

The cutter clamp extends to the toe of the plane as a complete sliding section to match the plane body. It carries an optional narrow fence for planing a bead on a tongued edge where the use of the standard guide fence would be impaired by the projecting tongue.

The plane body and sliding section each carries a knife-edge spur which slices the grain ahead when planing across the grain.

Multi-plane
A multi-plane is a combination plane with additional cutters. It will cut ovolo mouldings, window-sash mouldings, flutes and reeds. A slitting knife can be fitted in the plane to slice parallel strips of wood off the edge of a plank.

Using a scratch stock
Clamp the cutter between two identical pieces of plywood screwed together to form a simple stock with a built-in guide fence. Leaning the tool away from you, scrape the wood with the projecting part of the cutter until the stock comes to rest on the work.

PLOUGH-PLANE CUTTERS

CUTTER-CLAMPING SCREW

Plough plane

FENCE

CUTTER-DEPTH ADJUSTMENT SCREW

CUTTER CLAMP

BEAD FENCE

Combination plane

COMBINATION-PLANE CUTTERS

BLADE-DEPTH ADJUSTMENT SCREW

Multi-plane

BLADE

MULTI-PLANE CUTTERS

BEAD FENCE

FENCE

CAM FENCE STEADY

Scratch stock
A scratch stock is a home-made moulding tool. Simply file the reverse shape of the required moulding in the edge of a piece of broken hacksaw blade.

USING THE PLANES

Clamp the cutter in a plane and measure from it to set the guide fence and depth gauge. Settle the plane on the work at the far end, supporting the guide-fence assembly with your left hand. Start with short strokes, gradually working backwards until the plane is taking full-length shavings.

Support the guide-fence assembly with your left hand

Cutting grooves
A groove is usually planed with the grain and often in the edge of a piece of wood. Any of the planes can be used. You can cut a groove across end grain, but to avoid splitting the edge at the end of the stroke, mark the work with a mortise gauge and chop out the waste at the far end with a saw and chisel before you use the plane.

Cutting a housing
A housing is a groove across the grain. Guide the body of a combination or multi-plane with a straight batten pinned to the work. Adjust spurs to score both sides of the housing.

Cutting a rebate
To cut a rebate, set up any of the planes to cut a groove, but adjust the guide fence to bring the cutter to the edge of the work. You can cut wider rebates in stages by working back into the work one blade-width at a time.

Cutting a tongue and groove
Cut the tongue first with the special cutter clamped in a combination plane or multi-plane. Because the cutter has its own built-in depth stop there is no need to attach one to the plane itself. Set the guide fence to centre the tongue on the edge of the work. Match the grooving cutter to the planed tongue.

Cutting beads
To cut a bead along a tongued edge, fit the special narrow guide fence which automatically positions a beading cutter to plane the moulding on the very edge of the work just above the tongue. A bead can be cut at a distance from a square edge using the standard guide fence.

Cutting an ovolo
Cut an ovolo like a rebate. To mould all four edges of a solid-wood panel, plane across the grain at both ends first, then plane with the grain down both edges.

Cutting a window sash
Cut a window-sash moulding on the edge of a plank, planing first one half, then turning the work over to plane the other half. Finally, cut the moulding from the plank with the slitting knife.

Cutting a flute
Cut a flute like a bead, using the plane's depth gauge and standard guide fence.

Cutting reeds
A reed cutter produces a series of parallel beads in one go. Set up the plane as for a bead or flute.

Sharpening cutters
Sharpen plane cutters on an oilstone, like chisels, but with a single grinding angle. These small cutters are easier to sharpen when clamped in a honing guide. Use a fine slipstone to sharpen the curved cutting edges.

Clamp cutters in a honing guide

Plane cutters

1 Tongue
2 Window-sash moulding
3 Ovolo
4 Bead
5 Reeds
6 Flute
7 Rebate
8 Groove

CHISELS & GOUGES

Chisels and gouges rank with saws and planes as essential woodworking tools. They are primarily for removing waste wood from joints, although the lighter versions are also used to shape and trim workpieces. Strong stocky chisels and gouges are sometimes driven with a mallet when a lot of wood has to be removed, but most of the time the tools are used with hand pressure only.

Firmer chisel
The firmer is the most basic general-purpose chisel. Its rectangular-section blade is strong enough to be driven through tough woods with a mallet. Firmer blades are made in regular increments from 3 to 38mm ($\frac{1}{8}$ to $1\frac{1}{2}$in) in width, but a 50mm (2in) wide chisel is also available.

Bevel-edge chisel
The underside of the blade is flat like the firmer, but a shallow bevel is ground on the two long edges on the upper face. This makes a lightweight tool which should only be driven by hand, but it is ideal for chopping out the waste from dovetail joints. Bevel-edge chisels are made in the same range of sizes as firmers.

Paring chisel
A paring chisel is an extra-long bevel-edge chisel for chopping the waste out of housing joints.

Cranked paring chisel
The cranked neck of this chisel enables a woodworker to keep the blade flat on the work even when paring in the centre of a wide board.

Skew chisel
The end of the blade is skewed to an angle of 60 degrees to produce a slicing action at the cutting edge as the chisel is driven forward. This makes for smooth cutting, even through difficult grain, and the pointed tip is especially useful for cleaning out awkward corners. The range of blade widths is limited to 12, 18 and 25mm ($\frac{1}{2}$, $\frac{3}{4}$ and 1in).

Chisel handles▶
There has always been a wide variety of chisel handles, largely as a result of regional preference. Plastic handles are so tough that they will withstand being driven with a metal hammer – a practice which would ruin a wooden handle.

Firmer chisel

Bevel-edge chisel

Cranked paring chisel

Paring chisel

Skew chisel

1 Carving-pattern handle

2 Octagonal handle

3 Plastic handle

4 Reinforced handle

Styles of chisel handle
The cylindrical, but slightly bulbous, carving-pattern handle (1) is functional and ergonomic. Octagonal handles (2) are designed to prevent a chisel rolling off a bench, and plastic handles (3) are often moulded with subtle 'flats' for the same reason. The butt end of a wooden handle is sometimes reinforced (4) with a hoop of metal to stop the wood fibres splitting under the constant hammering of a mallet.

Hardwoods like boxwood, ash and beech have always been used to make chisel handles, but there has been an increasingly popular trend to mould them from plastics.

HOW CHISELS ARE MADE

Chisels vary in detail from type to type and from manufacturer to manufacturer, but they are essentially tools with stiff metal blades attached to roughly cylindrical straight handles. The joint between blade and handle is critical chisel design.

Blades

The average bench chisel has a blade 125 to 175mm (5 to 7in) long. Some woodworkers prefer the feel of the short heftier version, the butt chisel, with a blade length of 75 to 100mm (3 to 4in). Special-purpose chisels have blades up to 250mm (10in) long. The tip of a chisel blade is ground with a single bevel to form the cutting edge.

HANDLE

TANG

HOLLOW SOCKET

FERRULE

NECK

BLADE

Strongly-constructed chisels

The critical joint

A chisel blade narrows noticeably at the 'neck' just before the handle. At this point most blades are forged into a spike or 'tang' which is driven into a wooden handle or moulded into a plastic one. The junction between handle and blade is reinforced with a metal collar known as a ferrule.

Alternatively, the neck flares out again where it is formed into a hollow socket into which the handle fits.

STORING AND USING CHISELS

Storing chisels

It is bad practice to store your chisels loose in a tool chest. Keep them wrapped in a canvas roll with individual pockets for each chisel or store them in a tool rack behind your bench. You can buy a magnetic tool rack or make your own from two strips of wood or plywood separated by short spacer blocks. Screw it to the wall and drop the chisel blades into the slots formed between the two strips. Some woodworkers prefer to fit plastic protectors over the tips of their chisels. These tight-fitting sleeves incorporate a ring for hanging the tools from pins or pegs driven into the workshop wall.

Store chisels in a wall rack

1 Steadying a chisel

Horizontal paring

When paring wood laid flat on a bench, hold the chisel handle with your index finger extended towards the blade. Keep your forearm in line with the chisel and tuck your elbow into your body. With your free hand, grip the blade behind the cutting edge between thumb and forefinger. This grip not only guides the tip of the tool, it also controls the force applied to the chisel by acting as a brake on the blade. Rest the other fingers of the same hand against the work to steady the tool (1).

Take up a position in front of the bench with your forearm and chisel parallel with the floor. With your feet apart, use the weight of your body to move the chisel forward (2).

If you require extra force, strike the end of the handle with the ball of your hand (3).

3 Exerting extra force

Tapping with side of mallet

Driving with a mallet

To drive a chisel with maximum force, strike the end of the handle squarely with the face of a mallet. There are, however, many situations where the weight of the mallet alone will exert enough force. For delicate work, grip the shaft just below the head and tap the chisel with the side of the mallet.

Vertical paring

Trim end grain towards the bench top with the chisel held vertically. Grip the handle with your thumb over the end and control the blade with thumb and forefinger as before. Use your shoulder to apply steady force to the chisel.

Vertical paring

FOREARM AND CHISEL PARALLEL WITH FLOOR

HANDS BEHIND CUTTING EDGE

2 Correct stance

FEET APART

MORTISE CHISELS

Cutting deep mortises requires a chisel which is designed for the job. Ordinary bench chisels are either too weak or would jam in the cut.

A typical range of gouge profiles

6mm (¼in)
9mm (⅜in)
12mm (½in)
16mm (⅝in)
18mm (¾in)
25mm (1in)

LEATHER WASHER ABSORBS SHOCK OF HAMMERING WITH A MALLET

Sash-mortise chisel
Lock-mortise chisel
Registered mortise chisel
Drawer-lock chisel

Sash-mortise chisel

A sash-mortise chisel has an extra-thick blade for heavy-duty work. It is strong enough to be used as a lever to force the waste out of a deep socket and its wide sides help to keep it square to the mortise. Being markedly tapered from neck to tip prevents the blade jamming in the work. This type of chisel is made in four sizes from 6 to 12mm (¼ to ½in).

Registered mortise chisel

Originally made for shipbuilders, the registered mortise chisel is available in widths up to 38mm (1½in) for constructing substantial framing. A leather washer between the handle and blade absorbs the shock of hammering with a mallet.

Lock-mortise chisel

The swan-neck curve near the tip of the blade enables a woodworker to clean out the waste from the bottom of a deep mortise. Having cut the mortise with a standard mortise chisel, choose a lock-mortise chisel of the same size or slightly smaller to finish the job.

Drawer-lock chisel

This is an all-metal cranked chisel designed for cutting lock mortises and hinge housings in confined spaces where it would be impossible to wield an ordinary chisel. It has two cutting edges – one at right angles to the shaft, the other parallel with it. Holding the chisel on the work, strike the shaft with a hammer just behind the cutting edge.

Using a drawer-lock chisel

FIRMER GOUGES

A gouge is a chisel with a blade curved in cross section. The tip is ground to a bevel on the outside (out-cannel) or on the inside (in-cannel).

An out-cannel gouge is used to scoop out hollows, while an in-cannel or scribing gouge is used for trimming curved shoulders such as those on the end of a chair rail joining a round leg. The average range of sizes for both types of gouge is 6 to 25mm (¼ to 1in).

In-cannel gouge　　**Out-cannel gouge**

Using an out-cannel gouge
This gouge scoops hollows

Using an in-cannel gouge
This gouge trims shoulders

JAPANESE CHISELS

Japanese chisels are made with the same laminated-steel construction used for plane blades. It provides a hard hollow-ground back supported by a thick shock-absorbing strip of soft steel. Combining the tang and socket method of construction makes the strongest possible joint between blade and handle. All Japanese chisels have hardwood handles and most are fitted with a reinforcing hoop at the butt end.

Oiri-nomi (Bevel-edge chisel)
The standard bench chisel is bevel-edged, but unlike its Western equivalent it is strong enough to be mallet-driven. Blade width varies from 3 to 42mm ($\frac{1}{8}$ to $1\frac{3}{4}$in).

Shinogi-nomi (Dovetail chisel)
The triangular cross-section blade is ideal for chopping out the waste from between the pins and tails of dovetail joints. Shinogi-nomis are 3 to 12mm ($\frac{1}{8}$ to $\frac{1}{2}$in) wide.

Usu-nomi (Paring chisel)
Japanese paring chisels are designed to be used with a two-handed grip. The blades, thinner than standard oiri-nomis, range from 3 to 42mm ($\frac{1}{8}$ to $1\frac{3}{4}$in).

Kote-nomi (Cranked paring chisel)
The cranked neck of this chisel allows a woodworker to clean up long rebates and housings.

Mukomachi-nomi (Mortise chisel)
The Japanese mortise chisel has a thick square-section blade capable of cutting deep sockets. It is available from 6 to 18mm ($\frac{1}{4}$ to $\frac{3}{4}$in) wide.

Mori-nomi and Sokozarai-nomi (Hooked mortise chisels)
These special-purpose tools are used with a mortise chisel to clean up the bottom and sides of a blind mortise. Both chisels are hooked for easy waste clearance.

Chokkatu-nomi (Corner chisel)
This is a very specialized tool for cleaning up the corners of large mortises. Each half of the 90-degree cutting edge is 9, 16 or 25mm ($\frac{3}{8}$, $\frac{5}{8}$ or 1in) wide.

Uchi-hagane-nomi (Firmer gouge)
Similar in every way to the Western out-cannel gouge, sizes of the firmer gouge range from 3 to 30mm ($\frac{1}{8}$ to $1\frac{1}{4}$in) wide.

Oiri-uramaru-nomi (Scribing gouge)
The Japanese in-cannel gouge, used for scribing rounded shoulders, is ground with a flat bevel. Blade sizes are identical to out-cannel gouges.

Labels: 1 · 2 · 3 · 4 · 5 · 6 · 7 · 8 · 9 · 10
TWO-HANDED GRIP · BEVEL-EDGED BLADE · TRIANGULAR-SECTION BLADE · STIFF SQUARE-SECTION BLADE · CRANKED NECK · TWO-HANDED GRIP · WASTE-CLEARANCE HOOK · 90-DEGREE CUTTING EDGE · OUT-CANNEL BLADE · IN-CANNEL BLADE

Japanese chisels
1 Oiri-nomi
2 Usu-nomi
3 Mukomachi-nomi
4 Mori-nomi
5 Sokozarai-nomi
6 Oiri-uramaru-nomi
7 Shinogi-nomi
8 Kote-nomi
9 Chokkatu-nomi
10 Uchi-hagane-nomi

IRON HOOP · HARDWOOD HANDLE · FERRULE · TANG · HOLLOW-GROUND BLADE

Japanese-chisel construction

SHARPENING STONES

Maintaining a sharp edge on a tool is of paramount importance. Compared with a blunt tool, a really sharp chisel or plane not only leaves a superior finish, but handles better without resistance and cuts with a clean crisp sound. With sharp tools woodwork is a pleasure – with blunt tools it is a chore.

A plane iron or chisel comes ready-ground from the factory, but it cannot be described as sharp. Before it will perform satisfactorily the blade must be honed on a sharpening stone and as soon as its performance drops below an acceptable level, honed again.

Once a cutting edge is damaged by being chipped or misshapened by repeated honing, the original factory-made bevel must be reproduced by grinding the tool on a grinding wheel or coarse stone.

Woodworking tools are kept sharp by wearing away the metal to form a thin cutting edge on specially dressed blocks of abrasive stone. The best natural sharpening stones are expensive, but very acceptable results can be achieved on cheaper synthetic stones. Depending on the nature of the stone, it must be lubricated during the sharpening process with either water or oil. This prevents the steel overheating, and keeps the fine stone and metal debris in suspension to stop it clogging the abrasive surface of the stone.

Oilstones
Most woodworkers sharpen their edged tools on a rectangular block of stone lubricated with oil. Natural Arkansas stones are generally considered to be the finest oilstones available. The mottled-grey Soft Arkansas stones are coarse and will remove metal quickly for shaping edged tools. The white Hard Arkansas stones hone the tools to a sharp edge, but for an extra-fine edge use Black Hard Arkansas stones.

The equivalent synthetic oilstones, made from aluminium-oxide or silicon-carbide grit, are categorized as coarse, medium and fine.

Some woodworkers have a stone of each grade mounted on the bench so that they can move quickly from one to another. However, it is more economical to buy two stones of different grades glued back to back. These combination stones are usually a union of coarse/medium or medium/fine grades. You can also buy combinations of man-made and natural stones.

Carver's stones
Waterstones moulded with shaped profiles to match the common carving tools are made in coarse, medium and fine grades.

● **Mounting bench stones**
Ideally, mount your sharpening stones on a separate bench alongside your workbench so that they are always to hand. Storing a stone in its own box keeps the surface dust-free.

Nagura stone

Japanese waterstone

Diamond stone

Combination oilstone

Carver's stone

Black Hard Arkansas

Hard Arkansas

Cone slip

Soft Arkansas

Stone files

Diamond sharpening stones

Tough, durable sharpening 'stones' are made with a grid-like pattern of diamond particles bonded in a plastic base. They are made in extra-coarse, coarse and fine grades. Diamond stones can be used to flatten worn waterstones and natural oilstones.

Diamond-spray sharpening

Spraying diamond particles onto a special ceramic tile produces a sharpening slurry for all edged tools. A spray can of 45-micron particles is for general sharpening. Fine (14-micron) and extra-fine (6-micron) particles are also available, but you need a separate tile for each grade.

Diamond-spray kit

Slipstones and files

Small shaped stones are required for honing gouges and carving chisels. Natural and man-made waterstones and oilstones are made as slipstones and in the various grades. Teardrop-section and cone slips are the most useful, but there are special-ized square-edged and knife-edged stones plus a range of shaped stone files with square, round and tri-angular sections.

Combination waterstone slips are made for honing drawknives, axes and garden tools.

Shaped slipstones

Japanese waterstones

Japanese waterstones, both natural and synthetic, cut very quickly and are avail-able in grades of fineness which go far beyond those for oilstones. They range from 800 grit at the coarse end, through 1000 grit as a medium/fine grade, to fin-ishing grades of 4000, 6000 and 8000 grits. Natural waterstones are prohibi-tively expensive and only the most discerning crafts-man would have natural stones in a range of grits. Most woodworkers are satis-fied with man-made stones, but may have a slip of natural finishing stone. Combina-tion stones are available in the usual pairings.

To improve the cutting action of a waterstone, build up a slurry on its wet surface prior to sharpening by rubbing it with a chalk-like Nagura stone. This is es-pecially useful when honing on one of the hard extra-fine finishing stones.

CARING FOR SHARPENING STONES

Keep your oilstones covered to prevent a build-up of dust on the surface. Eventually an oilstone will become clogged with oil and metal dust. As soon as it no longer cuts effectively, scrub the surface with paraffin and coarse sacking.

Soaking a waterstone

Before you use a waterstone it must be loaded with water by immersion. A coarse stone can take four or five minutes before it is saturated, but a hard fine stone will take some-what less.

Store a waterstone in a specially fitted vinyl box to prevent the moisture evaporating so that it is always ready for use. Alternatively, keep it immersed in a can of water. It is imperative to stop a waterstone freezing or it will almost certainly crack.

Truing sharpening stones

Eventually all sharpening stones become hollow after repeated honing. Flatten an oilstone by grinding the sur-face on carborundum powder with water or oil on a sheet of glass. Resurface a waterstone by rubbing it on a piece of wet 200-grit silicon-carbide paper taped to a sheet of glass.

Flattening a sharpening stone

Sharpening-stone grades

Sharpening stones are graded in different ways. The various grading methods are listed below to compare one system with another. Every woodworker needs at least one medium and one fine stone.

GRADE	MAN-MADE OILSTONES	NATURAL OILSTONES	JAPANESE WATERSTONES
Extra-coarse			100 and 220 grits
Coarse	Coarse	Soft Arkansas	800 grit
Medium	Medium	Hard Arkansas	1000 grit
Fine	Fine	Black Hard Arkansas	1200 grit
Extra-fine			6000 and 8000 grits

Strops

Having honed your tools on a sharpening stone, use a strop to remove any remain-ing trace of the burr, leaving the cutting edge razor sharp. Use a simple strip of thick hide or a proprietary com-bination strop with one side covered in fine emery stone and the other three with coarse to fine leather. Lubricate all but the final leather surface with a fine stropping paste.

Stropping paste

Combination strop

SHARPENING CHISELS AND PLANES

The grinding process at the factory leaves a new plane iron or chisel with minute scratches on the back of the blade and across the cutting bevel. As a result, the actual cutting edge is serrated and incapable of very fine work. Both the back and bevel must be honed on medium and fine stones in order to remove the grinding marks and leave a perfectly sharp edge.

Flattening the back of a new blade
Lubricate your stone and hold the blade flat on its surface, bevelled side up. Rub the blade along the stone, maintaining pressure with your fingertips to stop it rocking. Repeat on a fine stone until the metal shines.

Flatten the back of a new blade

Sharpening the cutting edge
Bench-plane blades and chisels are ground with a bevel of about 25 degrees. Some woodworkers like to hone this bevel for cutting softwood, but the edge is too weak for hardwoods. A secondary bevel of 35 degrees is honed on the very edge of the blade to strengthen it. You will find this process makes for fast sharpening because you are removing very little metal.

Grasp the blade, bevelled side down, in your right hand with index finger extended along one edge. Place the fingertips of your left hand on top of the blade, slipping your thumb beneath and across it **(1)**.

Place the grinding bevel on a lubricated medium-grade stone and rock the blade until you can feel the bevel is flat on the surface. Rocking on the cutting edge, lift the blade slightly in order to hone the secondary bevel.

Keep your wrists rigid to maintain a constant angle and rub the blade up and down using the full length of the stone.

Turn a plane blade at an angle so that the whole of the cutting edge is in contact with the stone **(2)**. When honing a narrow chisel, move it from one side of the stone to the other to avoid wearing a hollow in the centre **(3)**. Hone very narrow chisels on the edge of the stone.

Once you have honed a bevel about 1mm ($\frac{1}{32}$ in) wide, move on to a fine stone and hone the edge again. Honing raises a burr on the flat back of the blade. If you stroke your thumb over the edge you can feel it **(4)**. Remove the burr by honing the back flat on the stone, give the bevel a few light strokes, then hone the back once more. This process breaks off the burr, leaving a sharp edge.

Hone a secondary bevel
A small bevel honed on the cutting edge strengthens the blade.

1 Holding a blade for honing

2 Angle blade to cover a stone

3 Move a chisel across a stone

USING A HONING GUIDE

Honing by hand is fast and efficient, but if you cannot master the technique you can clamp plane blades and chisels in a device which will hold them at the required angle to a sharpening stone. There are many different styles of honing guide, but they all perform the same function.

Using a honing guide
Maintain pressure on the cutting edge to grind the bevel.

4 Feel burr with your thumb

SHARPENING GOUGES

To hone an out-cannel gouge turn your stone cross-ways and rub the tool from side to side along the stone, describing a figure-of-eight to even out the wear (1). Remove the burr raised on the inside of the gouge with a lubricated slipstone (2).

Use a similar slipstone to hone a bevel on an in-cannel gouge (3). Remove the burr by holding the tool flat on a bench stone and move it from side to side while rocking the blade (4).

Carving gouges are sharpened in a similar way. Use knife-edge slipstones or stone files to hone the cutting edges of special carving chisels like the V-shaped parting tools and the squarish gouge-like macaronis and fluteronis.

1 Honing an out-cannel gouge

2 Remove burr with a slipstone

3 Honing an in-cannel gouge

4 Remove burr on an oilstone

SHARPENING JAPANESE BLADES

Japanese planes and chisels are sharpened in a similar way to Western blades, but there are significant differences as a result of their peculiar construction. As each blade is laminated with a hard-steel cutting edge, there is no need to hone a secondary bevel to strengthen it.

The hollow grinding on the back of every blade creates a narrow border of metal which is easy to keep flat on a stone. Eventually, repeated honing of the bevel wears into this hollow so that the cutting edge is no longer continuous. Maintaining this hollow is achieved by flattening the back after every honing. However, this wears away the blade relatively quickly and is somewhat laborious when sharpening wide chisels and plane irons. Japanese craftsmen prefer to recreate the hollow periodically by hammering some metal into the narrow border behind the cutting edge.

Flattening a new blade
As with Western blades, the backs of new chisels and planes are flattened before the bevel is honed for the first time. Because the metal is so hard, this is done by grinding on a steel flattening plate, using a pinch of coarse carborundum or silicon-carbide powder mixed with a little water.

Hold the blade flat on the surface at right angles to the plate using a short length of softwood to apply pressure. When the narrow border surrounding the hollow is an even colour and texture, repeat with finer powder.

Wipe the blade clean and move on to a medium sharpening stone to continue to flatten the back. Finish the job on a fine stone until the metal shines like a mirror.

Flattening a blade
Grind the back of a blade, using a length of wood to apply pressure.

Sharpening the edge
Sharpen the cutting edges of Japanese blades like their Western equivalents, but hone the whole width of the bevels. Do not hone secondary bevels on the cutting edges.

Maintaining the hollow back
Recreating the leading edge of the hollow back is a skilled process. Traditionalists rest the back of the blade on the edge of a block of wood. A square hammer is used to tap the bevel, pushing metal out of the back to fill the hollow edge. Blows must be within the soft part of the bevel. The hard cutting edge is brittle and will chip if struck with the hammer.

Once the hollow is refilled, the back is flattened on a grinding plate as already described. (See left).

Blade-hammering jig
Because the hammering process requires practice, a special jig is often used. A heavy metal bar, guided by a hollow tube, is dropped onto the bevelled edge which is backed up by a metal anvil. Alternatively, have your Japanese blades reshaped by a professional.

Maintaining a hollow back
One way is to tap the soft-metal bevel with a hammer.

METAL BAR ACTS LIKE A HAMMER

ANVIL

BLADE CRAMP

BLADE

Repeated honing wears into blade hollow

Hammering the soft-metal bevel re-forms the edge

Blade-hammering jig
A jig provides an easier way to maintain a hollow back to a blade.

GRINDERS

For centuries, chipped or worn blades have been reground on 100 to 200 grit coarse bench stones. Although this method is still perfectly adequate, *many woodworkers prefer to repair the edges of chisels and plane irons on a high-speed bench grinder or a slow-speed motorized whetstone.*

High-speed grinder

A standard bench grinder has a $\frac{1}{4}$ to $\frac{3}{4}$hp electric motor driving two aluminium-oxide grinding wheels at about 3000rpm. The majority of grinding wheels are between 125 and 200mm (5 and 8in) in diameter. The larger wheels are best for grinding blades because a small-diameter wheel produces an exaggeratedly hollow-ground bevel. Wheels are interchangeable, but most grinders are supplied with one coarse-grade and one fine-grade wheel.

All high-speed grinding wheels are guarded to prevent accidents and have transparent plastic spark deflectors to protect your eyes. An adjustable tool rest is mounted in front of each wheel.

Every grinder must be bolted securely to a bench before it is used.

High-speed grinders sharpen a blade quickly. With a range of grinding wheels, wire brushes and buffing mops, they can also shape, clean and polish all manner of metalwork.

Rubberized abrasive wheels

Having ground a bevel on a blade, it is normally honed to a sharp edge on a bench stone. However, you can hone chisels, gouges and plane irons on a bench grinder using a neoprene-rubber wheel with silicon carbide embedded in it. The 100 to 150mm (4 to 6in) diameter wheels are resistant to oil and water and are available in coarse, medium and fine grades.

You grind a blade with the wheel turning towards you, but a rubberized abrasive wheel must be spinning away from you when honing or the blade will damage the relatively soft material. If you cannot reverse the direction on your bench grinder you can trail the blade on the side of the wheel.

Using a motorized whetstone

WATER RESERVOIR

TAP   STONE DISC

TOOL REST

SWITCH

Motorized whetstone

COARSE-GRADE WHEEL

SLOW-SPEED WHETSTONE

TOOL REST

MOTOR HOUSING

HIGH-SPEED GRINDING WHEEL

SWITCH

Combination grinder

Motorized whetstone
The common problem of overheating blades is avoided by using a slow-speed motorized whetstone. A stone disc turns at only 500rpm and is lubricated by a continuous stream of water from a reservoir mounted on the machine. A 1000 grit general-purpose stone is fitted as standard, but it is a simple matter to swap this for, say, a 180 or 6000 grit stone. The latter stone is used to hone a fine cutting edge on a blade.

Combination grinders
There are several machines which provide some of the advantages of both high-speed grinding and slow whetstone sharpening. At one end of the machine, for example, is the familiar aluminium-oxide wheel, while at the other end is a clutch-operated whetstone turning in a water bath. Blades are sharpened on the edge of this type of whetstone.

Other machines combine a standard wheel with an abrasive grinding belt. With their larger surface area, belts do not heat quite as quickly as a high-speed stone. If a belt clogs, it is replaced.

MOTOR HOUSING

SPARK DEFLECTOR

TOOL REST

FINE-GRADE WHEEL

High-speed grinder

Star-wheel dressing tool

SWITCH

Grinding wheels

DRESSING A WHEEL

Aluminium-oxide grinding wheels will not cut efficiently when the surface becomes 'glazed' – i.e. clogged with metal particles.

A new clean surface is produced by holding a star-wheel dressing tool against the spinning wheel. Alternatively, dress the wheel with a carborundum block.

Using a dressing tool

GRINDING A CHISEL OR PLANE IRON

Use a coarse grinding wheel to reshape a badly worn blade, then change to a finer grade.

Before you grind a new bevel on a plane or chisel check the cutting edge with a try square (1). If it has worn unevenly, use a very fine felt-tip pen to mark a line square to the long edges of the blade.

1 Check the edge with a square

Set the tool rest about 3mm ($\frac{1}{8}$in) from the grinding wheel, check the adjusting clamps are all tight, then switch on the machine.

Wearing protective spectacles, dip the blade in water and place it, bevel downwards, on the tool rest. Gradually feed the cutting edge against the wheel and as soon as it touches, move the blade from side to side, keeping it moving the whole time to stop it overheating (2). Dip it in water every few seconds.

2 Grind the edge square

When you have ground the blade square, switch off and adjust the tool rest to present the blade at an angle of 25 degrees to the wheel.

Switch on and proceed as before, this time grinding an even bevel across the width of the blade (3). Don't press too hard and keep the blade cool by dipping, or use a fine plant spray while grinding the blade with one hand. If you allow the metal to heat to a temperature at which it turns blue, it will have lost temper and will not hold a sharp cutting edge for very long. The only remedy is to grind the blade beyond the blued area.

3 Grind a bevel on the blade

SPOKESHAVES

A spokeshave leaves the same finish as a bench plane, but because the sole or 'face' of the tool is so narrow it is not as easy to control and a certain knack is required before it will cut smoothly on every stroke. Being designed to smooth curved components, the spokeshave is the only tool for the job in certain situations. But some of the more specialized spokeshaves are not essential as an ordinary bench or block plane can achieve the same results, if a little slowly.

SPECIALIZED SPOKESHAVES

A craftsman, be he cooper, wheelwright or carpenter, would once have made special-purpose spokeshaves for himself. Tool catalogues still list some spokeshaves which may not be essential to the average woodworker, but can speed up a particular process or make it that much easier to accomplish.

Half-round spokeshave
Having a deep concave face and blade, this is a useful tool for shaping rounded legs and rails. You could do the same job with a bench plane or flat-face spokeshave, but this tool removes more wood per stroke.

Radius spokeshave
This is an excellent tool for scooping out deep hollows like those in a shaped wooden chair seat.

Combination spokeshave
This is a dual-purpose spokeshave, having a half-round spokeshave mounted alongside a straight one. It is convenient when shaping work with a frequently changing profile which otherwise entails swapping one tool for another.

Chamfer spokeshave
This spokeshave has adjustable fences for accurately cutting chamfers up to 38mm (1½in) wide. The tool is held at 45 degrees to the top face of the work.

STANDARD SPOKESHAVES

Round-face spokeshave
This spokeshave has a convex face and is used to smooth a concave-shaped piece of wood. No other tool will do the job as well.

The spokeshave cutter is like a miniature plane blade held in place by a simple cap iron. On basic spokeshaves, blade-depth adjustment is achieved by moving the blade up and down by hand until it looks about right before clamping it with the locking screw on the cap iron. More precise adjustment is possible on spokeshaves having a screw on each top corner of the blade.

Straight-face spokeshave
This spokeshave is identical in every way to the round-face version except for its narrow flat face designed for skimming a convex curve. Once again, the work must be positioned in such a way that you can shave the wood in the direction of the grain.

Types of spokeshave
1 Standard spokeshave
2 Combination spokeshave
3 Chamfer spokeshave
4 Half-round spokeshave
5 Radius spokeshave

Until you develop the right 'feel', a spokeshave will either skid across the surface without taking a shaving or try to bury its cutter in the wood. Practise on scrap softwood before working on expensive hardwoods.

Controlling a spokeshave
Spokeshaves cut on the push stroke. To have precise control over the angle of the blade to the work, take the tool in both hands with your thumbs resting on the back edges of the handles. With the tool resting on the work, rock it slightly backwards and forwards on its face until it is taking a shaving cleanly.

Cut in the direction of the grain only, even if it means turning the work in the vice to shave the curve in two directions.

Controlling a spokeshave

Sharpening a spokeshave cutter
A spokeshave cutter is honed on a bench stone like a plane or chisel, but it is difficult to hold such a short blade at a constant angle to the stone. Either clamp it in a honing guide or make a temporary 'handle' by cutting a slot in a piece of wood into which you can jam the top edge of the cutter.

Grind a new bevel on a coarse bench stone in the same way or clamp the cutter in a plier wrench to hold it firmly for power grinding.

Grinding a spokeshave cutter

Straight face

Round face

BLADE ADJUSTMENT

FENCE-CLAMPING SCREWS

BLADE

CAP IRON

1   2   3   4   5

DRAWKNIVES

The drawknife ranks with the axe and adze as being one of the earliest-known woodworking tools. It was used by many different craftsmen, from the shipwright to the chairmaker, for quickly shaping components which might then be more finely finished by plane or spokeshave. A drawknife is rarely used today except by those woodworkers who appreciate the speed with which one can reduce a blank to size for carving or turning. It is, however, a versatile tool which, in the hands of a skilled worker, can be used to make curved chairbacks, arms and so on.

Drawknife
Over the centuries, different patterns of drawknife were developed to meet the needs of specialist craftsmen or as a result of local styling. Even today there are several variations on the theme. A basic drawknife might have a straight or curved blade which is bevelled on one edge. The metal at each end of the blade is forged into a pointed tang which is bent at right angles and fitted with a turned wooden handle.

CURVED-EDGE BLADE

Drawknife (German pattern)

FORGED TANG

TURNED HANDLE

Swedish push knife

Drawknife (English pattern)

CUTTING EDGE

Inshave

CUTTING EDGE

Scorp

Swedish push knife
A modern derivation of the drawknife, this tool has a short 100 × 25mm (4 × 1in) blade and two straight handles. It is used on both the push and pull stroke.

Inshave
This drawknife is in the shape of a tight curve for working deep hollows. Inshaves are usually bevelled on the outside of the curve.

Scorp
A scorp is a one-handed inshave for work such as wooden bowls and spoons.

USING A DRAWKNIFE

When using a drawknife, extend your thumbs along the handles to stop the tool twisting in your hands and to help you control the angle of the blade to the work. A drawknife cuts on the pull stroke in the direction of the grain. Pulling the blade diagonally across the work produces a slicing action for cutting through difficult wood.

Shaping with a drawknife
If you are working a convex shape, hold the tool bevel upwards. Turn the tool over when cutting a concave shape or the bevel will drive the blade deeply into the wood.

Holding the work
When using a drawknife, craftsmen traditionally hold the work in a shaving horse – a long stool with a built-in foot-operated cramp (1).

However, it is quite possible to stand at the end of a standard workbench to shave work clamped by one end in a vice (2). Alternatively, use a home-made breast bib – a small board cut from sawn timber and suspended on a piece of string hung round your neck. One end of the work is supported on the edge of a bench and it is held firmly by pressing against the opposite end with the breast bib (3).

● Sharpening a drawknife
Hold the drawknife upright, resting one handle in a bench vice. Hone with a lubricated sharpening stone, using small circular strokes.

1 Traditional shaving horse

2 Clamp workpiece firmly

3 Using a breast bib

SHARPENING A SCRAPER

Any square-cut piece of steel will scrape wood to some extent. It will probably produce dust only, and if it does take a shaving it will be discontinuous and ragged, leaving a poorly finished surface. A cabinet scraper is carefully filed, stoned and burnished until it is left with a tiny burr on its long edges which acts like a miniature plane iron.

Making a square edge

Clamp a new scraper in a vice and use a smooth metal file to 'draw-file' its long edges square. Use your fingertips to guide the file and stop it rocking (1) while pulling it along the edge of the scraper.

1 Draw-file the edge

Honing with a slipstone

Having filed the edge smooth and shiny, use an oiled slipstone like the file to hone the scraper. Turn the stone frequently to avoid wearing a groove in its surface. Stone each side of the scraper to remove the burr (2).

2 Smooth with stone

Creating a burr

To raise a burr, first hold the scraper on a bench top close to its edge and stroke the face firmly with a burnisher four or five times (3). Then turn the scraper over and repeat the process.

To turn the burr at right angles, hold the scraper on end and, with the burnisher held at about 85 degrees to the face, make two or three firm vertical strokes (4).

When the cutter is not cutting cleanly, raise a new burr. There is no need to square the edge again until it is rounded or damaged.

3 Raising a burr

4 Turning the burr

SCRAPERS

A sharp metal scraper which removes paper-thin shavings leaves a finish on a piece of wood which is superior to that left after sanding where the grain is clogged with dust. This is even more true when working 'wild' or irregular grain which would become torn by even the most finely set plane. A scraper is also used to remove patches of hardened glue and other blemishes.

Cabinet scrapers

GOOSE-NECK

BASIC

CONCAVE/CONVEX

BLADE

BLADE-CLAMPING BAR

THUMBSCREW

Scraper plane

Hook scrapers

BLADE

BLADE

Burnishers

Cabinet scrapers

The basic scraper for working flat surfaces is a simple rectangle of tempered steel. It is supplied as a cropped blank upon which a scraping edge must be raised before it is ready for use.

Goose-neck and concave/convex scrapers are made for finishing mouldings and other shaped work.

Hook scrapers

A hook scraper with a wooden handle is easy to use and comfortable to hold. The disposable blades are replaced as soon as they become blunt. Long-handled versions of the hook scraper are available for heavy-duty work on wooden floors, boats and so on. When using a hook scraper (which cuts on the pull stroke only), hold it at an angle to the surface.

Scraper plane

A cabinet scraper is hard on the thumbs, especially when it gets hot enough to burn them. A scraper plane is a simple cast-metal jig designed to make the job easier and more comfortable. A scraper blade is clamped to the stock at the optimum angle and is bent into a curve by a centrally placed thumbscrew.

Unlike a standard cabinet scraper, which is cropped with a square edge all round, the scraper-plane cutter is ground at an angle of 45 degrees on two edges. Hone these edges on a stone and raise a scraping burr as for a cabinet scraper.

Clamp the blade in the tool with the bar and retaining screws, then adjust the curve with the thumbscrew until the blade is taking the required shaving – the greater the curve, the coarser the shaving.

Burnishers

Burnishers made from hardened steel with a round, oval or triangular section, are used to raise a burr on a scraper.

WOOD RASPS & FILES

Rasps and files are used rarely in the woodwork shop except perhaps by carvers. A rasp, in particular, removes wood very quickly and is frequently used by carvers for preliminary shaping, especially as it is possible to cut both with and against the grain. Rasps leave a rough surface and files of the same shape are employed to improve the finish.

Scraping technique
Lean the scraper away from you and push the tool to take a shaving **(1)**. Vary both the angle and the curve until the scraper is removing the required amount.

An almost flat scraper skims the surface; a more pronounced curve cuts deeper for removing blemishes.

To scrape a surface flat, cover a wide area by working across it diagonally in both directions with the grain before finishing parallel with the grain. Scrape away from an edge, or alongside an obstruction, by pulling the tool towards you **(2)**.

1 Bending a scraper
Bend a scraper with your thumbs to finish a flat surface.

2 Pulling a scraper
Pull the scraper to scrape into a corner.

Rasps
The surface of a rasp is covered with individual teeth which cut on the forward stroke. The size and distribution of teeth determine the degree of coarseness, or cut, of the rasp. There are slight variations in the way the cut is described from one manufacturer to another but, broadly speaking, there are bastard, second-cut and smooth rasps, the bastard cut being the most coarse.

There are flat and round rasps, but the most versatile is the half-round rasp. All versions are made in 200, 250 or 300mm (8, 10 and 12in) lengths, but you will find a 250mm rasp a good general-purpose tool.

Wood files
A wood file has rows of closely packed sharp ridges which 'plane' off the high points of the roughened timber left by a rasp. File cuts are also described as bastard, second-cut and smooth, but they are all relatively fine compared with a rasp. For an even finer finish, wrap abrasive paper around a file.

Surform tools
Surform tools are a relatively recent development of the rasp. The thin perforated blades are made by punching out regularly spaced teeth with their sharp cutting edges facing forward, leaving holes in the metal through which the wood shavings pass. This enables a Surform tool to cut faster than a regular rasp, without clogging.

There is a range of Surform planes and files, but they are merely variations on the basic principle. The simplest and most generally useful tools are the round hollow file and the flat file.

WIRE BRISTLES

File cleaner

COARSE-FIBRE BRUSH

PERFORATED
BLADE

Needle files

File handle

Half-round rasp

Half-round file

Flat Surform file

Round Surform file

Rifflers

Rifflers
Rifflers are miniature double-ended files specially designed for working in tight corners and confined spaces. Choose rifflers with rasp heads at one end and file heads at the other.

File cleaners
When file teeth become clogged with wood debris the tool can no longer cut. The wire bristles on the back of a file cleaner loosen the packed wood shavings which are then cleaned out with the coarse brush.

File handles
Always fit a handle over the pointed tang of a file or rasp. To use an unprotected tool is inviting an accident. If the tool catches and stops suddenly, you could drive the tang through the palm of your hand.

Drive a handle onto the tang by tapping it on a bench **(1)**. Remove an old one by holding the file in one hand and striking the front edge of the handle with a block of wood **(2)**.

Using a file or rasp
Place the fingertips of your hand near the point of the file to steady it. Apply pressure on the forward stroke only.

1 Tap handle on bench

2 Removing a handle

DRILLS & BRACES

The versatility of the power drill, especially since the introduction of the variable-speed models, has made the hand drill and brace far less commonplace today.

And yet these tools still have their place in the workshop. They are uncomplicated, lightweight, quiet and completely independent of a power source.

Bradawl
The bradawl is perhaps the simplest hole borer of all. It does not remove wood, like a drill, but merely displaces it by forcing the fibres apart. It is used to make a starter hole for inserting a screw or to hold the point of a drill on its centre-mark.

By placing it across the grain, the sharp screw-driver-like tip is used to sever the fibres as the awl is pushed into the wood, avoiding the possibility of splitting the grain. Twisting the tool opens up the hole.

Sharpen the tip on the edge of a bench stone.

Gimlet
The gimlet does a similar job to the bradawl, but it is capable of making deeper holes by cutting and removing wood like a drill bit.

Hand drill
Cranking the drive handle of a hand drill rotates the chuck via a system of gear wheels. The chuck contains three self-centring jaws which, depending on the model, clamp twist drills up to 9mm ($\frac{3}{8}$in) in diameter. With some hand drills the drive mechanism is kept dust-free by encasing it completely within a cast-metal shell.

Using a bradawl
To open up a screw-starter hole, twist the tool from side to side as you push it into the wood.

LEADSCREW

FLUTE REMOVES WASTE FROM HOLE

Gimlet

Bradawl

Hand drill

Dowel bits

GEAR WHEELS

DRIVE HANDLE

CHUCK

Countersink bit

JAWS

Twist drills

HAND-DRILL BITS

Buy good-quality drill bits only. Cheap drills not only blunt quickly, but they are often ground inaccurately.

Twist drills
A twist drill is a simple cylindrical drill bit with two helical flutes (spiral grooves) to clear the waste out of a hole. The flutes culminate in two cutting edges forming a pointed tip. The tips of most drill bits are ground to an angle of 59 degrees for boring into metal. An angle of 45 degrees is recommended for drilling wood but, rather than have two complete sets of drills, most woodworkers are prepared to use high-speed metal drills.

The average set of twist drills comprises a range of sizes from 1 to 13mm ($\frac{1}{16}$ to $\frac{1}{2}$in) although a hand-drill chuck will not accept a drill larger than 9mm ($\frac{3}{8}$in).

Dowel bit
This is a twist drill with a central leadpoint and two spurs to stop the bit being deflected by wood grain. It will even bore end grain accurately for dowel joints.

Countersink bit
A countersink bit cuts a tapered recess to accept the head of a woodscrew so that it lies flush with the surface of the work. A clearance hole for the screw shank is bored first to automatically centre the countersink bit.

Twist-drill tip

Dowel-bit tip

Countersink tip

BRACE BITS

The jaws in a brace chuck are designed to hold special-purpose square-shanked bits. Some braces are made with universal jaws which will also accept round-shanked twist drills.

Centre bit
The solid-shank centre bit is used for boring shallow holes. The single spur on one side of the bit scores the edge of the hole before the cutting edge on the other side enters the work. This ensures a crisp hole. The leadscrew in the centre pulls the bit into the work. Centre bits are made in a range of sizes from 6 to 50mm ($\frac{1}{4}$ to 2in).

Auger bits
A solid-centre auger bit is similar in principle to a centre bit, but it has a helical twist which keeps it on line in a deep hole and brings the waste to the surface. Also, it has two spurs and two cutting edges. A Jennings-pattern auger bit has a double helical twist.

Solid-centre bits are made in sizes from 6 to 38mm ($\frac{1}{4}$ to 1$\frac{1}{2}$in) in diameter. The range of Jennings-pattern bits is more limited – up to 25mm (1in) only.

Expansive bit
An expansive bit is adjustable to cut a hole of any diameter between limits. The calibrated spurred cutter is held in place by a spring-loaded packing piece or, on some models, a toothed dial. Generally there are two sizes of bit capable of cutting holes from 12 to 38mm ($\frac{1}{2}$ to 1$\frac{1}{2}$in) and 22 to 75mm ($\frac{7}{8}$ to 3in) in diameter.

Countersink bit
Used like the hand-drill countersink bit, this has a square shank to suit the standard brace chuck.

Screwdriver bit
This bit adapts a brace into a heavy-duty screwdriver capable of generating considerable torque for inserting large screws.

Brace
A brace is driven by cranking its frame in a clockwise direction while pressure is applied to the round handle at the rear of the tool. The circle described by moving the frame is known as the sweep, and the size of a brace is given as the diameter of its sweep. Most woodworkers use a 250mm (10in) brace, but they are made with sweeps as small as 147mm (5$\frac{7}{8}$in) and as large as 300mm (1ft).

Most braces are made with a ratchet mechanism just behind the chuck so that the tool can be used in places where a complete sweep is impossible. Having driven the bit as far as possible in a clockwise direction, a movement in reverse operates the ratchet, leaving the chuck stationary until the clockwise movement is resumed to drive the bit further. Adjusting a cam ring on the ratchet mechanism reverses its action or locks it solid.

HANDLE

FRAME

RETAINING SPRING

JAWS

The components of a brace chuck

The sweep of a brace

RATCHET MECHANISM

CAM RING

HANDLE

Ratchet brace

CHUCK

JAWS

Jennings-pattern bit

Solid-centre auger bit

Expansive bit

Expansive bit with dial

Centre bit

Screwdriver bit

DRIVING TIP AT EACH END

Countersink bit

DOUBLE HELICAL TWIST

HELICAL TWIST

PACKING PIECE

DIAL

LEADSCREW   SPUR

CUTTING EDGE

COUNTERSINK ROSE

CALIBRATED SPURRED CUTTERS

USING A HAND DRILL AND BRACE

A hand drill is primarily used to bore small holes for fitting woodscrews or dowels. Being designed specifically for woodwork, a brace has more uses. With a sharp bit fitted in its chuck, it will bore even large-diameter holes effortlessly.

1 Using a key to operate chuck

2 Opening a hand-drill chuck

Fitting a bit in a hand drill
Some hand-drill chucks are opened and closed by a key, just like an electric drill (**1**).

To operate the jaws of an average hand drill, hold the chuck in one hand, then crank the drive handle anti-clockwise (**2**). Load a twist drill into the chuck and tighten the jaws by turning the drive wheel clockwise. Check the twist drill is centred in the jaws before using the tool.

Depth stop
Wrap a strip of coloured tape around a drill as a guide to the depth of a hole.

Using a hand drill
Place the tip of the twist drill accurately on the work, then move the drive handle gently back and forth until the drill enters the wood. Crank the drive handle freely to bore a hole of the required depth.

To avoid breaking small drills, let the weight of the tool drive it into the wood, supporting it in an upright position without applying any force to the handle.

Using a hand drill

Fitting a brace bit
Lock the brace ratchet by centring its cam ring, then hold the chuck firmly while turning the frame clockwise. Drop a square-shanked bit into the open jaws and tighten them by reversing the action of the frame.

Using a brace
Hold the brace upright with one hand while turning the frame with the other (**1**). To make sure you are drilling vertically, ask an assistant to tell you if the drill leans forwards or backwards while you concentrate on stopping it leaning sideways. You can stand a try square on the bench as a guide, but it is difficult to keep your eye on the square and drill at the same time.

You can also use a brace in a horizontal position by steadying the round handle against your body.

The leadscrew of the bit will pull it into the wood. When you have reached the required depth, crank the frame anti-clockwise a couple of turns to release the leadscrew, then pull on the tool while moving the frame back and forth to extract the bit and clear the waste from the hole.

If you are drilling right through the wood, either clamp a block of wood on the far side to stop the work splitting as the bit emerges, or turn the work around as soon as the lead screw appears and finish the hole from that side, using the small exit hole as a pick-up point (**2**).

1 Keeping a brace upright

2 Pick up exit hole

SHARPENING DRILL BITS

All drill bits will stay sharp enough to work efficiently for a long time, but if you find you have to apply excessive pressure to bore a hole, sharpen the bit in the appropriate manner.

Brace bits
Sharpen auger and centre bits in the same way, using a small flat or triangular file known as a needle file. Put a sharp edge on each spur by stroking its inner face with the file (**1**). Never file its outer edge. Holding the leadpoint on the bench, sharpen the cutting edges (**2**).

Sharpen the cutter and spur of an expansive bit with a similar file.

Twist drills
There are several electric drill-sharpening machines which do a perfect job. All you have to do is drop the drill point-first into the machine and switch on.

Also, there are special jigs for sharpening drills. The drill is clamped at the required angle while the jig is rolled across abrasive paper.

Most woodworkers sharpen twist drills by rotating their tips against a bench-grinder wheel (**3**). Don't press too hard and concentrate on grinding each side evenly to keep the point in the centre of the drill.

Dowel bit
Touch up the cutting edges and spurs of a dowel bit with a pointed needle file. Take care to sharpen both sides equally.

1 Sharpening spurs

2 Sharpening cutting edges

3 Grinding a twist drill

HAMMERS

Although a cabinet-maker uses well-cut glued joints to construct fine pieces of woodwork, every worker needs a selection of hammers to build mock-ups and rough framing. In addition, simple butt, mitre and lap joints are secured with nails or panel pins.

Cross-peen hammer
Most cabinet-makers and carpenters favour a medium-weight – 300 to 350g (10 to 12oz) – cross-peen hammer for general work. It takes its name from the narrow wedge-shaped part of the head opposite the striking face, and is used for starting nails held between finger and thumb. The head is wedged tightly onto a tough ash or hickory shaft.

Pin hammer
A pin hammer is a light-weight (100g/3½oz) cross-peen hammer used to drive small nails, panel pins, tacks and staples.

Claw hammer
It is worth having at least one (550g/20oz) claw hammer in your tool kit. It is heavy enough to drive large nails with ease and its split peen (claw) is designed to extract bent ones. A curved claw is mostly used, but there is also a straight-claw or ripping hammer for dismantling frames and packing cases.

Pulling nails puts a considerable strain on the shaft/head joint. If you think you will be pulling a lot of long nails, choose a hammer with a tubular steel or GRP (glass-reinforced plastic) shaft permanently fixed to the head to form a one-piece tool. A vinyl or rubber sleeve is moulded onto the shaft, providing a comfort-able non-slip handgrip.

The traditional adze-eye claw hammer is strong enough for most purposes. A pre-shrunk hickory shaft is forced into the extra-deep socket (eye) where it is spread with hardwood and iron wedges.

CROSS PEEN

SHAFT

Cross-peen hammer

STRIKING FACE

Cross-peen hammer (Continental pattern)

Pin hammer

Pin hammer (Continental pattern)

CLAW

Adze-eye claw hammer

SOCKET

CLAW

Steel-shafted claw hammer

NON-SLIP HANDGRIP

TUBULAR-STEEL SHAFT

Nail set
This square-tipped punch is for driving panel pins and nails below the surface of the timber. Point diameters range from 1.5 to 4mm ($\frac{1}{16}$ to $\frac{5}{32}$in). Use a punch which is slightly smaller than the head of the nail.

MALLETS

Except for certain plastic-handled chisels, you will need a wooden mallet to drive chisels and gouges. A carpenter's mallet is also used to assemble joints, but a soft-faced mallet is less likely to mark work.

Carpenter's mallet
The shaft and head of a carpenter's mallet are both cut from solid beech. The head is tapered so that when the tool is swung naturally, one of the striking faces hits the work or end of a chisel squarely. The socket is also tapered to match the flared end of the shaft so that the head tightens by centrifugal force with every blow.

Soft mallet
A mallet with a soft rubber head can be used to assemble or dismantle joints without fear of denting the wood.

Tapered mallet head
A mallet head tapers towards the handgrip.

SOLID BEECH HEAD

FLARED SHAFT

Carpenter's mallet

Soft mallet

RUBBER HEAD

USING HAMMERS

There's no real trick to using a hammer, but it takes patience and practice before you can drive a nail quickly and surely without bending it or bruising the wood.

Setting a nail
To start a nail and make sure it is aimed in the right direction, hold it between finger and thumb and tap it once or twice with a hammer until it stands unsupported with the point buried in the wood.
Set small nails or panel pins with the peen of a hammer (1). If you don't own a cross-peen hammer, push the nail through thin card to set it (2). When the nail sits firmly, tear the card away and drive it home.

1 Drive small pins with a peen

2 Support a pin with thin card

Driving a nail
You should be able to swing a well-balanced hammer with the minimum of effort. Hold the tool by the end of the shaft and swing your arm from the elbow, keeping your wrist fairly firm. If you find you have to slip your hand up the shaft towards the head to swing the hammer comfortably it is too heavy for you. Keep your eye on the nail and strike it firmly with square blows. It should be possible to drive any nail home with a few strokes only. If you are having trouble sinking the nail, either the hammer is too light or the work is flexing and needs backing up with something heavy.

Raising a bruise
If you dent or 'bruise' the work with a heavy hammer blow, immediately soak it locally with warm water and let the wood swell, raising the crushed fibres flush with the surface. Let the wood dry and sand it smooth.

Sinking a nailhead
Overcome bruising by stopping about 1mm ($\frac{1}{16}$) short of the surface and sink the nail with a nail set. Hold the nail set upright between thumb and fingers, using your ring finger to steady the tip of the tool on the head of the nail. Tap the nail set firmly with a hammer until the nail is flush, or drive it just below for filling and painting.

Steadying a nail set

Secret nailing
To disguise a nail-fixing in clear-finished timber, lift a sliver of wood with a gouge, then drive a nail below the surface with a nail set and glue the sliver back down with a cramp to cover the sunken head.

Hide a nail below a sliver

Avoiding a split
Nailing close to the end of a piece of wood will often result in a split along the grain as the nail forces the fibres apart. Blunting the point of the nail with a hammer blow makes it act like a punch, driving a piece of wood ahead of itself instead of splitting it. This simple method works for softwood, but for hardwood drill a pilot hole just smaller than the nail itself.

CARING FOR HAMMERS

If the face of a hammer gets dirty and greasy it will skid off a nailhead, bending the nail and bruising the work. Keep the face clean by rubbing it on a piece of fine emery cloth or abrasive paper. Keep a vinyl or rubber handgrip grease free by scrubbing it with a nailbrush dipped in a solution of mild detergent and warm water.

Fitting a new shaft

If you break a wooden shaft, chisel or knock out the remaining stump, then plane a new shaft to make a tight fit in the hammer-head eye.

Make two or three sawcuts (depending on the size of the hammer) across the top of the shaft and at a slight angle (**1**). Saw down about two-thirds the depth of the eye. Fit the head on the shaft and tap the other end firmly on the bench to set the head (**2**). Saw off any part of the shaft protruding from the top of the head, then drive iron hammer wedges into each sawcut to spread the shaft (**3**). If the wedges do not lie flush, grind them down on a bench grinder.

1 Make two sawcuts in shaft

2 Tap shaft to set head

3 Spread shaft with wedges

PULLING NAILS

No matter how experienced you become you will inevitably mishit the occasional nail and bend it over. Don't try to straighten it in situ because the next blow will almost certainly bend it again and probably drive it sideways into the wood. Extract the bent nail and replace it with a new one.

Pincers

Tack lifter

Pincers

A claw hammer is ideal for pulling large nails with heads, but pincers will enable you to get a better grip on panel pins and small oval nails.

Tack lifter

The small curved claw of a tack lifter is for prising upholstery tacks holding webbing and fabric.

Using a claw hammer

To draw a partially driven nail, slide the claw under the nailhead and lever on the shaft. On show wood, protect the surface with thick card (**1**). If the nail is too long to extract with one pull, raise the hammer on a block of wood (**2**).

Remove old nails from dismantled framing either by tapping the points to drive the heads clear of the surface or jam the claw onto the protruding shaft of a nail so that it bites into the metal, then pull the nailhead right through the timber.

1 Protect surface with card

2 Use block to pull a long nail

Pulling with pincers

Hold the pincers vertically and grip the nail with the jaws resting on the work. Squeeze the handles together and rock the pincers on one of the curved jaws to extract the nail. Pull a long nail in stages or you will bruise the wood by levering the nail sideways.

Removing tacks

Work the claw of a tack lifter under the fabric or webbing beneath the head of a tack, then push on the handle.

SCREWDRIVERS

The most important point to remember when choosing a screwdriver is that its tip must fit the screw slot – consequently, you will need the same tool in a range of sizes. When it comes to style, select the handle that feels most comfortable, remembering that the smooth bulbous ones will provide the best grip despite the apparently functional appearance of fluted, waisted and faceted handles.

Cabinet screwdriver

The cabinet screwdriver is the customary woodworking tool. Its oval-section hardwood handle fits the human hand to deliver maximum torque at the driving end. Traditionally the blade has a wide, flat heel which fits in a slot in the ferrule.

The design has been modified of late with a cylindrical blade passing straight into a wooden or plastic handle.

The blade of a cabinet screwdriver flares at the tip, but this is sometimes ground back so that the tip tapers.

Fluted-handled screwdriver

Some woodworkers prefer the type of driver that was developed for the electrical and automotive industries. The relatively slim handle can be spun with the fingertips and the often-parallel tip will fit the full width of a screw even when it is located at the bottom of a deep hole. The tip will remain the same shape no matter how many times it is reground.

Cross-head screwdrivers

In order to improve the grip between tool and screw, these cylindrical-bladed screwdrivers have pointed tips ground with four flutes to fit the cross-shaped slots in the heads of special screws. There are three common makes – the Phillips-head driver which fits into a simple cross, the Posidriv-head which is designed to fit into a cross incorporating a small square at its centre, and the very similar Supadriva which will hold a screw unsupported on its tip while you locate it in its pilot hole. It is best to match each type of driver to its own brand of screw and always make sure the tip fits snugly or you are sure to damage the slots.

Ergonomic handgrip
Choose a screwdriver with a large handle that fits in the palm of your hand.

WOODEN HANDLE

FERRULE

FLAT HEEL

Modern cabinet screwdriver

CYLINDRICAL BLADE

FLARED TIP

Traditional cabinet screwdriver

Fluted-handled screwdriver

Ratchet screwdriver

Posidriv screwdriver

Phillips screwdriver

Supadriva

CHROME-VANADIUM

Offset screwdrivers

Offset screwdriver

This is a cranked bar of metal, ground at each end to form a straight or cross-head tip. It is used in spaces too small for conventional screwdrivers.

Stubby screwdriver
This is a screwdriver of any type designed for inserting large screws in restricted spaces. It has a short blade with a wide tip and a full-width handle.

Jeweller's screwdriver
Use this miniature screwdriver for fine work like screwing small hinges to a box lid. With the index finger applying pressure to the revolving head, the knurled shaft of the screwdriver is turned between thumb and other fingers.

Ratchet screwdriver
A ratchet screwdriver with a straight or cross-head tip allows you to insert or remove a screw without having to change your grip on the tool. A small thumb slide on the ferrule changes the ratchet action for clockwise or anticlockwise movement. Moving the thumb slide to its central position locks the mechanism, and the tool will then act like a conventional screwdriver.

Spiral ratchet screwdriver
This screwdriver is designed for speed. Straight pressure on the handle is converted by spiral grooves along the inner shaft to a rotational movement at the tip. The spring-loaded shaft works with a pump action, extending each time pressure is released. The direction of movement is controlled by a ratchet, and a lock-ring fixes the shaft in a retracted position so that the tool can be used like a standard ratchet screwdriver. The chuck takes interchangeable bits with straight or cross-head tips of various sizes. To load the screwdriver, pull the chuck back, insert a bit and release the chuck.

When using the screwdriver in its pump-action mode, always steady the chuck with one hand to stop the tip slipping out of the screw slot and being driven into the wood.

RATCHET MECHANISM

Stubby screwdriver

SPRING-LOADED SHAFT

Spiral ratchet screwdriver

REVOLVING HEADS

CHUCK

BIT

Jeweller's screwdrivers

SELECTING A SCREWDRIVER

Select a screwdriver with a tip that fits the screw slot exactly. It will drive the screw with the minimum of effort without damaging either the screw head or the work.

If a screwdriver tip is too wide (1), it will score the surrounding wood as you drive it home. If it is too narrow (2), you won't be able to generate enough torque to turn the screw but it will probably damage the slot.

Test a cross-head screwdriver by placing its tip in the screw head, then twist the very end of the handle with your fingertips. If the driver is too large it will ride out of the slots. If it is too small it will rock back and forth. A driver of the right size will fit snugly in the head without movement.

Don't try to turn cross-head screws with a straight-tip screwdriver. It will almost certainly strip-out the centre of the cross.

1 Wide tip scores wood

2 Small tip damages slot

INSERTING A WOODSCREW

It is possible to drive a screw into softwood without any preparation, but there is always the danger of splitting the timber or the screw may jam part way. It is much better to open up the fibres with a bradawl or, better still, drill pilot and clearance holes to guide the screw and reduce friction. The latter procedure is essential when screwing into hardwood.

PILOT HOLE   COUNTERSINK

CLEARANCE HOLE

Drilling pilot and clearance holes
For the pilot hole use a drill slightly narrower than the screw's thread, followed part way by a clearance hole the same diameter as the screw shank. If necessary, countersink the top of the clearance hole before inserting the screw. If a screw is too tight, remove it and lightly grease the shank.

Counterboring a screw
If you have to sink a screw below the surface of the wood – to pass through a deep rail, for example – counterbore it by drilling the large hole first with an auger bit, followed by pilot and clearance holes.

Removing a damaged screw
To remove a damaged screw, choose the largest driver that will fit the slot snugly. Regrind the tool to remove the corners of the tip if that is the only way to make it fit.

Try tapping the end of the screwdriver with a mallet. This sometimes helps to budge a stubborn screw.

Another way is to heat the screw head with a soldering iron. Heat expands the metal, and when it has cooled again you may find the screw has loosened.

If all else fails, use progressively larger drills to bore out the screw.

Removing a screw
Grind corners off a large driver tip.

Repairing screwdrivers
A screwdriver with a worn rounded tip is useless. Either sharpen it with a file and bench stone or regrind the tip on a bench grinder. Hollow-grind each side on the wheel (1), then grind the tip square.

It is virtually impossible to regrind cross-head screwdrivers yourself. You can touch up a damaged tip with a small file, but replace a badly worn screwdriver.

1 Repairing damaged tip
Hollow-grind each side of a screwdriver tip on a bench grinder.

CRAMPS

Every workshop needs a variety of cramps – long bar or pipe cramps for 'gluing-up' large constructions, web or mitre cramps for mitred picture frames, and several fast-action or G-cramps for gluing small jobs and to provide an 'extra hand' when you want to assemble awkward components. Collecting a range of cramps is expensive, but you can acquire them gradually as needed or even hire them.

T-section bar cramp
Extra-large cramps are cast with T-section bars for rigidity.

Bar cramp

The bar or sash cramp is an essential piece of wood-working equipment for clamping glue-jointed frames, carcasses or solid-wood panels while the adhesive sets. A screw-adjusted jaw is fixed permanently to one end of a rigid steel bar. Another jaw, known as the tail slide, is free to move along the bar to accommodate the size of the work-piece. The tail slide is held in the required position by a tapered steel pin located in one of a series of holes along the bar. Bar cramps sized 450 to 1200mm (1ft 6in to 4ft) are readily available, but longer cramps can be hired for the exceptionally large job. These longer cramps usually have T-section bars for extra rigidity. Most wood-workers, however, buy a straight extension bar to lengthen a standard bar cramp or bolt two of them end to end.

Fast-action bar cramp

Both the adjustable jaw and the tail slide are free to move on a fast-action bar cramp. As the screw is tightened on the work both jaws rock over and jam on the bar. There are several versions of this type of cramp, but they all work on a similar principle. Fast-action cramps can be adjusted in seconds to fit the workpiece.

Cramp heads

Large, custom-made bar cramps can be made using cast-iron cramp heads designed to fit onto a piece of timber 25mm (1in) thick.

ADJUSTABLE JAW

TAIL SLIDE

ADJUSTABLE JAW

SCREW-ADJUSTED JAW

ADJUSTABLE JAW

Fast-action cramp

WOODEN BAR

TAIL SLIDE

TAPERED RETAINING PIN

Pipe cramp

TAIL SLIDE

Cramp heads on wooden bar

CAM-ACTION LOCKING LEVER

STEEL PIPE

TAIL SLIDE

Bar cramp

Pipe cramp

American woodworkers prefer to construct a frame or carcass cramp from cramp heads and a length of steel pipe. One end of the pipe is threaded to take the adjustable jaw. The movable tail slide is locked anywhere along the pipe with a cam-action lever. Other models have a one-way clutch mechanism which tightens as load is applied to the tail slide. The cramp heads are made in two sizes to fit 12 or 18mm ($\frac{1}{2}$ or $\frac{3}{4}$in) pipe. A 12mm ($\frac{1}{2}$in) cramp is cheaper, but will bend more under load than the 18mm ($\frac{3}{4}$in) pipe.

USING BAR CRAMPS

Gluing and cramping a workpiece should be undertaken calmly and with confidence. Consequently, carry out a dry assembly to practise the procedure to ensure the workpiece assembles accurately and to check you have all the tools and equipment you need. Try to get an assistant to handle the other end of long cramps. As you run through the sequence, decide who will be responsible for the details of each stage.

Plan your work to make the assembly the last job of the day. The glued work can be left undisturbed overnight, by which time the adhesive has set. However, leave this crucial and irreversible stage until the next morning rather than rushing it or having to leave the glued work in an unheated workshop in freezing conditions.

Cramp up the piece in a series of sub-assemblies. To construct a table underframe, for example, glue the legs to the end rails first. When the glue has set and you have cleaned up the assembled endframes, join them with the side rails to complete the underframe.

1 Align block with joint

2 Misaligned block opens joint

3 Align cramps with rails

4 Check diagonals of frame

MOVE CRAMPS IN THIS DIRECTION

LONGEST DIAGONAL

5 Squaring up a frame

Clamping a frame

Adjust a bar cramp for each side of a square or rectangular frame. Cut softwood blocks to protect the work from the metal jaws and to place the force applied by the cramps directly in line with the joints **(1)**. A badly placed block will distort a joint and open the shoulder line **(2)**.

Paint glue thinly and evenly on all mating surfaces of the joints. Applying too much glue is not only wasteful but can hold the joints open or cause the wood to split due to hydraulic pressure.

Assemble the frame, align the cramps with the rails **(3)** and gradually tighten the jaws until the glue is squeezed out of the joints. Wipe excess glue from the surface with a damp cloth.

Checking for wind

Make sure the frame is not 'in wind' (twisted) by looking across it to see if one rail seems to be aligned with the other. To straighten out a twisted frame, lift one end of a cramp to correct the distortion, then check for alignment again. If necessary, slacken the cramps slightly and force the frame back in line.

Checking for square

You can use a try square to check the joints are clamped square. However, it is better to make sure the whole frame is square by gauging the diagonals. Make two pinch rods (slim battens, each planed to a point at one end). Hold the pinch rods side by side and slide them until the points nestle in two opposite corners of the frame **(4)**. Holding the pinch rods together, lift them out of the frame and fit them into the other diagonal. If the diagonals are not equal, slacken the cramps and set them at à slight angle to squeeze the longest diagonal, bringing the frame back to square **(5)**, and then check the diagonals again.

Web cramp

A length of nylon webbing 25mm (1in) wide is wound around a workpiece and pulled taut by a ratchet mechanism. The web applies equal pressure to the four corners of a mitred frame and can be used to clamp a stool or chair with turned legs – a difficult job with bar cramps. Tighten up the cramp by turning the small ratchet nut with a spanner or screwdriver. Wait till the glue has set, then release the tension by pressing the lever.

NYLON WEBBING

RATCHET NUT

RELEASE LEVER

Web cramp

Mitre cramp

A mitre cramp holds individual mitred joints while glue sets. Insert any reinforcing nails or screws before releasing the cramp. Larger mitre cramps have jaw capacities of 112mm (4½in).

Mitre cramp

SMALL CRAMPS

G-cramp
A most useful and versatile addition to a workshop, the G-cramp is used for all kinds of gluing procedures and to hold work firmly on the bench. G-cramps are made with jaw capacities ranging from 28 to 300mm (1⅛ to 12in).

Long-reach G-cramp
This is a G-cramp with a throat depth approximately double that of the standard cramp, for use when work needs to be clamped well in from the edge.

Edge cramp
This special-purpose G-cramp is for clamping lippings onto boards. Edge cramps are especially useful on a curved edge which is difficult to clamp with a bar cramp. With the edge screw retracted, they can be used as normal G-cramps.

Fast-action cramp
This is a short version of the fast-action bar cramp and performs the same function as a G-cramp, but can be clamped onto the work very quickly – useful when the glue is 'going off' rapidly.

Cam cramp
The cam cramp is a fast-action lightweight cramp with wooden jaws. Having slid the movable jaw up to the work, clamping force is applied by cocking the cam lever. Each jaw is cork-lined to protect the work.

Handscrew
Handscrews are rarely found in workshops these days, despite their unique feature of jaws that can be closed at a variety of angles to clamp tapered or irregularly shaped workpieces.

Using edge cramps
Clamp a lipping onto a curved edge with these special-purpose G-cramps.

LONG-REACH G-CRAMP · SHOE · SCREW · TOMMY BAR · G-CRAMP · EDGE SCREW · Edge cramp · SOFT JAWS · MOVABLE JAW · Cam cramp · CAM LEVER · Fast-action cramp · MOVABLE JAW · HANDLE · JAWS · Handscrew · HANDLE

USING SMALL CRAMPS

Using a G-cramp
Spin the threaded screw between fingers and thumb until the circular 'shoe' contacts the work, then apply pressure by screwing up the tommy bar or thumbscrew. As the shoe is attached with a ball joint it automatically adjusts to accommodate angled work. Use a softening block to protect the work as the edge of the shoe dents the wood very easily.

Adjusting a G-cramp
Spin the screw to close the jaws, then tighten with the tommy bar.

Using a handscrew
To adjust the cramp, hold a handle in each hand and rotate the tool to open or close the jaws. Slip the cramp onto the work, then tighten both screws to apply pressure. Being made of wood, the jaws are less likely to bruise the work, but take the precaution of sandwiching paper between them and the timber to make sure that the tool is not accidentally glued in place.

Adjusting a handscrew
Rotate the tool to open or close the jaws.

POWER

Not many years ago most home workshops were equipped with little more than a power drill and a few attachments that would convert it into a circular saw, jigsaw and orbital sander. Today the picture is completely different. Woodworkers now recognize the superior quality of modern power tools and are much more inclined to invest in purpose-made tools rather than rely on underpowered attachments. Modern power tools have lightweight insulated bodies. They are better designed and more powerful than their predecessors, and most of them can be bench-mounted to create what is in effect a serviceable miniature machine shop. Another important development has been the invention of battery-powered cordless tools.

TOOLS

As yet the batteries do not store sufficient electricity to drive powerful motors for long periods. But they are adequate for less demanding work, such as drilling and inserting screws, and cordless tools are quiet, efficient and comfortable to use.

POWER DRILLS

The electric power drill is the most widely sold and used power tool on the market. Not only is it an invaluable woodworking tool, it is also an indispensable DIY tool found in nearly every home for general household maintenance. Manufacturers try to satisfy the huge demand for power drills by producing an immense range of tools, from cheap 'throwaway' *drills to more sophisticated and powerful professional models. The woodworker needs a drill which falls somewhere in the middle of the range – a tool which is accurate and reasonably versatile. Most people buy one powered by mains electricity, although quiet cordless drills are popular for small-bore drilling and inserting screws.*

MAINS-POWERED ELECTRIC DRILLS

When choosing a mains-powered electric drill, look for features that give you the most effective tool for a reasonable price. Theoretically, tools made primarily for the professional may do jobs faster and they can run for long periods without noticeable reduction in performance – but in reality many professionals are quite satisfied with good-quality tools built to meet the requirements of the discerning amateur.

Chuck capacity
The drill bit is held in place by a chuck. Most chucks are operated by a toothed key which opens and closes three self-centring jaws designed to grip the shank of the bit. The 'chuck capacity' describes the maximum size of shank the chuck will accept and corresponds to the maximum diameter of hole the drill is capable of boring in steel. The same drill will bore holes two or three times larger in wood. This is achieved by fitting large woodworking bits with reduced shanks. Most drills have a chuck capacity of 10 or 13mm ($\frac{3}{8}$ or $\frac{1}{2}$in).

Fast-action chucks
Some top-of-the-range professional drills are fitted with fast-action chucks that need no key. Instead, when the chuck is pulled back it opens automatically and special bits with grooved shanks are inserted; then when the chuck is released, it grips the bit. Bits for this type of drill are made in a range of sizes, all with the same shank size. For use with ordinary drill bits, the chuck takes an adaptor.

● **Motor size**
Manufacturers normally specify the drill's motor as having a power input of so many watts. A 500 to 600W drill capable of producing about 3000 rpm is suitable for general work.

Mains-powered electric drill

Labels: DEPTH STOP · HAMMER-ACTION SWITCH · ALL-PLASTIC BODY · CHUCK · INTERNATIONAL STANDARD COLLAR · REVERSE-ACTION SWITCH · SECONDARY HANDLE · VARIABLE-SPEED TRIGGER · OPTIMUM-SPEED SELECTOR · TRIGGER-LOCK BUTTON · CHUCK KEY · BOSCH CSB 500 RE · 500W · Beton ⌀ max 15 mm · electronic

USING POWER TOOLS SAFELY

If you treat power tools with respect and handle them carefully, you should never have an accident. Always follow these basic safety procedures, whatever tool you are using:

● Do not wear loose clothing or jewellery which could get caught in the moving parts of a tool. Tie back loose hair.
● Wear protective eye shields whenever you are doing work which could throw up debris.
● Never carry a power tool by its cable or use the cable to pull the plug out of a socket.
● Check the cable and plug regularly for wear or damage.
● Unplug power tools when not in use and before making adjustments or changing accessories and attachments.
● Keep children away from areas where power tools are in use. Lock tools away when you have finished work.
● Always clamp work securely.
● Do not use power tools in the rain or in very damp conditions.
● Keep handles and grips dry and grease-free.
● Don't throw used batteries from cordless tools into water or a fire, as they are likely to explode.

Speed selection

You will find that your drill performs a particular function best at a particular speed. There are several systems for controlling and selecting speed. Some basic drills have from two to four fixed speeds selected by means of a switch. Others have a two-speed trigger control – a slow speed being achieved by depressing the trigger partway and full speed by depressing it completely. The trigger can be locked in either position.

More and more drills now have variable-speed trigger control. With this type of control, the speed varies from zero to maximum according to the amount of pressure applied to the trigger. On some drills the movement of the trigger can be limited by selecting an optimum speed with a built-in dial. This is a useful feature for inserting wood-screws, which is best done at a slow controlled speed.

Nowadays very few drills are fitted with gears as a means of controlling the speed – most are now controlled electronically. The best electronic speed-control systems maintain the selected speed even when load is applied to the drill bit, and internal torque compensators prevent the motor being damaged if the bit jams in the work.

Drill manufacturers recommend a range of speeds at which their tools will perform best; but as a general guide, select a slow speed for masonry or metal and a fast speed for wood.

Secondary handle and depth stop

Most drills can be fitted with an additional handle that clamps onto the collar at the most convenient angle. Choose one with an integral stop that comes to rest against the work when the drill bit has reached the required depth. Some secondary handles serve as storage magazines for spare drill bits.

Reverse action

Many power drills have a switch that changes the direction of rotation in order to remove screws.

Hammer action

Although never used for woodworking, it makes sense to buy a drill fitted with a hammer action so that you can bore holes in brick, stone and concrete. Operated by a switch, either before or during drilling, the hammer action delivers several hundred blows per second behind the drill bit to break up masonry as work progresses. It is essential to use special percussion drill bits and to make sure they are held firmly in the chuck.

Electrical insulation

The all-plastic body of a power drill protects the user from electric shock should a fault occur within the tool. This is known as 'double insulation'. When a tool is described as having 'full insulation', not only are you protected but the motor is safe from damage even if you inadvertently drill into an electric cable.

Collar size

A drill that has an inter-national-standard 43mm diameter collar directly behind the chuck will fit accessories or attachments made by other manufac-turers subscribing to the same system. This gives you the option to buy cheaper or better-quality equipment than is made by the drill's manufacturer.

Trigger lock

A small button on the handle of the drill is pushed in to lock the trigger for continuous running. Squeezing the trigger releases the lock.

CORDLESS DRILLS

Within their limits, cordless drills are excellent tools. They are lightweight, silent-running and convenient, doing away with the need for a long extension lead in order to reach a work site at a distance from the mains.

Most have a chuck capacity of 10mm ($\frac{3}{8}$in) but are not really suitable for drilling holes larger than 8mm ($\frac{5}{16}$in) in metal, although they will drill holes up to 12mm ($\frac{1}{2}$in) in diameter in wood. They will also drill masonry, provided the bit is sharp and of good quality.

There are both fixed-speed and variable-speed models; all models are fitted with reverse action for use as powered screwdrivers. Because cordless drills generate less torque than mains-powered drills, even the fixed-speed models are easier to control when driving screws.

To ensure that a cordless drill cannot be operated accidentally, especially during transit, there is an on/off safety switch.

Some models are supplied with a wall-hung storage rack incorporating a charging unit. So long as the tool is replaced every evening, it is always charged up. Other models have removable battery packs which plug into a charger. With this method you can always have a spare pack charged and ready for use.

Whatever system you choose, it normally takes 12 hours to fully recharge a cordless drill – unless you buy a rapid charger, which will complete the job in an hour. A drill or battery pack can be recharged several hundred times before it needs replacing.

Long exposure to heat or storing a seldom-used tool in freezing conditions can ruin a cordless drill.

SPEED-RANGE SELECTION SWITCH

CHUCK

Cordless drill

REVERSE-ACTION SWITCH

TRIGGER

ON/OFF SAFETY SWITCH

BATTERY PACK

Wall-hung charging unit
This type of cordless drill is recharged by replacing it in a wall-hung storage unit.

DRILL BITS AND ACCESSORIES

As a woodworker you will need a complete set of twist drills up to 13mm ($\frac{1}{2}$in) in diameter, but it is probably best to buy reduced-shank and other larger woodboring bits as the need arises. Accessories merely extend the usefulness of a power drill and are not considered essential workshop equipment. One exception is a vertical drill stand, which – unless you have a proper drill press – is necessary for drilling accurately and square to the face of the work.

Twist drills
Although twist drills are designed for metalwork, they are also good general-purpose woodboring bits. Carbon-steel drills are perfectly adequate for woodwork but, since you will almost certainly want to drill metal at some time, it is worth investing in the more expensive high-speed-steel bits. Twist drills from 13 to 25mm ($\frac{1}{2}$ to 1in) diameter are made with reduced shanks to fit standard power-drill chucks.

Keep twist drills sharp and, before you use them, pick out any wood dust which has become packed into the flutes.

Twist drills are not easy to centre. With hardwoods, it pays to mark the centre of the hole first, using a metalworking centre punch. To avoid splintering the wood, take the pressure off the drill as the bit emerges from the far side of the work. Alternatively, clamp a piece of scrap timber to the back face.

Dowel bits
The dowel bit is a twist drill with a centre point to prevent it wandering off line, and two spurs that cut a clean-edged hole.

Spade bits
These are relatively cheap bits for drilling large holes, from 6 to 38mm ($\frac{1}{4}$ to 1$\frac{1}{2}$in). The long leadpoint makes for very positive location at the centre of the hole, even when drilling at an angle to the face of the work.

Forstner bits
These are superior-quality drill bits which leave exceptionally clean, flat-bottomed holes. They are available up to 50mm (2in) in diameter. A Forstner bit will not be deflected by knots or wood grain, and will bore overlapping holes and holes that run out to the edge of the work without difficulty.

Countersink bits
A countersink bit makes a tapered recess to accept the countersunk head of a woodscrew. Drill the pilot and clearance holes first to centre the point of the countersink bit, then run the drill at a fast speed for a clean finish.

Drill-and-countersink bits
This type of bit drills a pilot hole, shank-clearance hole and countersink in one operation. The range of sizes available matches the most common woodscrews.

Drill-and-counterbore bits
These perform like drill-and-countersink bits but in addition drill a neat counterbored hole which can be filled with a wooden plug to hide the screw head.

Plug cutters
Driving a plug cutter into the side grain of timber cuts a cylindrical plug of wood to match exactly the hole left by a drill-and-counterbore bit. Cut plugs from timber which closely matches the colour and grain pattern of the work.

● **Spirit level**
Clamp a small spirit level to the drill collar to help you drill square to the work. For horizontal drilling, keep the bubble centred between the lines; for vertical drilling, centre it in the glass end of the spirit level.

Twist drills

Reduced-shank twist drill

Dowel bit

Spade bit

Masonry drill

Forstner bit

Hole-saw blades

Countersink bit

Drill-and-countersink bit

Drill-and-counterbore bit

Plug cutter

BACKING PLATE

SAW BLADE

Hole saw

DRILL BIT AND RETURN SPRING

Masonry drills

Masonry drills are steel twist drills with brazed tungsten-carbide tips that are designed to bore into brick, stone or concrete.

Percussion drills

These are masonry drills with shatter-proof tips designed to withstand the vibration produced by a hammer-action power drill.

Hole saws

A hole saw is a cylindrical-shaped saw blade held in a plastic or metal backing plate which is clamped to a twist drill passing through its centre. Hole saws are sold in sets ranging from 25 to 89mm (1 to $3\frac{1}{2}$in) in diameter.

Secure the shank of the bit in the chuck. The saw blade spins very much faster than the bit, so select a slower speed than you would normally use for drilling into wood and feed the blade into the work at a steady rate.

Screwdriver bits

Flat tips and all patterns of cross-head tips are available as screwdriver bits for power drills. It is possible to drive screws into wood without having to drill pilot and clearance holes, but it often helps to drill a pilot hole to ensure that the screw does not wander off line and the wood doesn't split.

When inserting or extracting a screw, select the slowest speed and maintain pressure on the drill the whole time to stop the bit jumping out of the slot.

Screwdriver bits

SPINDLE

CHUCK

SHEATHED DRIVE CABLE

Flexible drive

A flexible drive enables the user to work with drill bits and rotary files or rasps in areas which would be inaccessible with a full-size drill. It consists of a drive cable sheathed in a flexible casing, with a spindle at one end and a small chuck with a short pen-hold grip at the other. The spindle end fits into the chuck of a standard power drill, which ideally should be clamped in a bench stand. Flexible drives have chuck capacities of 6 to 8mm ($\frac{1}{4}$ to $\frac{5}{16}$in).

Rotary rasps
Coarse rotary rasps fitted in the flexible-drive chuck are ideal for complicated shaping.

Dowelling jig

A dowelling jig is a device which guides a drill bit square and true, and provides a means of repeating hole-spacing in the two components of a dowel joint. Choose a jig which is sturdy, well-made and capable of jigging solid-wood rails and wide boards for cabinet-making. One such jig has a fixed head or fence from which all measurements are taken, joined by two steel rods to a sliding fence which clamps the device to the work. Adjustable drill-bit guides are clamped to the rods to place the dowel holes in the required positions.

Very wide boards can be dowelled by using the jig with the end fences removed. Hold the side fences of the drill-bit guides against the work and space holes accurately along the board by locking the first guide over the last-drilled hole with a dowel peg.

Vertical drill stand

A vertical stand converts a portable power drill into a serviceable drill press. Pulling down on the feed lever lowers the drill bit into the work. If the stand is fitted with a return spring, the drill is lifted automatically to its initial position when you release the feed lever.

Make sure the stand you choose has a sturdy, rigid column and a positive clamp to hold the drill itself. It should also have a wide, heavy base which can be bolted to a bench. Slots in the base enable you to attach small vices to it to hold metal components for drilling, but you can also use the slots for bolting a home-made wooden fence to the base which will help you to position the work directly below the drill bit.

A depth gauge on the stand limits the travel of the drill when you want a stopped hole. When drilling right through the work, place a piece of chipboard or plywood under it to prevent splintering on the underside of the wood.

SLIDING FENCE

DRILL-BIT GUIDE

STEEL ROD

DRILL-BIT GUIDE

STEEL ROD

FIXED HEAD

Dowelling jig

Dowelling a board
Remove the end fences to drill holes in the edge of a wide board.

DEPTH GAUGE

RETURN SPRING

FEED LEVER

DRILL CLAMP

COLUMN

Vertical drill stand

BASE

JIGSAWS

Although some manufacturers claim too much for it, the jigsaw is undoubtedly a versatile tool. It will cut any man-made board and rip or crosscut solid timber reasonably well, but its ability to make curved cuts is its real advantage. When fitted with the appropriate blade, a jigsaw will also cut sheet metal and plastics. Jigsaw attachments for electric drills are still made, but they are almost certain to be phased out in the near future due to an overwhelming preference for purpose-made saws.

MAINS-POWERED JIGSAWS

In the past, jigsaws had a poor reputation among serious woodworkers because the narrow blades tended to wander off line and to bend under load, which made it virtually impossible to make an accurate, square cut. But well-designed jigsaws now have precisely balanced electric motors and plunger mechanisms which produce very little vibration. So long as the blade is sharp, this type of saw is comfortable to use, relatively quiet and a lot easier to control. A basic no-frills jigsaw is perfectly adequate for woodwork, but if you are prepared to pay more you can have a more versatile machine.

Orbital action

A basic jigsaw moves the blade straight up and down. Saws with orbital action cut faster by advancing the blade into the work on the upstroke, and minimize wear on the saw teeth and clear the kerf at the same time by moving the blade backwards on the down-stroke. The degree of oscillation is adjustable to select the best-possible action to suit the material being cut. On maximum advance, the blade cuts easily and quickly through softwoods and plastics. Orbital action is gradually reduced for thick sections of softwood and hardwoods, chipboard and soft metals; and finally to zero movement for steel and thin sheet materials.

● **Motor size**
Nearly all mains-powered jigsaws have 350W motors capable of a top speed of about 3000 strokes per minute. The more powerful motors of professional-range saws are designed to cope with cutting thick steel rather than produce a faster stroke rate.

TRIGGER

STROKE-RATE SELECTOR

TRIGGER-LOCK BUTTON

HANDGRIP

BLADE GUARD

BOSCH

PST 60 PEA

380W · max 60 mm · electronic

BLADE

ORBITAL-ACTION SELECTOR

SHOE

Mains-powered jigsaw

DUST-EXHAUST PORT

USING A JIGSAW SAFELY

Follow the basic safety procedures for power tools already described, but take extra care with a jigsaw.

- Check that the intended path of the blade is clear below the work.
- Make sure the flex trails behind the tool, never in front of the blade.
- Use sharp blades only. Blunt blades have to be forced through the work.
- Never curl your fingers around the workpiece near the line of cut.
- Relieve the pressure on the saw as you are about to finish a cut – to avoid sudden acceleration as the blade leaves the kerf.
- Switch off and wait until the blade has completely stopped moving before you put the saw down.

Depth of cut
The average jigsaw will cut softwoods and hardwoods up to 50mm (2in) thick. It will also cut non-ferrous metals up to 12mm ($\frac{1}{2}$in) and steel up to 3mm ($\frac{1}{8}$in) thick. Professional-range tools handle only slightly thicker timber, but they are able to cut through 20mm ($\frac{3}{4}$in) aluminium and 10mm ($\frac{3}{8}$in) steel.

Dust extraction
On most jigsaws a jet of air from behind the blade clears the sawdust from the cutting line. This system is sufficient for most woodworking applications; but if you are working for prolonged periods or on woods with toxic dust, buy a jigsaw with a dust-extracting facility. This is a flexible hose which plugs into the back of the saw and sucks dust from the cutting area into a domestic vacuum cleaner.

Electrical insulation
Choose a jigsaw with an all-plastic casing which insulates the user from electric shock should a fault occur within the motor.

Speed selection
Single-speed jigsaws operate at high speed the whole time and are primarily woodworking saws, so cannot be expected to cut metal for a prolonged period without overloading the motor.

Some jigsaws are made with dials to select a particular stroke rate, between 500 and 3000 strokes per minute, to suit the material being cut. But on a true variable-speed jigsaw the stroke rate is controlled by the amount of pressure applied to the operating switch or trigger, although this too can be limited by a dial selector.

Generally, top speed is reserved for cutting wood, the mid-range for plastics or soft metals, such as aluminium, and the low speeds for steel and ceramic tiles. But in practice, the sound of the saw and the ease with which it cuts are your best guide to the most suitable stroke rate.

The best saws have built-in electronic feedback to monitor the stroke rate and ensure that a constant speed is maintained within reasonable limits when the tool is cutting.

If you run a jigsaw on its slowest speed for an appreciable time, it may overheat – so every now and then let the saw run free at top speed for a couple of minutes so the motor can cool down.

Trigger lock
A button on the handle is depressed to lock the trigger for continuous running. This feature reduces tension and fatigue when making long, complicated cuts.

Scroller jigsaw

BLADE-STEERING KNOB

BLADE-ANGLE LOCK

SCROLLING FACILITY

Although, with an appropriately narrow blade, any jigsaw will cut intricately curved shapes, it is necessary to turn the whole saw in the direction of the cut or adjust the position of the work. However, on a scroller jigsaw the blade can be steered independently by a knob mounted on the top of the tool; it can also be locked facing forwards, backwards or sideways. When scrolling, care must be taken to keep pressure directly behind the cutting edge or the blade will distort and break.

CORDLESS JIGSAWS

Large cordless jigsaws are available for the professional worksite but very few manufacturers make models designed for the amateur-woodworker market. The advantages of a saw without a trailing flex are obvious – but a cordless jigsaw is relatively expensive and it is not as powerful as a saw operated on mains electricity. Its depth-cutting capacity for all materials is about half that of a mains-powered jigsaw; and, when cutting 18mm ($\frac{3}{4}$in) chipboard, it will run efficiently for only 15 minutes before it needs recharging. This is only a minor inconvenience if you keep a spare battery pack fully charged.

Make sure any cordless jigsaw you buy has a safety lock that prevents it being switched on accidentally.

Splinter control
As the blade cuts on the upstroke, it tends to lift splinters on both sides of the kerf on the upper surface of the work. Consequently, it is important to cut with the 'good' surface face down unless your jigsaw supports the wood as it is cut. This is achieved on some models by sliding the shoe or baseplate backwards until the blade fits into a narrow slot in the metal. Other models are supplied with a plastic insert which fills the space around the blade.

Insert prevents splintering

JIGSAW BLADES

All jigsaws are designed for easy blade replacement, primarily because the blades are never resharpened but are replaced as soon as they become blunt or are broken. In addition, different blades are available for cutting a variety of materials and woodworking blades are made with specific tooth configurations for a finer, faster or cleaner cut.

Although manufacturers describe their blades in different ways, a basic understanding of their construction and specification will enable you to select the appropriate blade for a particular job.

Blade length
This describes the length of the cutting or toothed section of the blade. It varies from 50 to 100mm (2 to 4in). Since you will usually be using the top half of the blade only, blade length isn't important for most purposes – but when you want to cut thick timber, choose a blade length 15 to 20mm ($\frac{5}{8}$ to $\frac{3}{4}$in) longer than the maximum thickness of the wood.

Size of teeth
Some manufacturers specify tooth size by the number of teeth that fit into a 1in length of blade; others use the engineering term 'pitch' – which describes the gap between two teeth, measured from point to point in millimetres. Thus a blade can be described as having 10 teeth per inch (TPI) or a pitch of 2.5mm.

As a rough guide, the smaller the teeth the finer the cut; and as tooth-size increases, so does the speed at which the blade will cut.

Set of tooth
The slot cut by a saw blade is known as the 'kerf'. If a blade cut a kerf equal to its own thickness, it would most probably break due to the strain imposed on it by too much friction. Consequently, blades are designed to cut a slightly wider kerf so as to provide a minimum clearance. This is achieved by setting the teeth in one of the following ways.

Saw or side set Alternate teeth are bent sideways to right and left, in the traditional method adopted for handsaws. However, this can only be achieved with relatively large teeth and is reserved for blades designed to cut quickly, leaving a rough-edged kerf.

Ground blades To produce a finer cut, this type of blade is made with teeth that have no set in the true sense; instead, to provide clearance, the blade behind the teeth is ground away to a thinner section. Ground blades cut very clean kerfs in man-made boards as well as solid timber. A blade which has a slight side set in addition to being taper-ground will cut a little faster.

Wavy set Blades with extremely small teeth are made to cut a wider kerf by having a serpentine cutting edge. Wavy-set blades are designed for cutting metal but are also useful for making a clean, narrow kerf in plywood and blockboard.

Changing a jigsaw blade
Follow the manufacturer's instructions for changing the blade, and always make sure the roller guide is supporting the blade from behind.

● **Cutting metal**
Cutting sheet metal, even if it is thin, is a slow process and you should not be tempted to force the saw to increase the speed of cut. Run a thin film of oil or turpentine ahead of the blade as a lubricant. Wear safety spectacles and ear protectors.

● **Cutting plastic laminates**
To reduce the chipping of plastic-laminated chipboard, fit a laminate-cutting blade with reversed teeth. Alternatively, use a fine metal-cutting blade – but turn the board over and sandwich it between two sheets of hardboard.

USING A JIGSAW

The reciprocal action of a jigsaw will set up vibration in the work unless it is clamped to a bench or held down firmly on sawhorses. This is especially true of sheets of thin hardboard or plywood, which should be supported on both sides of the cut line by planks of wood resting on sawhorses.

Freehand sawing
Rest the front of the shoe on the work, with the blade just clear of the edge and aligned with the cut line. Switch on the saw and advance the blade into the wood just on the waste side of the line. Push the saw through the work at a steady rate, but do not force it. Slow down for the last centimetre ($\frac{1}{2}$in) or so, supporting the offcut as it is severed.

Starting a freehand cut

Cutting parallel to an edge
An adjustable side fence fitted to the shoe guides the saw blade on a path parallel to a straight edge. Make sure the fence clamp is secure and that the fence itself is aligned accurately with the blade. If it isn't, the blade will not cut true and it may burn the work or even break. You can extend a short fence by screwing a longer hardwood strip to it.

Set the fence by measuring from its inner face to the blade – or, with the blade aligned with the cut line, slide the fence against the edge of the work and tighten the fence clamp. Switch on and advance the blade into the work, pressing the fence against the edge throughout the length of the cut.

Press fence against the work

Constructing a temporary fence
When the cut line is too far from an edge to use the side fence, run the side of the shoe against a batten clamped to the work.

Run shoe against guide batten

Cutting a bevel
The shoe on a jigsaw can be adjusted to any angle up to 45 degrees on either side of the blade. Slightly slacken the shoe-clamping screws, tap the shoe with a screwdriver handle to the required angle indicated on the tilt gauge, then retighten the clamps.

It is difficult to guide an angled saw freehand, so

Cut a bevel using a fence

Cutting a square hole

Beginning a plunge cut

Making curved cuts
Cut the waste into sections if a curve is especially tight.

Cutting a circle
Convert the side fence into a compass for cutting a circle.

if possible, use the side fence or clamp a guide batten to the work.

Cutting an aperture
To cut a round aperture in a board, first drill a starter hole for the blade just inside the marked area; then lower the blade into the hole, switch on, and cut the aperture in one pass.

To cut a square hole, follow the same procedure; but cut into each corner and back off about 25mm (1in), then make a curved cut to bring the blade in line with the next side of the hole. Finally, remove the triangular waste left in each corner by sawing back in the opposite direction.

Making a plunge cut
Instead of drilling a starter hole, you can plunge-cut with a jigsaw to begin to cut an aperture. Tip the saw onto the curved front edge of the shoe with the blade clear of the work; then switch on and pivot the saw on the shoe, gradually lowering the blade into the wood until the tool is upright and the shoe is flat on the work. Always make a plunge cut in the waste, not too close to the cut line.

Making curved cuts
Very tight bends should be cut with a scrolling blade, but sweeping curves can be cut freehand with virtually any blade in the range. If a blade begins to strain on a tight bend, make straight cuts in the waste up to the cut line first. This causes the waste to drop out in sections as the cut proceeds, which gives greater clearance for the blade.

To cut a perfectly circular hole or disc, convert the side fence into a compass by attaching to it a 'point' supplied as part of the accessory. Press the point into the centre of the circle and pivot the running saw about it.

JIGSAW BLADES FOR WOODWORK

EFFECTIVE LENGTH	TOOTH SIZE/ PITCH	SET	USE
75mm (3in)	8TPI/3mm	Side set	Hard and softwood up to 60mm (2½in) thick. Especially good for ripping with the grain. Rough cut.
75mm (3in)	6TPI/4mm	Ground & side set	As above, but with a clean cut.
75mm (3in)	6TPI/4mm	Ground	Hardwood, softwood and man-made boards up to 60mm (2½in) thick. Very clean cut.
50mm (2in)	12TPI/2mm	Wavy set	Man-made boards up to 30mm (1¼in) thick. Very fine cut.
50mm (2in)	12TPI/2mm	Wavy set	For cutting tight curves in wood and man-made boards up to 20mm (¾in) thick.
75mm (3in)	10TPI/2.5mm	Ground	Reversed teeth to cut on the down stroke. For plastic-laminated boards.
60mm (2⅜in)	6TPI/4.5mm	N/A	Tungsten-carbide-tipped teeth, especially good for coping with the high glue content of chipboard.
70mm (2¾in)	N/A	N/A	Half-round, flat and triangular files. For wood and man-made boards.

METALWORKING BLADES

EFFECTIVE LENGTH	TOOTH SIZE/ PITCH	SET	USE
75mm (3in)	12TPI/2mm	Ground	Non-ferrous metals up to 10mm (⅜in) thick. Very clean cut.
75mm (3in)	8TPI/3mm	Side set	High-speed-steel blade, for mild steel up to 6mm (¼in) and non-ferrous metals up to 20mm (¾in) thick.
50mm (2in)	20TPI/1.2mm	Wavy set	High-speed-steel blade, for mild steel and non-ferrous metals up to 1.5mm (1/16 in) thick.

OTHER MATERIALS

EFFECTIVE LENGTH	TOOTH SIZE/ PITCH	SET	USE
54mm (2⅛in)	N/A	N/A	Tungsten-carbide-coated for GRP and ceramic tiles.
75mm (3in)	N/A	Knife-ground	Soft rubber, cork, cardboard, carpet and plastics.

CIRCULAR SAWS

Even when a woodworker has a fully equipped machine shop with a table saw, you will often find he or she also owns a portable circular saw for the con- *venience of being able to work on site or for converting large man-made boards, which can be difficult to handle on a fixed saw unless it has a large table.*

● **Motor size**
As one would expect, the size of the motor increases in proportion to the diameter of the blade – not to produce more speed but to provide more torque to overcome the extra leverage applied to a large blade as it cuts its way through the wood. As a general rule, the larger the motor for a given diameter of blade, the better the performance of the saw.

SAWDUST-EXHAUST PORT — HANDGRIP — TRIGGER — CUTTING-DEPTH SCALE — TILT SCALE AND CLAMP — DEPTH CLAMP — SECONDARY HANDLE — PIVOTING BLADE GUARD — RIVING KNIFE — BLADE — SIDE FENCE — CUT-LINE SIGHT — SOLE PLATE

Mains-powered circular saw

MAINS-POWERED CIRCULAR SAWS

A woodworker turns to a circular saw because he or she wants to be able to rip and crosscut hardwoods, softwoods and man-made boards especially accurately. Consequently, buying a circular-saw attachment for a power drill is a waste of time and money – since the power output of the average electric drill cannot compete with even the smallest purpose-made circular saw, and the attachments are usually so small and flimsy they cannot be relied upon for accurate work. A purpose-made tool capable of more than your present requirements is a much wiser investment, especially if there is a chance you will want to convert it into a table saw by bolting it to an appropriate accessory or workcentre.

CUTTING DEPTH OF TYPICAL BLADES	
Blade diameter	**Cutting depth**
130mm (5in)	40mm ($1\frac{1}{2}$in)
150mm (6in)	46mm ($1\frac{7}{8}$in)
160mm ($6\frac{1}{2}$in)	54mm ($2\frac{1}{8}$in)
190mm ($7\frac{1}{2}$in)	66mm ($2\frac{5}{8}$in)
210mm ($8\frac{1}{2}$in)	75mm (3in)
230mm (9in)	85mm ($3\frac{3}{8}$in)

Dust extraction
A great deal of wood dust is produced by a powerful circular saw. It makes the workshop floor slippery, it's uncomfortable when it gets caught in your clothing and dust-laden air is unhealthy as well as unpleasant. Saws fitted with an exhaust port in the upper guard throw the sawdust sideways. You can either collect the dust in a bag plugged into the port or insert a nozzle connected to a vacuum cleaner.

Tilting blade
By slackening a clamp, the body and blade of the saw can be tilted to any angle up to 45 degrees. The angle can be read on a quadrant scale, but it is worth measuring the angle on a trial cut if the bevel must be exact. The maximum cutting depth of the saw is reduced when the blade is angled.

Safety lock
To prevent the saw being switched on accidentally, it is fitted with a safety lock button which must be depressed with the thumb before the trigger can be operated. Circular saws are not fitted with trigger-lock buttons for continuous running, but manufacturers of table-saw attachments supply clamps or straps to hold the trigger down.

Guards
The upper part of the blade is enclosed by a fixed guard. As the saw advances into the work, the pivoting lower guard is pushed back by the edge of the wood to reveal the blade. When the blade clears the work, the spring-loaded guard snaps back to enclose it again. Before using a circular saw, make sure the pivoting guard operates smoothly.

Anti-locking clutch
Clamping flanges on each side of the blade act as an anti-locking clutch. Should the blade jam suddenly they allow it to slip, protecting the drive mechanism from damage.

Electrical insulation
An all-plastic body enclosing the motor protects the user from electric shock.

Handles
A comfortable ergonomic grip and a secondary handle near the toe of the tool give you positive and safe control over the saw.

Depth of cut
Although a circular saw is often designated by the diameter of its blade, this is not a clear guide to the actual cutting capacity of the blade. The table opposite gives the cutting depth of a typical range of circular-saw blades. At the very least, most woodworkers need a saw that will cut timber 50mm (2in) thick. At the upper end of the range, the size and weight of the tool becomes a consideration. A 230mm (9in) saw, for example, is heavy and tiring to use for prolonged periods. On the other hand, when it is mounted in a workcentre its weight is no longer a disadvantage.

Adjusting the depth of cut
You can adjust the depth of cut by raising or lowering the body of the saw in relation to the sole plate. A scale is provided for reading off the depth of cut, but many woodworkers prefer to use the work itself as a guide. With the pivoting guard withdrawn, lay the sole plate on the work with the blade resting against the edge (1). Release the depth-adjusting clamp and raise or lower the blade until it projects about 3mm ($\frac{1}{8}$in) below the work, then tighten the clamp.

To cut through a piece of wood partially, mark the depth on the side of the work and adjust the blade to coincide with it (2).

1 Blade adjustment to sever work

2 Adjustment for partial cut

2-3mm ($\frac{1}{16}$-$\frac{1}{8}$in)   2-3mm ($\frac{1}{16}$-$\frac{1}{8}$in)

Riving knife
As solid timber is ripped longitudinally, tensions are released within the grain which can cause the kerf to close behind the blade. To prevent a circular-saw blade jamming in the kerf, a metal riving knife is mounted directly behind it. The riving knife should be adjusted to within 2 to 3mm ($\frac{1}{16}$ to $\frac{1}{8}$in) of the blade. Similarly, the tip of the knife should be 2 to 3mm above the lowest saw tooth.

CORDLESS CIRCULAR SAWS

Cordless-tool technology has not yet developed sufficiently to produce a really serviceable circular saw. At present, batteries small enough to be portable do not supply enough torque to drive a large blade through thick timber. Even so, a battery-operated saw is heavier than the equivalent mains-powered version. It is also more expensive. A professional who has to work on a site where there is no mains electricity may have use for a cordless saw, but it offers few advantages to the average woodworker.

Cordless circular saw

CIRCULAR-SAW BLADES

If you want to rip fence posts or crosscut siding, a reasonably cheap saw blade will do the job; but if you want a finish straight from the saw that requires very little planing and sanding, you have to use a top-quality blade. A first-class blade is absolutely essential if the saw is to be mounted in a work-centre for accurate joint cutting.

The PTFE coating on a blade reduces friction – thus increasing the life of the blade itself, lessening the wear on the saw drive mechanism and decreasing the risk of scorching the work.

Tungsten-carbide-tipped teeth produce a better finish and stay sharp ten times longer than standard saw teeth.

The blades shown below are typical woodworking blades. Depending on the size and make of your circular saw, you can also buy special blades for cutting metal, plastic and masonry.

1 Pointed-tooth blade
2 Fine-tooth blade
3 Ripsaw blade
4 Chisel-tooth blade
5 Carbide-tipped blade

Pointed-tooth blade
A multiple-toothed blade suitable for crosscutting solid timber. It leaves a reasonable finish.

Fine-tooth blade
For a fine cut in chipboard and plastic-laminated boards. It cuts relatively slowly.

Ripsaw blade
A blade with large tungsten-carbide-tipped teeth ideal for ripping softwood; it also cuts hardwoods and man-made boards. Having very few teeth, it does not produce a first-class finish.

Chisel-tooth blade
A medium-priced universal saw blade suited to ripping and crosscutting softwoods, hardwoods and man-made boards.

Carbide-tipped universal blade
A top-quality universal saw blade which leaves an extremely fine finish when crosscutting or ripping solid timber and all man-made boards, including laminate-faced materials.

Changing saw blades
Follow the manufacturer's instructions for changing a saw blade, and make sure you replace it with one having the correct bore diameter (the diameter of the hole in the centre). When fitted, ensure the teeth at the bottom of the blade face away from the riving knife. Always have blunt circular-saw blades sharpened by a professional.

USING A CIRCULAR SAW

Since the teeth of a circular-saw travel upwards when they cut timber, any tearing of the grain will be on the upper surface of the work. A good-quality blade will keep tear-out to the minimum, but as a precaution turn the work 'good' side down.

Support the work carefully, either clamped to overhang a bench or, better still, on sawhorses. To avoid having to move sawhorses when making a long through cut, nail battens to the top of them. You can make one continuous pass with the saw without cutting into the sawhorses, but make sure the nails are placed well away from the line of cut.

Cutting freehand
Circular saws are made with a small notch in the sole plate to act as a sight when cutting freehand. Make a few trial cuts to discover the relationship between the sight and the kerf left by the saw. When cutting freehand, keep safely on the waste side of the line. On some saws a second sight is provided to act as a guide when cutting a 45-degree bevel.

Hold the tool in both hands and rest the front section of the sole plate on the work, with the sight aligned with the cut line. Switch on, and advance the saw steadily into the work. At the end of the cut, let the guard close, switch off, and let the blade come to rest before laying the saw aside.

Align the sole-plate sight with a marked line for a freehand cut

Ripping parallel to an edge
All circular saws are supplied with a rip fence which guides the blade to cut a parallel-sided strip from the edge of a piece of wood or board. A well-made fence is sturdy, with a positive mounting and clamp which hold it perfectly parallel to the blade. It can be fitted to either side of the saw, and on a large circular saw you can screw a hardwood strip to extend the length of the fence.

Use the scale on the fence arm to set the fence, then make a trial cut to check the measurement. When ripping, cut at a steady rate, keeping the fence pressed against the edge of the work throughout.

Keep a circular-saw fence pressed against the edge of the work

Ripping with a guide batten

When you need to cut a parallel strip which is too wide for the rip fence, clamp or temporarily nail a straight batten to the work to guide the edge of the sole plate. Keep the plate pressed against the batten during the cut.

Ripping against a guide batten

Grooving and rebating

Cutting a groove or rebate with a portable saw is a laborious but accurate process. Set the fence to cut the two sides of a groove (1) or the inner edge of a rebate (2). Reset the fence to remove the waste gradually by making successive passes with the saw (3 and 4).

1 Cut both sides of a groove

2 Or make one cut for a rebate

3 Remove the waste in sections

4 Do the same for a rebate

Crosscutting

Square and angled crosscuts (1) are made by clamping a guide batten to the work.

To cut a number of boards to the same length, nail a stop batten to the bench and butt the squared ends of the boards against it, with their uncut ends overhanging the edge of the bench. Clamp a guide batten across all the boards (2) and trim them all with one pass of the saw.

1 Making an angled crosscut

2 Crosscutting several boards

Making a crosscutting T-square

You can make a permanent guide for crosscutting by gluing and screwing two stout battens together in the form of a letter 'T' (1). Hold this T-square against a scrap board and run the sole plate of the saw against the crosspiece to trim the end off the 'stock' (2). Aligning the trimmed end with a marked line (3) automatically sets up the blade to make the cut on the waste side of the line. Stick a strip of coarse abrasive paper to the underside of the crosspiece to increase its grip on the work – but if you still can't hold the T-square steady with one hand, clamp it in place.

1 Form a letter T

2 Trim the stock

3 Align the stock with cut line

TABLE-SAW CONVERSIONS

Most manufacturers supply a bench to convert their portable circular saws into table saws. The saw is bolted upside down to the underside of the bench, with its blade protruding through the table top.

In theory, a table saw has certain advantages. It leaves both hands free to control the work; it should have better guides and fences; and you can use a large, heavy saw safely and without getting tired. Unfortunately, however, most bench conversions are much too small to be practical and, unless they are supplied with extension arms, there is no possibility of passing man-made boards across them. Moreover, the guides and fences are often flimsy or will not slide smoothly; and the guards are sometimes inadequate or so clumsy that the user is tempted to remove them.

Any table saw must have a strong, stable underframe and an accessible on/off switch. Pulling away a saw-trigger clip with a length of string is not an adequate substitute for switching off in an emergency.

A serious woodworker would be better advised to spend a little extra to purchase a good-quality work-centre, which will not only serve as an excellent table-saw base but will also convert to a spindle moulder or shaper table by swapping the saw for a router.

Never clamp a circular saw upside down on a bench or fix the handgrip in a bench vice in an attempt to use it as a makeshift table saw. If the blade jams or the user slips while passing a length of wood across the saw, the tool could be wrenched off the bench.

● **Storing blades**
Preserve non-PTFE-coated blades with a light coating of acid-free grease or oil when in long-term storage, and clean them before using again.

BISCUIT JOINTERS

A biscuit jointer is a specialized miniature plunge saw developed to make a form of tongue and groove joint for cabinet construction. The joint works like a dowel joint but, instead of a round peg in a hole bored in the wood, a flat oval plate or 'biscuit' of compressed beech fits into a slot cut by a circular-saw blade. When water-based PVA glue is introduced to the joint, the wooden plate expands to fill the slot and forms an extremely strong bond. Round dowel holes need to be perfectly aligned if the two joint components are to fit snugly. With a biscuit joint, however, slight lateral adjustment is possible by tapping one component sideways.

The biscuit jointer can also be used to cut grooves for drawer bottoms or to trim wall cladding, panelling or floorboards.

Depth of cut
A biscuit jointer has a variable depth of cut, from 0 to about 22mm ($\frac{7}{8}$in). The depth scale should be marked with the dimensions required to accommodate standard-size biscuits. If you are trimming the edge of a piece of wood, adjust the blade depth until the teeth just break through the underside surface.

Plunge action
Depending on the model, a biscuit-jointer blade is lowered into the work by pivoting or pressing down upon the spring-loaded motor housing.

Guide fence
To guide the blade parallel to a straight edge, the biscuit jointer is fitted with an adjustable fence. Some jointers are supplied with an additional bevel fence for cutting a groove in a 45-degree mitre joint.

Cutting guide
A notch or line cut in the base or fence indicates the centre of a plunge-cut slot for jointing.

Dust extraction
Sawdust can be extracted into a collecting bag or into a vacuum cleaner.

Secondary handle
The motor housing acts as the main handgrip, but a biscuit jointer comes with one or sometimes two secondary handles for convenient control of the tool.

On/off switch
The on/off switch will be situated on the motor housing, either underneath for operation by the index finger or on top for the thumb.

● No-load speed
Because the blades are so small, biscuit jointers run at up to 10,000rpm to drive the saw teeth at a sufficient speed to produce a clean, accurate cut.

BLADES

Biscuit jointers are fitted with miniature 100 to 105mm (4 to 4$\frac{1}{4}$in) diameter circular-saw blades with tungsten-carbide-tipped teeth. Jointing and grooving blades cut a 4mm ($\frac{5}{32}$in) slot, and slimmer blades are available for trimming wood to length.

BISCUITS

Compressed-beech biscuits are manufactured in three sizes: for board thicknesses of 6 to 12mm ($\frac{1}{4}$ to $\frac{1}{2}$in); 13 to 18mm ($\frac{1}{2}$ to $\frac{3}{4}$in); and 19mm ($\frac{3}{4}$in) and over. Barbed plastic biscuits are available for test assemblies.

MOTOR HOUSING

BLADE GUARD

DEPTH SCALE

SAWDUST-EXHAUST PORT

GUIDE FENCE

CUTTING-DEPTH ADJUSTER

MOTOR-HOUSING RETURN SPRING

SECONDARY HANDLE

Biscuit jointer

Jointing methods

CUTTING BISCUIT JOINTS

Biscuit jointing is perfectly suitable for cabinet or frame construction using man-made boards and solid timber with butt, mitre or edge-to-edge joints.

Making a butt joint

Having drawn the centre line of the joint on the work, mark along it the central points of the biscuit slots, spaced about 100mm (4in) apart. Set the cutting depth to suit the biscuits you are using and adjust the guide fence to align the blade with the centre line.

Align the cutting guide with the central point of each slot, press the fence against the edge of the work and plunge the blade to make the cut **(1)**.

To cut a slot in the edge of a matching component, place the work on a flat surface and lay the jointer on its side **(2)**. Edge-to-edge joints are cut in the same way.

To cut slots across the central part of a board, hold the matching component on edge and draw a line along one side. Tip the component to that side and align it with the marked line. Use the component as a fence to plunge the slots across the board **(3)**; then, without moving the matching component, cut slots in its edge as described above.

Cutting a mitre joint

If the biscuit jointer is supplied with a bevel fence, you can cut slots for a mitre joint with the workpiece laid flat on a bench **(1)**.

If the jointer has a right-angle fence only, clamp the work with the joint overhanging a bench and run the fence along the outer edge of the bevel **(2)**.

Cutting a groove

To cut a continuous groove, adjust the jointer as for cutting a butt joint. Place the tool at one end of the work, switch on, and plunge the saw. Feed the tool to the end of the groove, raise the blade and then switch off.

1 Plunge blade to cut each slot

2 Slotting matching components

3 Cutting slots across a board

1 Using a jointer with a bevel fence

2 Jointing a mitre with a standard fence

Cutting guide in fence indicates centre of slot

Compressed-beech biscuits

Wood-trimming blade

Jointing blade

USING A BISCUIT JOINTER SAFELY

Follow the usual safety procedures recommended for power tools. In addition:

- Do not plunge a blade into the wood until the motor is running.
- Use sharp blades only and discard any that are cracked or bent.
- Do not apply side pressure to a spinning blade in order to slow it down or bring it to a stop.
- Never run the tool with the blade guard removed.
- When cutting a groove, feed the jointer at a steady rate away from you against the rotation of the blade.

BLADE ROTATION

Cutting a groove   DIRECTION OF FEED

PORTABLE PLANERS

A portable planer is not the tool for very precise work. However, it is excellent for quickly planing a baulk of timber to size ready for skimming with a bench plane. It is also a boon for joinery work, such as *relieving the bottom of a door to clear a fitted carpet or planing a bevelled rebate on a window sill. When mounted in a special-purpose bench stand, it makes a passable surface planer or jointer.*

● **Motor size**
Motor size varies a great deal from planer to planer, but a no-load speed of 12,000 to 14,000rpm is average.

Rebating depth
A depth gauge fitted to the body of the tool determines the maximum depth of a rebate cut by the planer. The smallest planers will rebate no deeper than 8mm ($\frac{5}{16}$in), but the maximum rebate depth for most planers is between 20 and 25mm (between $\frac{3}{4}$ and 1in). A side fence regulates the width of the rebate.

HANDGRIP

TRIGGER-LOCK BUTTON

TRIGGER

SLIDER TO RETRACT GUARD

DRIVE-BELT CASING

EXHAUST PORT

SECONDARY HANDLE

CUTTING-DEPTH DIAL

REBATE DEPTH GAUGE

INFEED SOLE

ANGLE INDICATOR

SIDE FENCE

Portable electric planer

Cutting depth
Small planers will remove from 0 to 1mm (0 to $\frac{1}{32}$in) in one pass, and larger models have a maximum cutting depth of 2mm ($\frac{1}{16}$in). Professional-range planers will plane up to 3mm ($\frac{1}{8}$in) deep, but they cost 50 per cent more than the average planer and the extra cutting depth alone is not worth the cost.
Cutting depth is selected by raising or lowering the front or infeed section of the sole. At a zero setting both sections of the sole are flush. Choose a planer fitted with an adjusting dial or knob which operates smoothly and indicates the depth setting clearly.

Planing width
The width of a planer sole matches the length of the cutters exactly. The majority of planers are 82mm ($3\frac{1}{4}$in) wide.

Secondary handle
A secondary handle placed over the toe of a planer helps to control the tool and keep the infeed section of the sole flat on the work.

Dust extraction
Power planers throw out so many shavings that it is worth fitting a collecting bag to the exhaust port, or attaching a vacuum-cleaner hose when the tool is clamped upside down as a jointer.

BEVEL-CUTTING GROOVE

Cutter-block guard
A retractable guard protects the user and the cutter block.

Cutter-block guard
Choose a planer with a guard that completely covers the cutters until it is pushed back by the wood to reveal the revolving cutter block as the planer is advanced into the work. It protects not only the user but also the cutters from damage should the planer be laid on the bench before the cutter block stops spinning. The guard can be withdrawn manually for cutter changing by operating a slider on the body of the tool.

Bevel-cutting groove
The 'V' groove machined along the centre of the infeed sole locates the planer on the 90-degree corner of a piece of wood to guide the tool when planing a bevel. A side fence with a face that adjusts for any angle from 90 to 45 degrees helps to keep the tool at the required angle as the bevel widens.

Electrical insulation
Choose a double-insulated planer with a plastic casing.

Trigger lock
The on/off switch or trigger can be locked for continuous running by depressing a button on the hand grip.

PLANER CUTTERS

The cylindrical cutter block holds a balanced pair of cutters or blades. There are three types of cutter, all double-sided.

Straight cutter
A general-purpose tungsten-carbide straight-edged cutter.

Straight cutter with rounded corners
For planing a surface wider than the planer. The rounded corners do not leave steps in the wood.

Wavy-edge cutter
Designed to leave a 'tooled' surface on 'rustic' joinery.

POWER PLANING

Whenever possible, plane in the direction of the grain. If the grain is 'wild', adjust the planer to take a finer cut. For the best finish, make two or three passes with a finely set plane rather than remove the same amount of wood in one go.

Place the infeed sole on the work, with the cutter block clear of the wood. Press down on the tool with the secondary handle, lining up the planer with the work. Switch on and advance the planer at a steady rate. At the end of the pass transfer pressure from the secondary handle to the rear of the planer, so that the tool does not 'dip' and take a deep scoop out of the end of the work. To correct a mistake of this kind, set the planer for a fine cut and carefully plane the wood below the level of the damage.

Check the work with a try square. Some woodworkers find that the side fence helps them to keep the planer square to the work.

To flatten a wide board, plane diagonally across the work in two directions, overlapping the passes each time. Finally, plane parallel with the long edges.

Planing a rebate
Adjust the side fence and depth gauge to the rebate dimensions (1). Plane to the required depth, keeping the fence pressed against the work throughout.

To plane a bevelled rebate, proceed as above but set the angle indicator to tilt the planer. It is vital to keep side pressure on the planer when bevelling, so that the tool does not keep on sliding down the slope (2).

Converting to a jointer
When a portable planer is bench-mounted upside down, work can be passed across it using both hands. With the side fence attached, it is possible to plane square shoulders on the work – but portable planers, unlike purpose-made jointers or surface planers, are not usually long enough to guarantee a perfectly straight edge on a long board.

If you buy a portable planer specifically for bench-mounting, examine the way the cutters are guarded before you make your final choice. Ideally, choose a planer already fitted with a retractable guard, so that the cutter block is covered until the work is pushed across the tool. Also, make sure that when the side fence is adjusted to leave just enough sole to accommodate the width of the work, an unguarded section of cutter block will never be exposed except to the work itself.

Planers without integral guards are supplied with a spring-loaded guard as part of the bench stand. This guard is pushed aside as the work is passed across the planer. However, check that when the side fence is fitted it does not hold the guard open, partly exposing the cutters.

Changing planer cutters
A good planer is designed to make changing the cutters as easy as possible. A cutter should be replaced when both sides are blunt. The usual practice is to slide the new cutter into the machined groove in the cutter block (1), then use a strip of wood to align the end of the cutter with the edge of the sole (2). Tightening two or three screws clamps the blade in the groove.

1 Fit cutter in block

2 Align cutter with sole

DEPTH-GAUGE SETTING

SIDE-FENCE SETTING

1 Planing a rebate

2 Planing a bevelled rebate

ADJUST TO WIDTH OF WORK

SIDE FENCE

RETRACTABLE GUARD

A bench-mounted planer

Some guards are pushed aside by the work

POWER ROUTERS

The power router has taken the place of a whole family of moulding, grooving and rebating planes. Unlike many other power tools, it can be fitted with a cutter and adjusted ready for use in about the same time as it takes to prepare a handtool for the same kind of job. With a powerful motor driving a cutter at high speed, the finished results are precise and professional in appearance. In principle, all routers are constructed similarly. A cutter is mounted directly below a motor housing fitted with a handle on each side, and the whole assembly sits on a roughly circular base through which the cutter protrudes. The main difference between routers lies in the way the cutter is fed into the work to cut a stopped groove or a housing. There are fixed routers which are suspended above and lowered into the work as one unit. Plunging routers are made with the motor housing mounted above the base on spring-loaded columns. When the base rests on the work, downward pressure on the handles feeds the cutter into the wood.

● **Lightweight plastic body**
Modern routers have a lightweight plastic motor housing which insulates the user from contact with live components.

Collet capacity
The shank of a router cutter fits into a tapered collet secured by a lock nut. Collet sizes are usually 6 or 8mm ($\frac{1}{4}$ or $\frac{3}{8}$in), but larger routers have a collet capacity of 12mm ($\frac{1}{2}$in). Some routers can be fitted with interchangeable collets of different sizes. Collet capacity is not the same as cutter diameter, which varies considerably according to its shape and function.

Handgrips
A fixed router has two large ergonomic handles for steering the tool along the intended path. On a plunging router, one of these handles acts as the plunge lock. A short anti-clockwise turn releases the mechanism, the router is then lowered to the required depth and the handle is tightened to lock the tool. At the end of the operation, the plunge lock is released to allow the router to rise automatically.

Electronic feedback
Some top-of-the-range routers are made with an electronic feedback system which prevents a drop in speed when the tool is under load by feeding more power to the cutter. In addition, optimum speed can be selected to suit the size of cutter or type of operation. Reducing the speed, for example, increases the life of an expensive large-diameter cutter and reduces the risk of scorching the wood when doing intricate routing freehand.

On/off switch
Ideally the on/off switch should be in reach without having to release your grip on the handles.

Base
It is an advantage if the base has a non-stick surface so that the tool slides smoothly across the work.

DEMOUNTABLE PLASTIC BODY

ON/OFF SWITCH

DEPTH STOP

FIXED HANDGRIP

PLUNGE-LOCK HANDLE

BODY CLAMP

COLLET

CUTTER

DEPTH SCALE

SPRING-LOADED COLUMN

SIDE-FENCE CLAMPS

Plunge router

Depth of cut
In theory, it is possible to cut a groove to the limit of the length of the cutting edges on a chosen cutter. However, deep grooves should be cut in stages, especially in hardwoods and with large cutters, in order to produce a clean finish and avoid overheating the motor. A narrow 6mm (¼in) cutter, for example, will cut a groove 6mm (¼in) deep in one pass, but a groove of the same depth should be cut in two equal stages when using a wide 19mm (¾in) cutter.

A depth stop fitted to all plunging routers limits the downward movement of the motor housing, thus controlling the depth of cut. Some machines are made with a means of setting the depth stop to two or three progressive stages for routing deep grooves, but the depth of any plunging router can be fixed partway by operating the plunge-lock handle mounted on the side of the tool.

Choose a model with a clear and precise depth scale, and check that the plunge mechanism operates efficiently and smoothly.

Progressive depth cutting with a fixed router involves switching off and resetting the depth of the cutter for each stage.

Motor size and speed
The great majority of routers have a fixed no-load speed, which can be anything between 22,000 and 27,000rpm. Except in special circumstances, a high speed of around 26,000rpm is required to produce a clean finish – especially as the speed drops considerably as soon as a cutter encounters hard wood. Motor size varies a great deal from router to router, but the larger ones will maintain a high cutting speed without strain. A motor with a power input of less than 450W will be hard-pressed to produce a satisfactory finish.

USING ROUTERS SAFELY

Very few accidents occur with routers provided sensible precautions are taken. Plunging routers are especially safe to use because the cutter is withdrawn into a comparatively shielded position between the support columns.

The following tips are specific to routers but general power-tool safety practice is also applicable.

● Advance a router steadily into the work using light pressure only.
● Always operate a router with both hands.
● Withdraw a plunging-router cutter after every operation and before switching off.
● Make sure the cutter has stopped spinning before laying a fixed router aside.

RISE-AND-FALL MOTOR HOUSING
ON/OFF SAFETY SWITCH
DEPTH MARKER
TRIGGER-LOCK BUTTON
TRIGGER
MAIN HANDGRIP
DEPTH SCALE
DEPTH-ADJUSTMENT CLAMP
SECONDARY HANDLE
BASE
CUTTER

Fixed router

141

ROUTER CUTTERS

Pressed-steel cutter

High-speed steel cutter

Tungsten-carbide-tipped cutter

High-speed-steel router cutters are more than adequate for the average woodworker, but tungsten-carbide-tipped cutters stay sharp longer especially when routing chipboard or plastic-laminated materials. You can hone the cutting edges of high-speed-steel cutters with an oiled slipstone until they eventually need to be resharpened by a professional. But take care to avoid overheating high-speed-steel cutters, which turns them blue so they lose temper and become so soft that they have to be replaced. Tungsten-carbide-tipped cutters can only be sharpened by a company with a specialized grinding machine.

There is a range of cheap pressed-steel cutters which, although they cannot compare with high-speed-steel cutters in quality, will allow you to experiment with different types of cutter without having to spend a great deal of money. They are also useful for the amateur woodworker who wants to cut a particular moulding once only and does not need a cutter that will have to perform for a whole production run.

GROOVE-FORMING CUTTERS

Straight cutter · V-grooving cutter · Veining cutter · Core-box cutter · Dovetail cutter

The following basic router cutters can make recesses both with and across the grain:

Straight cutter
Cuts square-section grooves and housings. You can buy straight cutters with either single-fluted or double-fluted cutting edges. The double-fluted variety leaves a better finish.

V- grooving cutter
Used mainly for freehand lettering or engraving for signs and wall plaques.

Veining cutter
For narrow round-bottomed grooves.

Core-box cutter
For wider round-bottomed grooves.

Dovetail cutter
For cutting dovetail joints with the appropriate accessory and for dovetail housings.

EDGE-FORMING CUTTERS

Cove cutter · Rebate cutter · Roman-ogee cutter

● **Plunge-cut router cutters**
If you intend to plunge-cut with a router cutter larger than 9mm (³⁄₈in) in diameter, make sure it has a cutting edge that extends right across its base.

Edge-forming cutters are made with a pilot tip which rides against the edge of the work, making a guide or fence unnecessary. Fixed pilot tips can burn the wood due to friction, but in normal circumstances skimming the edge with a finely set plane removes the blemish. However, this can be uneconomical in commercial production and special ball-bearing-tipped cutters are made to run against the edge without burning.

Trimmer cutter · Rounding-over cutter · Beading cutter · Chamfer cutter

Cove cutter
For a decorative scalloped edge, or for cutting a rule joint for the top of a drop-flap table.

Rebate cutter
Cuts a rebate without having to use a side fence on the router.

Roman-ogee cutter
Produces a specific decorative moulding.

Trimmer cutter
Cutter with ball-bearing pilot for trimming plastic laminates flush with the edge of a board.

Rounding-over cutter
Produces a simple radiused edge. If set lower, cuts an ovolo bead (a radiused edge with a stepped shoulder).

Beading cutter
Similar to a rounding-over cutter, but it cuts two shoulders on the beading.

Chamfer cutter
Cuts a 45-degree bevel. One cutter makes different-size chamfers, depending on its depth setting.

HONE THIS FACE
HONE THIS FACE

Honing a router cutter
To put a sharp edge on a high-speed-steel cutter, hone the inner faces only. Do not touch the outer faces, which alters the diameter of the cutter.

Fitting a cutter
Before using a spanner to loosen the collet lock nut in order to fit a router cutter, immobilize the spindle connected to the motor.

On some expensive routers the on/off switch is used to lock the spindle, but with most machines you either use a second spanner or a short metal pin passed through a hole in the spindle in order to hold it still (1).

Depending on the design of the router, you may be able to stand the machine upside down on a bench to change a cutter, or it may be easier to remove the motor housing from its base assembly. Whichever method you use, unplug the router first.

If a cutter is jammed in the collet, free it by rocking it gently from side to side, taking care not to injure yourself on the edges.

Before inserting a cutter, make certain the collet is free of wood dust. Once you have inserted it, use a spanner to tighten the collet lock nut, with the spindle immobilized.

1 Loosening the collet nut
A pin is sometimes used to immobilize the router spindle.

ROUTING GROOVES AND HOUSINGS

A true groove runs in the direction of the grain and is used a great deal in woodwork to hold drawer bottoms, the backs of cabinets, edge-to-edge joints and so on.

A housing is a groove which runs across the grain – for joining fixed shelves to the sides of a bookcase, for example. A groove or housing can run through the work from one edge to another, or it may be stopped at one or both ends.

Although a variety of techniques can be employed to ensure the accuracy of the work, the manipulation of the machine remains more or less the same – the only differences depending on whether you are using a fixed or plunging router.

Making a through housing or groove
If you are using a plunging router, lower and lock the mechanism. Rest the base on the work with the cutter clear of the edge and then switch on. Advance the tool into and through the work at a steady rate until the cutter emerges at the other end. Switch off and let the cutter come to rest before lifting the base off the work.

Making a stopped groove or housing
When using a fixed router, switch on and lower the whole machine until the cutter drills a hole in the work a short distance from one stopped end (1). Pull back the router to the nearest end, then advance the tool to the far end and lift the cutter clear of the work (2).

Before switching on a plunging router, lower the cutter to the surface of the work and position it precisely over one end of the groove or housing. Lift the cutter, switch on and plunge the cutter to its maximum depth (3). Advance the tool to the far end, release the plunge mechanism (4) and then switch off.

If necessary, cut the ends of a stopped groove or housing, using a chisel to trim them square.

Cutting a groove parallel with an edge
Most grooves, be they for drawer runners or a plywood back panel, are usually parallel with and quite close to the edge of the work. Manufacturers supply all routers with a bolt-on side fence which can be adjusted to position the cutter the required distance from the edge.

With the tool unplugged, stand the router on the work and align the cutting edge of the cutter with one side of the groove drawn on the surface (1). Adjust the side fence to touch the edge of the work (2), and tighten its clamps.

Cut the groove as described above, keeping side pressure on the fence throughout the operation (3).

You can extend a side fence for greater control by screwing a strip of hardwood onto the face of the fence.

Cutting a through groove
Start with the cutter clear of the wood and switch off at the far end before lifting the router.

1 Plunge and pull back   **2 Advance and lift at end**

3 Plunge to maximum depth   **4 Advance to end and release**

DRAWN LINE MARKS EDGE OF GROOVE

CUTTING EDGE

1 Align cutter   **2 Slide fence up to edge**   **3 Cut the groove**

Cutting a housing using guide battens

Clamp a batten across the work to guide the base when routing a housing across a wide board (1). Choose a batten long enough to project beyond both edges of the work, and keep the router pressed against it.

To cut a housing wider than the cutter, clamp two guide battens to the work parallel with one another and positioned to align the cutter first with one side of the housing then with the other. Always make the first pass against the batten on your right-hand side, then move the router over to cut against the left-hand batten (2). This way the rotation of the cutter helps to pull the router against the batten.

To cut a barefaced dovetail housing, substitute a dovetail cutter for the straight cutter after the first pass (3).

1 Cutting a housing using a guide batten

RIGHT-HAND BATTEN

LEFT-HAND BATTEN

2 Cutting a wide housing

CUT THIS SIDE WITH A STRAIGHT CUTTER

CUT THIS SIDE WITH A DOVETAIL CUTTER

3 Cutting a barefaced dovetail housing

CUTTING MOULDINGS AND REBATES

Solid panels and frames are often moulded for decorative purposes, to lighten their appearance, or to make a safe rounded edge. Rebates are more functional – being used to recess a panel in a frame, for example.

Rebating with a straight cutter

It is possible to cut a rebate with a straight cutter by running a guide fence along the opposite edge of the work. The same method can be used to cut a chamfer with a V-grooving cutter or a cove with a core-box cutter.

Rebating with straight cutter and guide fence

Moulding with edge-forming cutters

Moulding or rebating the edge of a wide panel is achieved by using an edge-forming cutter with a pilot tip. Practise on scrap timber to develop a light touch, which keeps the pilot tip in contact with the work without burning.

Mould the outer edge of a panel in an anti-clockwise direction, to ensure the rotation of the cutter keeps pulling it into the work (1). If the panel is made of solid timber, mould the end grain first then the side grain (2). This ensures that if the cutter tears out the end grain at the far edge of the board, the damage is remedied as the sides of the board are moulded. To mould end grain only, clamp a strip of scrap wood to the far edge to support it.

1 Moulding the edge of a panel

MOULD END GRAIN FIRST

2 Moulding a solid-wood panel

FINISH WITH SIDE GRAIN

144

Moulding or rebating inside a frame

It is sometimes convenient to rebate or mould a picture or mirror frame after the bare frame has been assembled. The outer edge can be moulded as described opposite, and the inner edge rebated using an edge-forming rebate cutter or by screwing a 90-degree triangular block of wood to the side fence (1). It is essential that the apex of the triangle is centred on the cutter (2).

Move the machine on a clockwise path when routing the inside of a frame. The cutter will leave rounded corners – but you can chop them square with a chisel, if you wish.

1 Cutting an internal rebate
Screw a triangular guide block to the router fence.

2 Centre the triangle on the cutter

ROUTING CIRCLES AND SHAPES

Using commercially made guides or home-made jigs and templates, it is possible to cut intricately shaped work and perfect circles, discs and curves.

Cutting circles

With the addition of a centring pin the side fence of most routers can be converted into an adjustable trammel bar for rotating the machine about a central point so you can cut circular grooves or mould the edge of a disc.

The average fence is ideal for detailing small work such as cheese or bread boards. For larger work (for example, to mould the edge of a circular table top) bolt the router to one end of a strip of plywood, cut a hole or slot for the cutter and drive a nail through the strip to act as a centring pin.

Use double-sided adhesive tape to stick a small patch of plywood to the work, to hold the point of the centring pin and avoid leaving a hole in the wood.

Routing with a template

Routing against a template provides a quick and easy means of making identical components – and once you are satisfied with the accuracy of the template, a perfect result is guaranteed every time.

To assist faithful reproduction of the shape of the template, router manufacturers supply template guides for their machines. A template guide is simply a cylindrical collar that surrounds the cutter and is bolted centrally on the base of the router. The collar runs against the edge of the template so that the cutter follows its shape exactly (1). When making a template, you need to allow for the difference between the diameter of the collar and the diameter of the cutter itself (2).

Cut a template from a stable sheet material such as plywood, hardboard or MDF. You can either pin it to the wood or fix it with double-sided tape.

Freehand routing

Signwriters and low-relief carvers use a router to engrave lettering or pictures on a flat piece of wood. A V-grooving cutter is often used for freehand work because even hardwoods offer very little resistance to its pointed tip. Straight or veining cutters are also suitable, but you will need to adjust the router to take a shallow cut only. Since a free-flowing action is essential, choose a style of lettering that allows you to keep the router on the move. Regular lettering is best cut with a template.

A plunging router is much better than a fixed machine for freehand work; to be able to lift and replace the cutter effortlessly is a considerable advantage.

Cutting a circle using the fence as a trammel bar

2 Allow for the diameter of the collar

1 Routing against a template

Cut free-flowing lines for freehand work

CUTTING JOINTS WITH A ROUTER

Cutting joints is a lot easier if you convert a router into a shaper or spindle moulder by bolting it upside down in a workcentre. However, it is possible to cut a number of joints with a hand- *held router by using a combination of techniques described in the sections on routing grooves and housings and cutting mouldings and rebates.*

Rebated and grooved joints

Lap joints, barefaced housings and halving joints are all variations on a basic theme. By clamping several components together flat on a bench you can cut any one of these joints, using a straight cutter in a router run against a guide batten.

Lap joint

Cutting a dovetailed tongue

Dovetail housing joints

Cutting a dovetail housing joint by hand is a long, difficult process, whereas cutting both components with a router and a dovetail cutter is extremely simple.

Cut the housing against a guide batten, then clamp the mating component between two pieces of scrap timber. Use a side fence to guide the cutter along both sides of the component to leave a dovetailed tongue which matches the housing exactly.

Tongue and groove joints

Use a straight cutter to rout a square tongue on the edge of a board, following the method described above for making a dovetailed tongue. Cut a matching groove down the centre of the other component, using a wooden strip clamped to both sides to provide a wide flush surface to support the base of the router.

Barefaced housing

Halving joint

Cutting a centred groove

Mortise and tenon joints

A mortise is no more than a short groove and is cut as described above but, being a stopped groove, it is much easier to achieve with a plunging router. When lowering a fixed router onto the work and removing it from the finished mortise, it is all too easy to damage the sides of the joint.

To make matching tenons, lay the components side by side and cut all the shoulders simultaneously, using a clamped batten to guide the router (1). Remove the rest of the waste, working with the router freehand. Turn all the components over, butt the newly cut shoulders against a stop batten nailed to the bench (2) and repeat the process to complete the tenons.

Dovetail housing

1 Cut the first set of shoulders

Tongue and groove

STOP BATTEN

2 Butt them against a stop batten

Mortise and tenon

Rule joints

A rule joint is the traditional way to join the folding flaps to the top of a gate-leg table. It supports the edge of the flap when it is raised, and hides the special table hinges when folded. The knuckles of the hinges must be set directly below the shoulder of the joint. Mould the edges with matching rounding-over and core-box cutters.

Rule joint   **Align hinge knuckle with shoulder**

Dovetail joints

Special templates and matching template guides are made for cutting dovetails with hand-held routers. Most of them cut lapped dovetails only. Although a machine-cut dovetail may not be as attractive as one made by hand, it is just as strong and very much faster to make. Detailed instructions for assembling jigs are supplied by the manufacturers, but basically the two matching components are clamped together in the jig, slightly offset and inside out (1). Design the width of the components so that the dovetails and pins are centred on each piece of wood.

Fit a dovetail cutter in the router and guide it in and out of the template fingers (2). Remove the components and turn them the right way round (3) ready for assembly.

1 Clamp components slightly offset and inside out

2 Cut the joint with a router   **3 Assemble the joint**

POWER SANDERS

Power sanders take most of the effort out of finishing timber, but even the orbital machines – the so-called 'finishing sanders' – will not produce a surface that a craftsman would consider ready for polishing or varnishing. A period of hand sanding is necessary to remove minute scratches left by the machines.

HANDGRIP

TRIGGER

SANDING BELTS

DUST-EXHAUST PORT

BOSCH
PBS 60

TRACKING-ADJUSTMENT KNOB

SECONDARY HANDLE

Belt sander

BELT-TENSION RELEASE LEVER

BELT

ROLLER

BELT SANDERS

These have a continuous belt of abrasive-covered cloth held taut between two rollers. A flat bed or 'platten' mounted between the rollers holds the paper against the work. The motor drives the rear roller only, but the front roller is adjustable to control the tension and tracking of the belt. Belt sanders remove timber very quickly and are used to sand large areas of wood and man-made boards. They are also used to finish metal and to remove old paintwork.

Belt size
Belt sanders are specified according to the size of the abrasive belt. A small light-weight machine will have a belt about 60mm (2⅜in) wide and 400mm (1ft 4in) long. Larger machines have belt sizes of 75 × 533mm (3in × 1ft 9in) and 100 × 620mm (4in × 2ft). Large belt sanders are heavy and can be tiring to use for pro-longed periods.

Belt speed
Most sanders have a 'no-load' speed of between 180 and 380m per minute (585 and 1235ft per minute). Variable-speed models can be set as low as 150m per minute (487ft per minute) for heat-sensitive materials, such as paint, and can be adjusted to high speeds for timber and boards.

Belt replacement
Changing the belt is a simple process on most machines. The tension is released by pulling a lever on the side of the sander; then, having removed the old belt, the new one is slipped over both rollers. The arrows printed on the belt must point in the same direction as those on the sander housing, since the joint on the belt will start to open up if it is fitted the wrong way round. The new belt is tensioned by pushing back the lever.

With the sander running, the tracking-adjustment knob is used to move the belt sideways until it is centred on the rollers and covers the platten.

Dust extraction
All belt sanders are supplied with a dust-collecting bag. This is an essential safe-guard when sanding wood, but the bag must be re-moved when finishing metal, to avoid the risk of fire caused by sparks.

Electrical insulation
Choose a sander with a plastic body that insulates the user from electric shock.

Continuous running and on/off trigger
The on/off trigger can be locked for continuous run-ning by pressing a button on the handgrip.

Secondary handle
It would be difficult to lower or lift the sander from the wood without the use of a secondary handle on the front of the machine. How-ever, it is convenient if the secondary handle can be removed for sanding up to an obstruction.

Sanding frame
On some machines it is possible to fit an adjustable sanding frame surrounding the belt. This limits the depth of cut, which makes for accurate sanding over a large surface and protects thin veneers.

SANDING BELTS

Use a coarse-grade belt on rough work, following up with a medium-grade and finally a fine-grade belt to remove the scratches left by the previous grade.

A torn, clogged or worn belt will damage the work and should be changed as soon as practicable.

Bench-mounted belt sanders

1 Sanding long edges

2 End-grain sanding

3 Shaping with a belt sander

A typical range of sanding-belt grades	
Grit 40	Very coarse
Grit 60	Coarse
Grit 80	Medium
Grit 100	Medium
Grit 150	Fine
Grit 240	Very fine

Using a belt sander

Switch on and lower the machine onto the work. As soon as the abrasive touches the surface, move the sander forwards; if you hold it in one place, it will leave deep scratches in the wood that may prove difficult to remove. Sand with the grain, in parallel overlapping strokes. To remove paint or smooth very rough wood, sand across the grain at 45 degrees in two directions, then finish parallel with the grain.

Take care to keep the machine flat on the work as you sand up to the edges of a board. It is very easy to round over the edges. With veneered board in particular, it is worth pinning narrow softwood battens around the edges, flush with the surface, to make sure you do not sand the edges through to the core.

Lift the machine off the work before you switch off.

Fixed applications

Belt sanders can be clamped to a bench in various positions. Clamped upside down with an optional fence (**1**), the tool can be used to sand long square or bevelled faces. Stood on end, it can sand end grain (**2**); and laid on its side, it can be used for shaping work (**3**).

ORBITAL SANDERS

On an orbital sander a strip of abrasive paper is stretched across a foam-rubber pad which covers the entire baseplate of the machine. An electric motor drives the plate with a continuous tight elliptical motion. A few machines are made to switch to a straight reciprocal stroke to remove the swirls of fine scratches left on the surface by this orbital motion. Other sanders are made with a random orbital action which breaks up the regular pattern of scratches, making them less noticeable. Sanding attachments for power drills are clumsy tools which lack many of the features built into more sophisticated purpose-made machines.

Sanding-sheet size

Although strips of abrasive paper are made specifically to fit sanding machines, they are based on a proportion of the standard-size sheet used for sanding by hand. The larger machines are known as $\frac{1}{2}$ or $\frac{1}{3}$ sheet sanders, with actual sanding areas of 260sq cm (40sq in) and 167sq cm (29sq in) respectively. Small palm-grip models are made as $\frac{1}{4}$ sheet sanders, with a sanding area of 110sq cm (17sq in).

Sanding rate

The sanding rate of an orbital sander is specified in orbits per minute. A fixed rate of about 20,000 to 25,000 opm is normal, although there are variable-speed sanders that can be adjusted to rates as low as 6000 opm for working on heat-sensitive plastics and paintwork. Sanding rates can be pre-selected, or varied by the amount of pressure applied to the trigger. If you intend to use a sander for woodwork only, a variable-speed model has limited advantages.

Tool weight

Even $\frac{1}{3}$ sheet sanders are relatively lightweight – and the palm-grip machines designed to be operated with one hand, which weigh about 1kg (2lbs) only, are exceptionally easy to use.

1/2 sanding sheets

Secondary handle

The secondary handle fitted to some of the larger orbital sanders is not really necessary. Placing the palm of your free hand on top of the motor housing gives sufficient control and adds more than enough weight.

Trigger lock

All orbital sanders are made with a trigger lock for continuous running.

Dust extraction
The better orbital sanders are made with integral dust-extraction systems. Ducts and channels in the baseplate suck dust from around the edge of the machine and deposit it in a dust-collecting bag. Some manufacturers supply a dust shroud that surrounds the baseplate for connection to a vacuum cleaner. Other models can be connected to a vacuum cleaner via a hose attachment in place of the dust-collecting bag.

Electrical insulation
Plastic bodies not only make for lightweight sanding machines but also insulate the user from live electrical components.

ORBITAL DISC SANDER

When a sanding disc moves eccentrically while simultaneously rotating, the surface of the wood is left virtually scratch-free. The rubber backing pad on this type of sander is flexible enough to cope with concave and convex surfaces.

Keep the tool moving while sanding a workpiece.

SECONDARY HANDLE

MOTOR HOUSING

BOSCH

Hubzahl/Stroke rate/Oscillations 1/min. 20 000
Schleifblatt/Paper size/Surface mm 115 × 280
Für Trocken- und Naßschliff. Holz, Kunststoff, Metall.
For dry- and wet sanding. Wood, plastics, metal.
Pour ponçage à sec et à l'eau. Bois matière, plastique, métal.

TRIGGER-LOCK BUTTON

TRIGGER

HANDGRIP

Orbital sander

PAPER-CLAMP RELEASE LEVER

HANDGRIP

PAPER-CLAMP RELEASE LEVER

ON/OFF SWITCH

FOAM-RUBBER PAD

1/4 sanding sheets

PAPER CLAMP

Palm-grip sander

149

SANDING SHEETS

Sanding sheets, regardless of size, are made in a range of grades which are used in sequence from coarse to fine.

Change to a finer paper as soon as the scratches left by the previous grade disappear. Coarse grades are suitable for sanding sawn softwood and other rough work. Medium to fine grades produce a good finish ready for a light hand sanding. On thin veneers use very fine grades only.

Abrasive grit is packed closely together on 'closed-coat' paper for fast general-purpose sanding. 'Open-coat' papers have widely-spaced grit for sanding resinous softwoods which would clog other papers very quickly.

Some sheets are ready-perforated to increase the efficiency of dust extraction. Alternatively, special-purpose templates are available to punch holes in standard sheets of abrasive paper.

Usually sheets are held by a clamp at each end of the baseplate, but there are also self-adhesive strips which stick onto the baseplate pad.

Cordless sanders
Professional-range cordless sanders work just as efficiently as mains-powered machines and weigh little more. But they are so expensive that they are only worth considering if there is no possibility of working near a supply of electricity.

A typical range of sanding-sheet grades	
Grit 40	Very coarse
Grit 50	Very coarse
Grit 60	Coarse
Grit 80	Coarse
Grit 100	Medium
Grit 120	Medium
Grit 150	Fine
Grit 180	Fine
Grit 240	Very fine
Grit 280	Very fine
Grit 320	Very fine
Grit 400	Very fine

Using an orbital sander

Keep an orbital sander moving up and down the work in overlapping parallel strokes. When using coarse grades of paper, take care not to round over the edges of the work or sand through veneers. There is no need to apply excessive pressure to the sander – the weight of the tool is in itself usually sufficient to sand the work efficiently.

Finishing with an orbital sander
Sand lightly with overlapping parallel strokes.

Using a palm-grip sander
This type of sander is light enough to be used overhead.

SAFETY AND SANDING

Provided the user follows the basic safety procedures recommended for power tools, an orbital sander is perfectly safe to operate.

- Wear safety goggles and a lightweight face mask when sanding overhead.
- Always unplug a sander before changing paper.

DISC SANDERS

Flexible-disc sanders made to fit into the chuck of a power drill are often used for sanding floors and old paintwork – but they leave deep cross-grain scratches and so are unsuitable for serious woodwork. A bench-mounted rigid-disc sander, on the other hand, is a useful tool in any workshop.

POWER DRILL

ABRASIVE-PAPER DISC

FENCE

SUPPORT TABLE

BENCH-CLAMPING SCREWS

Bench-mounted sander

A bench-mounted sander is a power-drill accessory used for sanding end grain and for shaping wooden components. It has a rigid metal sanding plate to which you glue abrasive-paper discs. A support table adjustable from horizontal to 45 degrees is bolted across the plate. With the work resting on the table you can shape work freehand (1). An adjustable fence that slides across the support table is used for accurately sanding square or bevelled end grain (2).

Use the 'down' side of the disc only – so that the work is driven onto the support table by the rotation of the machine. Keep the work moving and, to avoid burning it, refrain from applying excessive pressure.

1 Freehand sanding
Rotate the work on the table as you lightly press it against the sanding disc.

2 Using a fence
Accurately finish square or angled ends with the fence locked at the required angle.

WORKCENTRES

Power-tool manufacturers offer various accessories for converting portable circular saws, routers and jigsaws into bench-mounted tools, but the results rarely live up to the expectations of a serious wood-worker. In many cases the worktable is too small to support man-made boards, and the fences and guides are often short and flimsy. These accessories may be cheap to buy, but they cannot compare with a well-designed workcentre which provides a generous-size saw table or spindle-moulder facility, plus the opportunity to use the tools in the more usual over-head mode for crosscutting wide workpieces.

Workcentres are relatively lightweight and port-able. They incorporate universal mounting plates which accommodate any well-known power saw or router – and most woodworkers find it more efficient to have each tool permanently fixed to its own plate for immediate substitution in the workcentre.

ESSENTIAL FEATURES

When you select a work-centre, make certain it has the following features:

- Strong construction, with a rigid underframe supporting the workcentre at a comfortable work height.
- Generous-sized table, with an optional extension to handle full-size sheets of chipboard, blockboard etc.
- Efficient blade and cutter guards – since unless they work well and adjust easily, the user tends to disregard them. A riving knife fixed behind the blade to keep the saw kerf open is an essential safeguard, too.
- Rigid fences that will not distort as the work is passed over the cutter or blade.
- A sliding crosscut/mitre fence that runs smoothly. It should have a wide face to support the workpiece and should be mounted as close to the blade as practicable, so that overhanging work doesn't bend as it is cut.
- Fences with easy-to-read calibrated scales for accurate settings.
- Easy conversion from table to overhead mode and from one tool to another.
- An accessible on/off switch, since having to reach under the workcentre to unplug or turn off a tool may not be fast enough in an emergency.
- An ample crosscutting facility in the overhead mode for wide man-made boards.
- In the overhead mode power tools must be able to slide smoothly without any sideways movement.
- A workcentre that doubles as an assembly bench is useful in a small workshop.

- Options to fit a jigsaw, face-plate sander, planer or drill stand make for a more versatile workcentre – but they are of only minor consideration compared with circular-saw and router performance.

Workcentre in table-saw mode

Workcentre in overhead mode

THE WORKCENTRE AS A TABLE SAW

Although a good workcentre should be able to take any size of circular saw, you will get the best results if you fit a first-class tool with a 230mm (9in) tungsten-carbide-tipped blade. If the saw is to cut true, there must be no arbor float – that is, a tendency for the blade-mounting shaft to move in and out ever so slightly, causing the blade to wander off line.

Ripsawing
The manufacturer will supply full instructions for assembling a workcentre as a ripsaw. Once assembled, adjust the saw-blade depth so that it just breaks through the surface of the wood, and then lower the blade guard to within 6mm ($\frac{1}{4}$in) of the work. Also, make sure the rip fence is set exactly parallel to the blade. Should the outfeed end of the fence be set closer to the blade than the infeed end, the work will jam and will be flung back towards you by the blade.

When ripping a wide board, keep the work pressed against the fence with one hand while supporting the offcut with the other **(1)**. Push steadily but not too fast, trying to keep the work moving throughout the operation. Don't pause, otherwise slight steps in the cut edge may result.

When the cut is completed, push the work clear of the blade. Never pull back the workpiece or offcut while the blade is moving. Have an assistant help you pass a large board over the table.

When ripping a narrow board, use a notched push stick to pass the wood between the blade and fence **(2)** while holding the work against the fence with a small offcut of man-made board.

Ripping partially dried timber
Stresses within partially dried wood can be released when it is ripped, causing the kerf to spring open. This can force the work sideways against the blade which will jam or throw the wood. As a safeguard, provide a clearance by clamping a block of wood to the rip fence at the infeed end.

1 Ripping a wide board
Keep it pressed against the fence and support the offcut.

2 Ripping a narrow board
Use a push stick to feed the work.

1 Crosscutting using a sliding fence

2 Crosscutting one half of a mitre joint

Crosscutting
Cut work to length by holding it firmly against the face of the sliding fence with one hand while feeding it smoothly with the other **(1)**. A small offcut could be thrown back by the blade or it could get jammed between the blade and the sides of the slot in the table. If you have to remove 5 or 6mm ($\frac{1}{4}$in) of wood or more, do so in two one-blade-width stages. This way the offcut is reduced to sawdust with each cut.

To cut a mitre, set the required angle and follow the same procedure **(2)**.

Cutting joints
By lowering the blade to cut partway through the thickness of the work it is possible to cut tenons, tongues and grooves, rebates and lap joints. Always cut the shoulders first, then remove the waste one blade-width at a time.

TABLE-SAW SAFETY

- Keep fingers clear of the blade and use a push stick whenever necessary.
- Don't lean over a spinning blade to retrieve an offcut or workpiece.
- Make sure both workpiece and offcut are supported throughout the operation.
- Always wear goggles or other eye protection.
- Don't wear loose clothing.
- Remove jewellery, and tie back long hair.
- Work in a tidy, well-lit environment.
- Fit extraction equipment or a dust-collecting bag to a table saw whenever that is possible.
- Unplug the tool after work.
- Always keep unsupervised children away from a workcentre when in use.

THE WORKCENTRE AS AN OVERHEAD SAW

With a circular saw fitted to a workcentre in the overhead mode you can make any of the crosscuts and joints that are possible with a hand-held power saw – but in a fraction of the time, since there is no need to set up guide battens. The overhead-saw mode is especially well-suited to crosscutting and bevelling wide boards.

Crosscutting wide boards

Having mounted the circular saw and adjusted the blade to the required depth, always slide it the full length of its travel to make sure the blade is unimpeded throughout the operation.

Hold the work firmly against the crossfence and feed the saw smoothly and gently until you have severed the wood. Always switch off and allow the blade to stop spinning before pulling the saw back.

Crosscutting a wide board or panel
Hold the work against the fence and feed the saw smoothly.

Multiple crosscuts

To cut several identical workpieces to the same length, align their square-cut ends, tape them together, then crosscut them as described above.

Crosscutting identical pieces
Align their ends and cut them all with one pass of the saw.

Cutting housings and rebates

To cut a housing or rebate across a board, raise the saw to cut partway through the workpiece, then crosscut each shoulder line before removing the waste one blade-width at a time.

If you need to cut a matching housing or rebate across several pieces of wood, tape them together beforehand.

Raise the saw to cut a housing

Cutting bevels

To cut bevels across a workpiece, first place a flat packing piece beneath it to raise it from the worktable. Tilt the saw to 45 degrees, then make one pass with it. The slot cut across the packing piece with the tip of the saw blade serves as a guide to positioning the subsequent workpieces.

Place a flat packing piece beneath a bevel-cut workpiece

PACKING PIECE

WORKPIECE

BEVEL

Kerfing

Kerfing in order to bend a thick piece of wood is particularly easy with an overhead saw. The sawcuts must be spaced evenly; and you need to cut almost through the work, leaving a strip of wood 2 to 6mm ($\frac{1}{16}$ to $\frac{1}{4}$in) thick untouched.

To space the kerfs, first take a batten that is deeper than the workpiece and screw it to the crossfence of the workcentre. Then make a single pass with the saw to cut a notch in the batten, and make a pencil mark on the batten to serve as a guide to the kerfs' spacing **(1)**. After you have made the first kerf in the workpiece, align the cut you have just made with the pencil mark and make the next cut. Repeat this procedure until you have made enough kerfs to bend the wood.

BATTEN

PENCIL MARK

NOTCH

KERFS

WORKPIECE

1 Kerfing against a crossbatten

SAFETY PROCEDURES

Using a circular saw mounted on a workcentre is usually safer than operating a hand-held one. However, the following safety measures are important.

- Concentrate at all times, and never use a power saw when you are tired.
- Always double-check your settings and run through your planned procedure in your mind before switching on the saw.
- Clamp or hold the work firmly.
- Always wear eye protection when sawing.
- Keep both hands clear of the blade.
- Having cut through a workpiece, switch off before pulling back the saw, since a small offcut is sometimes thrown by the blade.

ROUTING WITH A WORKCENTRE

You can cut housings, even in wide boards, quickly and easily by using a router in the overhead mode. For grooves, rebates and edge mouldings, assemble the workcentre as a spindle moulder, following the instructions supplied by the manufacturer.

The workcentre in spindle-moulder mode

Cutting grooves and rebates

To cut a longitudinal groove or a rebate in the edge of a workpiece, set the two guide fences in line and adjust the depth of the router cutter as required. When rebating, always feed the work against the rotation of the cutter (**1**). Place both hands on top of the workpiece and keep it pressed against the fences while you are feeding it over the cutter (**2**).

1 Cutting a rebate
Feed the work against the rotation of the cutter.

SPINDLE-MOULDER SAFETY

- Use the cutter guard whenever possible.
- Never trail your fingers or thumbs behind the work when you are feeding it over a cutter.
- When edge-moulding or rebating, feed against the rotation of the cutter; feeding in the same direction as the rotation may result in the work being snatched out of your hands. You can draw an arrow on the work table to remind you.
- Always keep your router cutters sharp.
- Remove large amounts of waste by making two or more passes.
- Always wear some form of eye protection.

2 Feed the work with both hands

Cutting a mortise

To cut a mortise, set up the workcentre for grooving. Hold the work against the fence and lower it onto the spinning cutter to start the mortise (**1**). Feed the work to the end of the mortise, then lift it off the cutter (**2**). To cut a series of identical mortises, clamp a stop block to the fences, one behind and one ahead of the work (**3**).

1 Lower the work onto the cutter   **2 Lift the mortise off the cutter**

3 Cutting identical mortises

Trimming a square edge

Even a sharp saw blade can leave a chipped edge on a plastic-laminated board. Use a straight router cutter to trim the edge perfectly clean and square. Adjust the outfeed fence until it is exactly level with the arc of the cutter. The position of the infeed fence determines the depth of cut (**1**).

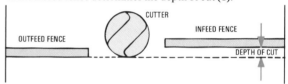

Trimming a laminated board

Moulding an edge

When using a pilot-tipped cutter to edge-mould a workpiece, set the fences close to the cutter as a safety measure and use the pilot tip to guide the work in the usual way (**1**).
If you prefer to feed straight work against the fences, adjust them so the pilot tip is just behind the line of the fences (**2**).
Whatever method you use, always feed the work against the rotation of the cutter.

1 Moulding a curved edge with a pilot-tipped cutter

2 Moulding a straight edge against the fence

MACHINE TOOLS

Many modern woodworking machines offer such a fine degree of accuracy and quality of finish that they provide an incentive to attempt projects that would be difficult or daunting by hand. Powerful machinery also makes light work of ripping, crosscutting and planing heavy baulks of timber to size, and most machines are designed to make the cutting of identical components easy and precise. Virtually all woodworking machines are potentially hazardous. It is therefore essential to follow safety procedures to the letter and to fit some form of dust extraction. You should also never allow your concentration to lapse, nor be tempted to push a machine beyond safe limits. Machine tools are made with either three-phase or single-phase motors. However, to have three-phase wiring run to your workshop is both unnecessary and expensive, whereas single-phase machines can be connected to ordinary domestic circuits.

TABLE SAWS

In its basic form a table saw comprises a rotary saw blade protruding through the centre of a flat worktable or bench. Fitted with fences and guides, it is primarily used to cut solid timber and man-made boards to size. Despite its seemingly limited function, the table saw is usually the first machine a woodworker buys and it becomes the centre of machine-shop activity, since workpieces are returned to the saw again and again as they are squared, shaped, grooved, mitred and joined.

Saw-blade diameter
Table saws for the home workshop are made with blades from as little as 140mm (5½in) up to 300mm (1ft) in diameter. The most important factor – maximum depth of cut – is determined by how much of the blade can protrude above the table, and that is only about one third of its diameter. For serious woodworking you need to consider buying a saw with a 250mm (10in) or preferably a 300mm (1ft) blade.

The blade is usually raised or lowered by means of a handwheel or crank handle. For the cleanest cut and to prolong the life of the blade, adjust its height so that the teeth are about 6 to 9mm (¼in to ⅜in) above the surface of the work.

Saw-blade angle
By operating another handwheel or crank the blade can be tilted to any angle from vertical to 45 degrees to the table. Having adjusted the blade, before switching on always check the position of the guard and fences to make sure they will not retard its movement. Also, read the manufacturer's instructions to determine whether you should remove the table insert or lower the blade before adjustment. Choose a machine with a graduated scale which indicates the angle of the blade clearly.

Table insert
A small section of the table immediately surrounding the blade is removable to facilitate the changing of blades. This 'table insert' has a slot through which the blade protrudes. Occasionally a poorly made saw is supplied with a table-insert slot which is too wide, so small offcuts become jammed between it and the blade. It may be possible to replace a poorly fitting insert with one made from stable wood or board in which the blade cuts its own slot.

Riving knife
When timber is seasoned unevenly, it can become 'case-hardened' as a result of the moisture content varying throughout its thickness. As soon as case-hardened timber is cut, it begins to move due to the release of stresses created within it. If this movement causes partially sawn timber to close up and pinch a revolving saw blade, the workpiece will be thrown back towards the operator with considerable velocity. For this reason, a curved metal blade known as a riving knife is bolted directly behind the blade to keep the saw kerf open. The riving knife is adjustable to suit blades of different diameters. When adjusted correctly it should be approximately 3mm (⅛in) from the saw teeth at its lowest point, no more than 8 or 9 mm (⅜in) from the teeth at its tip and a maximum of 2 to 3mm (⅛in) below the highest point of the saw blade. Once set, the riving knife cants with the saw blade and automatically follows its vertical movement.

3mm (⅛in)

3mm (⅛in)

Recommended riving-knife settings

Blade guard
A sturdy metal guard is suspended directly over the blade to prevent the operator touching it accidentally and also to restrain the workpiece if it is lifted from the table by the motion of the saw. The guard is bolted onto the riving knife or suspended from an adjustable arm. Adjust the guard as close to the work as is practicable.

Electric motor
Being stationary machines, table saws are equipped with relatively large electric motors more than capable of driving a blade at a speed which will leave a clean-cut edge on the work. However, the larger table-saw motors are less likely to be strained by the cutting of thick, dense hardwood. A 1.5kW (2hp) motor is adequate for a machine fitted with a 250 to 300mm (10 to 12in) blade.

Worktable
The main requisite of a saw table is that it should be rigid and flat. Consequently, the best saws are made with cast-metal or ground fabricated-steel tables. A cheaper folded-metal table is acceptable provided it is rigidly braced. Choose a saw with a generous-size table or one that is equipped with extension pieces to support a full 2.44 × 1.22m (8 × 4ft) board.

Rip fence
A workpiece is run against a rip fence to guide it on a straight path as it is sawn from end to end. It is essential that the fence is sturdy and inflexible. To this end some fences are held at both the front and back of the saw table, but this is not essential provided that the fence is constructed with a well-designed single mounting. The fence should be capable of very fine adjustment from side to side, with a clear graduated scale. Fore and aft adjustment is a useful feature found on few table saws designed for the home workshop.

The rip capacity – the distance between the fence and the blade – varies considerably from saw to saw. Ideally, choose a saw capable of halving a full-size man-made board, but you will find many saws have a smaller capacity.

BLADE GUARD

SAW BLADE

MITRE FENCE

RIP FENCE

RIP-FENCE SCALE

RIP-FENCE LOCK

CAST-METAL TABLE

RIVING KNIFE

BLADE-ANGLE CRANK

FENCE-ADJUSTMENT CONTROL

ON/OFF SWITCHES

BLADE-HEIGHT CRANK

STARTRITE tilt arbor

Table saw

Mitre fence
An adjustable mitre fence slides on a path parallel to the blade in a slot machined in the table. It is used when crosscutting timber from 90 to 45 degrees. The fence must run smoothly without being slack, and it should be marked with a clear scale to indicate its angle.

Sliding table
A standard mitre fence is adequate for relatively small-scale work, but it is difficult to crosscut a wide board unless the table has a section that slides parallel to the blade and has an adjustable fence attached to it. Sliding crosscut tables are sometimes supplied as accessories to saws made for the home workshop.

On/off switches
Choose a saw with easily accessible on/off switches.

1

2

- **Cleaning a saw blade**
  Clean wood resin from a
  saw blade with a rag
  soaked in cellulose
  thinner or white spirit.
  Alternatively, you can
  use an oven cleaner.

- **Dado head**
  Two universal blades
  are combined with
  special waste-removal
  blades to construct a
  dado head for cutting
  wide grooves or housings.
  See radial-arm saws.

3

4

1 Ripsaw blade
2 Crosscut blade
3 Universal blade
4 Carbide-tipped blade

TABLE-SAW BLADES

*Special-purpose ripsaw or crosscut blades are mainly used
when a machine is set up to perform one function for a period of
time. A universal or combination-tooth blade is a better choice
for the average home workshop, since the chore of repeatedly
changing the blade, perhaps every few minutes, would soon
become tedious. Despite its additional cost, a carbide-tipped
universal blade is even better. It rips and crosscuts solid timber,
leaving a superb finish, and is ideal for cutting chipboard and
plywood, which quickly blunt ordinary steel blades. Always
follow the manufacturer's instructions for changing blades.*

Ripsaw blade
A ripsaw blade has large
alternately set chisel-like
teeth with deep gullets
between them for clearing
large amounts of waste. It
is designed to cut with the
grain only.

Crosscut blade
Crosscut teeth are much
smaller than those on a ripsaw blade and are shaped
to saw across the grain without tearing it out. Hollow-
ground blades, which are
reduced in thickness towards
their centres, are made to
produce a top-quality finish
and are sometimes known as
'planer blades'.

Universal blade
Universal blades, which are
made to cut both with and
across the grain, have groups
of crosscut teeth separated by
a rip tooth and a deep gullet.
A universal blade will not
perform quite as well as a
special-purpose blade.

Carbide-tipped blade
This type of blade has no
'set' in the conventional
sense. Instead, a wide tip of
tungsten carbide is brazed to
each tooth to provide the
necessary clearance in the
kerf or sawcut. Carbide-
tipped blades are often slotted to prevent distortion as
the blade expands through
heating. To reduce whistling
caused by the blade moving
through the air at speed, the
hole at the root of each slot is
plugged with soft metal.

Sharpening table-saw blades
When a blade becomes blunt
you will smell burning and it
becomes more difficult to
feed the work. A blunt blade
is also more likely to jam
and throw the work back
towards the operator. Send
a blunt blade to a specialist
for sharpening or for the
replacement of a damaged
carbide tip.

WOBBLE WASHERS

A pair of tapered wobble
washers causes the edge of
the saw blade to move from
side to side as it revolves, in
order to cut a groove wider
than the normal kerf. (Alternatively, you can fit a dado
head – see radial-arm saws.)
Rotating the washers in
opposite directions changes
the angle of the blade so as
to increase or reduce the
width of the groove. It is
necessary to remove the
riving knife and to substitute a table insert with a
wider slot in place of the
normal one. If the blade
guard is attached to the riving knife, fit a hold-down
unit when using wobble
washers.

Wobble-washer assembly

RIPSAWING ON A TABLE SAW

Ripsawing is used to reduce solid timber to width by cutting more or less parallel to the grain. The work is always run against the rip fence and never cut freehand, in order to avoid the risk of twisting the workpiece and jamming the blade in the kerf. Man-made boards are ripped in the same way. The riving knife and blade guard must be in position when ripsawing.

Adjusting the rip fence

A rip fence that extends in one piece across the saw table is ideal for cutting stable man-made boards. However, when sawing solid timber there is always the chance that this type of fence will cause an accident. Just as the partially cut kerf in case-hardened timber could close on the blade were it not for the riving knife, so similar stresses locked in the timber can make the kerf spring open until pressure against the rip fence forces the workpiece against the side of the blade, causing it to jam and possibly throw the workpiece. If the fence is capable of fore and aft adjustment, it should be withdrawn until its far end is about 25mm (1in) behind the leading edge of the exposed part of the blade **(1)**, providing clearance to the right of the blade. Alternatively, clamp or screw a block of timber to a one-piece fence **(2)** to provide similar clearance. Whatever type of fence is fitted, it must be set parallel to the blade.

Adjust the rip fence to the width of cut according to its graduated scale, then make a test cut in the end of a piece of scrap timber to check the setting. If you cannot trust the scale, use a rule to measure from the fence to one of the saw teeth set towards the fence. Before you switch on, check that the fence is securely clamped.

1 Withdraw a two-piece fence

2 Fix a block to a one-piece fence

Ripping a wide board

Use both hands to rip a wide board – applying pressure with one hand directly behind the work but out of line with the blade, while holding the work against the fence and down onto the table with the other. Feed the work at a steady rate, and do not attempt to retrieve the offcut until the blade has stopped moving.

Have an assistant help you support a very wide board when ripsawing, making it clear that you will guide the workpiece and control the feed rate.

Ripping a narrow board

As you approach the end of a ripcut in a narrow board, feed the work with a push stick – a strip of hardwood notched at one end, with a rounded handgrip at the other – and use a second push stick to apply pressure against the rip fence. Store your push sticks near the table so they are always to hand when needed.

Bevel ripping

To rip a bevel along a workpiece, before you switch the table saw on, tilt the blade to the required angle and check that the blade is not touching the guard or rip fence. Feed the work as for a normal ripcut.

Cutting a tapered workpiece

To saw a tapered workpiece, cut a notch in the side of a plywood or chipboard jig to hold the wood at the required angle to the blade. Keep the jig pressed against the rip fence while feeding it in the normal way.

Ripping a waney-edge board

It is impossible to run a waney edge against the rip fence with any certainty of achieving a straight ripcut. To help keep the cut straight, pin a sheet of thin plywood to the underside of the workpiece so that it projects slightly beyond the waney edge and acts as a guide.

Coping with a waney edge

Ripping a wide board

Use push sticks to rip a narrow board

Tilt the blade to cut a bevel

Cutting a wedge

CROSSCUTTING ON A TABLE SAW

When cutting workpieces to length on a table saw, use the mitre fence or a sliding crosscut table to guide the wood past the blade. A sharp blade will produce such a clean cut that the end grain may need no further finishing. Keep the blade guard and riving knife in position, even though the knife is not essential for crosscutting.

Fix a wooden strip to the fence

Crosscut by sliding the fence

Crosscutting with a mitre fence

The adjustable mitre fence on the average table saw is relatively short, but it is often drilled so you can screw a longer hardwood fence to its face. Once the wooden fence itself is crosscut on the table saw, it also acts as a backup to the work to prevent the grain splitting out at the back as it is fed past the blade. Alternatively, as a temporary backup, sandwich a piece of scrap timber between the factory-made mitre fence and the workpiece.

Hold the work firmly against the fence with both hands, and feed it relatively slowly into the blade. If the workpiece is too short to be held with both hands, clamp it to the fence.

MAKING MULTIPLE CROSSCUTS

Many woodworking projects require several identical components. Rather than crosscut individually marked workpieces one at a time, set up one or two stops to locate the wood accurately in relation to the blade and make repetitive cuts.

Making identical offcuts

It is tempting to butt the end of the work against the rip fence to ensure that offcuts to the right of the blade are of equal length. However, an offcut caught between the fence and a revolving blade can be thrown back into the face of the operator. The correct method is either to withdraw the rip fence clear of the blade or to clamp a spacer block to the fence to act as an end stop for the work, leaving a clearance to the right of the blade (**1**).

To make the cut, slide the work sideways until it butts against the block and feed it into the blade, then repeat the process to make identical offcuts.

Making identical workpieces

Using the mitre fence, cut each piece of wood square. Clamp a block of wood to the extended mitre fence to act as a stop for the squared end of each workpiece (**2**), then feed them past the blade to cut them to length.

1 Making identical offcuts

2 Cutting identical workpieces

Crosscutting on a sliding table

The friction between a large board or a long workpiece and the saw table can make crosscutting with a mitre fence a laborious procedure. A smooth-running, sliding crosscutting action makes for easy and accurate work, regardless of the size or weight of the workpiece. A sliding table is fitted with a longer-than-average crosscut fence that is adjustable to any angle between 90 and 45 degrees to the blade. Most fences are made with an adjustable end stop for use when making identical workpieces.

Cutting a mitre

To cut a mitre on a table saw, adjust the mitre fence to the required angle, then feed the workpiece past the blade in the normal way (**1**). Take care to hold the work firmly against the fence, to prevent it being drawn backwards by the blade.

To cut a compound mitre (one angled in two planes), first adjust the mitre fence then tilt the saw blade (**2**). To cut a mitre across the end of a board, tilt the blade to 45 degrees and set the mitre fence at 90 degrees to the blade (**3**).

1 Adjust the fence to cut a mitre

2 Tilt the blade to cut a compound mitre

3 Keep the fence square to mitre the end of a board

CUTTING REBATES AND GROOVES ON A TABLE SAW

When cutting a groove or rebate, on certain table saws it is necessary to remove both the blade guard and the riving knife. As a result, both procedures are more hazardous than standard ripping or crosscutting, so extra concentration and caution are required. Some table saws can be fitted with special vertical/horizontal 'hold-down' guards which surround the work in the vicinity of the blade. Alternatively, afford some protection by making a wooden lining for your rip fence incorporating a simple guard to cover the blade.

Fit a hold-down guard when grooving or rebating

The alternative is a handmade guard

Cutting a rebate

Two straightforward ripcuts produce a rebate on a workpiece. Make the first cut in the narrower face of the workpiece (**1**), leaving sufficient wood on each side of the kerf to provide adequate support. Reset the rip fence and blade height, then make the second cut to detach the waste from the workpiece (**2**). Make this second cut with the waste facing away from the fence, since a waste strip trapped between the blade and fence could be thrown back as the last few wood fibres are severed. Stand to one side when feeding work into the blade.

1 Making the first cut

2 Second cut removes the waste

Cutting a groove

A wobble saw allows you to cut a groove in one pass, using a push stick to keep your fingers clear of the blade. Without special equipment, make one sawcut to the required depth on each side of the groove (**1**), then adjust the rip fence sideways one kerf-width at a time to remove waste between (**2**).

Cutting a tongue and groove

Leave a centrally placed tongue on the edge of one workpiece by cutting two identical rebates. Make the first cut in the narrower face, then turn the wood end for end to cut the other side of the tongue (**1**). Remove the waste from both sides (**2**).

To saw a matching groove in another workpiece, adjust the fence to cut one side, then turn the work end for end to make the second cut before removing the waste (see left).

1 Make two saw cuts

2 Remove waste between them

1 Cut each side of a tongue

2 Then cut off the waste

KERFING ON A TABLE SAW

If you almost sever a strip of wood with regularly spaced sawcuts, that provides sufficient local flexibility to make a tight bend in a thick workpiece of solid timber. The exact kerf spacing is a matter of experimentation – but as a rough guide, the closer the spacing the tighter the bend. Adjust the height of the blade to leave an intact strip of wood between 2 to 6mm ($\frac{1}{16}$ to $\frac{1}{4}$ in) thick, depending on the flexibility of the work. On some saws no guard can be fitted – in which case, exercise extreme caution.

Accurate spacing is essential if the resulting curve is to be smooth and regular. Screw a temporary auxiliary wooden fence to the saw's mitre fence. Make one cut through the fence, then drive a nail into it to mark the kerf spacing and cut off the head of the nail (**1**).

Having made one kerf in the workpiece, slot the first kerf onto the nail and cut your second kerf. Slot that kerf over the nail and make your third cut, and so on (**2**).

Bend solid timber by kerfing

1 Make a jig for accurate kerfing

2 Drop each kerf in turn over the nail

CUTTING JOINTS ON A TABLE SAW

Through housing Barefaced housing

A table saw is capable of cutting a variety of woodworking joints with extreme accuracy. As the blade guard and riving knife may have to be removed, proceed with caution when using a table saw for cutting joints.

Halving joints
Both parts of a halving joint are cut in the same way. Clamp a spacer block to the rip fence and use it to align the shoulder of the joint with the blade. Adjust the blade to the required height and make the first cut **(1)**. Then remove the waste one kerf-width at a time, sliding the workpiece to the left against the mitre fence.

A cross halving joint is cut by a similar method, but use two spacer blocks – clamping one to the rip fence and the other to the mitre fence – to align both shoulders with the blade **(2)**. Having cut both shoulders, remove the waste as above.

1 Cutting a halving-joint shoulder

2 Use two spacer blocks to cut cross-halving shoulders

Halving joint

Cross halving joint

Mortise and tenon

Adding a support
If the saw has a low fence, glue a block to the tenon-cutting jig to stop it rocking.

Tenon joints
Having cut the mortises with a router or mortiser, cut the matching tenons on a table saw. Some saw manufacturers supply a tenoning cramp which slides along the machined mitre-fence slot. Alternatively, you can make a wooden jig to support a workpiece while you cut the tenon.

Screw and glue two strips of wood, precisely the same thickness as the work, to a piece of plywood approximately 400 × 200mm (1ft 4in × 8in) in size **(1)**. Make sure each strip is square to the long edge of the plywood, and leave enough room to fit a workpiece between one strip and the short edge **(2)**. Restrict screw-fixings to the top half of the jig, clear of the blade.

Clamp the workpiece to the jig and pass it across the blade to cut one side of the tenon **(3)**. Turn the work round to cut the second side.

Having cut one tenon, remove a short section of waste from each side **(4)** to test its fit in the mortise. If necessary, make adjustments to the fence setting before cutting any remaining workpieces.

Crosscut the shoulder lines **(5)**, clamping a spacer block to the rip fence to align each shoulder line with the blade. If need be, reduce the width of the tenons by cutting the shoulders first, then remove the waste one kerf-width at a time **(6)**.

1 Fix wooden strips to plywood

2 Allow space for workpiece

3 Cut one side of tenon

4 Remove a short section of waste from each side of tenon

5 Cut the shoulder lines

6 Reduce tenon width

Housing joints
Cut a simple through housing or the relatively narrow 'groove' of a barefaced housing joint in the same manner as a cross halving joint, or use a wobble saw to cut them in one pass. Cut the tongue on the other half of a barefaced housing like a halving joint.

Lap joints
Having sawn both of the components square, cut the tongued half of a lap joint like a halving joint.

Reinforced mitre joints
Having cut mitre joints on the table saw, cut slots for plywood tongues.

Slotting a mitred workpiece
Tilt the blade to cut a slot for a loose tongue.

Slotting a mitred frame
Modify the tenon-cutting jig to slot a wide mitre.

Finger joints

A finger joint is a decorative corner joint often used for box or drawer construction. Cutting it by hand is a laborious process, but with the help of a simple jig you can cut several joints in minutes on a table saw. Use a blade that cuts a wide kerf, or fit wobble washers to cut the spaces between the fingers. Work out the spacing so as to distribute the fingers regularly across each of the workpieces.

To make a jig, clamp a length of wood to the mitre fence and, having adjusted the blade height to just over the thickness of the work, cut a slot through the wood (1). Plane a strip of hardwood to a snug fit in the slot. Cut a piece of wood 50 to 75mm (2 to 3in) long off the strip and glue it into the slot to form a short projecting tongue (2).

Reposition the jig against the mitre fence and place the remainder of the planed strip between the blade and the tongue (3), then screw the wood to the fence and remove the strip.

Stand the first workpiece on end and butt it against the projecting tongue. Clamp the work (4). Feed the work across the saw, then drop the resulting kerf over the projecting tongue and saw another kerf (5). Continue in the same way until you have completed the row of fingers (6).

The fingers on the second workpiece must be offset to fit between the fingers on the first. Place this second piece on end as before, but sandwich the remainder of the wooden strip between it and the tongue (7). Remove the strip and make the first cut, then locate the cut over the tongue and saw the next kerf (8). Repeat the process across the width of the workpiece.

Glue and assemble the joint, then plane the slightly projecting fingers flush once the glue has set.

1 Make one cut in the jig

2 Glue a tongue in the slot

3 Place a strip of wood between the tongue and blade

4 Butt the workpiece against the tongue

5 Drop the kerf over the tongue and make a second cut

6 Complete the row of fingers

7 Sandwich a strip between the tongue and second workpiece

8 Locate the cut over the tongue and saw the next kerf

RADIAL-ARM SAWS

The radial-arm saw is first and foremost a crosscut saw, but it is the machine's versatility that makes it such an attractive proposition for the amateur wood-worker. The saw will rip, crosscut, bevel or mitre, and with slight modifications the same machine can be converted into a spindle moulder, overhead router, sander or drill. The blade and motor housing on a standard-pattern radial-arm saw is suspended below a metal arm mounted on top of a rigid column. The arm swings from side to side to present the blade at an angle to the work for cutting mitres. At the same time, the motor housing and blade can be tilted and pivoted to make compound-angle cuts. On one model, the arm is fixed while the table pivots below it. As the column is mounted to the rear of the worktable, a radial-arm saw can be installed against a wall. Most radial-arm saws stand on a bench or their own legstands, and some can be folded away and hung from wall brackets. Assemble and wire your saw according to the manufacturer's instructions.

Electric motor
The average radial-arm saw for the home workshop is fitted with an induction motor rated at about 1.1kW (1½hp). This is powerful enough to generate adequate saw-blade speeds of nearly 3000rpm, but is not capable of generating cutter speeds comparable with a purpose-made spindle moulder un-less the motor has a second 'arbor', or drive shaft, geared for high-speed work.

Saw-blade diameter
Radial-arm saws manufac-tured for the home workshop are usually supplied with 250mm (10in) blades.

Depth of cut
Most radial-arm saws have a possible maximum depth of cut of about 75mm (3in). The blade, along with the machine's arm, is raised or lowered by operating a crank situated either on top of the column or beneath the worktable.

Arm angle
The arm can be rotated left or right, after releasing the mitre clamping lever. A latch positively locates the arm for crosscutting at 90 or 45 degrees. A scale on top of the column indicates the angle of the arm.

DEPTH CRANK
ELECTRICAL FLEX
MITRE SCALE
MITRE CLAMPING LEVER
RADIAL ARM
MITRE LATCH
ON/OFF SWITCH
RIP SCALES AND RIP LOCK ON THIS SIDE OF MACHINE
CONTROL HANDLE
COLUMN
DeWALT POWER SHOP
DW 1251
SAWDUST EXHAUST PORT
BLADE-PIVOT LATCH
ANTI-KICKBACK ASSEMBLY
BLADE GUARD
BEVEL LOCATING PIN
ELECTRIC-MOTOR HOUSING
BEVEL CLAMPING LEVER
FENCE
BEVEL SCALE
WORKTABLE

Radial-arm saw

Saw-blade angle

You can tilt the saw blade to any angle between vertical and horizontal, having first released the bevel clamping lever and withdrawn a locating pin which engages automatically when the blade is at 90 or 45 degrees. Choose a machine with a scale that indicates the angle of the blade clearly.

Crosscut capacity

The maximum crosscutting width is determined mainly by the length of the arm. The crosscut capacity of home-workshop saws varies from 310 to 465mm (1ft to 1ft 6in). To make cuts up to 600mm (2ft) wide, you need to buy one of the smaller industrial radial-arm saws.

Rip capacity

The width of ripcut – up to a maximum of between 500 and 650mm (1ft 8in and 2ft 2in) – is selected by sliding the motor housing along the arm and locking it in position with a clamping lever or knob. Scales printed along the arm indicate ripcut width.

Blade guard

The blade on a modern radial-arm saw is enclosed by a 'gravity guard' which is raised automatically by the work during a sawing operation then drops back under its own weight at the completion of the process.

Riving knife

When ripping, to prevent case-hardened timber closing on the blade, lower the riving knife into position just behind the blade and secure it with the lock nut. When crosscutting, the knife is pushed back inside the blade guard.

Anti-kickback assembly

If a blade jams during a ripcut, it can throw the work back towards the operator. To prevent this happening, an anti-kickback assembly which has trailing teeth, or 'pawls', is mounted on the saw. The slightest backward movement of the work causes the pointed pawls to pivot downwards to restrain the wood. The anti-kickback assembly also acts as a hold-down device to prevent the workpiece being lifted off the table by the ascending saw teeth.

For ripsawing, raise or lower the anti-kickback assembly until the points of the pawls hang 3mm ($\frac{1}{8}$in) below the surface of the wood. For crosscutting, raise the assembly clear of the work.

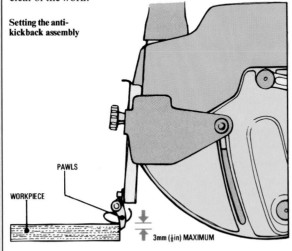

Setting the anti-kickback assembly

PAWLS

WORKPIECE

3mm ($\frac{1}{8}$in) MAXIMUM

Worktable

A simple worktable of high-density fibreboard or chipboard is fixed to the machine's metal base. Because the blade of a radial-arm saw must cut into the surface of the table, it is worth pinning or spot-gluing a sheet of thin plywood onto the chipboard or fibreboard. Make sure any metal fixings are out of range of the blade's movements.

Fence

A workpiece is crosscut against a fence running across the worktable. The same fence is used to guide the work during a ripsawing operation.

For crosscutting, the fence is sandwiched between the worktable and a spacer board – the blade being parked behind the fence between cuts. To increase rip capacity, the fence can be placed behind the spacer board.

The fence that comes with the machine is usually made from the same fibrous material as the worktable. However, you can replace it with one made from solid timber – in which case, make it longer than the original since end stops for making repetitive crosscuts can be clamped to an extended fence in order to accommodate longer workpieces.

On/off switches

The on/off switches are usually placed either at the end of the radial arm or on the main control handle, where they are within easy reach. Some saws are supplied with removable keys, so they can be rendered inoperable.

Dust extraction

Radial-arm saws create a great deal of dust, which is ejected through a rubber exhaust port on the blade guard. Some form of extraction is required in order to make sure the area surrounding the saw does not become slippery with loose sawdust.

USING A RADIAL-ARM SAW SAFELY

Always follow the general safety recommendations for working in a machine shop and take extra care when operating a radial-arm saw.

- Install the saw sloping backwards very slightly, so the blade and motor housing cannot slide towards the operator under their own weight.
- When crosscutting, make sure the hand holding the work is not in line with the blade.
- Always park the blade and motor housing behind the fence between crosscuts.
- Never rip without using the anti-kickback assembly and riving knife.
- Keep anti-kickback pawls sharp. Take care when ripping plastic-laminated board, since it may not provide sufficient grip for the pawls.
- Do not perform an operation freehand. Always use the fence or some other device that will hold the workpiece still and stop it rotating or twisting.
- Plan a ripcut so that the offcut is free to move sideways away from the blade.
- Do not stand directly in line with the blade when ripping.
- Have an assistant help you to support a long board.
- Don't rip short pieces of wood that will bring your hands close to the blade.
- Keep the blade guard in place and in good working order.

● **Setting up the machine** Support a radial-arm saw on a bench at a comfortable working height and allow enough clearance for your knuckles between column and wall when operating the depth-adjustment crank.

165

RADIAL-ARM SAW BLADES AND CUTTERS

Blades similar to those used on a table saw are available for radial-arm saws. A general-purpose or universal blade, especially one with tungsten-carbide-tipped teeth, is the best choice for a home workshop. Fitting wobble washers to make the blade move from side to side is one way to cut grooves and housings.

Dado head

A dado head fitted to the normal saw arbor provides a means of cutting grooves and housings up to 21mm ($\frac{7}{8}$in) wide in one pass. A dado head comprises two universal blades which cut both sides of a groove or housing simultaneously, while 'chipper' blades sandwiched between them remove the waste. Paper washers are inserted between the blades to make minute adjustments to the width of cut.

Chipper blades are sandwiched between dado saw blades

Tungsten-carbide-tipped saw blade

Dado head

MOULDING HEADS

A radial-arm saw is converted to a spindle moulder by replacing the blade with metal moulding heads that take two or three shaped cutters. A three-cutter head leaves a much cleaner finish on a workpiece. Each cutter is bolted securely into a slot in the moulding head. An extensive range of shaped cutters is available for radial-arm saws.

The machine can be set up with the moulding head revolving horizontally, in which case a special guard and fence have to be fitted. On some saws the moulding head can also be mounted vertically, like a saw blade, using the usual guard.

● **Changing blades and cutters**
Always follow the manufacturer's instructions when fitting blades and moulding heads on your radial-arm saw.

Moulding head and cutters

166

CROSSCUTTING ON A RADIAL-ARM SAW

In order to sever a workpiece completely, the saw blade must cut into the plywood table lining to a depth of about 1mm ($\frac{1}{16}$ in). This scored line passes across the table and through the fence. The notch cut in the fence makes an ideal guide when you need to line up a marked cut line on a workpiece with the blade. Both the anti-kickback assembly and riving knife must be withdrawn while crosscutting.

Making a square crosscut

With one hand, hold the work face side uppermost against the fence so that the blade will cut on the waste side of the marked line. Make sure all clamping levers are tight, except for the one that allows the blade and motor housing to travel along the arm. Switch on and steadily pull the saw towards you to just sever the work, then push it back and switch off.

Crosscutting is a relatively safe procedure, because the action of the blade tends to hold the work against the fence and down onto the table. However, the blade also has a tendency to pull itself towards the operator – a tendency that must be resisted by keeping your forearm in a straight line with the handle of the saw.

Making repetitive crosscuts

If you want to cut several identical workpieces to length, aligning the marked lines with a notch in the fence may not be sufficiently accurate. Instead, clamp a block of wood to the fence to act as an end stop for the workpieces – but never position the end stop so that it restricts the lateral movement of an offcut once it has been severed. Also, always make sure that sawdust does not become trapped between a workpiece and the fence or end stop.

Cutting a wide or thick board

Use an end stop when you want to cut a board that is wider than the saw's crosscut capacity or thicker than its maximum depth of cut.

Cut just over halfway through the work – then turn it over, press it against the stop and sever the wood with a second cut. This procedure is acceptable only when it is not important to preserve a face side.

Making a bevel crosscut

To make a bevel crosscut, first tilt the blade and clamp it at the required angle, then proceed as if you were making a square crosscut.

Cutting a mitre

To cut a mitre on the end of a workpiece, keeping the blade vertical, swing the arm to the required angle – usually 45 degrees – and clamp it in place. Holding the work firmly against the fence to make sure it cannot move during the operation, cut the mitre by pulling the saw towards the front of the table.

Hold the work firmly against the fence when making a square crosscut

Use a clamped end stop to make identical workpieces

Cut just over halfway through thick wood, then turn it over to sever it

Tilt the blade to cut a bevel

Swing the arm to one side to cut a mitre

RIPPING ON A RADIAL-ARM SAW

In order to cut a piece of timber to width, the blade of a radial-arm saw is turned parallel to the fence. For relatively narrow work-pieces, the blade faces the saw's column in what is called the 'inrip' position. To rip wider boards, the blade is turned to the 'outrip' position, facing away from the column.

Feeding the work
A workpiece must be fed into the blade against its direction of rotation. To feed the work in the opposite direction would result in the blade snatching the work, perhaps pulling the operator's hands towards it. When inripping, the work is fed from one side of the table (usually the right-hand side, but check the manufacturer's instructions); when outripping, it is fed from the other side since the blade is facing in the opposite direction. Both the riving knife and the anti-kickback assembly must be deployed whenever you are ripping timber.

Direction of feed
Always feed wood against the rotation of the blade.

Adjusting the blade
Slide the blade along the arm until the required width of cut is indicated on one of the rip scales. To make sure the setting has not been affected by tightening the clamping lever, make a test cut in the end of a piece of scrap timber. You can increase the rip capacity by placing the fence behind the table's spacer board. To sever a workpiece completely, the blade must be lowered until it cuts into the table lining to a depth of about 1mm ($\frac{1}{16}$in).

Ripping a workpiece to width
Check all clamping levers are tight, then switch on. Keeping the work pressed against the fence, use both hands to feed the work into the blade at a steady rate. Always use a notched push stick to feed a narrow workpiece that would bring your hands close to the blade. Have an assistant support or withdraw a long workpiece from the opposite side of the worktable.

Bevel ripping
To cut a bevel along one edge of a workpiece, proceed as if you were making a square ripcut, but tilt the blade to the required angle. Follow the manufacturer's instructions for setting the anti-kickback pawls for a tilted blade.

Use a push stick when inripping a narrow workpiece

Turn the blade away from the column to outrip a wide board

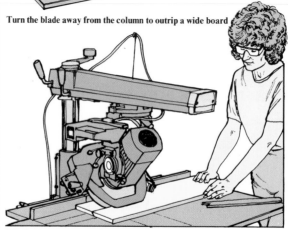

Tilt the blade to cut a bevel

CUTTING HOUSINGS, GROOVES & REBATES

It is possible to cut a groove or rebate parallel with the grain or a housing across a workpiece by using the standard saw blade to cut along both sides, then resetting the saw to remove the waste one blade-width at a time. However, it is much less laborious to cut grooves, housings and rebates with a wobble saw, or better still, a dado head.

Cutting a housing
Cut a housing with a dado head as if you were making a crosscut or mitre. Being considerably wider than a single saw blade, a dado head may exaggerate the machine's tendency to pull itself towards the operator – so be prepared to resist it. To repeat a housing on more than one workpiece, clamp an end stop to the fence.

Cutting a groove
Fit a dado-head combination to make up the required width of cut. Remove the riving knife, but keep both the blade guard and anti-kickback assembly in place. Select the inrip or outrip position for the dado head, as appropriate, then proceed as if making a ripcut.

Cutting a rebate
To cut a rebate along the edge of a workpiece, use the dado head as if you were cutting a groove.

KERFING

Bending a length of solid timber by kerfing is an easy procedure on a radial-arm saw set up for crosscutting.

You can make a simple jig for accurate kerf spacing by driving a nail into the fence and snipping its head off. Having made one kerf, shift the work sideways, slide the kerf onto the nail and then cut the next kerf. Instead of using a nail, you can make a pencil mark on the fence and align each cut by eye.

Use an end stop to position housings accurately

A dado head cuts a wide groove with one pass

Use a cut nail to gauge kerf spacing

CUTTING JOINTS ON A RADIAL SAW

Certain simple joints can be cut quickly and accurately on a radial-arm saw. Fit a universal blade, or save time by using a dado head for halving joints, lap joints and tenons.

Reinforced mitre joint

A plywood tongue is often used to reinforce a mitre joint. Having made two straightforward bevel cross-cuts, adjust the blade depth, then turn the work end for end and cut a slot for the tongue in each bevel. Use an end stop to ensure the slot is identically placed in both halves of the joint.

Halving joints

To make a halving or cross halving joint, first adjust the blade to cut halfway through the work, then make cross-cuts on the shoulder lines. Slide the work sideways against the fence, making successive crosscuts to remove the waste little by little.
   Use an end stop to repeat shoulder-line cuts accurately. In the case of a cross halving joint, clamp end stops at both ends of the fence – one for each of the shoulder lines.

Lap joints

Square both halves of the joint with a straightforward crosscut, then adjust the blade height and cut the lap in the same manner as a halving joint.

Cutting tenons

With the workpiece butted against an end stop, cut one side of a tenon as you would a lap joint, then turn it over and cut the other side.

Cut a slot for a mitre-reinforcing tongue

Cut a halving-joint shoulder first, then remove waste

Use an end stop to help cut both sides of a tenon

169

DRILLING WITH A RADIAL-ARM SAW

You can convert your radial-arm saw into a power drill by fitting a chuck with a capacity of 10mm ($\frac{3}{8}$in) to the arbor at the other end of the motor housing from the blade, which must be removed first.

Drilling side grain
To drill into the side of a workpiece, set up the machine so that the drill chuck faces the column. Construct a high fence to serve as a backup, and raise the workpiece on scrap wood. Use a clamped end stop to position the work accurately.

Hold or clamp the workpiece, then switch on and feed the drill into it by moving the motor housing along the radial arm (1). Drill a series of holes in line to remove the waste from a mortise.

Drilling end grain
To drill into end grain – to insert dowels, for example – turn the motor housing so that the drill bit is parallel to the fence and tighten all clamping levers. Raise the work on a temporarily constructed box or a piece of scrap timber, and feed it against the fence into the drill bit (2). Pin or clamp a block to the fence ahead of the work to act as a depth stop.

1 Feed the drill into side grain   **2 Feed end grain towards the drill**

ROUTING WITH A RADIAL-ARM SAW

Radial-arm saws are supplied with mounting brackets to take one or more of the most popular brands of power router.

Sliding the router back and forth along the radial arm is an excellent method for making stopped housings in a bookcase or staircase string.

Cut grooves or rebates along a workpiece by running it against the fence into a fixed router held in place by the saw's clamping lever. Cutting a stopped groove is less simple, since you have to lower and raise the router during the operation, using the depth-adjusting crank.

When moulding or rebating an edge, remember to feed the work against the rotation of the router cutter.

Cut stopped housings with a mobile router

USING THE MOULDING HEAD

If you intend to shape work with a moulding head, you must fit a special guard that encircles the cutters. You will also need to make a two-part fence and to take extra care to ensure every procedure is undertaken with safety. Few radial-arm saws are supplied with the vertical/horizontal hold-down guards which are a feature of purpose-made spindle moulders, so you may have to make a featherboard to hold narrow workpieces firmly against the fence (see opposite).

Always follow the manufacturer's instructions for setting up the machine and for fitting the cutters in the moulding head – since a serious accident could occur if a cutter works loose.

Making a fence for shaping
When the moulding head is mounted horizontally for shaping the edge of a workpiece, you need a two-part fence through which the cutters protrude. Clamp both halves of the fence between the worktable and the spacer board, adjusting them to provide just enough clearance for the cutters (1). When you are rebating or cutting a moulding that leaves part of the edge intact, both halves of the fence should be in line (2).

To support a deeply moulded edge, the outfeed half of the fence must be set forward (3). The simplest method is to plane two wooden strips to a thickness that exactly matches the amount of wood to be removed. Place one strip in front of the fence, and the other behind the outfeed half (4). Set the strips flush with the worktable.

1 Make a two-part fence for moulding

2 Rebating an edge
When only part of an edge is removed, keep fence in line.

3 Cutting a deep moulding
Offset outfeed section of fence to support the moulded wood.

4 Shift the two-part fence out of line with strips of wood

1 Moulding from above the work   **2 Moulding from beneath**

Adjusting the cutter height

Using the saw's controls, you can adjust the height of the cutters to mould a workpiece from above (1). However, moulding from underneath (2) has two advantages. Firstly, the work itself protects the operator from the cutters. Secondly, should the workpiece jump from the table for some reason, the cutters will not take a deeper bite out of it as they would if the moulding head was suspended above it.

Positioning the moulding head below the work can be achieved by cutting a hole in the worktable and spacer board, or by laying a board on the table to raise the work.

Moulding a wide board

Always feed the work at a steady rate against the rotation of the moulding head. Press the work against the fence, keeping both hands flat on the work – never trailing them behind or in line with the cutters. Don't try to remove too much wood in one go. Shape a deep moulding by making two or three shallow cuts and adjusting the moulding head between passes.

Moulding a wide board
Feed the work by hand

Moulding a narrow board

Don't feed a narrow board past the cutters by hand. With a jigsaw or band saw, make a featherboard by cutting curved fingers along the edge of a piece of wood. Screw the featherboard to the worktable to leave a tight sliding fit for the workpiece between the flexible fingers and the fence. Use a push stick to feed the work past the cutters. Don't try to mould a very narrow strip of wood – instead, shape the edge of a wider board, then saw off a strip the size you want.

Moulding a narrow board
Use a featherboard to hold the work against the fence.

USING A RADIAL-ARM SAW AS A SANDER

You can convert a radial-arm saw into a very serviceable sanding machine by adding disc and drum sanders. Both accessories are fitted in place of the standard saw blade.

Drum sanding

The small drum sanders available for radial-arm saws are ideally suited for finishing and shaping the edges of workpieces. With the drum mounted vertically, a contoured workpiece can be fed freehand against the abrasive surface. Separate the table and spacer board with wooden blocks to create a gap through which you can lower the drum level with the worktable surface. Tilt the motor housing to sand a mitred edge.

In order to sand a straight narrow workpiece with flat surfaces, set the drum horizontally and pass the workpiece under it.

Take care to feed the work against the rotation of the drum, or it will be snatched from your hands and thrown off the machine.

Contour sanding
Mount the drum vertically.

Use a fence for accurate disc sanding

Disc sanding

To sand end grain, swing the radial arm to one side and lower the motor housing to present the disc alongside a worktable extension. If you do not have room to construct an extension, raise the work by standing it on a temporary box or platform placed on the worktable. Clamp the arm at 90 degrees and adjust the disc so that it will revolve level with the platform.

Work against the 'down' side of the disc at all times, so that the work is held down on the table. Sand square or mitred work against a temporarily clamped fence, or use the disc to shape components freehand.

Sanding a straight edge
Set the drum horizontally.

Shape curved work freehand.

BAND SAWS

A band-saw blade is a continuous loop of metal driven over two or three large wheels. Because the thrust of the blade is always downwards onto the saw table, there is no danger of a kickback throwing the work towards the operator. For this reason, many woodworkers prefer the band saw to a radial-arm saw, even though it neither rips nor crosscuts quite as cleanly or as fast. The band saw has several other advantages. It can be used to cut curved components;

it will cut thicker timber than the average circular saw will; the wastage of timber is minimal thanks to the very narrow kerf cut by the blade; and it also costs less than a good table saw. A band saw takes up little floor space, and those designed for the home workshop are light enough to be manoeuvred into place without special lifting equipment. A good band saw runs relatively quietly – an advantage if your workshop is part of your house.

Depth of cut
Many band saws are sold by virtue of the fact that they are capable of cutting thick workpieces. The average home-workshop band saw will cut wood up to 150mm (6in) thick, but the slightly more expensive versions have a maximum capacity of 300mm (1ft). This facility makes a band saw the ideal machine for cutting large baulks of wood into planks or even into veneers.

Width of cut
The band saw's throat – the distance from the blade to the vertical frame member – determines its maximum width of cut. Throat size on most home-workshop band saws is about 300 to 350mm (1ft to 1ft 2in). If you are likely to cut wider boards, choose one of the smaller industrial band saws.

Cutting speed
The cutting speed of a band saw is measured by the number of metres or feet a point on the blade will travel in one minute. Top speed varies considerably from saw to saw, ranging from 220m (720ft) to 1220m (4000ft) per minute. On some band saws, slower speeds can be selected for cutting metals and hard plastics. Others are fitted with variable-speed control between limits. Manufacturers normally recommend the highest speeds for cutting wood, but be prepared to reduce speed if you sense the saw is straining when cutting very dense timber.

● **Electric motor**
Band saws for the non-professional market are made with 550 to 750W (¾ to 1hp) electric motors, quite powerful enough to cope with the demands made on them in a home workshop.

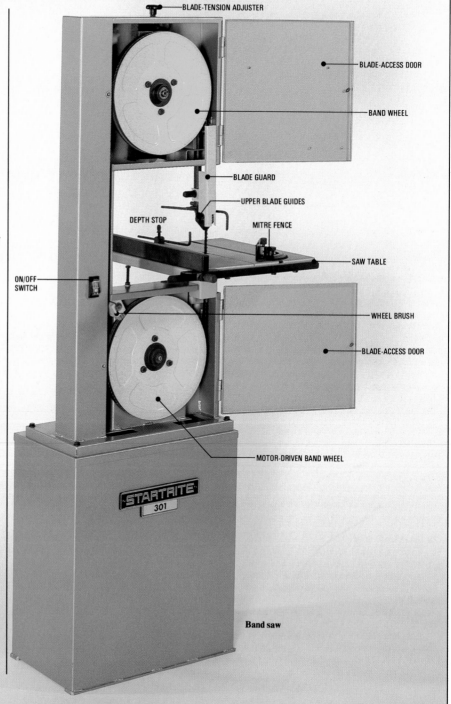

BLADE-TENSION ADJUSTER

BLADE-ACCESS DOOR

BAND WHEEL

BLADE GUARD

UPPER BLADE GUIDES

DEPTH STOP

MITRE FENCE

ON/OFF SWITCH

SAW TABLE

WHEEL BRUSH

BLADE-ACCESS DOOR

MOTOR-DRIVEN BAND WHEEL

STARTRITE 301

Band saw

Band wheels

All band saws have at least two wheels for the blade, one mounted directly above the other. The lower wheel is driven by the motor. Some saws have a third wheel which has the effect of increasing throat width, since the blade travels to one side before returning to the upper wheel. Three-wheel saws put a greater strain on blades, causing them to break more often. Band wheels are fitted with rubber, cork or PVC tyres to preserve the set of the blades.

If possible, choose a saw with a fixed brush mounted in such a way that it continuously cleans sawdust from the drive-wheel tyre while the machine is running, since accumulated dust can cause the blade to slip. Also look for band wheels mounted on sealed bearings – they never need lubricating.

Two-wheel band saw   **Three-wheel band saw**

Blade guides

Bearings or guide blocks support the blade on both sides and from behind so as to resist the tendency for it to be twisted and pushed off the band wheels by the action of cutting a workpiece. One set of bearings, mounted above the saw table, is moved up or down to accommodate the thickness of the work; and a fixed set of bearings is usually mounted below the table. Blade guides must be capable of adjustment to very fine tolerances.

Blade tension and tracking

The blade's tension is adjusted by moving the top band wheel up or down. Some saws are made with a scale that indicates the tension for each blade, but usually the correct blade tension has to be ascertained by experimentation and experience. The tracking is adjustable to ensure that the blade runs centrally on the band wheels.

Blade guards

Except for the part exposed to the work, the entire band-saw blade is enclosed by the machine's casing. The exposed section is shielded by a vertically adjustable guard.

Saw frame

The best band saws are constructed with a rigid heavy-gauge steel frame to resist the considerable tension applied to the blade. A saw cannot run true if the frame is flexible.

Saw table

The majority of saw tables are made from cast iron, ground fabricated steel or an aluminium alloy. They are machined perfectly flat or have grooves for faster sawdust clearance.

Every band-saw table tilts to 45 degrees for cutting mitres and bevels. A scale under the table indicates the angle of tilt. The average table is 400 to 450mm (1ft 4in to 1ft 6in) square.

Rip fence

Straight ripcuts are made against a short adjustable fence. Very deep or long workpieces may prove unstable when using the rip fence as supplied – in which case, extend the fence by screwing a higher wooden fence onto it. You will find it advantageous if the rip fence can be mounted on either side of the blade, particularly for bevel ripping when gravity will help hold the work against the fence on the tilted table. Some saws are made with a depth stop mounted ahead of the rip fence for cutting tenons and other joints to length.

Mitre fence

A mitre fence slides along a groove machined or cast in the saw table. By adjusting the angle of the fence, it is possible to make square or mitred crosscuts. Mitre fences are often too short, and should be extended with a wooden facing to support long workpieces.

On/off switches

As a safety feature, on/off switches are sometimes made with a removable key. On some models opening the blade-access doors automatically immobilizes the machine to ensure that the saw cannot be switched on accidentally when the blade and band wheels are exposed.

Foot brake

Floorstanding band saws are sometimes fitted with a brake to bring the blade to a stop after switching the machine off.

Dust extraction

A sawdust exhaust port below the table can be attached to the hose of a portable extractor.

USING A BAND SAW SAFELY

A band saw is a relatively safe woodworking machine providing you follow general safety recommendations and observe the following rules.

- Always adjust the blade guard and top guides as close as possible to the workpiece.
- Do not feed work with your thumbs directly in line with the blade. Use a push stick to feed a narrow workpiece.
- To avoid pulling the moving blade off the band wheels, never back out of a deep cut without switching off first.
- Should a blade break or slip from the band wheels while you are using the saw, switch off immediately and stand back. Do not open the blade-access doors until the machine has come to a stop.
- Replace blunt or damaged blades before you find you are having to feed the work with excess force.
- Wear gloves when coiling or uncoiling band-saw blades.

TYPES OF BAND SAW

The larger band saws stand on the workshop floor and have a one-piece frame. The smaller models are designed for mounting on a low bench. You can either buy a bench as an accessory or make your own.

Floor-standing band saw

Bench-mounted band saw

When you buy a band saw, it will probably be fitted with one of the wider saw blades available for that particular machine. However, a much wider range of blades is made for every band saw and even if you decide to continue using one or two blades only, it is worth knowing about the full range in case you want to perform a specific procedure on your saw which your standard blades cannot cope with.

Material
Band-saw blades are made from a tough flexible steel with a hard, brittle cutting edge that stays sharp and keeps its set for long periods even when sawing man-made boards. Hard-edged blades cannot be file-sharpened and are thrown away as soon as they become blunt.

Although relatively soft nickel-steel blades can be sharpened, reset and even rewelded when broken, the cost of professional repair and maintenance is such that the longer-lasting disposable blades are a better proposal.

Tooth size
In spite of metrication, saw-tooth size is specified by the number of teeth that fit into a 1in length of blade. For a given thickness, tough wood, chipboard and plywood require more teeth per inch (TPI) than resinous softwood. Also, bear in mind that small teeth tend to skid when cutting softwoods.

Generally, the best finish is achieved using relatively fine teeth with a high saw speed and a slow rate of feed. For faster cutting, fit a blade with larger teeth, then increase both the saw speed and feed rate.

Width of blade
Depending on the model of band saw, blades are available from 3 to 20mm ($\frac{1}{8}$ to $\frac{3}{4}$in) wide. Wide blades tend to hold a straight line better than narrow ones, and are selected for ripping timber and boards to width.

When you want to cut curves in timber, select the optimum width of blade to suit the minimum radius.

To save time in changing blades, most woodworkers fit a medium-width blade for general-purpose work.

Tooth shape
The shape of the saw tooth is designed either for faster cutting or a clean finish.

Regular teeth

Skip teeth

Hook teeth

Regular tooth This is the standard type of tooth for most band-saw blades. It will produce an accurate fine finish on most woods and man-made boards.

Skip tooth The shape of a skip tooth is similar to that of a regular tooth, but each one is separated by a wide gullet for better chip removal. The finish is relatively rough. Skip-tooth blades are particularly suitable for sawing deep workpieces.

Hook tooth This kind of tooth has what is known as a 'positive rake' – i.e. the leading edge of each tooth leans at an acute angle. A hook tooth is able to cut hard material quickly.

Tooth set
Band-saw teeth are bent sideways to cut a kerf wider than the body of the blade, thus providing a clearance which reduces friction in a straight cut and also permits the work to be steered on a curved path.

Standard set

Raker set

Wavy set

Standard set The teeth are bent alternately to left and right, as on the blades of most woodcutting saws.

Raker set Blades designed primarily for cutting curves have pairs of standard-set teeth separated by a single unset tooth.

Wavy set Groups of teeth set alternately to the left and right form a wavy cutting edge on this type of blade. It is the best sort of blade for cutting thin boards.

Special-purpose bands
Occasionally, you may want to cut materials that require special-purpose bands instead of the usual toothed blades. A band is fitted like a saw blade, but an abrasive one is backed up by a rigid plate bolted in place of the blade guides.

Straight knife-edge band

Scalloped knife-edge band

Wavy-edge band

Abrasive band

Knife-edge bands To cut upholstery foams, fabrics and cork, fit a straight, scalloped or wavy-edge knife band.

Abrasive bands These are narrow flexible bands covered with abrasive material for shaping and sanding straight and curved edges.

BLADE-WIDTH GUIDE

Select the width of blade to suit the minimum radius of a curved cut.

Blade width	mm	3	6	10	12	15	20
	in	$\frac{1}{8}$	$\frac{1}{4}$	$\frac{3}{8}$	$\frac{1}{2}$	$\frac{5}{8}$	$\frac{3}{4}$
Minimum radius	mm	8	25	38	62	100	136
	in	$\frac{5}{16}$	1	$1\frac{1}{2}$	$2\frac{1}{2}$	4	$5\frac{1}{2}$

CHANGING A BAND-SAW BLADE

Whether you need to replace a blade because it has become blunt or simply want to swap it for one of a different size or tooth configuration, the procedure is identical.

Replacing the blade

To change a blade, first remove the rip-fence guide rail and blade guard, then withdraw the blade guides. Lower the upper band wheel by turning the blade-tension adjuster, and lift the blade out of the machine.

Place the new saw blade over the top wheel and feed it onto the lower one while turning the wheels slowly by hand. The blade teeth should be facing the operator and pointing downwards towards the saw table.

Tension the blade just enough to take up the slack, then check the tracking by spinning the band wheels by hand. Professional sawyers like to have the blade running close to the front edges of the wheels (1), but it is normally safer to position the blade centrally (2). However, check the manufacturer's recommendations for tracking adjustment. Adjust the tracking device until the blade runs true.

Raise the top wheel until the correct tension is indicated on the appropriate scale or the unsupported section of the blade can flex no more than about 6mm ($\frac{1}{4}$in) to either side.

1 Some sawyers track close to the front edges of band wheels

2 It is safer to run a blade that is centred on the wheels

Setting the blade guides

Set both sets of blade guides in the same way. First, adjust the thrust bearing up to the back edge of the blade, leaving the minimum clearance so that contact is made only when load is applied to the blade.

Next, adjust the side bearings to leave a paper-thin clearance on each side of the blade (3). Each bearing should be level with the roots of the teeth when the blade is cutting (4). If you advance the bearings too far, they will destroy the set of the blade.

Finally, replace the guard, close the blade-access doors and reassemble the rip fence before switching on.

3 Side-bearing adjustment
Leave a tiny gap on each side.

THRUST BEARING
SIDE BEARING
4 Set bearings level with roots

FOLDING A BAND-SAW BLADE

Store band-saw blades by folding them in three coils and hanging them on pegs on the workshop wall. Until you have developed the knack of folding a blade, wear gloves to protect your hands and wrists.

With the teeth facing away from you, hold one side of the loop in each hand; at the same time, hold the blade lightly under one foot (1). Bring your hands together, allowing the top of the loop to bend towards the floor (2). Cross the blade over itself to form three coils (3), then let it fall lightly to the floor.

To unfold a coiled band, hold it securely while you separate the coils slowly and allow the blade to spring open away from you.

1 Hold the band in both hands and under one foot

2 Bring hands together to form a loop in the blade

3 Cross the blade over to form three coils, then let it fall

MAKING CURVED CUTS ON A BAND SAW

Sawing freehand by following a line marked on a workpiece is not difficult providing the blade is sharp and accurately set. If the blade is blunt or damaged, it is much more likely to wander and you will find yourself constantly correcting the line of cut, which inevitably puts a strain on the blade. Select the width of blade to suit the minimum radius you wish to cut, and plan the procedure to ensure that the bulk of the workpiece is able to pass through the throat of the saw.

2 Cutting a tight curve
Remove waste in sections.

1 Freehand cutting
Guide the work with both hands.

3 Cut waste first
Waste falls away as curve is cut.

Following a curve freehand

Feed the work into the blade, cutting at a steady rate on the waste side of the line, and follow the curve without twisting the blade in the kerf. As the blade approaches the end of the cut, keep your hands away from the cutting edge and, if need be, pass one hand behind the blade to guide the work (**1**).

If the blade begins to bind as you negotiate a tight curve, do not withdraw it. Instead, run it out to the side of the work through the waste and start the cut again. It may be necessary to perform a similar procedure several times to complete a curve (**2**).

If you suspect in advance that it will be impossible to complete a cut in one flowing movement, make short straight cuts through the waste so that it will fall away in sections as the curved cut progresses (**3**). Alternatively, drill clearance holes at strategic points so that you can turn the blade in another direction (**4**). If there's no escape route for a binding blade, switch off and slowly back out of the kerf.

4 Drill holes at strategic points to change direction

Cutting parallel curves
Feed the work against a rounded block clamped to the saw table.

Cutting parallel curves

Curved components often have parallel sides. To help cut one curve parallel to another, round over the end of a block of timber and clamp it to the saw table, leaving a clearance between it and the blade equal to the width of the finished workpiece. Run one of the curves against the rounded end of the block while following the other marked line with the saw blade.

Cutting identical components

To make identical components, cut several blanks and pin them together through the waste. Following the outline of the workpiece marked on the top blank, cut all the components in a single pass.

Cutting three-dimensional curves with a band saw

To cut a component that has three-dimensional curves (a cabriole leg, for example), mark out its shape on two adjacent sides of a square-section blank. Cut one side freehand, then replace the waste and tape it in position. Turn the workpiece through 90 degrees in order to cut the second curve.

Cutting a cabriole leg
Tape waste onto the workpiece before making the second cut.

RIPSAWING ON A BAND SAW

Making a ripcut parallel to another edge is a straightforward procedure – but unless the blade is sharp and set perfectly, it will tend to drift off line even when you are ripping against a fence. Also, make sure the blade guides are adjusted correctly and the tracking is true.

Ripping against the fence

With the work pressed against it, adjust the rip fence sideways until the blade is just on the waste side of the marked line. Switch on and feed the work at a steady rate, without forcing it. Keep the work-piece pressed against the fence throughout the cut.

Finish cutting a narrow workpiece by feeding it with a push stick, pressing diagonally towards the fence.

Ripping against the fence

Ripping against a block

If a blade persists in wandering when you are using the rip fence, employ a rounded guide block similar to that used for cutting parallel curves. Clamp it to the saw table, leaving the required clearance between blade and block, and make the ripcut freehand so that you can compensate for the sideways drift by slightly changing the direction of feed.

Ripping against a rounded block

Resawing timber

When resawing a piece of timber into thinner planks, fit a wide blade and use either the rip fence or a guide block. Hold the work against the fence with a block of scrap wood and feed with a push stick.

Bevel ripping

To cut chamfers along a workpiece, tilt the saw table and position the rip fence below the blade. If you cannot fit your fence on the downside of the blade, clamp a temporary wooden fence to the saw table for bevel ripping.

Cutting chamfers
Tilt the table for bevel ripping.

CROSSCUTTING ON A BAND SAW

Reasonably accurate crosscutting is possible on a band saw but the finish will not be as good as on a table saw. If appearance is important, you will need to plane or sand the end grain.

Hold the work firmly against the mitre fence and feed it past the blade by sliding the fence along its groove machined in the saw table. Don't force the pace or you will distort the blade.

Clamp a block to the rip fence to serve as an end stop when you want to saw several identical offcuts **(1)**.

To cut a number of work-pieces to the same length, extend the saw's mitre fence with a wooden facing and clamp an end stop to it. Butt the squared end of each workpiece against the end stop and cut it to length **(2)**.

Cut a mitre by adjusting the angle of the fence. To make a compound-angle mitre, tilt the saw table at the same time.

1 Making identical offcuts

2 Cutting identical components to length

CUTTING JOINTS ON A BAND SAW

Any joint that incorporates a tongue – a tenon, lap joint, barefaced housing, corner halving joint and so on – can be cut in a similar way. The procedure for cutting a tenon demonstrates the principle. To avoid having to back out of a deep cut, always saw the shoulders first so that when you cut alongside the tongue the waste will fall away.

Using an end stop clamped to the rip fence as a guide, crosscut the shoulder lines of the tenon.

Adjust the rip fence to saw alongside the tenon, with the waste facing away from the fence. Set the depth stop to complete the cut on the shoulder line. If your saw is not fitted with a depth stop, clamp a block to the fence ahead of the work.

To ensure that the tenon is centred on the rail, cut one side, then turn the work over and cut the other.

Cutting a tenon
Adjust the saw's depth stop to complete the cut on the tenon's shoulder line.

POWERED FRET SAWS

Powered fret saws are generally associated with model-making and lightweight craftwork, but the better-quality saws will cut relatively thick timber with ease and to a superb finish. The saw's reciprocal action derives from the hand-held fret saw, but the powered version leaves both hands free to guide the work – enabling you to work accurately and also to cut a very tight curve when required. To a large extent, *the fret saw's popularity is due to its safety record. Any blade that cuts wood can cut your fingers, but if you operate the saw with care and observe general machine-shop safety procedures, it is practically impossible to have a serious accident. Most powered fret saws are designed to be bolted to a bench at standing height. Make sure the bench is solidly built, or accuracy will be impaired by excessive vibration.*

Depth of cut
Even a reasonably small powered fret saw is capable of cutting 50mm (2in) wood, and the heavy-duty ones can handle timber of twice that thickness.

Saw table
Whether the saw table is made from cast alloy or pressed metal, it must be flat and rigid. Nearly all tables can be tilted for making bevel cuts, and some can be raised or lowered to utilize another section of the blade as one part becomes worn.

Throat
A fret saw's throat – the distance between the blade and the column behind the saw table – determines the maximum width of cut possible. A small powered fret saw has a throat of about 380mm (1ft 3in) or less, but you can buy larger saws that will cut boards 600mm (2ft) wide. In any case, blades can be turned through 45 or 90 degrees so that a long workpiece can be fed past the column.

Length of stroke
Even though a fret saw will cut quite thick material, the length of stroke – vertical movement of the blade – is relatively short. As a result, if you cut a lot of thin materials, you will blunt a short section of blade just above the table while the rest of the saw teeth remain untouched. To get more use out of the blade, raise the work on a table top made from chipboard or plywood 18mm ($\frac{3}{4}$in) thick.

Blade tensioner
Fret-saw blades are extremely narrow and must therefore be held taut to prevent them bending when load is applied. This is achieved by a strong spring acting on one end of the blade. On some saws, spring tension is adjustable to suit different blade sizes.

● Electric motor
The tiny 100W induction motor that powers the average machine fret saw is capable of generating blade speeds of between 2800 and 5750 strokes per minute. Some fret saws are supplied with variable-speed control.

Hold down
An adjustable hold-down stops a thin workpiece vibrating.

BLADE TENSIONER

DUST-CLEARANCE PIPE

HEGNER

TILTING SAW TABLE

BLADE

ON/OFF SWITCH

TABLE CLAMPING SCREW

Powered fret saw

MOTOR HOUSING

BELLOWS SUPPLIES AIR TO DUST-CLEARANCE PIPE

FRET-SAW BLADES

Blade guard
A blade guard on a fret saw is very simple, usually consisting of one or two vertical wire or plastic rods that form part of the hold-down. This type of guard is designed to stop you pushing your fingers against the blade. However, if you feed the work correctly, this should never happen. When cutting thick timber a fret saw is often operated without a blade guard of any description, especially since with some saws the hold-down with its integral guard is offered only as an optional accessory.

Hold-downs
To prevent a thin workpiece 'chattering', or vibrating noisily, fret saws are supplied with a hold-down to stop the work being lifted from the table by the action of the blade. A sprung hold-down will lift automatically as thin wood is fed towards the blade, but with thicker wood it may be necessary to lift the hold-down up onto the workpiece before you can begin to cut. A vertically adjustable hold-down is set to suit the individual workpiece before cutting starts.

Dust extraction
Dust-extraction systems are not normally supplied for powered fret saws – but, as the sawdust produced is very fine, if you suffer from respiratory ailments wear a face mask.

On/off switch
The on/off switch on most fret saws is of the simple toggle variety.

Dust clearance
A feature of the better-quality fret saws is a pipe mounted just behind the blade which blows sawdust away from the point of cut before it obscures your view of the marked line.

There are coarse 'coping-saw' blades with standard alternate-set teeth for ripping thick timber, but most of the blades made for powered fret saws have a skip-tooth arrangement – a deep gullet between each tooth – or else pairs of teeth separated by deep gullets. Skip-tooth or double-tooth blades will cut wood and soft metals, and you can also buy jeweller's blades for cutting hard ferrous metals.

BLADE-SIZE SELECTION

BLADE SIZE	TPI	MATERIAL THICKNESS
1 2	25 23	Veneers and wood up to 6mm ($\frac{1}{4}$in) Plastics up to 6mm ($\frac{1}{4}$in) Soft metals up to 1.5mm ($\frac{1}{16}$in)
3 4	20 18	Hardwoods up to 12mm ($\frac{1}{2}$in) Softwoods up to 18mm ($\frac{3}{4}$in) Plastics up to 6mm ($\frac{1}{4}$in) Soft metals up to 3mm ($\frac{1}{8}$in)
5 6	16$\frac{1}{2}$ 15	Hardwood from 6 to 18mm ($\frac{1}{4}$ to $\frac{3}{4}$in) Softwoods 6 to 25mm ($\frac{1}{4}$ to 1in) Plastics up to 12mm ($\frac{1}{2}$in) Soft metals up to 6mm ($\frac{1}{4}$in)
7 8 9	14 14 14	Hardwoods from 6 to 25mm ($\frac{1}{4}$ to 1in) Softwoods 6 to 50mm ($\frac{1}{4}$ to 2in) Plastics up to 12mm ($\frac{1}{2}$in) Soft metals up to 12mm $\frac{1}{2}$in)
10 11 12	12$\frac{1}{2}$ 12$\frac{1}{2}$ 12$\frac{1}{2}$	Hardwoods from 18 to 50mm ($\frac{3}{4}$ to 2in) Softwoods 18 to 50mm ($\frac{3}{4}$ to 2in) Plastics up to 18mm ($\frac{3}{4}$in) Soft metals up to 12mm ($\frac{1}{2}$in)
		The larger blades may have a similar TPI, but are made to different widths to cope with more intricate work.

Selecting the size of blade
Blade size is normally specified by the numbers 1 to 12, although not all manufacturers supply the complete range. Each size of blade is designed to cope with materials of different thicknesses, but the intricacy of cut will also affect your choice. Select a finer blade if the one you are using cannot negotiate a tight curve.

The chart above is intended as a guide to selecting the appropriate blade size, but the final compromise between smoothness of finish, speed of cut and durability of blade must be a matter of experiment and personal preference.

Fitting a blade
Follow the fret-saw manufacturer's instructions for fitting and tensioning a blade. The teeth of the blade should always point downwards towards the saw table.

Fitting a fret-saw blade
Make sure the saw teeth point towards the table.

MAKING CURVED CUTS ON A FRET SAW

Cutting a curved workpiece, even one that is quite intricately shaped, is a commonplace task on a powered fret saw. So long as you are using a blade of the right width, it is easy enough to follow a marked line freehand, always cutting on the waste side of the line to preserve the shape of the finished piece.

Cutting curves
Feed the work with both hands, holding it flat on the saw table while applying forward pressure into the blade. Keep your hands on either side of the blade, never directly in line with it. Be patient and feed the work slowly, allowing the blade to cut naturally. If you feel you are having to force the pace, change the blunt blade for a sharp one.

While concentrating on the point of cut, it is all too easy to distort a narrow blade by unintentional sideways pressure or by twisting the work. To allow the blade to spring back to its natural position, relax fingertip pressure very slightly while continuing to maintain control over the work.

Cutting an aperture
First, drill a small hole in the waste through which you can pass the blade; then, with the saw switched off, connect both ends to the saw. Switch on again and follow your marked line to complete the aperture, then release the blade to remove the workpiece.

Making bevel cuts
To make a bevel cut on a fret saw, adjust the angle of the saw table, then proceed as if you were cutting a square edge, taking extra care not to distort the blade. To avoid distortion, keep the feed pressure directly in line with the cutting edge.

Cutting an aperture

MAKING STRAIGHT CUTS ON A FRET SAW

A powered fret saw is not especially good for making straight cuts, but you can clamp a temporary wooden fence to the table to guide the work on its intended path. As most fretwork consists of a combination of straight and curved shapes, it is usually necessary to follow all marked lines by eye. To make a long straight cut, following the manufacturer's instructions, turn the blade to an angle that allows you to feed the work past the saw column at the rear of the table.

Cutting with a temporary fence

Combining straight and curved cuts
If the combination of straight and curved lines is such that you will need to change one blade for another, drill access holes at strategic points where the wider blade will have to be swapped for a narrow one and vice versa.

BLADE-ACCESS HOLES

Bore access holes to change blades

PLANERS

Having acquired a table or band saw, most woodworkers begin to think about buying a machine that will plane smooth surfaces on all four sides of a workpiece accurately. A production workshop is often equipped with two separate machines. The first is a surface planer or jointer for dressing the face side and face edge of a workpiece. The same workpiece then passes through a thicknesser which planes the remaining surfaces parallel to face side and edge. If there is no room or need for two planers, home woodworkers often opt for a planer/thicknesser which combines both functions in a single machine.

Maximum planing width
Planers are most often specified according to the widest workpiece you can plane on the machine – which is determined by the length of the cutters bolted into the revolving cutter block. Small special-purpose surface planers have short cutters – 150mm (6in) or less – but the average home-workshop planer/thicknesser will have a maximum planing width of about 260mm ($10\frac{1}{4}$in).

Cutter-block speed
The cylindrical block with its two or three balanced cutters revolves at a very high speed in order to produce a clean, smooth surface. Cutter-block speed is sometimes specified in revolutions per minute, but a more telling figure is the number of cuts produced per minute by the moving cutters. A three-cutter block will produce more cuts per minute than a two-cutter block revolving at the same speed. For a two-cutter block 12,000 cuts per minute is a respectable speed.

Combined length of tables
In order to be able to plane a perfectly straight edge on a workpiece, the overall length of the infeed plus outfeed tables should be as long as possible. The overall length of the average planer is about 1m (3ft 3in).

Fence
A rigid metal fence is essential for planing true square or bevelled edges on a workpiece. All fences can be tilted to any angle from 90 to 45 degrees to the tables. It is convenient if the fence automatically comes to a stop at both extremes, but check the settings with a try square or sliding bevel.

Maximum depth of cut
The cutter block is situated between two independently adjustable cast-metal tables. The height of the table to the rear of the cutter block – the outfeed table – should be adjusted so that it is level with the top of the circle described by the revolving cutters. The table in front of the cutter block – the infeed table – is lowered to produce the required depth of cut, up to a maximum of about 3mm ($\frac{1}{8}$in). A very shallow 0.5mm ($\frac{1}{32}$in) cut will produce a superior finish; but for speed, make two or three deeper cuts followed by one or more finishing cuts. Depth of cut is indicated by a scale next to the infeed table.

WORKPIECE

OUTFEED TABLE

INFEED TABLE

DEPTH OF CUT

Setting the depth of cut

CUTTER-BLOCK

Cutter-block guard

A planer's revolving cutters are capable of severing a finger-tip in a fraction of a second – so never operate the machine without the appropriate guard.

A bridge guard that is adjustable in height and which can be slid across the entire width of the cutter block is the ideal form of protection. Some planers are made with spring-loaded bridge guards which are lifted or pushed aside by the work as it is passed over the cutter block. This type of guard is superior to the simpler version that merely swings aside to expose the cutters.

In addition, there should be a guard behind the fence that is automatically drawn across the cutter block as the fence is adjusted sideways.

You should never attempt to rebate a workpiece without a vertical/horizontal hold-down guard, so your hands need not approach the cutters.

A hold-down guard
Fit this type of guard when planing a rebate.

OUTFEED TABLE

FENCE

CUTTER-BLOCK
BRIDGE GUARD

SECONDARY CUTTER-
BLOCK GUARD

INFEED TABLE

ELECTRIC-MOTOR HOUSING

DEPTH SCALE

DEWALT mod. DW 1150
PLANER-THICKNESSER

**Planer/thicknesser in
surface-planing mode**

DEPTH-OF-CUT
CONTROL

On/off switches
On/off switches should be accessible from either end of the machine so you can turn it off quickly in an emergency, no matter whether you happen to be surface-planing or thicknessing.

SURFACING TABLES

GUARD AND SHAVINGS DEFLECTOR

Planer/thicknesser in thicknessing mode

ON/OFF-SWITCH HOUSING

THICKNESSING TABLE

CUTTING-DEPTH ADJUSTER

FEED-SPEED CONTROL LEVER

CUTTING-DEPTH SCALE

MOTOR HOUSING

Width of thicknesser table
The average thicknesser table is about 250mm (10in) wide. Never attempt to plane a workpiece which is shorter than the width of the table. If a piece of wood is able to slew sideways, it may be splintered by the feed rollers and cutters, and pieces can be thrown out of the planer with considerable force.

Feed rollers
A thicknesser is equipped with two motor-driven spring-loaded feed rollers that pass the workpiece under the revolving cutter block and out the other end of the machine. The infeed roller, usually a horizontally ribbed steel roller, is situated in front of the cutter block and provides the main driving force. The outfeed roller, which is situated behind the cutter block, is smooth – so as not to mark the planed surface – and exerts less pressure on the work. When taking a very shallow cut, the parallel bruising left by a ribbed roller is sometimes detectable on the planed surface. For this reason, some planers are made with rubber-covered drive rollers.

Thicknesser feed rollers
1 Infeed roller
2 Chip breaker
3 Cutter block
4 Pressure bar
5 Outfeed roller
6 Workpiece

Maximum thicknessing depth
When a workpiece is passed through a thicknesser, it travels on a bed situated beneath the same cutter block used for surface planing. The thicknessing table on the average home-workshop machine can be raised or lowered to accommodate any workpiece up to a maximum thickness of 160 to 180mm (6 to 7in). Even though the thicknesser is power driven, never attempt to take more than 3 to 4mm ($\frac{1}{8}$in) in one pass.

Electric motors
A small 375W ($\frac{1}{2}$hp) electric motor is powerful enough for a special-purpose surface planer. However, on a thicknesser the motor is used to drive the feed rollers and cutter block simultaneously, so a larger 1.5 to 2.2kW (2 to 3hp) motor is required. On some models, the drive rollers can be disconnected from the motor so that its entire output is available for surface planing.

Thicknesser feed rate
Because an amateur woodworker is not primarily concerned with a fast throughput of work, he or she is more likely to be attracted by a planer that produces a good finish at the expense of speed – since a slow feed rate combined with a high cutter-block speed produces the best finish. Many thicknessers are therefore designed to feed the work at the relatively slow speed of about 5m (16ft) per minute. However, you can buy a thicknesser with a feed rate of 9m (29ft) per minute, which can be increased to 11m (36ft) per minute. As a general rule, feed hardwoods slowly but increase the feed rate for softwoods.

Anti-kickback device

If for some reason the drive rollers loose their grip on a workpiece, it may be thrown out of the machine by the cutter block and a serious accident can occur if you are feeding the work at the time. To prevent this, a row of pointed metal teeth or 'pawls' hang in front of the infeed roller. As the work travels under them, the pawls lift to allow free passage. Should the work begin to travel backwards, the pointed pawls catch in the wood surface and restrict its movement.

Dust extractor

Without an extractor, shavings are dumped onto the tables above and below the cutter block where they impair the efficiency and accuracy of the machine. Consequently, you have to stop the planer regularly to clear the accumulated debris. A hose attachment leading to a portable extractor solves the problem.

USING A PLANER/THICKNESSER SAFELY

Always operate a planer confidently but with extreme caution. An accident can happen so quickly that even the fastest reflexes will not save you from injury. It is therefore essential to cultivate a safe method of working and always observe general machine-shop safety procedures.

- Follow the manufacturer's instructions for fitting cutters, and always complete the procedure before you leave the machine. If you are distracted and forget to secure a cutter, a serious accident could result when you switch on the machine.
- Inspect the machine before you switch on to make sure nothing is likely to foul the cutter block.
- Never use a surface planer without a properly adjusted guard in position.
- Use a push block to feed a thin workpiece over the cutters. Never attempt to plane a piece of wood less than 6mm ($\frac{1}{4}$in) thick.
- Don't attempt to surface-plane a workpiece that is too short to be held firmly in both hands.
- Never trail your fingers or thumb behind a workpiece.
- Always feed work against the direction of rotation of the cutter block. When surface-planing, pass the work from infeed to outfeed table. Feed from the opposite end of the machine when thicknessing.
- Feed one workpiece at a time through a thicknesser. The feed-roller pressure may not be consistent across a number of pieces, and one of them could be thrown back by the cutter block.
- Don't try to force a workpiece through a thicknesser. Let the feed rollers work at their intended rate.
- When planing a workpiece of uneven thickness, set the depth of cut to cope with the thickest section first, then gradually raise the thicknessing table between passes until you are cutting the full length of the board.
- Don't feed work that is shorter than the width of the thicknessing table nor shorter than the distance between the feed rollers.
- When planing long workpieces, either have an assistant take the weight as they come off the machine or set up a roller stand or trestles to support the work.
- Never put your hands into a thicknesser to retrieve a workpiece or clear away shavings. Use a long push stick instead, to extend your reach.

PLANER CUTTERS

A few planers are made with double-edge disposable cutters similar to those used in portable power planers. However, the majority of machines are fitted with two or three single-edge cutters or 'knives' which need to be honed and sharpened at regular intervals.

Types of cutter

Planers for the home-workshop market are supplied with high-speed-steel cutters that are perfectly adequate unless you expect to plane a lot of chipboard or 'gritty' timbers like teak. When planing these materials, follow production-workshop practice and fit the more expensive tungsten-carbide-tipped cutters, which will hold a sharp edge much longer but must, when the time comes, be sent to a professional for sharpening. Even high-speed-steel cutters are sent for regrinding, but they can be honed in the meantime by running an oilstone along the cutting edges.

Fitting cutters

It is important to follow the manufacturer's instructions for fitting cutters to your planer. However, in principle, each cutter fits into a slot in the cylindrical block. In some cases the cutter rests on springs at the bottom of the slot, and height adjustment is simply a matter of holding the cutter down against their compression. The cutter is normally secured with a wedge-shaped bar clamp held tight by adjusting expansion bolts. Always double-check that the cutters are tight before you switch on.

Adjusting cutters

Each cutter must project from the block by exactly the same amount if it is to do its fair share of the work. If one cutter is set higher than another, it will do all the planing but a loss of finish will result. It is possible to buy special equipment for gauging cutter setting, but in a home workshop a straight batten is quite good enough. Always disconnect a planer from the supply of electricity before making adjustments to the cutters.

Adjust all the cutters by eye until they appear to project the required amount. Lower the outfeed table slightly, then rest the wooden batten on it overhanging one end of the cutter block. Mark the edge of the outfeed table on the batten **(1)**. Turn the cutter block slowly by hand, allowing the cutter to lift the batten and carry it forward, then mark the edge of the batten again **(2)**.

Move the batten to the other end of the cutter block, aligning the first mark with the edge of the table. Turn the block again. The same cutter should move the batten forward by exactly the same amount. If the second mark does not align with the table edge, adjust the height of the cutter at that end until it does.

Tighten the cutter bar clamp, then repeat the gauging process at each end to make sure that clamping has not altered the setting. Turn the block and set each cutter in the same way. Finally, raise the outfeed table until each cutter just scrapes the underside of the batten.

EXPANSION BOLT

COIL SPRING

CUTTER   BAR CLAMP

A typical planer cutter block

- **Cleaning the cutter block**
Before you fit new or reground cutters, clean wood resin from the cutter-block slots and bar clamps with a solvent such as cellulose thinner or white spirit.

1 Mark the edge of the outfeed table on a batten

2 Turn the cutter block, then make a second mark on the batten

SURFACE PLANING

To machine-plane a piece of timber, first prepare the face side and face edge on the surface planer then pass it through the thicknesser to plane the remaining faces.

Inspect the workpiece to select the most suitable faces to plane. If the workpiece is bowed, plane it with the concave face resting on the feed tables – it is virtually impossible to flatten a convex surface on a planer since the workpiece is sure to rock on the tables as you pass it across the cutters.

To achieve a smooth finish, orientate the wood so that the grain runs at an angle away from the cutters. Occasionally, when the grain runs in different directions, the decision may not be quite so straightforward – in which case, take a fine cut and if the planer tears the grain, turn the work round and try again.

Grain direction
Feed the work with the grain running at an angle away from the cutters.

Adjust guard to plane an edge

Raise guard to just clear the work

Planing face side

Lower the thicknesser table, then move the fence aside to accommodate the widest face of the workpiece and select the depth of cut by adjusting the infeed table.

Slide the bridge guard to cover the cutter block and, with the wood resting on the infeed table, raise the guard to just clear the workpiece.

Stand to the side of the infeed table and switch on. With your right hand flat on the work, feed the wood across the cutters (**1**). Apply just enough pressure to control the work. If you press a bowed or twisted workpiece flat on the infeed table, the cutters will remove an even layer from the surface – but as soon as you relieve the pressure, the wood will spring back to its distorted condition. Your intention should be to plane just those points in contact with the table, gradually removing more and more wood until the surface is flat.

As soon as the workpiece passes under the guard, shift your body weight to hold the work on the outfeed table with your left hand (**2**). Continue feeding the work at an even rate, transferring your right hand to the work on the outfeed table (**3**). Keep the work moving until you have completed the first cut. Return the workpiece to the infeed table and repeat the process until the face side is flat, then switch off.

1 Feed the work across the cutters

2 Shift your weight to the outfeed table

3 Transfer your right hand to the outfeed table

Planing face edge

Brush any shavings away from the fence, and check that it is perfectly upright and tightly clamped.

Lower the guard completely and slide it sideways to allow the work to pass between the guard and the fence with minimum clearance. Check to make sure your fingertips cannot slip between the end of the fence and the workpiece.

Switch on and, with the face side held firmly against the fence, pass the work from one hand to the other over the cutter block.

Pass work from hand to hand

Tilt the fence to plane a bevel

Planing a bevelled edge
Support work with your left hand.

Planing a bevel

To plane a bevel edge on a workpiece, tilt the fence to the required angle and slide the bridge guard sideways allowing the minimum clearance for the work.

In order to maintain an accurate bevel, you must prevent the bottom edge of the work sliding away from the fence. Use your left hand as a stationary guide – holding the work against the fence with your index finger and thumb while resting the other three fingers on the outfeed table – and feed the work with your right hand.

Planing a stopped chamfer

A stopped chamfer is often used as a decorative feature in furniture-making. A surface planer is the ideal machine for producing such a detail, but take professional tuition before attempting the process yourself. It involves lowering both tables by an equal amount, so you can cut the chamfer in one pass. Screw end stops to a long board, clamp it to the fence and tilt the fence to 45 degrees. Adjust the guard as if you were planing a normal bevel.

Butt one end of the work firmly against the rearward end stop, while holding the other end above the cutter block (1). With your fingertips on the very end of the wood, lower the workpiece slowly onto the cutter block. There will be considerable rearward force on initial contact with the cutters. Feed the work along the fence until it comes to rest against the forward end stop, then carefully lift the wood off the cutters (2) and switch off. For safety, plane a stopped chamfer on an overlong piece of wood – then cut it to length at each end after machining.

Stopped chamfers

1 Lower the work onto the cutter block

2 When the work touches the stop, lift it off the cutters

Planing end grain

To plane end grain, construct a jig similar to the one used for cutting tenons on a table saw. Make the whole jig from softwood – plywood will chip the edges of planer cutters. Clamp the work in the jig before passing it across the cutter block.

Support the work in a jig when planing end grain

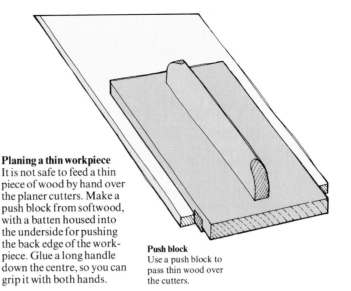

Planing a thin workpiece

It is not safe to feed a thin piece of wood by hand over the planer cutters. Make a push block from softwood, with a batten housed into the underside for pushing the back edge of the workpiece. Glue a long handle down the centre, so you can grip it with both hands.

Push block
Use a push block to pass thin wood over the cutters.

THICKNESSING

Having planed a flat face side and face edge, the work is ready for thicknessing, but don't waste time and money by turning more wood than necessary into shavings. Band-saw oversize workpieces close to finished width or thickness, then return them to the planer.

Preparing the thicknesser

Remove the fence, then lift and secure one or both surfacing tables, depending on the manufacturer's instructions. Swing the thicknesser's cutter-block guard and shavings deflector into position. Select the depth of cut by adjusting the thicknesser table to the necessary height indicated on its scale.

Feeding the work

Switch on and engage the automatic feed mechanism; then, standing slightly to one side of the machine, pass the end of the workpiece into the thicknesser until the feed rollers draw it under the cutter block. If the rollers do not take hold of the work, raise the table very slightly.

Move to the other end of the machine and withdraw the work, but don't attempt to accelerate the process by pulling the wood through the thicknesser.

Return to the infeed end of the machine and raise the table to take another cut, then repeat the process.

Planing a thin board

To plane a board thinner than the minimum depth of cut on a thicknesser, place it on top of a thicker board already planed to an even thickness and pass both boards through the machine together.

Planing an edge

If a workpiece is thick enough to be stable, you can pass it on edge through a thicknesser – but a thin workpiece can tip over as it is taken by the rollers, crushing the corners. If you suspect there is a possibility of damaging a workpiece, rip it to within 1mm ($\frac{1}{16}$in) of its final width on a table saw or band saw. If you are preparing several identical components, rip them all on the same setting. Take one workpiece to the finely set surface planer and plane the first 25mm (1in) of the sawn edge. Check the width and, if necessary, adjust the depth of cut and plane the same 25mm (1in) again. When you are satisfied with the width of the workpiece, pass the whole sawn edge over the cutters. Finally, with one pass, plane all the matching components to an identical width.

● **Cleaning the thicknesser**
Clean wood resin from the rollers and table of your thicknesser with a solvent such as white spirit or cellulose thinner. Polish the table with a dry cloth, and wax it occasionally to ensure smooth power feeding.

MORTISING ATTACHMENTS

Industrial workshops where cutting mortise and tenon joints is an integral part of a mass-production programme are equipped with heavy-duty mortising machines. These special-purpose machines are prohibitively expensive, but a good-quality mortising attachment that can be fitted to another machine, such as a drill press or planer, is a cheaper alternative which many amateur woodworkers find attractive.

HOLLOW-CHISEL MORTISER

A drill press can be adapted to cut mortises by fitting a hollow-chisel mortising attachment into the chuck.

The attachment includes a special auger drill in the centre of a square, hollow chisel that has four cutting edges. As it is plunged into the wood, the mortiser cuts a perfectly square hole – the auger drill boring out the waste just ahead of the chisel, which slices the corners square. To cut a long rectangular mortise, slide the workpiece sideways between each plunge of the chisel.

Although larger chisels are used in industrial production, home-workshop attachments are designed to take square chisels 6 to 18mm ($\frac{1}{4}$ to $\frac{3}{4}$in) wide.

Hollow-chisel mortising attachment

SHARPENING AN AUGER AND CHISEL

Mortising auger drills, like the ordinary auger bits used in a hand-cranked brace, are sharpened with a small file. The four cutting edges of the square chisel are sharpened simultaneously, using a special tool similar in design to a rose countersink but with a central pilot tip which keeps the tool centred in the chisel. Rotating the tool with a brace hones the chisel. Each chisel has to have its own matching sharpener.

Put a sharp edge on each spur with a small file

Holding the drill tip on a bench, sharpen the cutting edges

Hone the square chisel with a special tool

Using a hollow-chisel mortising attachment

Set the drill-press depth stop to determine the depth of the mortise. Plunge the chisel to cut a square hole against one shoulder line of the mortise (1), then slide the workpiece under the chisel and cut another hole against the other shoulder line (2). Finally, remove the waste between the holes with several plunges of the chisel (3).

Plunge a chisel at a firm but even rate. Don't force the pace when mortising hardwoods, since small chisels can be split by excessive pressure – but don't labour the process, either, or the chisel will overheat due to friction between it and the auger.

If you are going to cut a through mortise, place a strip of planed timber beneath the work. This will save the chisel being driven into the metal drill-press table and will also back up the workpiece, preventing the grain splitting as the chisel breaks through the underside of the wood. Alternatively, you can cut the mortise from both sides, by turning the work over.

1 Cut a hole at one end

2 Move to the other end

3 Remove the waste between

SLOT MORTISER

A slot mortiser incorporates a horizontally mounted milling cutter for machining workpieces.

This type of attachment uses the drive mechanism of another machine – typically a planer/thicknesser or a universal machine – and is fitted to a chuck at the end of the machine's cutter block. The chuck, similar to one on an electric drill, accommodates 6 to 16mm ($\frac{1}{4}$ to $\frac{5}{8}$in) diameter cutters with two cutting edges, one of which may be toothed.

A mortising table, to which the work is clamped, is mounted next to the cutter chuck. The table is able to slide sideways, moving the work relative to the stationary chuck, and travels back and forth to adapt to the depth of cut. The table is also adjustable in height and adjustable stops limit its travel, thus regulating the length and depth of the mortise. Lateral movement and fore-and-aft movement are controlled by levers.

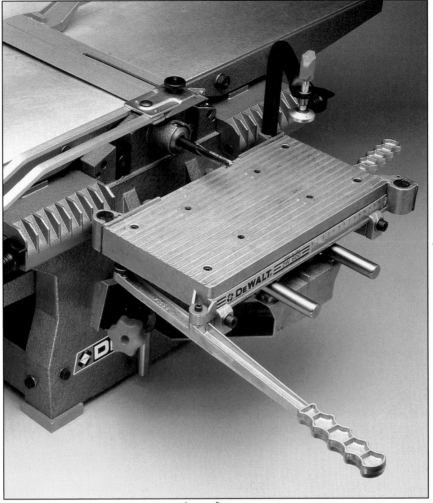

● **Sharpening milling cutters**
Sharpen a milling cutter by honing the inner faces of the cutting edges on an oiled slipstone. Do not hone the outer surfaces or you will alter the diameter of the cutter. Have cutters reground by an expert when they do not cut efficiently after honing.

Slot mortiser
This particular attachment fits onto a planer/thicknesser.

Using a slot mortiser
Cut a mortise in stages, plunging only as deep as the diameter of the cutter at one pass. To attempt to cut any deeper puts an unacceptable strain on the milling cutter, which may break under side pressure.

Having cut the mortise, you can either cut the shoulders square with a chisel or round over the ends of the matching tenon with a file or machine sander.

Cutting tenons with a mortising attachment
It is possible to remove the waste from both sides of a tenon with a milling cutter – but, since the cutter is not supported on two sides by timber, you must feed the work against its direction of rotation.

Cutting a mortise

Cut both sides of a tenon

DRILL PRESSES

A drill press is a heavy-duty stationary drilling machine. The drilling head, comprising the chuck for holding the drill bit, drive-belt mechanism and electric motor, is mounted on a rigid metal column. The column is supported by a heavy cast-metal base which is either bolted to a workbench or stands on the floor of the workshop. In the latter case, the column is long enough to raise both the drill and the worktable to a comfortable working height.

Chuck
A drill-press chuck has three self-centring jaws operated by a key and is identical in principle to the familiar power-drill chuck. Most drill-press chucks accommodate bits with shanks up to 12mm ($\frac{1}{2}$in) in diameter.

Drill-press vice
This small engineer's vice is for holding metal workpieces on a drill-press table.

BELT AND PULLEY HOUSING

DEPTH GAUGE

CHUCK

GUARD

COLUMN

MOTOR HOUSING

FEED LEVER

WORKTABLE

TABLE-HEIGHT ADJUSTER

BASE

Bench-mounted drill press

Electric motor
Stationary drills are made with induction motors rated between 187 and 750W ($\frac{1}{4}$ and 1hp). This type of motor is very efficient, but even so, it is best to buy a drill with at least a 250W ($\frac{1}{3}$hp) motor.

The motor's power is transmitted via a V-belt and pulley-wheel system to the spindle and chuck. Moving the rubber V-belt up or down stepped cone pulleys changes the speed in 4 or 5 increments between 450 and 3000 rpm.

The slowest speeds are selected for drilling metal or for boring large holes in hardwood. Increase the speed when working with softwood.

Worktable
A cast-metal worktable is cantilevered from the column. The table on some drills is raised or lowered by hand and clamped to the column in the required position by tightening a pinch bolt. Other drills are made with a rack-and-pinion system, the height of the table being adjusted by means of a crank handle.

Select a machine with a table that can be tilted to 45 degrees and which can be swung to one side by rotating it about the column in order to place a larger-than-average workpiece on the drill-press base.

A hole in the dead centre of the rectangular or circular worktable allows the drill bit to pass through a workpiece without damage. Fences, vices or jigs can be bolted to the table, using using the slots machined across it.

Drill-press base
For stability, the cast-metal base must be large and heavy. The upper surface is machined perfectly flat and is slotted to serve as a second worktable for large workpieces.

Throat
The throat – the distance from the centre of the worktable to the column – should be as large as possible. The throat capacity on home-workshop drill presses can be anything from 100 to 200mm (4 to 8in).

Feed lever
The drill bit is plunged into a workpiece by pulling down on the feed lever mounted on one side of the machine. Since it is spring-loaded, the lever returns automatically – but the mechanism can be locked with a clamp lever to run the drill in a lowered position, leaving both hands free for working.

Maximum depth of hole
The maximum depth of hole that can be bored on a particular drill press is determined by the vertical movement of the chuck. Maximum vertical movement varies from about 50 to 90mm (2 to 3$\frac{1}{2}$in) on bench-mounted machines, but you will probably be able to bore deeper holes on a floor-standing drill press.

Depth gauge
Drilling depth is controlled by setting a gauge. Mark the required depth on the side of the workpiece. Lower the chuck until the tip of the drill bit aligns with the mark, then set the depth-gauge stop to limit the vertical travel of the spindle and chuck.

Safety guard
If possible, buy a machine with a safety guard (usually made of transparent plastic) that drops down or swings across to shield the drill-press chuck. The guard prevents hair or loose clothing becoming caught in the rotating chuck. Closing the guard should also alert you to the presence of a chuck key accidentally left in the machine.

DRILL BITS

You will need a complete set of good-quality twist drills and dowel bits up to at least 10mm (⅜in) in diameter. However, as bits larger than that are relatively expensive, it is probably best to acquire them one at a time when the need arises.

Twist drills
Choose high-speed-steel twist drills, since these are equally suitable for wood and metal. Before boring a hole with a twist drill, mark the centre with a bradawl – or with a metalworking punch if you are drilling hardwood or metal.

Dowel bits
Dowel bits are designed to bore holes in end grain for dowel joints. They are also excellent general-purpose woodboring bits.

Power auger bits
Use power auger bits to drill deep holes in timber. An average set contains augers ranging from 6 to 25mm (¼ to 1in) in diameter.

Spade bits
These are relatively cheap bits for drilling holes from 6 to 38mm (¼ to 1½in) in diameter. The long leadpoints make for very positive location at the centre of a hole even when the workpiece is clamped to a tilted drill-press table.

Forstner bits
Forstner bits are expensive but they bore exceptionally clean flat-bottomed holes, and they are not deflected by knots or wild grain. Forstner bits are available in a wide range of sizes up to 50mm (2in) in diameter.

Countersink bits
Having drilled a clearance hole for a woodscrew, use a countersink bit to cut a tapered recess for the head. Select a high speed for a clean finish.

Drill-and-countersink bits
Made to match specific woodscrews, these bits drill a pilot hole, shank-clearance hole and countersink in a single operation.

Drill-and-counterbore bits
Set woodscrews below the surface of a workpiece by using a drill-and-counterbore bit. The neat hole above the screw can be filled with a specially cut wooden plug (see below).

Plug cutters
Drive these cutters into side-grain timber to make plugs for covering counterbored screws. Cut plugs from timber that closely matches the work in colour and grain pattern.

Hole saws
Cut a hole up to 89mm (3½in) in diameter by using one of a set of hole saws. Select a slow to medium speed and clamp the work firmly.

Dowel bit

Twist drill

Power auger bit

Forstner bit

Spade bit

Plug cutter

Countersink bit

Drill-and-countersink bit

Drill-and-counterbore bit

Hole saw

USING A DRILL PRESS SAFELY

Providing you follow general machine-shop safety procedures, a drill press is a relatively safe machine. However, you must take certain extra precautions.

- Always remove the chuck key after you have fitted a drill bit.
- Lower the safety guard before switching on.
- Hold the work securely on the drill-press table. If a drill bit catches, it can spin the work with serious consequences. Hold a wooden workpiece against the rigid column or a custom-made fence to resist the turning force, or clamp the work to the table.
- Always clamp a metal workpiece or hold it in a drill-press vice.

USING A DRILL PRESS

Having fitted a drill bit, adjust the worktable to bring the work to within a millimetre, or fraction of an inch, or so of its tip. Then set the depth gauge, centre the bit and switch on. Feed the bit into the work steadily – it isn't necessary to apply excessive force to a sharp drill bit. Slowly release the feed lever, allowing it to come to rest in the raised position before switching off.

Holding the work securely
To resist the turning force of the drill press, it is often possible to rest one end of a workpiece against the left-hand side of the column (1). Alternatively, use a G-cramp or small fast-action cramp to clamp the work firmly to the table of the drill press.

A simple wooden fence secured to the worktable with bolts and wing nuts is a useful device for positioning identical workpieces accurately. Butt the end of each workpiece against an end stop clamped to the fence (2).

Slide a workpiece along the fence when you want to drill a series of holes in line – in order to remove waste from a mortise, for example (3).

Cut a V-block on a table saw to serve as a cradle for drilling holes in a cylindrical workpiece (4).

1 Rest the work against the drill-press column

2 Use a fence and end stop to drill identical workpieces

3 Slide the work against the fence to drill holes in line

4 Use a V-block to cradle a cylindrical workpiece

- **Drilling a workpiece**
Place a piece of planed timber or man-made board beneath the work when you need to drill a hole right through it.

SANDERS

Most amateur woodworkers find portable orbital and belt sanders perfectly adequate for finishing wide flat panels or boards, but a bench-mounted belt-and-disc *combination will provide you with a means for shaping components and sanding end-grain timber, too. It is also ideal for finishing small workpieces.*

Sanding disc

A vertically mounted metal disc covered with abrasive paper is used for sanding square or radiused ends on a workpiece and also for sanding mitres.

The maximum width of work that can be sanded on a disc is somewhat less than half its diameter. Much larger discs are available in industry, but a 225mm (9in) disc is a reasonable choice for the home workshop.

Paper-backed abrasives are normally glued to the face of the disc with a special adhesive. When one wears out, simply peel it off and replace it with a fresh paper disc.

SANDING DISC
CROSSFENCE
SANDING BELT
WORKTABLE
TRACKING-CONTROL DEVICE
ROLLER
MOTOR HOUSING
ON/OFF SWITCH

Sanding machine

Sanding belt

An abrasive-covered cloth belt 100 to 150mm (4 to 6in) wide, stretched between two metal rollers, is used to sand the long edges or faces of a workpiece. Concave-shaped pieces can be sanded over one of the rollers. The belt is normally used horizontally with the work butted against a crossfence, but the belt can be tipped to a vertical position for sanding end-grain timber.

To remove a worn belt, release the tension by retracting one of the rollers. After fitting and tensioning a new belt, run the machine and centre the belt on the rollers by adjusting the tracking-control device.

Abrasives

Use 60 and 80 grit belts or discs for the initial sanding and shaping of components. Change to a 120 grit abrasive for light sanding or finishing.

● **Electric motor**
A single 250 to 375W (⅓ to ½hp) electric motor drives both the sanding disc and belt.

The belt can be set vertically

Worktable
A cast-metal worktable mounted next to the disc sander is fitted with a sliding mitre fence which presents the work to the disc at the required angle.

With the table tilted to any angle up to 45 degrees to the disc, the machine can be used to sand compound mitres. The same table can be repositioned to sand a workpiece against a vertically positioned belt.

On/off switches
Some sanders are equipped with individual on/off push buttons. However, many have a simple toggle or rocker switch. Make sure this type of switch is in the off position before plugging the machine into an electrical socket.

Dust extraction
If at all possible, fit a dust extractor to a sanding machine. The fine dust is detrimental to your health and creates a potentially explosive atmosphere in the workshop.

WORKING WITH A SANDER

Whenever possible, sand in the direction of the grain. Cross-grain sanding with either a disc or belt sander leaves scratches on the work that will be difficult to remove and impossible to disguise with clear varnish or polish.

Using a disc sander
Hold the work firmly against the mitre fence and press the grain against the 'down' side of the rotating disc. Keep the work moving back and forth, and don't press too hard or you will burn the end grain.

To shape a component on a disc sander, cut away most of the waste with a saw and then remove the mitre fence before sanding down to the marked line, using the table to support the workpiece.

Using a belt sander
To sand the side of a workpiece, butt the end against the crossfence **(1)**. Change the position of the work periodically, in order to maximize the life of the belt, and take care not to round over the edges of the workpiece.

To shape a curved piece, hold it against the roller at the end of the belt **(2)**.

If the size and shape of the workpiece permits, you can tip the belt upright and use its entire width for sanding the work **(3)**.

Sand end grain against the 'down' side of the disc

1 Butt a long workpiece against the crossfence

2 Shape a curved workpiece against the end roller

3 Tip the belt upright to sand end grain

WOODTURNING LATHES

Woodturning is far more than a simple machining process – at its best it becomes an art form. Successful lathe work requires not only the mastery of very special techniques, but also an appreciation of what constitutes a pleasing shape with flowing lines.

A lathe, unlike other woodworking machines, is rarely used merely to process a workpiece from one stage of its production to the next – complete objects, from a rough blank through to a polished article, can be created on the one machine.

BENCH-MOUNTED LATHES

Heavy floorstanding lathes may be the norm for industrial turning, but lighter bench-mounted machines are more popular for the home workshop. A rigid bed forms the backbone of the machine, with a drive mechanism housed in a fixed headstock at one end and a sliding tailstock at the other. The workpiece is suspended between the two and is rotated at speed against a hand-held cutting tool. Typically, lathes are designed for two methods of turning: between-centre turning for shaping spindles, table legs and other long thin workpieces, and one-centre or faceplate turning for bowls, boxes, egg cups etc.

Headstock
The headstock delivers turning force to the work via a drive spindle. The spindle is threaded at one or both ends to take a bowl-turning faceplate, and is hollowed out so it can accommodate a tapered drive centre for between-centre turning. A drive centre has a leadpoint and either two or four prongs which bite into the end grain of the workpiece.

MOTOR HOUSING
DRIVE SPINDLE
DRIVE CENTRE
ON/OFF SWITCHES
HEADSTOCK
TOOL REST
BENCH-MOUNTING BRACKET
QUICK-RELEASE HANDLE

SLOW   FAST
SPINDLE PULLEY
MOTOR PULLEY
Changing lathe speed

Lathe size
A lathe is specified according to the maximum length of workpiece it can accommodate between centres; also, according to its 'swing' – the maximum diameter of workpiece that can be turned over the lathe bed. The headstock on some lathes is designed to rotate through 180 degrees to allow for faceplate turning of larger work at the front or end of the lathe.

The maximum workpiece length can be anything from 500mm to 1.2m (1ft 8in to 4ft) on a bench-mounted lathe. Longer workpieces can be assembled by dowelling two or three pieces together. Using the lathe to turn a peg on one end of a piece to fit a hole in another ensures perfect alignment, and a well-placed bead or groove disguises the joint.

SWING   BETWEEN CENTRES
Dimensions of a lathe

Speed control
Most lathes use a belt drive to transmit power from a 375 to 750W ($\frac{1}{2}$ to 1hp) electric motor to the headstock spindle. Stepped pulleys provide three or four pre-set spindle speeds with a typical range of between 450 and 2000 rpm. Some more expensive lathes use electronic variable-speed control.

Use the lowest speed for rough-cutting workpieces and then move the drive belt up the speed range as work progresses. The size of the work and the type of wood you are turning also affect speed selection. There are no hard and fast rules, but use the chart on the right as a rough guide.

USING A LATHE SAFELY

A lathe is unique among woodcutting machines in that it does not incorporate a moving cutter or blade. Instead, a hand-held cutting tool is used to shape a spinning workpiece. One reason why the lathe appeals to the amateur woodworker is that it seems a relatively safe machine with little risk of injury to his or her fingers. However, if you neglect to develop safe working practices, a single mistake can cause the work to be hurled across the workshop – so always follow general machine-shop safety procedures and observe the following rules.

- Always work in good light.
- Keep the area around the lathe clear of loose objects and stacks of timber that could fall against a spinning workpiece.
- Select a speed setting suitable for the work.
- Never leave keys or spanners in a lathe chuck.
- Fit a guard around a three-jaw or four-jaw chuck.
- Before switching on, check that all clamps and fixings are secure and that the work is free to rotate.
- Switch off the lathe before adjusting the tool rest.
- Make sure a cutting tool is in contact with a tool rest before feeding it into the work.
- Remove the tool rest before sanding a workpiece.
- Never leave a lathe running unattended – it can appear to be stationary.
- Don't wear loose clothing, especially a necktie, when operating a lathe.
- Remove rings and necklaces before you use a lathe, and tie back long hair.
- Wear safety goggles or a full face guard to protect yourself from flying woodchips.
- It is difficult to fit a dust extractor to a lathe – so wear a mask, especially if you suffer from respiratory problems.

Headstock rotated for faceplate turning

Lathe bed
Bracket-mounted steel bars or tubes support the tailstock, tool rest and other accessories. There must be ample clearance between bed and bench for removing shavings.

Tailstock
The tailstock, which is clamped to the lathe bed with a quick-release lever, supports the end of a workpiece for between-centre turning. It is fitted with a sliding hollow spindle, controlled by a handwheel, that takes a tapered tailstock centre with a simple central point. If this point is fixed – a 'dead' tailstock centre – it must be lubricated with wax to prevent it burning the work. Alternatively, fit a revolving 'live' centre constructed with ball bearings.

Tool rest
An adjustable tool rest is used to support the blade of a turning tool just in front of a rotating workpiece.
A standard rest – between 200 and 300mm (8 and 12in) long – is slid along the lathe to the most convenient position as work progresses. An extra-long rest that spans the length of the lathe bed is supported by mounting brackets at each end. Curved or cranked tool rests are made for bowl-turning.

Bench-mounted woodturning lathe

TURNING TOOLS

Specially designed cutting tools are used for shaping work-pieces on a woodturning lathe. The stocky blades are fitted with long turned handles that provide the leverage required for control of the tools. Carbon-steel blades are relatively inexpensive and are easy to sharpen. So long as you do not turn abrasive woods such as teak or elm, a carbon-steel blade will hold its edge reasonably well. High-speed-steel tools stay sharp much longer, especially on hard or wet wood, but they cost considerably more.

Basic set of turning tools

There is no need to buy every tool available. Purchase the following to begin with, then add further tools to your basic set as need arises:

Roughing-out gouge – 25mm (1in)
Spindle gouge – 12mm ($\frac{1}{2}$in)
Bowl gouge – 9mm ($\frac{3}{8}$in)
Skew chisel – 18mm ($\frac{3}{4}$in)
Parting tool – 3mm ($\frac{1}{8}$in)
Round-nose scraper – 12mm ($\frac{1}{2}$in)

MEASURING AND MARKING TOOLS

In addition to a tape measure and rules, a woodturner requires special measuring, gauging and marking tools.

Compass
You will need a compass for marking out the diameter of the workpiece. It is not necessary to purchase an expensive compass, but choose one that will maintain its accuracy.

Calipers
These are essential for measuring the diameter of work-pieces. Outside calipers are used for gauging the diameter of between-centre work, inside calipers for measuring the inside diameter of bowls and other kinds of hollow ware.

Sizing tool
A sizing tool is designed for clamping onto the blade of a parting tool. It is used to determine the diameter of a cylindrical workpiece or spigot. Hooked over the workpiece, it guides the tip of the blade to cut the precise diameter that is required.

Roughing-out gouge
Being ground square across the tip, rough-ing-out gouges are used for turning square or octagonal stock to a cylinder. They are available in widths of 18, 25 and 32mm ($\frac{3}{4}$, 1 and 1$\frac{1}{4}$in).

Bowl gouge
These deep-fluted gouges allow heavy cuts to be taken when turning hollows. Standard bowl gouges range from 6 to 18mm ($\frac{1}{4}$ to $\frac{3}{4}$in). You can also buy an extra-long 18mm ($\frac{3}{4}$in) gouge for greater control when turning large-diameter bowls.

Spindle gouge
This round-nosed gouge takes over from the roughing-out gouge for general between-centre turning. Spindle gouges are available in a range of sizes from 6 to 25mm ($\frac{1}{4}$ to 1in) wide.

TURNING GOUGES
The blade of a turning gouge has a curved cross section and is ground on the outside only.

Roughing-out gouge

Spindle gouge

Bowl gouge

Ring tool

Square-end chisel

Skew chisel

RING TOOL
Ring tools are designed to eliminate the problem of catching the corners of a gouge in the work. The ring-shaped 'eye', or 'blade', is ground on the outside to form a cutting edge 12 or 25mm ($\frac{1}{2}$ or 1in) in diameter.

Square-end chisel
These chisels are used for finishing a workpiece when between-centre turning. Blade widths range from 6 to 32mm ($\frac{1}{4}$ to 1$\frac{1}{4}$in).

TURNING CHISELS
A turning chisel is the woodturner's equivalent of a plane. It is used to smooth a roughly turned workpiece and has a rectangular-section blade ground on both sides to form a square or skewed cutting edge.

Skew chisel
Like a square chisel, a skew chisel, can be used for smoothing between-centre work – but it is also used for shaping beads and pummels.

Compass

Inside calipers

Outside calipers

Sizing tool

Hook a sizing tool over the work

PARTING TOOLS

These tools are designed primarily for cutting through a workpiece and removing it from the lathe. Consequently, the blade – which usually has a rectangular section but may be faceted or oval-sectioned – is ground to a point that has a cutting edge parallel to its narrow faces.

Standard parting tool

This type of parting tool is either 3 or 6mm (⅛ or ¼in) wide.

Parting tool

Fluted parting tool

Full-round scraper

Domed scraper

Square-end scraper

Rounded side-cutting scraper

Diamond side-cutting scraper

Diamond-point scraper

Fluted parting tool

This is hollow-ground along one narrow face to form two sharp points that scribe the wood before the tool cuts. This leaves an exceptionally clean finish on end grain when the tool is held flute-down on the lathe rest. A fluted parting tool is usually 3mm (⅛in) wide.

Full-round and domed scrapers

These scrapers are used for working inside bowls and goblets. Blade widths range from 12 to 25mm (½ to 1in).

Square-end scraper

This type of scraper is used mainly on the outside of bowls or the flat bottom of a turned box. Square-end scrapers are made in the same range of sizes as the round and domed varieties.

Side-cutting scrapers

Rounded and diamond side-cutting scrapers are especially useful for working inside all kinds of hollow ware. Both types have a blade width of 18mm (¾in).

SCRAPERS

Ground to a shallow cutting angle, scrapers leave a smooth finish on end grain. When you turn a bowl, two areas of end grain are presented to the tool with each revolution of the lathe. For this reason, scrapers are used primarily for cutting bowls and for other deep hollowing operations.

Diamond-point scraper

This kind of scraper is usually ground to a 90-degree pointed tip. It is used for incising V-shaped notches in between-centre work and for cleaning up square corners. Blade widths range from 6 to 32mm (¼ to 1¼in).

SHARPENING TURNING TOOLS

Because the work spins so fast on the lathe, a turning tool cuts through a considerable amount of wood in a matter of seconds. As a result, you need to sharpen your tools every few minutes. Many woodturners use a power grinder to sharpen lathe tools; others prefer to hone them frequently on an oilstone. Perhaps the best method is to regrind the cutting bevels for most uses, but hone the ground edge razor-sharp for fine work.

Whichever method you adopt, locate your sharpening bench close to the lathe so you can sharpen your tools frequently. Use a star-wheel dressing tool to renew the grindstone's surface when it becomes clogged with metal particles, and keep a jar of cold water next to the grinder for cooling blades.

New gouges, chisels and scrapers come with their bevelled cutting edges ground to the manufacturer's recommended angles. These tools will continue to perform perfectly if you maintain the same angles on a grindstone, but woodturners often regrind their tools to different cutting angles and shapes according to personal preference.

Roughing-out gouge 45°

Spindle gouge 30° to 40°

Bowl gouge 40°

Chisel 30°

Parting tool 30°

Scraper 75° to 80°

Roll a gouge from side to side

Regrinding a gouge
Dip the tip of a gouge in the jar of cooling water and lower it bevel downwards onto the grindstone. As soon as the bevel touches the stone, roll the tool from side to side to grind the whole bevel evenly. Don't press the blade too hard, and cool the metal frequently in water. Recommended bevel angles are 45 degrees for a roughing-out gouge, 30 to 40 degrees for a spindle gouge and 40 degrees for a bowl gouge.

Regrinding a chisel
Sharpen both sides of a chisel, moving the tool from side to side to grind a straight cutting edge. Apply light pressure only to the tool, taking care not to grind away the points which would create a curved cutting edge, and cool the metal frequently. Grind a chisel to an included angle of 30 degrees, and hone the edge on an oilstone.

Regrinding a parting tool
Regrind a parting tool in the same manner as a chisel, to an included angle of 30 degrees.

Raise a burr on a scraper

Regrinding a scraper
Most turners use a scraper straight from the grindstone – but a more efficient cutting edge is produced if you hone the bevel afterwards, then raise a burr by stroking the edge with a burnisher. Grind a scraper to an angle of 75 to 80 degrees.

BASIC TOOL CONTROL

The way you stand and move your body while woodturning is as important as the way you hold the tool. Even basic tool control demands practice, so begin by turning test pieces in softwood until you get used to the feel of the tools and have developed a sensitive touch.

Working height
Construct a strong bench to support your lathe at a comfortable working height. A height that is perfectly comfortable for one woodturner will not suit another – but as a rough guide, mount your lathe so that the centre line of the workpiece is at elbow height.

Work should be at elbow height

Correct stance and tool control
When you are turning wood between centres, stand facing the lathe, balanced comfortably with your feet apart. Don't stand too far from the machine so you are forced to lean forwards – this soon becomes tiring and you are bound to lose an element of tool control. Hold the turning tool with its handle more or less in line with your forearm and your elbow tucked into your side.

Control the blade of the tool with your other hand, moving the tool from side to side along the rest. Cup your hand over the blade when rough-cutting (**1**); for more delicate work, use an underhand grip with your thumb on top of the blade (**2**). With either grip, tuck your elbow close to your body.

1 Overhand grip for rough-cutting

2 Underhand grip for delicate work

Correct stance
Stand close to the lathe with your feet apart and with the tool tucked into your body.

Poor stance
In this position you are forced to lean forwards with an inevitable loss of control.

Moving with the tool

When you're turning a basic cylinder, you must keep the tool moving on a path that's parallel to the work. If you move your hands and arms only, the tool will tend to swing in an arc. The correct method is to move your whole body in the direction of the cut, in a controlled but fluid manner. Try not to overtense your muscles nor grip the tool too firmly.

When working to the left, rotate your shoulders, twisting your body from the waist as you lean into the cut (**1**). Gradually transfer your weight onto your left leg – bending it to keep your balance as you straighten your right leg (**2**).

When working to the right, open your stance to enable you to hold the tool at the required cutting angle to the work (**3**).

If you are left-handed, the reverse stance and body action applies as you move to right or left.

1 Move with the tool
Twist your body from the waist as you lean into the cut.

2 Follow through
As you move, transfer your weight onto your left leg and bend your knee to maintain a balanced stance.

3 Changing direction
When working to the right, re-position your feet for good balance and a comfortable stance.

CUTTING WITH A WOODTURNING TOOL

Present a woodturning scraper square to the work and hold it more or less parallel to the floor. Many beginners use woodturning gouges and chisels in a similar fashion, scraping the wood rather than cutting it smoothly. Although this is an easy method to learn, it leaves a relatively rough surface that requires more sanding than should be necessary to achieve a satisfactory finish. Experienced woodturners use the tools with a slicing action – a technique that requires more practice, but one that all turners should aspire to.

Adjust the tool rest so that it is within 6 to 12mm ($\frac{1}{4}$ to $\frac{1}{2}$in) of the work and is positioned on its centre line. Turn the workpiece by hand to check work clearance. Switch on, then place the blade on the rest before any part of the tool comes into contact with the work. If you touch a spinning workpiece with an unsupported tool, the blade will be driven violently against the rest. This will almost certainly damage the work or tool, and may even result in injury.

Hold the tool at an angle, with its bevel resting on the wood (**1**), then slowly lift the handle to initiate the cut (**2**). Raising and lowering the handle of the tool gives you precise control over the depth of cut. As you move the tool sideways to the left or right while turning a cylinder, incline the whole tool to induce a slicing action (**3**). At the same time, roll the blade in the direction of the sideways movement so that the cutting edge does not catch in the work (**4**). If the tool is cutting correctly, it will produce fine shavings and leave a smooth surface that requires minimum sanding.

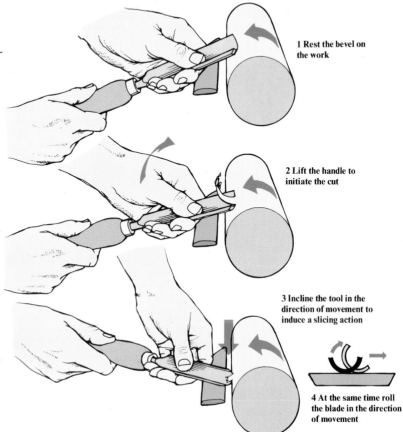

1 Rest the bevel on the work

2 Lift the handle to initiate the cut

3 Incline the tool in the direction of movement to induce a slicing action

4 At the same time roll the blade in the direction of movement

TURNING BETWEEN CENTRES

Between-centre turning is used to make cylindrical workpieces – for straight-forward chair or table legs, for example. This is a relatively simple procedure, though a woodturner will often want to produce more decorative work incorporating beads and hollows. All between-centre projects start in the same manner – by converting the square-section 'stock' on the lathe.

Preparing and mounting the stock

First prepare an accurately squared workpiece on a planer/thicknesser, and find its centre by drawing diagonals from corner to corner on each end (**1**). Draw the circumference of the finished workpiece on both ends of the stock with a compass, then mark both centres (where the diagonals cross) with a metalworker's centre punch (**2**) or bradawl. Use a tenon saw to cut a shallow kerf along both diagonals on one end to engage the drive-centre prongs (**3**).

An experienced woodturner will mount the stock in the lathe and remove its square corners with a gouge. However, a beginner will find it easier to plane off the corners to make an octagonal workpiece (**4**). Tap the drive centre into the kerfed end of the workpiece (**5**), then slip the tapered end of the drive centre into the headstock.

Slide the tailstock up to the work, locating the point of the tailstock centre in the central hole marked in the end grain. Clamp the tailstock to the lathe bed; then, after turning the handwheel to feed the 'centre' into the work, lock the handwheel.

Adjust the tool rest up to the work, then check clearance by revolving the workpiece by hand. Select a slow speed and check all fixings are tight before switching on. After running the machine for a few minutes, switch off and put an extra turn on the handwheel to make sure the tailstock centre is still secure in the work.

1 Draw the diagonals

2 Mark the centres

3 Cut shallow kerfs

4 Plane the stock to an octagon

5 Tap drive centre into the work

Turn the work to a cylinder with a roughing-out gouge

Turning the stock to a cylinder

Starting at one end of the workpiece, use a roughing-out gouge to remove the corners. Make very light cuts at first, moving the gouge smoothly along the tool rest. If necessary, switch off, move the rest and reduce the other end of the workpiece to the same diameter. Repeat the process until you have removed all the 'flats', leaving a cylindrical workpiece with a uniform diameter from one end to the other.

1 Use a skew chisel to smooth the work

2 Check the diameter with calipers

Smoothing with a chisel

Before switching on, adjust the tool rest again to suit the reduced diameter of the workpiece and practise holding the skew chisel correctly. While resting the cutting bevel on the wood, slightly rock the blade on the rest to lift the 'longer' point away from the work and incline the tool towards the direction of cut. Use the middle to bottom part of the cutting edge to make the cut (**1**).

With the lathe running, start at one end of the work by gently touching the surface of the wood with the chisel until you begin to produce shavings, then smoothly move the tool sideways. Keep the cutting depth constant throughout the pass. A correct cutting action will leave a smooth 'planed' surface. At regular intervals, switch off and check the diameter of the work with calipers (**2**).

1 Sand the work with folded paper

2 Or wrap a strip of paper over the work

Sanding a cylinder
In theory, a properly turned workpiece should not require sanding – the finish straight from the chisel should be perfect. In practice, most woodturners clean up the surface with a light sanding. Always wear a face mask when sanding on a lathe, since a great deal of fine sawdust is produced.

Tear a strip of fine-grade abrasive paper 75mm (3in) wide and fold it in three. Remove the tool rest, switch on and hold the abrasive pad against the revolving workpiece with your fingertips (**1**). Keep the paper moving along the work so you don't leave cross-grain scratches. Alternatively, hold both ends of an abrasive-paper strip and wrap it over the work (**2**).

Cutting the work to length
Replace the tool rest and mark each end of the work-piece by holding the point of a pencil against the spinning cylinder (**1**). Hold a parting tool square to the work, with its bevel rubbing on the waste side of the marked line. Slowly lift the handle of the tool to cut a deep slot in the wood (**2**). Leave a small-diameter 'neck' at the centre of the workpiece at each end (**3**). Remove the work from the lathe and cut through the waste with a tenon saw (**4**). Trim the end grain flush, using a sharp firmer chisel.

1 Mark the spinning work with the point of a pencil

2 Cut a slot with a parting tool

3 Leave a 'neck' at the centre   **4 Cut off the waste with a saw**

POLISHING ON A LATHE

You can apply a polish to turned work before taking it from the lathe. French polish is suitable as a sealer for all woods except oily open-grain timbers like teak or afrormosia. Choose transparent French polish for pale-coloured timbers, and button or garnet polish for darker woods.

Brush the liquid polish onto the workpiece (**1**), then select a slow lathe speed and switch on. Wear goggles or spectacles to protect your eyes from polish that might be thrown off as the wood starts moving. Use a bunched soft rag to rub the polish into the grain (**2**). Take special care to keep the cloth away from all moving lathe parts. While the work is still rotating, rub the surface with a stick of hard wax and burnish it with a clean rag.
  Apply teak oil to open-grain woods that do not require a gloss finish. Paint it on and burnish it with a rag, like button polish. On salad bowls, use edible vegetable oil or a commercial salad-bowl oil.

1 Brush polish onto the work

2 Rub the polish into the grain

DECORATIVE TURNING

If the workpiece is to incorporate beads and hollows as a form of decoration, it is not necessary to smooth or sand the wood accurately before shaping it. Simply turn the rough stock to a cylinder with a gouge, then mark out the beads and hollows.

BEADS, HOLLOWS AND FILLETS

A 'bead' is a rounded convex shape used for decorative purposes. Its counterpart, the 'hollow' or 'cove', is concave. The junction between hollows and beads is often demarcated by short shoulders known as 'fillets'.

BEAD FILLET HOLLOW **Typical decorative features**

Marking out beads and hollows
Use a straight rule and a pencil to mark out the positions of beads and hollows along the workpiece. When you switch on the lathe, your pencil marks will appear as continuous faint lines. Emphasise the marks by touching them with a pencil point while the lathe is running.

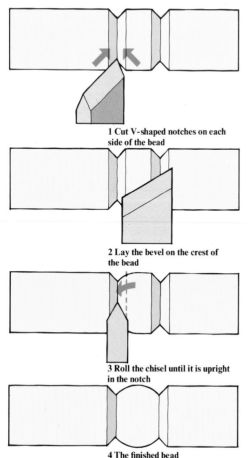

1 Cut V-shaped notches on each side of the bead

2 Lay the bevel on the crest of the bead

3 Roll the chisel until it is upright in the notch

4 The finished bead

Cutting beads
Place one narrow edge of a skew chisel on the tool rest, and touch the workpiece with the 'longer' point of the chisel to cut a 3mm ($\frac{1}{8}$in) groove on each marked line. This is achieved by lifting the tool's handle to lower the point slowly into the workpiece. Rock the chisel to one side then the other to open up the grooves into V-shaped notches (**1**). Remove about 3mm ($\frac{1}{8}$in) of wood on each side of the grooves.

To shape one side of a bead, lay the chisel's cutting bevel on the wood between the V-shaped notches (**2**), then gradually rotate the tool's handle to bring the blade upright in the centre of one of the notches (**3**). Cut the other side of the bead in a similar way. Repeat the action, taking very shallow cuts to smooth the bead and remove any remaining ridges. Check the 'horizon' of the workpiece to see the exact shape of the bead you are cutting (**4**). Keep the chisel square to the work – if you swing the handle sideways as you rotate it, you may catch the point of the tool in the wood.

TURNING FROM SQUARE TO ROUND

Turned table and chair legs are sometimes left square at one or both ends to receive mortise and tenon or dowel joints for the crossrails. Because this type of leg has to be turned from square-section stock, you need to be an experienced wood-turner before attempting this technique.

Cut the joints before you mount the stock on the lathe, and mark the shoulders of each section that are to be left square very clearly (**1**).

Use the point of a skew chisel to cut a V-shaped notch on the shoulder lines as if you were cutting a bead, then carefully roll the chisel to cut a half 'bead' on each side (**2**). Use a roughing-out gouge to turn the part of the stock between the squared ends to a cylinder, and finish it with a chisel and abrasive paper in the usual way.

1 Mount the jointed stock

2 Cut half 'beads' on each side of the centre lines

Cutting hollows and fillets
To turn hollows, use a 12mm ($\frac{1}{2}$in) spindle gouge or a bowl gouge which has its corners ground away to form a cutting tip with a rounded point. Remove some of the waste from between the beads by smoothly sweeping the tip of the gouge from side to side (**1**).

Use the point of a skew chisel to carefully shape a fillet on each side (**2**). Shape the hollow, starting on one side with the gouge rolled on the tool rest so that its flute is turned away from the bead. Slide the gouge towards the centre of the hollow, while rolling the blade and advancing the tip of the tool into the work (**3**). Shape the other side of the hollow in the same way.

Repeat the process, taking very shallow cuts with the gouge and always working 'downhill' from the outside of the hollow towards the middle. Check the horizon to see the true shape of the hollow. Finally, clean up the fillet on each side with a skew chisel, to leave a neat corner against the bead and a sharp edge to the hollow.

1 Remove some of the waste between beads with a gouge

2 Shape fillets with a chisel

3 Sweep a gouge 'downhill' to shape a hollow

TURNING WITH ONE CENTRE

When making items such as turned wooden boxes, egg cups and vases that have to be hollowed out, you need to remove the tailstock in order to turn the end grain. Consequently, the workpiece must be held securely at one end by one of several special chucks mounted on the headstock spindle.

Woodscrew chucks
One of the simplest chucks incorporates a threaded screw which is driven into a pre-drilled hole in the workpiece. The most basic chucks are made with a standard woodscrew, but the better-quality versions have a coarse purpose-made screw that bites securely into end-grain as well as side-grain timber. A screw chuck will hold relatively short workpieces only.

Woodscrew chuck

Cup chuck
A cup chuck has a hollow recess that will accommodate a cylindrical spigot turned on one end of a workpiece. Very often a cup chuck is designed to function by means of a good friction fit between it and the work. However, some chucks are made with provision for woodscrew-fixings for additional security. A cup chuck will support a workpiece that is too long for a screw chuck.

Cup chuck

Pin chuck
A pin chuck is designed to be inserted in a hole drilled in one end of a workpiece. A small-diameter metal pin rests in a shallow depression machined longitudinally in the chuck spigot. When stationary the spigot, together with the pin, slides effortlessly into the workpiece. Then as soon as the lathe is switched on, centrifugal force causes the pin to climb the sloping face of the depression and grip the timber.

Pin chuck

Three-jaw chuck
This type of chuck has three key-operated self-centring jaws that grip a cylindrical workpiece or spigot, or expand to grip a hollow workpiece. Although it has been used by generations of woodturners, this device is now losing its popularity owing to the distinct possibility of injuring one's knuckles on the protruding ends of the jaws while the lathe runs at speed. If you fit a three-jaw chuck to your lathe, protect yourself by mounting the appropriate guard.

Three-jaw chuck **Gripping internally** **Gripping externally**

Combination chucks
Recently, one-centre turning has been revolutionized by the development of combination chucks. These ingeniously engineered devices incorporate not only woodscrew, pin and cup-chuck facilities but also contracting collets which can grip a cylindrical workpiece or expand to fit a 'dovetail' recess turned in the base of a bowl or similar object.

Combination chuck **Gripping externally** **Gripping internally**

Turning a hollow workpiece
Rough out the stock between centres and turn the drive-centre end to fit whatever type of chuck you plan to use. Remove the tailstock, fit the workpiece to the chuck and skim the wood with a gouge to ensure it is turning centrally. Use a pencil to make alignment marks on the chuck and workpiece for exact replacement should you have to remove the work for any reason. Turn the tool rest across the work to hollow out the inside first, using a bowl gouge or scraper (**1**). When turning cross-grain wood, work the tool from the outside towards the centre; but work in the opposite direction, from the centre outwards, if you are turning end-grain timber. In either case, use the tool on the down side of the work only – i.e. the half which is moving downwards towards the tool rest. You can remove some of the waste beforehand by drilling out the centre. Check the internal diameter with inside calipers (**2**), then turn the outside and detach the workpiece with a parting tool.

1 Hollow the inside first

2 Check diameter with calipers

Drilling on a lathe
To bore a hole in the end of a workpiece, fit a drill chuck with a tapered shaft into the tailstock of the lathe. With the work held securely in a one-centre chuck, select a slow lathe speed and advance the drill bit by turning the tailstock handwheel. You can use a special saw-tooth machine centre bit, which cuts end grain cleanly, or an ordinary twist drill or a spade or Forstner bit.

Drill chuck **Saw-tooth machine centre bit**

FACEPLATE TURNING

Turning wooden bowls and containers has always been a popular aspect of lathe work – but because the workpiece is usually of a relatively large diameter bowl-turning demands a high degree of skill, especially when an experienced turner is pushing the craft to its limits to create fine thin-walled pieces. At that level, one slip of the tool can shatter the workpiece.

The bowl 'blank' must be fixed securely to the lathe, since a serious accident is a distinct possibility if a heavy workpiece works loose. A combination chuck provides the most sophisticated and probably the best method of clamping the work, but the traditional faceplate is much cheaper. This is a cast-metal disc, threaded at its centre to fit the lathe's drive spindle. The work is attached by passing woodscrews through holes in the plate. A 100 to 150mm (4 to 6in) diameter plate is normally supplied with a lathe, but larger ones are available as accessories. Select a plate that is as large as can be comfortably accommodated by the base of the workpiece.

Mounting the faceplate

If the turned piece is designed with a base thick enough to take stout woodscrews, you can attach the faceplate directly to the bowl blank. However, you will then have to accept screw holes in the base of the finished piece or plug them with timber after turning.

An alternative method is to screw the faceplate to a hardwood disc glued temporarily to the base of the workpiece. First, cut a square workpiece from well-seasoned knot-free timber and plane one side flat. Draw diagonals from one corner to another to find the centre, then use a compass to draw a circle slightly larger than the circumference of the bowl. Draw another circle representing the circumference of its base (1).

Cut a disc from hardwood 18mm ($\frac{3}{4}$in) thick, with the same diameter as the bowl's base. Cut another disc the same size from brown paper. This is to serve as a separator sandwiched between the wooden disc and the workpiece so the joint can be split when turning has been completed. Spread woodworking adhesive on both pieces of wood, then stick the paper to the wooden disc and glue both centrally on the workpiece (2). Apply a cramp and leave the glue to set.

Use your compass to draw the circumference of the faceplate on the disc, and attach the plate centrally with three or four No10 woodscrews. The screw threads should penetrate the full thickness of the wooden disc. Cut the waste off the workpiece on a bandsaw to leave a circular bowl blank (3). Attach the faceplate to the drive spindle – centrifugal force will tighten it on the spindle thread as the lathe starts up.

Woodturning faceplates

1 Use a compass to draw the base on the workpiece

2 Glue the wooden disc centrally on the workpiece

Screw a faceplate directly to a thick base

FACEPLATE

WOODEN DISC

PAPER SEPARATOR

BOWL BLANK

Or screw plate to a disc that is temporarily glued to workpiece

3 Cut the waste off the workpiece

Turning the outside of a bowl

Adjust the tool rest so it is centred on the edge of the bowl blank. Spin the work by hand to check that it is free to rotate, then select a slow speed and switch on.

True up the circumference of the blank with a roughing-out gouge, then change to a bowl gouge for shaping the outside of the bowl. Never be tempted to take deep cuts – always remove the waste gradually until you obtain the required shape.

Use a round-nose scraper to smooth the work. Lower the tool rest slightly and increase the lathe speed. Hold the chisel more or less square to the work, with its handle raised just above horizontal. Move the tool sideways, taking a light even cut.

Turning the inside of a bowl

Swing the tool rest round to align with the wide face of the workpiece, and begin to hollow out the bowl with the lathe running at a slow speed. Remember to work on the 'down' side only – the half of the workpiece that is moving downwards towards the tool rest (1).

Start removing the waste wood with a bowl gouge, cutting back towards the centre from a point halfway to the rim of the bowl (2). As you cut deeper, start a little closer to the rim with each pass of the tool and always work towards the centre of the bowl.

Once you have removed most of the waste, increase the speed of the lathe. Then, using a scraper, complete the shaping and smooth the inside of the bowl.

Sanding a bowl

Reduce the speed again, remove the tool rest and use a folded strip of abrasive paper to sand the surface (1). Use medium to fine paper, and keep the paper moving to avoid leaving scratches. When sanding the inside, trail the paper on the 'down' side only (2).

Use a scraper to smooth the outside of a bowl

1 Always work on the 'down' side of a spinning bowl

2 Work towards the centre of the bowl

1 Sanding the outside   2 Trail paper on the inside

CHECKING THE SHAPE OF A BOWL

As the work progresses, switch off the lathe from time to time to check the outer shape of the bowl or its depth and rim thickness.

Using a template
Hold a card template against the outside of the bowl to check its shape.

Measuring bowl depth
Hold a straightedge across the rim of the bowl, and use a steel rule to measure the depth of the bowl.

Checking the rim
Use calipers to measure the thickness of the bowl's rim. An experienced turner can reduce a rim to 3mm ($\frac{1}{8}$in) or less, but beginners should be less ambitious. A bowl is stronger if the thickness of the sides tapers from the base to the rim.

FINISHING AND DISMANTLING

Apply a polish or oil to the work while it is attached to the lathe, then unscrew the faceplate.

To remove the wooden disc from the base of the bowl, stand it on edge on a bench then place the tip of a sharp chisel on the joint line and tap it gently to split the paper separator. Scrape and finish the bottom by hand.

Split the disc from the bowl with a chisel

UNIVERSAL MACHINES

Ideally, a workshop should be equipped with individual woodworking machines adequately spaced apart so that even large workpieces can be passed from one machine to another. However, woodworkers with limited workshop room might consider an alternative occupying the minimum of floor space – a universal machine that combines several functions in one unit. Most universals comprise a table saw, surface planer, thicknesser, spindle moulder and horizontal borer/mortiser, built either as separate machines grouped around a single motor or as one machine with shared worktables and, on some models, shared fences. Avoid a cheap underengineered universal – it is best to choose one with specifications that compare favourably with those recommended for special-purpose woodworking machines.

Electric motors
Good-quality universals are fitted with one or more 1.5kW (2hp) electric motors. Clearly, a machine with an individual motor for each main function is preferable, since individual motors are subjected to less wear and changeover from one function to another can be implemented with the minimum of effort. Not surprisingly, this type of universal machine is relatively expensive.

More commonly, drive belts from saw, planer and spindle moulder have to be connected in turn to the pulley of a single motor. Where this can be achieved by the shifting of a lever on the outside of the machine, changeover is practically instantaneous, whereas having to change belts manually is tedious as well as time-consuming.

Changing from function to function
In order to prepare a universal machine for work, it is always necessary to remove certain fences, raise and lower blades or cutters, and to reposition guards – although these changes involve little more effort than setting up a special-purpose woodworking machine. If, however, you have to partly dismantle and reassemble your machine before you can undertake the next process, that will soon prove irksome and it is especially frustrating if you cannot move effortlessly from saw to planer and vice versa.

Control panels
In addition to the usual side-by-side on/off push buttons, a universal machine is normally fitted with emergency shut-off buttons at strategic points. The main control panel may also include a switch for selecting specific functions. The same selector switch is used to disconnect all motors when the machine is left unattended.

Universal machine

OPERATING A UNIVERSAL MACHINE

There is inevitably an element of compromise in the design of a universal machine – nevertheless, you should be able to operate each element of the machine efficiently, comfortably and, most important of all, safely. Follow the manufacturer's instructions for setting up the machine to perform any of its functions. Operating procedures are identical to those recommended for using the relevant special-purpose machines.

Ripping on the table saw

USING A UNIVERSAL MACHINE SAFELY

When using a universal machine, adopt the safe working practices that are recommended for individual table saws, planers, spindle moulders and mortisers. In addition to general machine-shop safety procedures, observe the following rules.

- Install a universal machine in a position where it can be operated and approached safely from all sides.
- Where possible, fit a dust extractor to the machine.
- If drive belts have to be changed manually, tuck away or hang up belts not in use well away from the motor's pulley and other moving parts.
- Support extra-long or very wide workpieces on trestles or a roller stand, or have an assistant take the work as it comes off the machine.
- After completion of a procedure, either withdraw blades and cutters into the machine's casing or enclose them completely with appropriate guards. Always remove a milling cutter as soon as you have finished mortising or boring holes.

Cutting a mitre using the saw's sliding table

Using the surface planer

Passing a workpiece through the thicknesser

Operating the slot mortiser

205

SPINDLE MOULDING ON A UNIVERSAL MACHINE

Spindle moulders are used primarily for cutting mouldings and certain woodworking joints. Basically, the machine comprises a cutter block that rotates at high speed on a vertical 'spindle', or shaft, projecting through a hole in the worktable. Adjustable fences guide the workpiece past the cutter block.

Special-purpose spindle-moulding machines are made for industry, but because of their price and somewhat limited role they are rarely bought by amateur woodworkers. On the other hand, a spindle moulder built into a universal machine often proves a welcome asset in a home workshop.

Spindle
The belt-driven spindle rotates at a speed between 4000 and 8000rpm. On some universal machines different speeds can be selected. Nowadays most manufacturers follow the international standard for spindle size, so spindles usually have a diameter of 30mm (1¼in). You can therefore use cutter blocks made by any company that has adopted the international standard, providing you do not run them faster than the specified speeds. This information is normally stamped on the cutter block.

The method for fitting cutter blocks varies from one model to another, so it is important to follow the manufacturer's instructions. In principle, the spindle is locked in position, usually by inserting a steel pin to stop it rotating, then the cutter block is lowered over the shaft. Spacer collars or rings are dropped onto the top of the cutter block before a locking nut or retaining screw on the end of the spindle is tightened to clamp the block in place. The spindle-locking pin is then removed. Spindle height is adjustable to position the cutters in relation to the work.

Guards
The spindle and cutter block are surrounded by guards and fences except for the parts of the cutters that shape the work. A metal casing encircles the rear of the spindle while adjustable vertical/horizontal hold-down guards hold the work firmly against the fence and worktable.

Guide fence
The guide fence is made in two halves, with a gap between through which the cutters protrude. Each half is adjustable sideways to give just enough clearance for the cutters.

When cutting a moulding that leaves part of the edge of the workpiece intact, both halves of the fence should be in line (**1**). When removing the edge entirely, the outfeed half of the fence is finely adjusted fore and aft to support the moulded edge (**2**).

A universal machine set up for spindle moulding

1 When part of the workpiece edge is intact, keep the two-part fence in line

2 Move the outfeed half of the fence forward to support an edge that has been cut away

Spindle moulding
The saw table is also used for spindle moulding.

SETTING UP THE MACHINE FOR SPINDLE MOULDING

It is essential to follow the manufacturer's instructions for converting your particular universal for spindle moulding, but a typical procedure is as follows.

Since the spindle shares a worktable with the circular saw, the saw guard and rip fence have to be dismantled and the blade retracted beneath the table's surface.

Raise the spindle, by operating the appropriate handwheel or crank, and fit the cutter block according to the manufacturer's instructions. Having fitted cutter guards and fence, make sure nothing is likely to foul the cutters, then switch on the machine.

*Even experienced machin-
ists approach a spindle
moulder with caution, since
it is arguably the most
dangerous machine in the
workshop. A cutter should
never work loose from a
well-designed block – but
if it does, it is thrown at a
lethal velocity. However,
an accident is more likely to
occur due to the cutters
throwing a workpiece back
towards the operator, so be
on your guard and take
precautions to avoid such
an eventuality.*

*If you have never had
experience of operating a
spindle moulder, it is
advisable to take tuition
from a recommended pro-
fessional machinist before
using one on your own.
In addition to general
machine-shop safety prac-
tices, always observe the
following rules.*

- Always use approved
  spindle-moulder guards
  and hold-downs.
- Only use sharp cutters.
  Discard cutters and
  blocks when damaged.
- Before switching on,
  check your settings and
  turn the spindle by hand
  (making sure the power
  is off) to ensure sufficient
  clearance all round.
- Always feed the work
  against the rotation of the
  cutter block.
- Use a push stick to feed
  narrow workpieces.
- Don't attempt to make
  a deep cut in one pass.
  Either mould it in stages
  or remove most of the
  waste beforehand on a
  saw or planer.
- Never attempt to mould
  across the end grain of a
  narrow workpiece free-
  hand. Clamp the work
  to a sliding table or
  mitre fence.

CUTTER BLOCKS AND CUTTERS

*Practically all spindle
moulders are supplied with a
cutter block designed to take
pairs of interchangeable
cutters or knives. The block
itself is roughly cylindrical,
since square blocks are now
generally considered to be
unsafe. A great variety of
shaped cutting tools is available for spindle moulders
built to the international
standard.*

Interchangeable-cutter block

Interchangeable-cutter blocks

The cylindrical metal block, approximately 100mm (4in) in
diameter, is slotted to accommodate two identical cutters.
A wedge-shaped clamp, tightened by bolts or machined
screws, holds each cutter securely in its slot. A peg or screw
passing through a hole in each cutter locates it precisely and
provides additional security against it working loose.

In addition to the vast range of ready-profiled cutters commercially available, you can buy blanks to grind your own.
To keep the cutting edges sharp, hone them lightly with an
oiled slipstone – but once they have become worn, have
pairs of cutters reground by an expert to ensure they remain
perfectly balanced.

The amount a cutter projects from the blocks is crucial, so
carefully follow any instructions stamped on or supplied
with cutters. Cutter projection must be limited so as to prevent violent kickback of the work, or even cutter failure,
as a result of trying to take too deep a cut in one pass. The
shape of the cutter block itself often limits the maximum
depth of cut (1). Alternatively, matching pairs of deflectors
are mounted just ahead of the cutters (2).

**1 A cutter block is designed to
limit cutter projection**

**2 Alternatively, deflectors are
mounted ahead of the cutters**

Wobble saw

Solid-profile blocks

Blocks and cutters are cast in one piece to make industrial-
quality solid-profile cutter blocks. This type of block has
three or four cutting edges that produce a superior-quality
finish. Solid-profile blocks last longer than conventional
interchangeable-cutter blocks, but are also considerably
more expensive.

Grooving cutters

Grooving cutters resemble heavy-duty rotary saw blades.
Some encircle the spindle and can be adjusted to cut grooves
of different widths. Others are designed for bolting into the
sides of a cylindrical cutter block.

Wobble saws

You can also buy small-diameter wobble-saw blades for
cutting grooves from 3 to 16mm ($\frac{1}{8}$ to $\frac{5}{8}$in) wide.

**Interchangeable-
cutter block**

Grooving cutters

Moulding cutters

Solid-profile block

MOULDING A WORKPIECE

Spindle-moulder cutters revolve at such a high speed that they invariably produce a fine finish. Nevertheless, if possible, feed the work so that the machine cuts in the direction of the grain. Disconnect the motor before making cutter adjustments.

1 Mould the work from below

2 Adjust the fence

3 Adjust the hold-down guard to fit the work

Having mounted the cutter block, adjust the spindle to mould the workpiece from underneath (**1**). In this position the workpiece itself offers extra protection by covering the rotating cutters; also, it is impossible to take a deeper bite out of the wood, even if the workpiece jumps slightly during the moulding process.

Holding the end of the work against a stationary cutter, adjust the fence to set the depth of cut (**2**). (Make a trial cut on scrap timber before you mould the actual workpiece.) Adjust each half of the fence sideways to leave the minimum clearance for the cutters.

Drop the upper hold-down onto the work and clamp it to provide a firm sliding pressure. Adjust the side-pressure plate similarly (**3**).

Check that the cutter block is free to revolve, then switch on. Press the work against the fence and feed it at a steady rate past the cutters. Keep the work moving and use a push stick to complete the process.

Moulding a short workpiece
It is dangerous to attempt to mould a workpiece which cannot be held comfortably in two hands on either side of the cutter-block opening in the fence. Instead, feed a longer workpiece through the machine, then cut it to the required length afterwards.

Cut a short workpiece from a longer board

Moulding a narrow strip
Either mould a wide board and rip a narrow strip from its edge (**1**) or mould both sides of a workpiece and rip it down the centre (**2**).

2 Mould both sides, then halve the work

1 Cut a strip from a wide board

MOULDING END GRAIN

To mould across the end grain of a workpiece, set up the machine in the usual way but remove the side-pressure plate. Adjust the hold-down to keep the work pressed against the worktable.

Clamp the work to the universal machine's sliding crosscut table. To prevent the grain being split from the back edge of the work by the revolving cutters, sandwich a piece of scrap timber between the work and the sliding-table fence. The scrap must extend to the tip of the workpiece. Both pieces of wood are machined together.

Moulding end grain using the machine's sliding table

Cutting joints
With the appropriate cutters, short tenons and finger joints can be cut to perfection on a spindle moulder. However, the special set of cutters and spacers required for finger jointing is expensive and may not be cost-effective, considering the number of times it is likely to be used in a home workshop.

MOULDING A CURVED WORKPIECE

In order to shape a curved workpiece on a spindle moulder, the standard fence and guards have to be replaced by a ring fence and hold-down. The work must be fed freehand into the cutters, which requires some experience if you are to avoid taking a dangerously deep cut that could result in a violent kickback. Unless you are already familiar with this technique, it is a wise precaution to take professional tuition before attempting it on your own.

A ring fence is required when moulding a curve

HOME

Some woodworkers are able to produce surprisingly immaculate work in a chaotic environment, but most woodworkers would agree that a clean, well-planned workshop is conducive to good working practices as well as being a safer and more pleasant place to work in. When planning the layout of your workshop, try to think ahead and make provision for your future needs. Suppose you have a fairly extensive kit of handtools and a few portable power tools at the moment; if you can foresee a time when you may want to install woodworking machines, allow space for them or at least make the layout easy to convert at a later date. Most woodworkers hoard oddments of wood that may come in handy — but a small

WORKSHOPS

workshop soon becomes cluttered if you try to save every offcut and there's no point in hoarding materials if you can never find them when they are wanted. It therefore pays to clear out your workshop ruthlessly every few months, keeping only those items that are really likely to be of use.

HOME WORKSHOPS

Unless you are starting from scratch it may not be possible to create a perfect working environment, but by careful planning you can convert an existing building such as a garage, outhouse or barn into an effective workshop. Ground-floor accommodation is essential if you plan to install heavy machinery, and it is more convenient for the delivery of boards and *lengths of timber. Ideally, a workshop should be located separately from your living quarters in order to reduce noise pollution and keep dust and fumes away from the house. Install thermostatically controlled heating, and possibly air conditioning, to keep the workshop at a constant temperature and also to control the humidity.*

Electrical sockets
Make sure you have plenty of electrical sockets mounted just behind the benches.

Narrow shelving
Store small packets and glass jars of screws and other fixings on narrow shelves, so that you can review your stock at a glance.

Tool storage
Store your handtools within reach of your bench. Hang them on dowel pegs glued into a sheet of plywood, or make a wall-hung tool rack.

Lighting
Space fluorescent lights evenly across the ceiling to provide shadow-free illumination. Choose 'daylight' tubes for accurate matching of colours and veneers. However, fluorescent lighting can create the optical illusion that moving machinery is stationary, especially when it is slowing down after being switched off.

Natural light
Ideally, natural light should come from the north, but unfortunately it is not always possible to be choosy.

Extractor
Install an extractor to expel unpleasant fumes.

● **Decoration**
Paint the ceiling and walls white to reflect as much light as possible into the work areas.

Dust extraction
To keep your workshop clean and to reduce health hazards, connect a portable dust extractor to your woodworking machinery. Small dust extractors are available for power tools.

Cupboard storage
Keep planes and hand-held power tools in a low cupboard.

Universal machine
If you have need for woodworking machinery but space is limited, you can install a unit that combines the functions of several machines.

Assembly area
Leave an open space where you can assemble cabinets or erect a temporary bench on sawhorses for light-weight assemblies and for finishing work.

Workbench
A sturdy workbench is essential. A cabinet-maker's bench fitted with vices is ideal, but you can build a simpler workbench of your own design against a wall.

First-aid kit
Mount a well-stocked first-aid kit in a conspicuous position.

Open shelving
Use open shelving for storing materials and finishes. Keep the bulk of inflammable materials in a separate shed.

Storing timber
Store solid timber and veneers on strong brackets securely bolted to studs.

Security
Fit workshop doors and windows with locks, not only to deter burglars but to keep inquisitive children away from dangerous chemicals and machinery.

Scrap storage
Store short lengths of scrap timber on end in plastic bins.

Storing boards
Store man-made boards on edge between a purpose-made open-stud partition and a workshop wall, so you can slide boards out without the others falling over. Site the stack in line with an access door.

PLANNING A MACHINE SHOP

The majority of people who do woodwork for pleasure, or even as a part-time earner, could never afford separate machine and hand workshops even though that would be the ideal arrangement. Consequently, most woodworkers have to find a way to fit a number of machines into a restricted space.

Measure your workshop and plot the ground plan on squared paper, then try various arrangements with scaled paper cutouts of the machines. The object of the exercise is to ensure you will have an unrestricted pathway for workpieces through each machine – and when you consider that you will want to be able to pass a full 2.44 × 1.22m (8 × 4ft) board across a table saw, it becomes obvious how important it is to allow sufficient working space around the machines.

One popular arrangement is to group the machines in the centre of the workshop, with their workpiece pathways at right angles to each other (see below). This layout works well provided you never have to operate all the machines at once, and with a one-person workshop that should never be necessary. It is clearly also an advantage to be able to run the electrical supply to a common area.

If the workshop is too narrow for this arrangement, it may be possible to arrange the machines in line but stagger them slightly so that a board passing over one machine will be supported by the worktable of a neighbouring machine – though you may have to adjust the height of the worktables to create a clear pathway. Alternatively, it may be convenient to position a portable roller stand on the outfeed side of a machine in order to support a long board or feed it over the table of the next machine in line.

To provide extra clearance you can align a machine with an open door or window, or even with a purpose-made port cut into the workshop wall, so long as protruding boards won't endanger passers-by. A lathe or drill press can be positioned against a wall, allowing the optimum clearance on both sides of the machines.

Fire prevention
Dispose of dust and shavings regularly, and never store oily rags in your workshop. Always have a good-quality fire blanket and extinguisher to hand, and fit a reliable smoke detector.

Fire extinguisher

Battery-operated smoke detector

The machine shop
One arrangement for a combined machine and hand workshop is to group the machines in the centre. The workpiece pathways cross at right angles.

1 Lathe
2 Bench
3 Dust extractor
4 Roller stand
5 Table saw
6 Planer/thicknesser
7 Drill press
8 Band saw

WORKBENCHES AND ACCESSORIES

A woodworker's bench is one of the most important pieces of equipment in the workshop. It is virtually impossible to produce quality work on a bench that is not sturdily constructed and fitted with well-machined vices, so choose your bench *carefully. Most workbenches are between 800mm (2ft 8in) and 850mm (2ft 10in) high but you can have higher or lower ones made to order. Some manufacturers offer left-handed benches that are mirror images of the standard format.*

Woodworker's bench

A good bench will have a hardwood worktop that is at least 50mm (2in) thick. Tough short-grain beech is the most common material for worktop construction, although birch, maple and African hardwoods are also used. Some Continental benches are made with a worktop partly constructed from plywood. Providing the plywood veneers are thick enough to withstand periodic scraping in order to clean glue and spilled finishes from the surface, a composite construction is not necessarily a disadvantage. You can choose a bench with a plain worktop, but the majority are made with a shallow tool well. This temporary-storage facility enables you to move a large workpiece or frame across the bench without sweeping handtools onto the floor. Other benches are supplied with a tool tray that can be bolted to the edge of the worktop. A slot or row of holes along the back edge of the bench for storing saws and chisels is yet another option.

One or two models are made with softwood underframes, but most benches are constructed entirely from hardwood. Look for a bench with mortise-and-tenoned endframes that are securely bolted to wide crossrails, and check that the underframe is stable enough not to distort when you apply sideways pressure to the worktop. Most manufacturers offer at least one simple drawer as an optional extra, and some benches are available with the underframe converted to a fully enclosed tool cupboard.

Woodworking vices

Every woodworker needs at least one large vice fixed permanently to the front edge of the worktop as close as possible to one of the legs of the underframe. This leg will prevent any flexing of the worktop caused by working wood clamped in the jaws of the vice. Continental-style vices are made with wooden jaws to grip the work without marking it. Another common style of vice has cast-metal jaws made to be lined with timber by the woodworker. Both types of vice can be operated by turning a large tommy-bar handle on the front jaw, but some metal vices are also equipped with a quick-release lever which disengages part of the screw mechanism, permitting the jaws to be opened and closed rapidly by a straight pull or push.

End vice

Better-quality benches are constructed with a vice built into one end of the worktop. An end vice provides clamping force along the bench to hold a workpiece between metal or wooden stops dropped into square holes cut into the vice and at regular intervals along one or both sides of the worktop. The workpiece can also be clamped upright in the jaws.

Holdfast

A holdfast is a portable 'vice' with a long shaft that fits into a large hole drilled in the worktop, lined with a metal collar. Turning a screw presses a pivoted arm down onto the workpiece, clamping it flat on the worktop. If you fit a second collar in a hole drilled in the bench leg, that will enable you to use the holdfast to provide support for a long workpiece held in a woodworking vice.

THICK HARDWOOD WORKTOP

MITRE BOX

TOOL-STORAGE SLOT

CAST-METAL VICE

BENCH HOOK

STURDY HARDWOOD UNDERFRAME

TOOL WELL

DRAWER

END VICE

SHOOTING BOARD

BENCH STOP

Cabinet-maker's bench

Continental-style wooden vice

WORKBENCH ACCESSORIES

Bench-mounted holdfast

Cutting wood directly on a bench damages the worktop. Instead, use an appropriate accessory that protects the worktop from sawcuts and chisel marks and also serves as a jig for the work and tool.

Bench hook
A hardwood bench hook is used for crosscutting short lengths of timber with a backsaw. A block fixed to the underside rests against the front edge of the bench and the work is held against a second block, or 'stop', fixed to the top. You can buy a ready-made bench hook or you may prefer to make one yourself by dowelling two blocks to a flat board.

Mitre box
This is a simple wooden jig for cutting mitre joints and square ends, using a backsaw. It has two raised sides with slots cut in them to guide the saw. The work is held against the far side of the box. On more expensive mitre boxes the slots are reinforced with adjustable nylon saw guides.

Saw square work on a bench hook

Cut mitred work in a mitre box

A simple mitre block

Mitre block
A mitre block is a simpler version of the mitre box, having only one raised side.

Shooting board
This type of jig is used for planing across end grain. It comprises two boards that are bonded together and staggered so that they form a wide rebate. The work is held against a wooden stop housed in the upper board while a bench plane is slid along the lower board to take a fine shaving. To trim mitre joints, plane them on a mitre shooting board, which has angled stops.

Mitre shooting block
A mitre shooting block is a jig with a movable clamping jaw designed to hold large mitred or squared workpieces so you can trim them with a sharp finely set plane. To hold the jig at a comfortable height, clamp the strip fixed to the underside of the shooting block in a vice.

Shooting board

Planing on a shooting board

Mitre shooting board

Mitre shooting block

A holdfast supports a long board

Sawhorses
These lightweight trestles are used singly or in pairs to support the work when sawing planks or boards. The legs are splayed and braced to provide a steady platform approximately 600mm (2ft) from the floor.

A typical sawhorse

FOLDING BENCH

If workshop space is too limited for a permanent bench, use one that folds flat for storage. The worktop comprises two huge vice jaws, one of which can be slewed to grip tapered workpieces or straightened up for parallel-sided wood. You can also clamp a workpiece to the top of the bench between plastic pegs. The bench unfolds to standard bench height for planing, or paring with a chisel, and may be lowered to a convenient height for sawing.

PLASTIC CLAMPING PEG

VICE JAWS

VICE CONTROLS

A folding bench can accommodate awkwardly shaped workpieces

Folding bench

213

HEALTH AND SAFETY IN THE WORKSHOP

Commercial and industrial establishments have to comply with strict regulations and restrictions safeguarding the health and safety of their workers. Although the same rules do not apply to home workshops, it makes sense to protect yourself from harmful fumes or dust, noise, and pieces of wood or metal thrown up by machine or power tools.

Safety spectacles **Goggles** **Face screen**

Hearing protectors **Face mask** **Respirator**

Safety spectacles
The lenses of safety spectacles are made from a tough impact-resistant polycarbonate. They not only protect your eyes from projectiles but also shield them from the dust and turbulence created by power tools. Side screens riveted to the frames provide added protection.

Goggles
Being designed to fit tightly against your face, goggles provide all-round eye protection. The lens is usually made from clear semi-rigid plastic and is fitted to a softer vinyl frame perforated to prevent condensation inside the goggles. Some goggles are designed for wearing over ordinary glasses.

Face screen
Total face protection is provided by the hinged plastic visor of a face screen. It is a particularly comfortable form of protection if you wear glasses.

Hearing protectors
Padded ear muffs or ear plugs protect your hearing from overexposure to noise that could cause long-term damage. Wear hearing protectors when operating noisy machinery.

Face mask
A simple mask with a replaceable filter protects your lungs from dust, non-toxic fumes and paint or varnish spray.

Respirator
A professional dual-cartridge respirator provides full protection against the harmful effects of paints, lacquers, adhesives and toxic dust. Interchangeable colour-coded cartridges are designed to filter specific materials. This type of respirator can be worn with goggles or safety spectacles.

DUST EXTRACTION

Sawdust and shavings left to pile up on the workshop floor constitute a serious fire hazard. The risk is increased when very fine dust is allowed to float in the air, contributing to a potentially explosive atmosphere. Moreover, dust makes the floor slippery, is harmful to your lungs and can ruin lacquered or varnished surfaces. Industrial workshops are equipped with purpose-built dust-extraction systems serving every individual machine. This type of installation is prohibitively expensive for the home woodworker, but simpler portable extractors are available to suit the smaller workshop.

◀ **Large-volume dust extractor**
Connect this type of extractor to woodworking machinery.

▼ **Industrial vacuum cleaner**
This machine doubles as a dust extractor for power tools.

Dust extractors
Mobile large-volume dust extractors are ideal for the small machine shop. Dust sucked through a flexible hose is filtered from the air by a woven-cotton bag mounted on top of the machine and is collected in a plastic sack below. The hose takes a variety of shaped mouthpieces designed to fit different woodworking machines. Some extractors can be equipped with dual hoses to service two machines simultaneously.

Industrial vacuum cleaners
A heavy-duty vacuum cleaner is an essential piece of workshop equipment. It is supplied with the usual range of hoses and nozzles which you can use for cleaning the floor and your woodworking machinery. When fitted with the appropriate accessories, the same machine can be connected directly to portable power tools, eliminating dust or shavings at source. In this mode, operation is by remote control, being activated by the power-tool switch.

JOINT

It is hardly surprising that many people regard joint-making as a measure of a cabinet-maker's skill, since the ability to cut fine joints takes practice and requires the mastering of a variety of accurate cutting techniques using saws, planes and chisels. However, the choice of joint is no less important than the quality of the making. The design must primarily be functional to provide strength, but it should also be in keeping with the overall style of the project. Most joints are designed to conceal the methods used to hold the parts together, while others such as decorative dovetails are made a feature. The following chapter illustrates the most common hand-cut joints and how to make them. Generally, dimensions have not been specified, as different projects require joints of different

MAKING

sizes. Instead, relative proportions are given to enable you to make sound joints to suit your requirements.

BUTT JOINTS

The butt joint is the simplest form of joint where one member meets another with no interlocking elements cut into the parts. It is not a strong joint and is often

reinforced in some way. Right-angled joints are used in the construction of light frames and small boxes. The jointing ends may be square-cut or mitred.

SQUARE-ENDED BUTT JOINT

Butt joints for boxes are made with the end of one member glued to the inside face of the other. For frames the end is glued to the edge. It is essential for the surfaces to be flat and the ends square.

Cutting the joint
Mark the length of the parts and square a shoulder line all round with a marking knife. Using a bench hook to hold the work, saw off the waste clear of the line (**1**).

Trim the end grain with a plane to provide the best surface for gluing. Use a shooting board to guide the plane, in order to ensure a square end (**2**).

Apply glue to the joint and clamp the parts together. Make sure the components are aligned properly as the joint has no means of locating itself.

1 Saw off the waste

2 Shoot the ends square

MITRED BUTT JOINT

A mitre halves the angle between the parts being joined. In most instances joints are made at 90 degrees so the common mitre is set at 45 degrees. End grain to end grain does not offer a good gluing surface; but the mitre's larger area, compared with the square butt joint, does compensate to some degree. The mitre is usually reinforced with nails or tongues.

The importance of accuracy
Mitres need to be cut accurately as gaps will show on the inside or outside if the mitre is not exactly half the angle. Use well-seasoned wood as a gap will open up on the inside of the angle if the wood shrinks after cutting the joint.

Inaccurate cutting causes gaps

Shrinkage can cause inside gap

Cutting the joint
Mark the cutting lines with a knife and mitre square on the face or edge. Square the lines onto the adjacent faces from the mitre angle. Cut off the waste with a tenon saw. To guarantee greater accuracy use a mitre box (**1**), particularly if cutting decorative mouldings which are more difficult to mark with cutting lines.

Trim the cut end with a plane and mitre shooting board (**2**). For wide boards use a mitre shooting block (**3**). If this is not available, set the work in a vice with a piece of waste wood at the back edge to prevent break-out (**4**).

Square-ended butt joint

Mitred butt joint

1 Cut off the waste

2 Plane the ends smooth

3 Use a mitre shooting block

4 Or use waste-wood backing

Reinforcing a square-ended butt joint

As the end grain does not glue well, additional reinforcement is usually required. You can use fine lost-head nails or blocks glued into the angle. Drive the nails into the joint dovetail-fashion to provide additional mechanical strength. In some cases the nails can be used in place of cramps when gluing up. If using glued-block reinforcement, rub-joint them into the angle and leave the glue to set.

Set nails at an angle

Rub-joint blocks into angle

REINFORCING A MITRED BUTT JOINT

The easiest way to reinforce a mitred joint is to glue it first and add the reinforcement when set. Use a mitre cramp or a web cramp for gluing up.

Using nails
For nailing, use panel pins or fine nails depending on the size of the joint. Sink the nailheads and disguise the holes, using matching coloured filler.

Using splines
For small joints, veneer or plywood splines can be set in sawcuts made across the corner. Make the cuts perpendicular, or angled for additional strength. Glue the splines into the sawcuts and trim them flush when set. Use splines of contrasting wood for a decorative effect.

Using a loose tongue
For larger mitres, a loose tongue or key can be fitted. Set a mortise gauge to the thickness of the tongue, which can be solid wood or plywood and about one-third the thickness of the frame material. Mark the gauge lines on the edges and centred on the thickness. Square lines across the end of the gauged lines the same distance from the corner on each edge.
 Set the joint in a vice with the shoulder line vertical. Carefully saw down each line and chop out the waste with a chisel, working from both sides towards the middle. Glue the loose tongue and plane it flush when set. If you are using a solid-wood loose tongue, its grain must run across the corner.

Integral reinforcing
A loose tongue is also used to reinforce a mitre before the joint is glued together. This type is more easily cut by machine, but can be made by hand.
 Make the tongue from 3mm ($\frac{1}{8}$in) plywood about 12mm ($\frac{1}{2}$in) wide or use solid wood, with the grain running across the width. Cut matching grooves by hand with a saw and chisel or with a plough plane. Centre the groove when the tongue runs with the mitre (**1**). When cutting across the mitre, set the groove nearer the inside of the angle to avoid leaving weak short grain (**2**).

1 Centre the groove **2 Set groove near the inside of the angle**

VENEER SPLINES

Splined joint

Loose-tongued joint

LOOSE TONGUE

Loose-tongued joint LOOSE TONGUE

LOOSE TONGUE OR KEY **Loose-tongued joint**

LAP JOINTS

The lap joint is a straightforward corner joint used for simple box and cabinet construction. Also known as a rebate joint, the plain end of one part is set in a *rebate cut in the other. It is the remaining wood left by the rebate that forms the lap and covers the end grain of the other member.*

SIMPLE LAP JOINT

This is not a particularly strong joint and needs pinning, but it is better than a butt joint in strength and appearance.

Cutting the joint
Cut the wood to length. Set a marking gauge to one-quarter or one-third the thickness of the rebated member. Scribe a line on the end and over the top and bottom edges, working from the face side (1). Reset the gauge to the thickness of the butting member. Run the gauge against the end of the rebate member to scribe a line on the back face and edges (2). Mark the waste with a pencil.

Set the rebate member in the vice. Saw down the lap gauge line to the shoulder line. Hold the work on a bench hook and cut across the shoulder line to remove the waste (3). Trim the rebate with a shoulder plane if necessary.

Apply glue to the joining parts, clamp together and secure with pins driven through the side member.

1 Mark the lap gauge line

2 Mark the shoulder line

3 Saw out the waste

MITRED LAP JOINT

The mitred lap is neater than the simple lap, but is more difficult to cut.

Cutting the joint
Mark and cut the lap as described (see left). Mark a 45-degree mitre on the edges of the lap (1). Square a line across the inside of the lap. Carefully plane off the waste down to the mitre line.

Using the marking gauge at the same setting, scribe a shoulder line on the inside and edges of the butting member, working from the end. Then, with the stock against the outside face, scribe a line across the end and over the edges to meet the shoulder line. Mark a mitre on each edge from the outside face to the point where the two gauge lines meet each other (2).

Hold the work flat on a bench hook and saw down the shoulder line to the mitre. Set it upright in a vice and saw down the gauge line to remove the waste. Reset the work in the vice and, using a shoulder plane, carefully shape the mitre (3).

1 Mark the lap mitre

2 Mark the edge mitre

3 Plane the mitre

● **Scarf joint**
A form of lap and mitre joint in one, this is used to join wood end to end. A long shallow taper in each part gives a large gluing area. Saw or plane the length of the taper to at least four times the thickness of the wood.

REBATE MEMBER

SIDE MEMBER

Simple lap joint

Scarf joint

REBATE MEMBER

BUTTING MEMBER

Detail of mitred lap joint

HALVING JOINTS

Halving joints are those which are cut in components of equal thickness and have half the thickness of the wood cut from each piece. They are relatively simple to cut and are used in frame construction where one member must cross or meet another in the same plane. The joint can be cut by hand with a saw and chisel or machine-cut. The methods shown here are for hand-cutting different forms of basic joint.

CROSS HALVING JOINT

This joint is the best to use when horizontal rails cross vertical members of a frame such as the divisions in a cabinet front or the glazing bars of a door or window.

Marking out the joint

It is conventional practice for the divider to run through, although the joint is equally strong either way.

Mark the width of the divider on the rail (**1**). Using a try square and marking knife, square lines across the face of the rail and carry them over and halfway down each edge (**2**). Turn the wood over and use the same procedure to mark the width of the rail on the back face of the divider.

Set a marking gauge to half the thickness of the wood and scribe a line on the edges between the marked lines, working from the face side of both parts (**3**). Mark the waste.

Cutting the joint

With the aid of a bench hook saw along the shoulder line to the depth of the gauged line. Be sure to keep just inside the waste side of the line as a slack joint is unsightly and weak. Make one or two extra sawcuts evenly spaced across the waste to make chiselling out the waste easier (**4**).

Set the work in a vice. Using a suitably sized chisel and a mallet, cut away the waste wood. Work towards the middle with the chisel held at a slight upward angle (**5**). Turn the wood around to cut from the other side. With most of the wood removed, pare away the remaining raised portion in the middle. Use the chisel vertically to sever any wood fibres along the base of the shoulder that were not cut by the saw. Check the cutout is flat, using the side edge of the chisel.

1 Mark the divider width

2 Square the cut lines

3 Gauge the edges

4 Saw across the waste

5 Chisel out the waste

CORNER HALVING JOINTS

These joints are simple to cut, but rely for their strength on the glue and may require extra support from screws or dowels. The mitred corner halving is a refined version, but is not so strong because of the reduced gluing area.

Corner halving joint

DIVIDER

RAIL

Cross halving joint

Mitred corner halving joint

GLAZING-BAR HALVING JOINT

The cutting of a halving joint in a moulded glazing bar is basically the same as that used for a cross halving joint, but there is the added complication of the moulded section.

Cutting the joint

Cut away the moulding on each side of the joint after marking its position. Cut down to the depth of the top face of the moulding. The width of the cutout is the same as the top face (**1**). As it is difficult to mark a line over the contoured surface, use a mitre box to make the sawcut (**2**).

Make a 45-degree mitre block for trimming the moulding. Clamp the block to the work and pare away the corners of the moulding with a chisel (**3**).

Now cut the halving joint in the remaining section of each part. The depth of the cutout in each should be level with the line of the moulding rebate (**4**).

2 Use a mitre box

3 Pare away the corners

4 Cut the cross halving

1 Width of cutout
Make the cutout the same width as the top face.

DIVIDER

RAIL

Glazing-bar halving joint

OBLIQUE HALVING JOINT

The oblique halving joint is cut in a similar way to the conventional cross halving joint, but the cutouts are set at an angle. The main difference is the marking out of the shoulder.

Marking out the joint

Making a 45-degree angle is very simple when using a mitre square. For any other angle it is necessary to use a sliding bevel set with the aid of a protractor or by taking the setting from an accurate drawing.

Mark one angled shoulder line on the face side of the bottom member. Place the top member on the line and mark its width (**1**). Scribe the second shoulder line on the mark. Square the lines halfway down each edge and mark a line between them with a gauge set to half the thickness of the wood.

Place the top member, face side up, in position and mark the width of the bottom piece on both its edges (**2**). Mark the cutout on the underside with the bevel or square.

Cutting the joint

Saw and chisel out the waste from both parts as for a cross halving, but working at the marked angle.

1 Mark top member's width

2 Mark bottom member's width

TOP MEMBER

BOTTOM MEMBER

Oblique halving joint

'T' HALVING JOINT

This relatively strong framing joint is used where one member intersects the other, finishing flush on the outside edge.

Marking out the joint

After marking the cutout on the cross member of the 'T' as described for cross halvings, cut the end of the upright member square and mark the width of the cross member on its underside. Square the line onto the edges and run a gauge line along each edge and along the end (1).

1 Gauge the edges and end

Cutting the joint

Saw and chisel out the waste from the cross member (2). Saw down first the gauged line on the waste side and then the shoulder line to remove the waste from the upright member (3).

2 Chisel out the waste

3 Saw down the gauge line

UPRIGHT MEMBER

CROSS MEMBER

'T' halving joint

DOVETAIL HALVING JOINT

The dovetail halving is similar to the 'T' halving joint, but is stronger as it can resist pulling forces better.

Marking and cutting the joint

The upright member forming the tailpiece is cut first. Mark out and cut the end lap, as described for the 'T' halving. Mark out the slope of the dovetail with a template (1) or set it out with a rule. Saw or pare away the waste depending on the size of the wood (2).

Lay the dovetailed end on the cross member and mark its shape on the face side (3). Square the lines down the edges and gauge the depth line between them. Then saw and chisel out the waste.

1 Mark the dovetail slope   **2 Pare away the waste**   **3 Draw around the shape**

UPRIGHT MEMBER

CROSS MEMBER

Dovetail halving joint

EDGE-TO-EDGE JOINTS

Edge joints are used to join relatively narrow boards to make up wider boards or panels for table tops or cabinet work. The edge may be plain or shaped. The shaping of the edge is to increase the gluing area, provide reinforcement and a means of interlocking the *edge, which is a help when gluing up. Whichever method is used, they all rely on the strength of the glue joint. Modern glues are very strong and, providing the jointing edges are accurately cut, even the plainedged butt joint will be stronger than the wood itself.*

PREPARING THE WOOD

Start with the boards planed to thickness. Where possible use quarter-sawn wood as this is more stable than wood sawn through and through.

1 Alternate the growth rings

2 Number each board clearly

Selecting and arranging the boards

If you have no choice, or have chosen through and through for its surface figure, select the boards so the direction of the growth rings alternates (1). Also select the boards for colour and arrange them so the grain of the wood runs in the same direction, otherwise final cleaning up of the surface will be more difficult. Number each board on the face side (2) and, when working them, keep the numbers facing the same way.

EDGE-TO-EDGE BUTT JOINTING

When making a joint between two boards, it is standard practice to plane the meeting edges square to the face side.

Checking for square

Use a try plane or the longest plane available to true each edge (1). Constantly check each edge for square, using a try square. Test the edge is straight with a metal straightedge (2).

1 Plane the edge true

2 Test the edge is straight

Irregular boards

A slight hollow is acceptable if the boards are going to be cramped together, but if a rubbed joint is to be used they must be straight.

Slightly concave edges (1) are acceptable for clamping as the extra pressure at the ends will be released by shrinkage and helps counter end-splitting.

Convex edges (2) are unacceptable, as closing the ends with cramps sets up stresses which are likely to cause end splits.

1 Slightly concave edges are acceptable

2 Convex edges are unacceptable

LOOSE TONGUE

Butt joint

Tongue and groove joint

Loose tongue and groove joint

CLAMPING EDGE-TO-EDGE JOINTS

Planing boards to fit
Planing individual boards straight and square is not easy. A way of making the squareness of the joint less critical is to plane both edges together. Set the two boards level in a vice, back to back with the face sides outwards (3). Plane the edges straight. If the edge is not quite square the boards will still fit together and produce a flat surface (4).

When joining three or more boards edge to edge, the inner boards have both edges planed to fit. Using the back-to-back technique to true the edges, set the first and second board in the vice and plane the edges. Remove the first board, rotate the second and back it up with the third board. Plane the edges of each pair in this way (5).

Before gluing up, check the boards for fit by setting them in cramps. This will also pre-set the cramps in readiness for gluing up, which must be done as quickly as possible.

The number of cramps you use will depend on the size of the work, but you should use at least three for most panels. Place 'softening', pieces of scrap wood, between the cramp heads and the edge of the boards. Set the boards out on battens laid across the bench.

Gluing up
Apply a thin film of glue to the jointing edges. Place a cramp across each end about a quarter of the board's length in from each end (1). Keep the cramps clear of the surface to prevent any reaction with the glue staining the wood. If necessary, tap the joints with a hammer and block to set them flush (2).

Turn the panel over and place a cramp across the middle (3). This cramp not only pulls the joints together, but also counters any tendency for the panel to bow. Wipe away surplus glue which is squeezed from the joints.

Leave the work in the cramps until the glue has cured. If you need to remove the clamped work from the bench it can be stood against a wall, but make sure it is supported evenly to avoid distortion.

1 Set the cramps across the top

2 Tap the boards flush

3 Turn and clamp the panel

3 Set the boards back to back

4 Out-of-square edges will fit

5 Rotate each board in turn

TONGUE AND GROOVE JOINTS

The best tool to use for hand-cutting a tongue and groove joint is a combination plane. Start by cutting the tongue, using a tonguing cutter.

Cutting the tongue
Set the work in the vice with the face side towards you. Adjust the plane's fence to centre the tongue on the edge (1). You can check this by making a light indentation, then reversing the plane with the fence against the other face. If the blade aligns with the marks, it is on centre. Set the depth stop on the cutter and plane the tongue, starting at the forward end (2).

Cutting the groove
To cut the groove, fit the ploughing cutter which matches the width of the tongue into the plane. Sit the cutter on the edge of the tongue and adjust the fence (3). Set the depth stop to produce a groove slightly deeper than the tongue. Place the board in the vice and cut the groove.

1 Centre the cutter

2 Start planing at the end

3 Adjust the plane for grooving

Using a loose tongue
An alternative tongue and groove joint can be made with a loose plywood tongue or spline. This is set in a groove cut in both halves of the joint. The joint can be cut with any of the grooving planes, with a table saw or router.

HOUSING JOINTS

Housings or dadoes are wide, shallow grooves cut across the grain of panels. They are used primarily in the construction of cabinetwork to retain fixed shelves or dividers. Various versions of the joint can be made using handtools or hand-held machine tools. The through housing is the most common and the simplest to make. The best type for strength is the dovetail housing, which uses mechanical strength as well as that provided by glue. Both types can be stopped so the end of the groove does not show on the front edge of the side panel.

THROUGH HOUSING JOINT

Housings may be cut in manufactured board or in panels made from edge-to-edge-jointed solid-wood boards. Prepare the surfaces and edges, and select and mark the face side and edge. If manufactured boards are to be veneered, apply lippings and veneers before cutting the joints.

1 Mark the shelf thickness

3 Chisel out a guide groove

5 Chisel out the waste

2 Gauge the housing depth

4 Saw along the line

6 Router-plane the groove level

Marking out the joint
Measure and mark the bottom line of the groove to position the joint on the inside face of the side panel. Mark the width of the groove from the thickness of the shelf member (1). Using a marking knife and a large try square, scribe cutting lines across the width of the side panel and square them onto the edges. Make the edge marks not more than one-third of the thickness.

Set a marking gauge to 5 to 6mm ($\frac{3}{16}$ to $\frac{1}{4}$in) or not more than one-third the thickness of the panel. Scribe a line between the marks on both edges (2).

Cutting the joint
Using a wide chisel, pare out a shallow wedge-shaped groove from the waste side of the cutting line (3). Use the resulting shoulder to guide a fine-toothed dovetail saw and carefully saw down to the gauged line (4). If you are not confident with a saw, you can clamp a batten along the line to help guide the saw.

Remove most of the waste from a narrow panel with a chisel (5) and finish with a hand router plane to level the groove (6). Work from both edges towards the centre in order to prevent edge break-out. For wide panels, use the router plane to remove all the waste. Do not try to remove the full depth of the groove in one cut. Make several passes, resetting the cutter until the full depth is reached.

SIDE PANEL

Single-sided dovetail housing

SIDE PANEL

SIDE MEMBER

Through housing joint

SHELF MEMBER

SHELF MEMBER

HORIZONTAL MEMBER

SIDE PANEL

SHELF MEMBER

SIDE PANEL

SHELF MEMBER

Barefaced housing joint (corner)

Stopped housing joint

Stopped dovetail housing

DOVETAIL HOUSING JOINTS

The dovetail housing may be made with one or both sides of the groove cut at an angle. The single-sided version is easier for hand-cutting. The double-sided type lends itself to machine cutting. It takes accurate cutting as the tailpiece has to slide into the housing from one end.

Single-sided dovetail housing
Set a marking gauge to one-third of the thickness of the side panel and scribe a shoulder line on the underside of the shelf end **(1)**. Square the line onto the edges. Make a mark on both edges 3mm ($\frac{1}{8}$in) in from the underside face. Mark the slope of the dovetail from the end corner to this mark **(2)**. Saw along the shoulder line to the bottom of the slope. Pare out the waste. Use a home-made guide block if you need to cut a number of joints **(3)**.

Mark the width and position of the shelf on the side panel with a pencil. Square the lines onto the edges.

Gauge the housing depth on the edges. Mark the dovetail outline on the edge of the side panel, using the shelf as a guide. Saw along the line at the marked angle. Use a guide block if required to help maintain the angle **(4)**. Remove the waste with a bevel-edge chisel and then a router plane.

Stopped dovetail housing
Follow the instructions as outlined for the standard stopped housing, but use the dovetail procedure.

Cut both sides of the housing and shelf end at an angle for a double-sided dovetail housing.

1 Mark the shelf underside

3 Pare the dovetail angle

2 Mark the dovetail slope

4 Use a guide when sawing

STOPPED HOUSING JOINT

The groove of a stopped housing is not run through, but stopped some 9 to 12mm ($\frac{3}{8}$ to $\frac{1}{2}$in) short of the shelf width. (The end of the shelf is notched by a corresponding amount.) The front edge of the shelf may finish flush with the front edge of the side panel or be set back from it.

Marking out the joint
Mark the width of the groove, as described for the through housing, to match the depth of the shelf. Set a marking gauge to the depth of the groove and mark the back edge of the side panel. With the same setting, gauge a line around the front edge of the shelf. Cut the notch with a saw **(1)**. Mark the length of the groove from the end of the shelf **(2)**.

Cutting the joint
To cut the groove, first chop a cutout or drill a line of overlapping holes at the stopped end to the required depth. Use a Forstner bit where possible, as it has a short centre spike. Trim the waste from the drillings **(3)**. Saw along the scribed lines towards the cutout and remove the waste with a router plane.

1 Cut the notch

2 Mark the groove's length

3 Trim the drilled cutout

BAREFACED HOUSING JOINT

The barefaced housing, often referred to as a barefaced tongue and groove or barefaced tongue and rebate joint, is stronger than the standard housing and can be used as a corner joint. The shoulder formed by the rebate on the shelf member means the groove depth is less critical and removal of wood when cleaning up the surfaces does not result in a slack joint.

Marking out the joint
To make a barefaced joint at a corner, first of all mark the thickness of the horizontal member on the inside face of the side member, then square this line across the face and onto the edges.

Set your marking gauge to not more than one-third of the thickness of the side member. Mark the rebate shoulder line on the face side and edges of the horizontal member **(1)**. Then gauge the width of the tongue across the end of the horizontal member and onto the

edges to meet the first gauge lines, working from the inside face **(2)**. Saw the waste from the rebate, and use a shoulder plane to clean up if required.

Align the inside face of the horizontal member on the line marked on the side member. Mark the width of the housing from the tongue and square a line across the face and onto the edges. Gauge the depth of the housing on the edges, and then cut the housing as described (see opposite).

1 Mark the rebate shoulder

2 Mark the tongue width

MORTISE & TENON JOINTS

The mortise and tenon joint has a long tradition in the construction of timber frames. One member slots into another to provide a strong mechanical joint which was used to full advantage in traditional timber-framed buildings. It is now rarely used in building construction, where economics dictate a lower specification. The joint has been refined by joiners and furniture-makers over centuries, and various forms have been developed. The mortise and tenon joint has a large gluing area and is widely used for tables and chairs, where maximum strength is an important consideration.

PROPORTION OF MORTISE TO TENON

The proportion of the mortise and its corresponding tenon is important to the strength of the joint. The form of the joint is largely determined by the section of the tenoned member.

In most instances the tenoned member is a rectangular-sectioned rail with its width set in the vertical plane. Sometimes the rail is used with its width set in the horizontal plane. In any event the sides or cheeks of the tenon are cut in the vertical plane to give the maximum long grain for gluing to the mortise sides (below). For rails set horizontally, two or more tenons may be required as the thickness of the tenon should not exceed its width.

The thickness of a tenon is usually one-third the thickness of the wood where two members of equal thickness are being joined. Its precise thickness is actually taken from the chisel used for cutting the mortise. A thin tenon is relatively weak in 'shear' and a wide mortise will produce thin sides that could split out under twisting forces.

Where a tenoned member is jointed into a thicker member than itself the tenon may be as much as half the thickness.

The width of the tenon is usually the full width of the rail. Where this would be excessively wide, as with a rail in a large panelled door, the tenon is divided into two and is known as a double mortise and tenon.

The length of the tenon is mainly determined by the design of the joint. The tenon for a through mortise will match the width of the mortised member. For a stopped (or 'stub') mortise and tenon the length is usually about three-quarters of the width of the mortised member.

Tenons
Tenons are cut with their sides or cheeks following the grain of the mortised stile or leg.

THROUGH MORTISE AND TENON JOINT

The through mortise and tenon is widely used for frame construction. The end grain of the tenon shows on the edge of the frame stiles. The joint needs accurate cutting for good appearance. Wedges can be used to provide extra strength, and as a decorative detail if made of contrasting wood.

Marking out the joint
Cut the tenon member to length; a little waste can be left to be planed off after gluing up. If the work requires tenons at each end, set out the distance between the shoulders of the tenons precisely. Square the shoulder lines all round with a marking knife (1).

1 Square the shoulder lines

Mark the position of the mortise on the edge of the mortise member; then the width of the mortise, using the tenon member as a guide (2). Square the lines all round using a pencil.

2 Mark the mortise width

Select a mortise chisel, remembering the mortise should be approximately one-third the thickness of the wood. Set the pins of a mortise gauge to the width of the chisel. Now set the stock of the gauge to centre the mortise on the edge of the wood. The gauge should be set and worked from the face side. Scribe the gauge lines between the width marks on both edges (3). Mark the tenon with the gauge at the same setting. Working from the face side, scribe the lines from the shoulder line on one edge, over the end and back down to the shoulder line on the other edge (4). If the tenon member is thinner than the mortise member reset the stock of the gauge only.

3 Gauge the mortise lines

Cutting the mortise
Always cut the mortise before the tenon. It is easier to adjust the tenon to the mortise, if required. Clamp the work to the bench. It is a good idea to place a piece of waste wood under it to protect the bench.

4 Gauge the tenon lines

Position yourself in line with the work to enable you to check the mortise chisel is held upright. Start in the middle, with the bevel facing away from you **(5)**. Drive the chisel with a mallet to a depth of about 3mm ($\frac{1}{8}$in). Work backwards in approximately 3mm ($\frac{1}{8}$in) steps and stop 2 to 3mm ($\frac{1}{16}$ to $\frac{1}{8}$in) from the end. This is to provide waste for the chisel to lever against when cleaning out the chippings. Turn the chisel around and work towards the other end. Remove the chopped waste by levering it from both ends using the chisel bevel-side down **(6)**.

To prevent splitting out the underside, cut halfway through the work only. Cut the remaining waste from the ends with the chisel held vertically, bevel-side in **(7)**. Turn the wood over. Shake out any loose chippings and clear the surface before clamping it down, as trapped pieces can bruise the face. Chop out the waste in the same way to meet the first cutout.

Drilling the mortise
As an alternative to chopping out the waste a mortise can be cut using a drill. The chisel is used to finish the cutout squarely.

Use a drill press or hand power drill in a drill stand. This will give better control and greater accuracy than trying to drill freehand.

Fit a drill bit that matches or is close to the thickness of the mortise. Clamp a board fitted with a guide fence to the base of the drill stand, and set it to centre the drill on the mortise.

Adjust the depth setting to drill halfway through the wood. Drill a hole at each end of the mortise **(1)**, then drill a series of slightly overlapping holes between them **(2)**. Turn the wood over and, with the same face against the fence, drill through the other side.

Place the work on some waste wood and clamp it to the bench. Clean out the waste and cut the ends square with a mortise chisel.

5 Start the cut in the middle

6 Lever out the waste

7 Trim the ends square

1 Drill each end first

2 Drill overlapping holes

Cutting the tenon
Set the work in a vice at an angle, with the end facing away from you. Using a tenon saw, cut down the waste side of each line keeping the cutting edge parallel with the bench **(1)**. Stop on the shoulder line taking care not to overrun.

Reset the work in the vice so it faces you and cut down the other tenon line **(2)**. Then place the work upright in the vice and saw down level with the shoulder **(3)**.

Hold the work on a bench hook and saw along the shoulder line to remove the waste. The tenon should fit the mortise straight from the saw. If it is too tight, pare the cheeks of the tenon with a chisel. Take care to keep the tenon symmetrical.

1 Saw down the tenon line

2 Reset and saw the other side

3 Finish level with shoulder

WEDGED THROUGH MORTISE AND TENON JOINT

A mortise and tenon joint is strong by virtue of the relatively large gluing area. Mechanical strength can be improved by fitting wedges. A standard through mortise and tenon can be fitted with a pair of wedges in two ways. They can be fitted at the ends or set in sawcuts within the tenon.

Fitting the wedges
Working from the outside edge, cut a shallow taper at each end of the mortise. Cut the wedges from the tenon waste to be slightly steeper than the taper. Make two sawcuts across the tenon about the thickness of the tenon from each edge, if using the inset method. Drill a hole at the end of the sawcut to prevent splitting.

When the joint is glued up, apply glue to the wedges and drive them in alternately to keep them level. Once they have set, trim and plane the ends flush.

TENON MEMBER

TENON MEMBER

MORTISE MEMBER

MORTISE MEMBER

Through mortise and tenon joint

WEDGES

Wedged mortise and tenon joint

DOUBLE MORTISE AND TENON JOINT

The double mortise and tenon is used for frames which have wide rails where the width of the mortise needed to take a single tenon would weaken the stile. The centre rail of a panelled door is usually jointed in this way. The joint described here is for a through double mortise and tenon in a square-edged stile and rail.

Marking out the joint

Start by measuring and marking the tenon shoulders on the rail. Scribe the lines all round with a marking knife and try square. Lay the rail on the edge of the stile and mark its width and position, then square the marks all round the stile with a pencil.

Set the pins of a mortise gauge to the width of a mortise chisel which is approximately one-third the thickness of the stile. Set the stock of the gauge to centre the pins on the edge. Mark the gauge lines between the width marks on both edges of the stile, but use only light pressure on the outside edge, and mark the end of the tenon member with the gauge at the same setting.

The joint has two in-line tenons separated by a gap. In order not to weaken the rail, a haunch is left between them to give support to the tenon shoulder. The width of the tenons and the corresponding mortises will be determined to some degree by the width of the rail. As a guide, make the width of each tenon not less than four times its thickness. If this leaves a gap between them more than one-third the width of the rail, increase the width of the tenons.

Set a marking gauge to the required dimension and, working from each edge in turn, mark the width of the tenons. Run the lines across the end and down both faces to meet the shoulder line.

Mark the length of the haunch, which is equal to the thickness of the tenon, across one edge. Square the line down both faces. Mark the waste as shown (1) in order to visualize the shape of the tenons.

Lay the rail in position on the mortise member and mark off the tenons (2). Square the marks all round and mark the mortise waste.

1 Mark the waste for clarity

2 Mark off tenon widths

3 Saw haunch waste

4 Saw tenon sides

5 Cut the waste between tenons

6 Saw along the shoulder line

Cutting the joint

Chop out each mortise as previously described for a through mortise and tenon. If there is sufficient clearance, run a tenon saw down the gauge lines on the inside edge for removing the waste from the haunch cutout (3). Pare out the waste to the depth of the haunch. If sawing first proves difficult, then chop out the waste in the usual way.

Set the tenon member in a vice and cut the tenons by first sawing down the inside edges of each and stop on the haunch line. Next, saw the sides of the tenon, finishing level with the shoulder line (4). Now cut the waste from between the tenons using a coping saw (5). Saw along the shoulder line to remove the remaining waste (6). Glue and wedge the joint as described for a through mortise and tenon joint.

Double mortise and tenon joint

Twin mortise and tenon joint
Heavy construction

TWIN MORTISE AND TENON JOINT

Twin mortise and tenon joints, like the double version, give maximum strength, but are used where the mortise is cut into the face rather than in the edge of the mortise member. The proportion of the joint will depend on whether it is for a heavy frame or a lighter construction such as a drawer rail.

Marking out the joint

Measure off and mark the shoulder line all round the end of the tenon member. The thickness of the tenons are marked out across its width. As a guide, make the tenon thickness and the gap between them the same.

Make a mark not less than 6mm (¼in) from each edge. Divide the distance between them into three to give the tenon thickness and provide a gap between **(1)**; in practice, you will have to adjust the tenon thickness to the width of the nearest mortise chisel. Set a mortise gauge to the width of the chisel, and its stock to the required distance from the pins. Mark the tenons, working from both edges of the tenon member **(2)**.

Lay the marked end of the tenon member in position on the mortise member and mark off its width and the tenon lines **(3)**. Square the width lines all round with a pencil. Gauge the mortise lines between them. If the mortise member is wider than the tenon member, reset the gauge stock.

Cutting the joint

Chop out each mortise as previously described for a through mortise and tenon joint. Saw down the sides of each tenon in the usual way. Saw along the shoulder lines to remove the waste from both sides. Cut out the waste between the tenons with a coping saw **(4)** and trim the shoulder square with a chisel. You can also remove the middle waste by first drilling through it at the shoulder and then sawing down the sides of the tenon. You will still need to trim the shoulder with a chisel.

1 Set out the tenon thickness

2 Gauge the tenons on the end

3 Mark off the tenon lines

4 Cut out the waste

PINNED MORTISE AND TENON JOINT

The pinned mortise and tenon joint is like a multiple version of the twin tenon. It provides a strong carcass joint for vertical partitions or shelves.

Tenon pins

The tenons or pins are usually square in section and evenly spaced. They may be cut through or stopped. Through pins are often wedged with the sawcut made diagonally across the pin **(1)** or square across the grain.

Marking out and cutting the joint

Mark and cut the joint using a similar method to making the twin tenon joint. A stopped housing may also be incorporated for a neater and stronger joint **(2)**.

1 Wedges set diagonally   **2 Stopped housing type**

MORTISE MEMBER

TENON MEMBER

Twin mortise and tenon joint
Light construction

TENON OR PIN MEMBER

MORTISE MEMBER

Pinned mortise and tenon joint

STUB OR STOPPED MORTISE AND TENON JOINT

The stub or stopped mortise and tenon joint is made with a blind mortise so the tenon does not show on the outside face. It is commonly used in furniture construction where a high standard of finish is required. The depth of the mortise needs to be about three-quarters of the width or thickness of the mortise member in order to leave a reasonable amount of wood at the blind end. Skilled Japanese 'shoji' (sliding-door) makers, however, take pride in cutting deep mortises leaving only paper-thin wood at the end. The method described here is the typical Western technique.

Marking out the joint
Measure the width of the mortise member to calculate the depth of the mortise and the length of the tenon. The length of the tenon is about three-quarters of the wood's width **(1)**.

Using a try square and a marking knife, scribe a shoulder line all round the tenon member at the required distance from the end of the wood **(2)**.

Set a mortise gauge to the width of the chisel and adjust the stock to centre the pins on the edge of the work. Scribe the tenon lines over the end and mark the waste.

Mark the position and width of the tenon member on the inside edge of the

mortise member **(3)** and square the lines across, then scribe the mortise gauge lines between the squared lines.

To establish the depth of cut for the mortise, apply a band of self-adhesive tape around the blade of the chisel. Set the tape a little over the length of the tenon from the cutting edge **(4)**.

Cutting the joint
Saw the waste from the tenon as previously described. Chop out the mortise, working from one side only. Stop when the tape guide is level with the surface **(5)**. Ensure that the bottom is level.

TENON MEMBER

MORTISE MEMBER

Stub or stopped mortise and tenon joint

1 Measure width of wood

2 Mark the shoulder line

3 Mark off tenon-member width

4 Apply tape depth guide

5 Chisel down to the tape

WEDGED STUB OR STOPPED MORTISE AND TENON JOINT

Stub mortise and tenon joints can be fox-wedged for additional strength. The parts must be accurately cut as once the joint is assembled it cannot be parted for adjustment.

Fitting fox wedges
The ends of the wedges are pressed against the blind end of the mortise, which should not be less than 9mm (⅜in) thick. Make two sawcuts in the tenon about 6mm (¼in) from each edge and drill a small hole at the end.

Make two wedges the same width and length as the tenon and a full 3mm (⅛in) at the thickest end. Carefully chisel a tapered undercut at each end of the mortise, making the tapers no more than 3mm (⅛in) at the blind end.

Apply glue to the wedges and the joint itself. Start the wedges in the sawcut and assemble the joint. Press the joint together with a cramp, using waste-wood blocks under the cramp heads. As the wedges are driven further into the sawcuts they spread the tenon so that it fits tightly in the mortise.

3mm (⅛in)

Fox wedging
The hidden wedges spread the tenon inside the mortise, locking it in place.

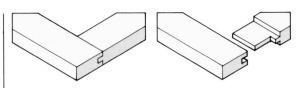

HAUNCHED MORTISE AND TENON JOINT

A mortise and tenon joint at the corner of a typical rectangular frame presents a particular problem if the outside edges are to finish flush. For the rail to be well supported the tenon should be full width, but this would mean the mortise would be open-ended, like a bridle joint, and relatively weak. The haunch is used to overcome this problem. It allows the width of the tenon to be reduced and the mortise to be set below the end of the mortise member. The haunch can be square or sloping.

The sloping or 'secret' haunch is used where appearance is important, such as for the frame of a panelled cabinet door or the joint between the seat rail and front leg of a chair. The haunched mortise and tenon is usually stopped in furniture construction and cut through in joinery work.

Marking out the joint

The proportion of the haunch in relation to the mortise and tenon is important if the joint is to perform satisfactorily. As a general guide, the width of the haunch is not more than one-third the width of the tenon, while the length of the haunch is equal to the thickness of the tenon (**1**).

The basic method that is described here is for a stub mortise and tenon, using a square haunch between members that are of equal thickness.

First, mark the length of the tenon, normally three-quarters of the mortise member's width, from the end of the tenon member. Square the tenon shoulder line all round with a marking gauge. Set a mortise gauge to the width of your chisel and adjust the stock to centre the pins on the edge of the work. Scribe the tenon lines around the end. Mark the width of the tenon with a marking gauge set to two-thirds the width of the tenon member (**2**). Scribe the line on both faces and the end, working from the inside face edge. Mark the length of the haunch on the top edge. Square a line across the top and down the sides to meet the top line of the tenon (**3**). Mark the waste by hatching.

Cut the mortise member to rough length, leaving about 18mm (¾in) extra wood at the end of it. The 'horn', as the extra wood is known, gives support to the

end of the wood while the mortise is cut. The horn is sawn off after the joint is glued and set.

Transfer the tenon-width lines to the edge of the mortise member (**4**) and square them across. Scribe the thickness of the mortise on the edge with the mortise gauge, running the lines through to the end and over onto the end grain (**5**). Set a marking gauge to the length of the haunch and scribe a line on the end between the mortise gauge lines (**6**). Hatch the waste wood.

Cutting the joint

Remove the waste from the mortise before cutting the haunch. If using a chisel, apply a marker tape to it to gauge the depth of the cut. Set the drill stand depth stop if drilling out the waste.

Now make the cutout for the haunch. Set the mortise member in a vice and saw along the gauged lines to the depth mark on the end (**7**). Cut the groove from the end, holding the chisel parallel with the work (**8**). Take out thin slices rather than chopping out the waste in one piece, thus avoiding cutting too deeply because of uneven grain.

Cut the tenon by first sawing down the gauged sides. Set the work upright in the vice and saw down the top line of the tenon. Reset the work horizontally in the vice and saw away the corner waste following the haunch line. Finally saw along the shoulder lines to remove the remaining waste.

Try the tenon in the mortise. If the shoulder does not seat properly, then deepen the mortise or the haunch groove as appropriate. After gluing, saw off the horn flush with the edge.

Haunched mortise and tenon joint

Sloping haunch

The sloping haunch is marked out and cut in a similar way to the square haunch, but with slight changes. Use the same marking method on the tenon member, but add a line for the slope of the haunch (**1**). Saw along this line when cutting away the corner waste.

When marking out the gauge lines on the mortise member, there is no need to carry them onto the end grain. Chisel out the slope for the haunch after chopping out the mortise (**2**).

1 Mark the slope

2 Chisel the slope

1 General proportion guide

3 Mark the haunch-length line

5 Gauge the edge and end

7 Saw down to end mark

2 Mark the tenon-width line

4 Transfer the tenon lines

6 Mark the haunch length

8 Chisel out the waste

GROOVED-FRAME MORTISE AND TENON JOINT

The frame of a panelled cabinet door is usually grooved to take the panel. The square haunched mortise and tenon serves to give support to the rail, but also fills the end of the groove in the stile. The thickness of the tenon and the corresponding mortise is made to match the width of the groove. The width of the groove is usually one-third the thickness of the frame members and is centred on the edge following the normal convention for setting out mortise and tenon joints. This may not always be the case, however, and the thickness and position of the joint may vary according to the size and position of the groove. For hand-cutting, the groove may be cut before or after the joint.

Marking out the joint
Set a mortise gauge to the required width of the grooving-plane's cutter and matching mortise chisel. Set the stock and scribe the groove on the inside edges of the rails and stiles. Carry the lines onto the end of the rails and stiles, and follow the procedure for marking the square-haunched mortise and tenon. In addition, set a marking gauge to the length of the haunch and use it to mark the depth of the groove on the end and sides **(1)**. This line represents the bottom edge of the tenon. Alternatively, determine the depth of the groove first and mark the length of the haunch to match. When transferring the tenon dimensions onto the mortise member, remember the width of the mortise is reduced to take the smaller tenon which is cut down by the depth of the groove **(2)**.

Cutting the joint
Follow the procedure given for the haunched mortise and tenon – but before you cut the shoulders, cut the bottom line of the tenon. It is not necessary to chisel out the waste from the haunch cutout in the stile. This will be removed when the groove is made after cutting the mortise. Plane the groove in the rails and stiles. Try the joints for fit, then cut and fit the infill panel before you glue the joints.

HAUNCH LINE

GROOVE-DEPTH LINE

1 Mark cutting lines

2 Mark the mortise

REBATED-FRAME MORTISE AND TENON JOINT

The frames of glazed cabinet doors are rebated rather than grooved to allow fitting and removal of the glass. The glass is held in the rebate by a bead. A haunched mortise and tenon joint in a rebated frame requires the tenon member to have one long and one short shoulder. The short shoulder fills the space left by the rebate. Like the grooved frame, it is easier to mark out and cut out the joint before cutting the rebates.

Marking out the joint
Mark the width and depth of the rebate on the inside edge of the mortise and tenon members with a marking gauge. Set the depth to two-thirds the thickness of the members to correspond with the line of the tenon. Referring to the methods set out for marking the haunched mortise and tenon, measure and mark the long shoulder line on the face of the tenon member. Pencil the line onto the top and bottom edges. Measure the width of the rebate from this line to mark the short shoulder on the inside face and square it onto the edges. Measure and mark the length and width of the haunch from the short shoulder line, and then use the mortise gauge to mark the thickness of the tenon.

Transfer the tenon width lines to the mortise member and mark the thickness of the mortise. Extend the gauged lines onto the end and mark the depth of the haunch cutout taken from the long shoulder line on the tenon member. Last of all, mark the waste area.

Cutting the joint
Cut the joint in a similar way to the grooved-frame joint. Plane the rebate after cutting the joint. Cut the remaining waste from the haunch cutout as described for the haunched mortise and tenon joint.

LONG-SHOULDER LINE

HAUNCH LINE

HORN

REBATE LINE

SHORT-SHOULDER LINE

REBATE LINE

TENON MEMBER (RAIL)

MORTISE MEMBER (STILE)

Grooved-frame mortise and tenon joint

TENON MEMBER

MORTISE MEMBER

Rebated-frame mortise and tenon joint

MOULDED-FRAME MORTISE AND TENON JOINT

When making mortise and tenon joints in framing with rebated and moulded edges it is necessary to mitre or scribe the moulding. It is usual for the depth of the rebate and the moulding to coincide, thus allowing the moulding to be cut away with a chisel to give a flat shoulder. Trim the stile moulding to match the width of the rail. Mitre or scribe the ends of the moulding after cutting the joint.

TRIM MOULDING TO WIDTH OF RAIL

Cut away stile moulding

ANGLED MORTISE AND TENON JOINT

Haunched and plain mortise and tenon joints are used in the construction of chair frames. Sometimes a chair design will have the front wider than the back. If the side rails are jointed into the front and back legs the rails must be set at an angle. Various solutions may be used depending on the proportions of the parts. The tenon may be on the same axis as the rail or set at an angle to it. It may also be necessary to offset the tenon to make a barefaced mortise and tenon joint.

Mark out the joint similarly to the conventional square joint, but use an adjustable bevel set to the required angle. Draw a full-size plan of the joint from which to set the bevel.

Angled mortise
For ease of marking out and maximum tenon strength it is better to have the tenon on the same axis as the rail, so the mortise is cut at an angle. To enable the chisel or drill to be held vertically for easier alignment and control make a simple jig to hold the mortise member at the required angle. Plane a short board to the same angle as the tenon shoulder and then glue a fence along the edge.

Barefaced tenon
When the face of the rail and leg are required to finish flush, an angled mortise can weaken the side of the leg.

In this case, make a barefaced tenon to set the mortise away from the edge.

Angled tenon
In some instances you may prefer to cut the mortise square and angle the tenon. This sets the tenons on each rail parallel with each other which makes it easier to fit the assembled back and front frames of the chair when gluing up.

Take care not to make the angle excessive as short grain will weaken the tenon. Use a set square held against the bevel to mark the tenon as you will not be able to use the mortise gauge.

Angled mortise
Make a simple jig to allow the cutting tool to be vertical.

Making a jig
Fix a fence to an angled baseboard.

LEG
JIG

Barefaced tenon
Use a barefaced tenon to avoid the mortise weakening the leg.

Angled tenon
Angled tenons make assembling a frame easier when gluing up.

MORTISE MEMBER (STILE)

TENON MEMBER (RAIL)

Barefaced tenon

Angled tenon

Moulded-frame mortise and tenon joint

CORNER MORTISE AND TENON JOINT

Mortise and tenon corner joints, as used in the construction of a table or a chair, are marked out and cut in the way described. In the case of the mortise member (the leg), the mortises are marked on adjacent faces. It is usual for the joint to be symmetrical and the mortises to meet. To allow the tenon members (the rails) to fit, it is better to mitre the ends of the tenons than to cut them short. The larger gluing area gives a stronger joint.

Round-leg corner joint
Set out and cut the mortises before turning the leg. Scribe the tenon shoulders with a gouge to fit the curve.

LOOSE-WEDGED MORTISE AND TENON JOINT

The loose-wedged mortise and tenon is demountable and is used in the construction of Tudor-style refectory tables. It is similar to the traditional and stronger tusk tenon used in building construction, but the furniture version does not usually include the tusk element. The proportion of the joint should provide an adequate shoulder on the tenon member and a strong tenon that will resist being split by the wedge. The wedge is usually set vertically, but it can also be fitted horizontally. The following is one method which you can adapt to suit your requirements.

Marking out the joint
The length of the projecting end of the tenon should be at least one and a half times the thickness of the mortise member. Calculate the total length of the tenon and square the shoulder line all round the tenon member (**1**). Gauge the width of the tenon to be not less than one-third the width of the tenon member (**2**). Mark the thickness of the mortise member from the shoulder line and square the line all round (**3**). Mark the waste.

Mark the width and position of the tenon on the mortise member and square the lines all round, then centre and gauge the thickness of the tenon between the lines (**4**).

Cutting the joint
Drill or chop out the mortise, working from both sides. Saw off the waste from the tenon member. Fit the tenon into the mortise;

this should be a sliding fit. With the shoulder up tight, mark the thickness of the mortise member on the top of the tenon (**5**). Take the joint apart and mark the length of the wedge mortise to equal the thickness of the mortise member, but set it about 3mm ($\frac{1}{8}$in) in from the first line (**6**). Square the lines all round the tenon. Set a mortise gauge to one-third the thickness of the tenon and mark the thickness of the mortise (**7**). Make a single sloped wedge to fit, about three times the width of the tenon. Make the slope 1–6. Hold the wedge on the side of the tenon level with the inner mortise line and mark the slope (**8**). Square the line onto the bottom of the tenon. Chisel out the mortise, taking exta care with the angled face. Assemble the joint and tap in the wedge in order to draw the joint up tight.

1 Mark the tenon-shoulder line

2 Gauge the tenon width

3 Mark mortise-member thickness

4 Gauge thickness of tenon

TENON MEMBER (RAIL)

TENON MEMBER (RAIL)

MORTISE MEMBER (LEG)

Corner joint

MORTISE MEMBER

WEDGE

TENON MEMBER

Loose-wedged mortise and tenon joint

5 Mark the top of the tenon

6 Mark 3mm (⅛in) inside line

7 Gauge wedge-mortise thickness

8 Mark the slope of the wedge

BRIDLE JOINTS

The bridle joint is grouped with the mortise and tenon joints by virtue of the methods by which it is marked out. However, the methods used to cut the joint also make it similar to the halving joint. The tenon element of the bridle joint is usually one-third the thickness of the wood, but it can be more where a rail is T-jointed into a thicker leg member.

Marking out the joint
To make a corner joint, mark the width of the mortise member on the end of the tenon member. Allow for a little waste to be planed off after gluing up. Square the shoulder lines all round with a marking knife. Use light pressure on the edges.

Mark the width of the tenon member on the mortise member and square the shoulder line using a pencil. Set a mortise gauge to one-third the thickness of the tenon member. It is not necessary to set the gauge to the width of a chisel as usual for a mortise and tenon, but it can help when cleaning up the shoulder of the mortise cutout.

Set the stock to centre the pins and gauge the tenon lines over the end. Mark the mortise-member cutout in the same way, and mark

the waste on both parts as they look identical at this stage (**1**).

Cutting the joint
Select a drill which is close to the width of the mortise and drill a hole just inside the shoulder line, working from both edges (**2**). Set the work in the vice and saw down to the hole on the waste side of the gauged lines (**3**). Pare out the remaining waste level with the shoulder line (**4**). Alternatively, using a tenon saw, cut down the gauged lines first, then cut out the waste with a coping saw. Cut the tenon as you would for a mortise and tenon.

To mark and cut a 'T' bridle joint (**5**), basically follow the procedure above, but use the halving-joint method to cut the waste from the tenon member.

1 Mark the waste on both parts

2 Drill close to the shoulder

3 Saw down to the hole

4 Pare out the remaining waste

5 Cut 'T' bridle joints similarly

TENON MEMBER

MORTISE MEMBER

Corner bridle joint

MORTISE MEMBER

TENON MEMBER

'T' bridle joint

DOWEL JOINTS

The dowel joint is relatively simple and quick to cut. Basically it is a butt joint reinforced with wooden pegs glued into holes drilled in both of the parts being joined. It is used to make a variety of joints for frame and carcass construction. The dowel joint is widely used by furniture manufacturers as a cost-effective substitute for the mortise and tenon. For handwork the joint does not require complicated marking out and, if using a dowelling jig, marking out is minimal.

Dowel rod
Dowel rod is a round-sectioned moulding, available in a range of diameters from 6 to 47mm ($\frac{1}{4}$ to $1\frac{7}{8}$in). For most work you will only need the 6, 8, 10 and 12mm ($\frac{1}{4}$, $\frac{5}{16}$, $\frac{3}{8}$ and $\frac{1}{2}$in) diameters. Check the quality, as it is not always round due to moisture changes or inaccurate machining.

DOWELS

Dowels are made from even-textured hardwoods such as beech, birch, maple or ramin. You can cut your own from commercially produced dowel rod or use ready-made dowels; or, if neither suits your purpose, make them entirely using a dowel former.

Cutting dowels
Use a fine-toothed saw to cut the dowels to length. Steady the wood with a bench hook or mitre box. To avoid break-out of the wood fibres rotate the dowelling as you cut. If making a number of dowels, set up an end stop to gauge the length.

Cut a groove down the length of each cut dowel using the saw. This is to release the hydraulic pressure from the hole as the dowel is glued in. Failure to do this can cause the wood to split. Finally, chamfer the ends to make inserting the dowels easier. You can either use a special dowel-chamfering tool or a sander, or a pencil sharpener for the smaller sizes.

Ready-made dowels are supplied cut to length. They are chamfered and grooved all round with straight or spiralled flutes.

A dowel former is a thick steel plate with standard-sized dowel holes drilled through it. It is used to produce purpose-made dowels from lengths of roughly sized wood that are driven through the appropriate hole. You can either make your own former to produce smooth round dowels or use a proprietary former which has serrated holes that create relief flutes as the wood is driven through.

The length of the dowel will vary according to the size of the wood into which it is fitted. As a guide, make the length not less than five times the diameter. The longer the dowel, the greater the gluing area will be. The diameter of the dowel can be half the thickness of the wood.

Boring the dowel holes
The strength of the dowel joint is dependent on the fit of the dowel in the hole. The hole must be clean and true and the correct depth. It can be drilled using a brace and auger bit or a dowel bit in a power drill. If you use a hand-held method, stand so you are looking down the centre line of the holes (1), since it is critical to keep the drill upright in the thickness of the wood.

For greater accuracy use a proprietary dowelling jig. Various types are available with a choice of drill-guide bushes which not only keep the drill upright but accurately position the holes on the individual parts.

The holes must be of consistent depth and only slightly deeper than half the length of the dowel. Use a proprietary depth gauge or make your own gauge with a wooden or rubber sleeve which can be cut or positioned as required.

Countersink the holes to aid assembly. If you find you have drilled a hole out of square, fill it with a plug and redrill it.

Marking the joint
Unless you intend to make a number of dowel joints it is sufficient to mark out the joints using conventional methods.

For edge-to-edge joints, place the boards in a vice with the edges flush and face sides out. Evenly space the positions of the dowels and square the lines across. Set a gauge to half the thickness of the boards and scribe a centre line on each, working from the face sides (2).

The number and spacing of the dowels used in frame joints depends on the width of the rail. Two dowels are usually used. The spacing between the dowels is not critical, but you should inset the dowels not less than 6mm ($\frac{1}{4}$in) from the edges.

Prepare and mark the face side and edge of the rail and stile members. Mark their lengths. Plane the ends of the rails square on a shooting board. You can leave the stiles overlength. Set each joint's rail and stile in a vice with the surfaces level and face sides out. Square lines across both members. Set a marking gauge to half the thickness of the rail and mark a centre line on each part, working from the face side (3). Centre the drill where the lines cross.

Dowel rod

Prepared dowel

Fluted dowel

Carcass joint

Edge-to-edge joint

Framing joint

1 Stand in line with the edge

2 Mark the centre lines

3 Mark rail and stile centres

4 Make a right-angled jig

5 Insert centre points

6 Mark the stile

Using centre points

Another marking method, which is easier to use for awkwardly shaped parts, is to use centre points to mark one part from another. You can either make your own or buy proprietary dowel centre points.

For the panel pin method, mark the positions on one part. For edge-to-edge joints, use either edge. For the frame-corner joint described here, fit the points into the end of the rail.

Drive the pins into the centre marks and crop off the heads. Lay the rail and stile on a flat surface and push them together to offset the nail points on the inside edge of the stile. You can make a simple jig to help keep the parts in line (**4**).

Using proprietary dowel centre points, first mark and drill the end of the rail. Then insert the appropriate-sized centre point in each hole and press the parts together (**5**).

Using a template

When making a number of identical dowel joints, a template will speed up marking out. Cut a hardwood fence-block to the width of the rail member. Make a sawcut across its centre to receive a thin steel plate. Before epoxy-gluing the plate into the slot, mark and drill small guide holes through it at the required setting.

Use a pointed tool to mark the centres through the holes. Always hold the template's fence against the face side. Finally, mark the end of the rail and then invert the template to mark the stile (**6**).

Using a dowelling jig

A dowelling jig is designed to clamp onto the work to position and guide the drill accurately. Some are preset and have fixed guide holes for 6, 8 and 10mm ($\frac{1}{4}$, $\frac{5}{16}$ and $\frac{3}{8}$in) dowels, while others have interchangeable steel guide bushes which can be adjusted to various settings.

DOWEL FRAMING JOINT

Using the adjustable-type jig, set the drill-bit guides on the slide rods to the required spacing to suit the width of the rail. Take the measurements from the jig's fixed head. Set the fences on the drill-bit guides to centre the holes on the thickness of the wood. Locate the jig on the end of the rail and clamp it in place with the sliding fence. Make sure the fixed head and fences are set against the face side and face edge. Drill the holes to the required depth (**1**).

Remove the sliding fence and, without altering the other settings, invert the jig and clamp it to the inside edge of the prepared stile using the cramp provided. Drill the matching holes in readiness for the dowels (**2**).

DOWEL CARCASS JOINTS

The jig can be fitted with a range of slide rods, allowing wide boards to be jointed. In addition, extra drill-bit guides can be purchased to enable more holes to be drilled without resetting the two guides supplied as standard.

Fit appropriate-sized bushes in the guides to suit the thickness of the board. Set the end bushes about 25mm (1in) from the edges and the others about 75mm (3in) apart.

For a corner joint, set the fences to centre the holes on the thickness of the board. Clamp the jig to the end with the sliding fence. Drill the holes (**1**).

Clamp the end of the other board in the top of the jig. Release the lower clamp screw and invert the board with the jig attached. Drill the stopped holes on the inside face (**2**).

For a 'T' joint, set out and drill the end as before. Remove the fences and clamp the jig across the other board with the bushes centred on a line drawn across for the purpose (**3**). Always keep the fixed head against the face edge.

CARCASS MITRE JOINT

Mitre the ends of the boards. Set the jig in place as described for the corner joint, but following the slope of the mitre. Set the fences to place the bushes close to the inside face where the board is thickest. Drill the holes, then transfer the jig to the other board (see above).

1 Drill the rail holes

2 Drill the stile holes

1 Drill end holes

2 Drill the stopped holes

3 Centre jig on marked line

Drill stopped angled holes

● **Gluing the joint**
Apply a little glue to the jointing faces and into each hole with a brush or stick. Dip the ends of the dowels in glue as they are inserted into the holes. Tap them home with a mallet and set the assembly in cramps, as required.

DOVETAIL JOINTS

Dovetail joints, perhaps more than any other type, express what wood joints are all about. In most examples the interlocking wedge-shaped elements of the joint are clearly demonstrated, leaving you with no doubt that the joint would hold together even if it were not glued. Traditional drawer-making is a classic example of the use of the dovetail joint, the inherent strength of the joint's tails and pins being used to resist the pulling forces applied to a drawer front.

Dovetail joints can be made in a number of ways. Some exploit the decorative nature of the repetitive shapes, while others hide them completely. All are a challenge to the maker.

THROUGH DOVETAIL JOINT

The through dovetail is a traditional joint for joining the ends of solid-wood boards. It is commonly used in the construction of boxes and cabinetwork. Through dovetail joints can be cut by hand or machine. A power router and a special jig are used for machining dovetails. Although functional, the even spacing of the machine-cut dovetails is regarded by traditionalists to be less attractive than the well-proportioned hand-cut dovetail joint described here. The through dovetail is the simplest type to make, but it still takes very careful marking out and cutting.

1 Plane the ends square

2 Mark the shoulder line

Marking the tails
Mark the face side, face edge and each pair of ends that are to be jointed. Accurately cut the components to length and plane the ends smooth and square. The use of a shooting board will make the planing easier **(1)**.

Set a cutting gauge to the thickness of the wood. Mark the shoulder line for the tails all round the end of the tail member **(2)** and on the sides of the pin member. Where the gauge lines could mar the finished work, use a fine pencil line and a try square instead. Next, mark the tails. The size and number can vary according to the width of the boards being joined and the type of wood (softwood needs coarser and fewer tails than hardwood), as well as the appearance of the finished joint. As a general guide, for good appearance the tails should be the same size and equally spaced, but wider than the pins.

Start by squaring a pencil line across the end 6mm (¼in) from each edge, then divide the distance between the pencil marks into an even number of equal parts. Measure 3mm (⅛in) on each side of the marks and square pencil lines across the end **(3)**. Mark the slope of the tails on the face side using an adjustable bevel or a dovetail template. Mark the waste to avoid confusion later.

PIN MEMBER

TAIL MEMBER

Through dovetail joint

3 Mark the ends of the tails

Cutting the tails

Set each piece of wood in the vice at an angle so that one side of every tail is vertical.

Using a dovetail saw, cut down one side of the tails. Keep close to the line on the waste side **(4)** and take care not to go beyond the shoulder line. After re-positioning the work in the vice, cut down the other side of the tails.

Set the work horizontally in the vice and cut away the corner waste, following the shoulder line **(5)**. Remove most of the waste from between the tails with a coping saw **(6)**. Pare out what is left with a bevel-edge chisel, working from both sides towards the middle and finishing level with the shoulder line **(7)**.

4 Saw the sides of the tails

5 Saw off the corner waste

6 Remove the waste between tails

7 Pare out remaining waste

Marking the pins

Rub chalk on the end grain of the prepared wood and set it vertically in the vice. Lay the cut tail member in position, checking that the 'face marks' correspond **(8)**. Line up the edges and shoulder line of the tails precisely on the chalked end and mark their shape with a scriber or knife **(9)**, then square the lines down to the shoulders on each face of the wood **(10)**. Mark the waste with a pencil.

8 Align the tailpiece accurately

9 Mark round the tails

10 Mark the sides of the pins

Cutting the pins

Set each piece vertically in the vice. Saw down to the shoulder line, following the angles marked from the tails **(11)**. Keep the sawcut on the waste side so it just shaves the marked line. Remove most of the waste from between the pins with a coping saw, then trim down to the shoulder line with a bevel-edge chisel. Work from both sides towards the middle. Clean out the corners holding the chisel at the angle of the pins **(12)**.

Assembling the joint

Dovetails are cut to be a close fit and should be fully assembled once only. To check the fit, partly assemble the joint and trim any tight spots. Clean up the inside faces of the parts prior to gluing. Apply glue to both halves and tap the joint together, using a hammer and a piece of waste wood to protect the surface **(13)**. If you are working on a wide joint, tap across the width as you go in order to keep it level. Wipe away any surplus glue before it sets. When the glue has set, clean up the joint with a smoothing plane, working from the edges towards the middle so as to prevent the end grain breaking out.

11 Saw the sides of the pins

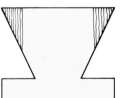

12 Angle chisel to pare corners

13 Tap the joint together

DOVETAIL ANGLES

The angle of a dovetail should not be too steep or too shallow.

Excessive slope on a dovetail will give weak short grain on the corners **(1)**, while an insufficient slope can reduce the interlocking strength of the joint **(2)**. Mark out the proportions of the slope on a piece of wood and set a sliding bevel to the angle, or use a template. Make the slope 1–8 for hardwoods and 1–6 for softwoods.

1 Excessively sloped

2 Insufficiently sloped

Hardwood angle

Softwood angle

DECORATIVE THROUGH DOVETAIL JOINT

A well-proportioned and accurately cut through dovetail joint makes an attractive feature which is often exploited in the design of a cabinet's construction. Decorative through dovetails are used to enhance this feature and express the skills of the maker. The design of the joint follows basic principles, but the proportion and disposition of the joint's elements is open to interpretation. The example shown here uses fine-cut pins and half-depth dovetails.

2 Set out the tails

Marking the tails
Pencil or lightly gauge the shoulder line all round the end of the tail member. Set the try square or the gauge to the thickness of the pin member. Mark the shoulder line of the small dovetails to half the thickness **(1)**. Where the line is to be cut, which is established after marking the tails, enhance the pencil line with a marking knife or deepen the gauge line.

Set out the size and position of the tails and mark the slope with a template **(2)**. The fine pins are created by placing the tails close together. The distance between them needs to be no more than the thickness of the saw kerf. You can measure and mark the tails directly on the wood or work out the design on paper and transfer the dimensions to the tail member. Square the lines onto the end and mark the waste area **(3)**.

Cutting the tails
Cut away the waste in the same manner as a through dovetail, using a dovetail saw and coping saw. Finish the cut along the shoulder line, paring from both sides with a bevel-edge chisel.

Marking the pins
Chalk the end of the pin member. With the cutting gauge set to the length of the small tails, mark the thickness line of the small pins on the end **(4)**. Mark the pins from the tail member using the tip of the saw **(5)** or a scriber. Square the lines down to the shoulder line on each face and mark the waste.

Cutting the pins
Remove most of the waste with a dovetail saw and coping saw, and trim the shoulder line with a chisel. To cut the small pins to size, first clamp the work to the bench on a flat board. Make a cut across the grain close to the shoulder line **(6)**. Carefully pare away the waste, working with the grain **(7)**. Then repeat the operation and finish level with the gauged shoulder and thickness line. Glue and assemble in the same manner as a conventional through dovetail.

3 Mark the ends of the tails

4 Mark thickness of small pins

1 Mark small dovetail shoulder

5 Mark the pins with a saw

6 Cut across the grain

PIN MEMBER

TAIL MEMBER

7 Pare out the waste

Decorative through dovetail joint

MITRED THROUGH DOVETAIL JOINT

A mitred edge is sometimes incorporated with a through dovetail joint to allow the edge to be moulded. The depth of the mitred portion is dependent on the contour of the moulding.

Marking the tails
Gauge the shoulder line on the two sides and bottom edge of the tail member. Mark the mitre shoulder line on the top edge **(1)**.

Measure down from the top edge the depth required for the moulding. Gauge a line at this level across the end and round to the shoulder line **(2)**.

Make a light pencil mark 6mm ($\frac{1}{4}$in) below the first mark and also 6mm ($\frac{1}{4}$in) up from the bottom edge. Divide the distance between these marks and set out the tails as required. Mark the waste to be cut away.

Cutting the tails
Saw down the sides of the tails and the moulding depth line and remove the waste with a coping saw. Trim the shoulders with a bevel-edge chisel. Leave the mitre waste at this stage.

Marking the pins
Lightly gauge a shoulder line on both sides of the pin member. Mark the mitre shoulder line on the top edge. Chalk the end and mark the pins and mitre waste from the tail member.

Square the tail lines down to the shoulder lines on each face and to the mitre waste line on the inside face only. Mark the waste.

Cutting the pins
Cut the waste from between the pins. Then cut away the mitre waste from the top corner **(3)**. Finally, saw off the mitre waste from the tail piece **(4)**. Plane the top edge to the required moulding before assembling the joint.

1 Mark the mitre line

2 Gauge the moulding-depth line

3 Cut away the pin-mitre waste

4 Cut the tail-mitre waste

REBATED THROUGH DOVETAIL JOINT

A box featuring through dovetails and having the bottom panel set in a rebate requires the joint to be modified if a gap is not to show at the bottom corner. This is done by projecting the shoulder of the tail member to fill the rebate.

Marking the tails
Gauge the tails' shoulder line on the sides and over the top edge. Gauge the rebate depth line along the inside edge, over the end and round to the shoulder line on the face side **(1)**. Also mark the inside face of the pin member at the same setting. Reset the gauge, if necessary, and mark the width of the rebate on the edge of both parts **(2)**.

Make one pencil mark on the tail member 6mm ($\frac{1}{4}$in) below the intended depth of the rebate and another at 6mm ($\frac{1}{4}$in) from the opposite edge. Set out the tails between the marks.

Square a line over the rebated edge of the tail member to match the rebate on the pin member **(3)**, and mark the waste.

Cutting the tails
Saw down the sides of the tails and the rebate depth line. Remove the waste with a coping saw and chisel.

Marking the pins
Gauge a shoulder line on both sides of the pin member. Chalk the end and mark the pins from the tail member, using a scriber or sharp pencil. Mark the waste.

Cutting the joints
Cut the sides of the pins and remove the waste with a coping saw and chisel. Plane the rebate on both pin and tail members. Finally, cut off the waste from the projecting shoulder of the tail member **(4)**.

1 Mark the rebate-depth line   **3 Square a line over the edge**

 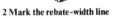

2 Mark the rebate-width line   **4 Saw off projecting waste**

PIN MEMBER

TAIL MEMBER

Mitred through dovetail joint

TAIL MEMBER

PIN MEMBER

Rebated through dovetail joint

LAPPED DOVETAIL JOINT

The lapped dovetail joint is used in cabinet construction where the dovetail joint is needed for strength but not to be seen from one side. The joint is typically used for traditional drawer construction. It is similar to the through dovetail to execute except for the marking and cutting of the pins.

Marking the tails

The thickness of the lap must first be determined before the tail member is cut to precise length. As a guide, the lap can be one-third the thickness of the pin member but not less than 3mm ($\frac{1}{8}$in). Set a cutting gauge to the length of the tails (the thickness of the pin member less the lap) and mark the shoulder all round the prepared end of the tail piece. Then set out the dovetails and mark the waste.

Cutting the tails

Cut away the waste with a dovetail saw and coping saw and trim the shoulders with a bevel-edge chisel.

Marking the pins

With the cutting gauge set to the length of the tails, gauge the lap line on the end of the pin member, working from the inside face.

Reset the gauge to the thickness of the tail member and mark a line across the inside face, working from the end. Chalk the end of the pin member and mark the pins from the tails (1). Square the lines down to the inside shoulder line and mark the waste.

1 Mark the pins from the tail

Cutting the pins

Set the work upright in the vice. Hold the saw at an angle and cut down the waste side of the lines (2). Stop on the lap and shoulder lines. Saw out some of the waste from the corners while you have the wood set up in the vice (3).

Clamp the wood to the bench on a flat board. Chop out the waste with a bevel-edge chisel. Make a series of alternating cuts, first across the grain (4), then with the grain (5). Start the cross-grain cuts away from the shoulder line and work back to it as the waste is removed. Carefully trim away the waste from the corners with a narrow bevel-edge chisel.

2 Saw at an angle

3 Saw out some of the waste

4 Cut across the grain

5 Pare out the waste

DOUBLE-LAPPED DOVETAIL JOINT

The double-lapped dovetail is used for cabinet or box construction where the dovetails are required to be hidden. All that is seen of the joint is the end grain of one lap. The lap may be on the tail or pin member. The method you adopt will determine which way round the parts are marked. If the lap is on the pin member, the pins must be cut first and the tails marked from them. The method described here has the lap on the tail piece.

Marking and cutting the tails

Start with the wood cut to length and the ends planed square. Set a cutting gauge to the thickness of the pin member and mark the shoulder line on the inside face and edges of the tail member.

Set the gauge to the width of the lap and mark the end and edges from the outside face. Gauge the rebate depth line on the inside and edges at the same setting from the end (1).

You must now cut the rebate before you can mark the tails. Saw away the rebate waste keeping close to the line (2). To help keep the saw on line, chisel a groove on the waste side of the line. Trim the rebate with a shoulder plane (3).

Set out the width and positions of the tails and mark the slope with a template (4). Square the lines on the end. Mark the waste. Saw and chisel out the waste as for a lapped dovetail.

Marking and cutting the pins

Gauge the width of the lap on the end of the pin member. Set the gauge to the thickness of the tails and mark a line on the inside face, working from the end. Chalk the end and mark the pins from the tails (5). Square the lines down on the inside face. Mark the waste, then saw and chisel it out.

LAP

PIN MEMBER

TAIL MEMBER

Lapped dovetail joint

1 Gauge the rebate-depth line

2 Saw away rebate waste

3 Trim the rebate

4 Mark the tails

5 Mark the pins from the tails

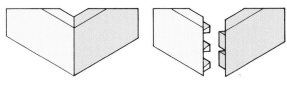

MITRED DOVETAIL JOINT

The construction of this dovetail joint is completely hidden by the mitred laps and is often referred to as a secret mitred dovetail. It is used in fine work and requires careful marking and cutting. The members being jointed must be the same thickness and need to be cut to length. The tails can only be marked from the pins, which are cut first.

Marking and cutting the joint
Set a cutting gauge to the thickness of the wood and mark a shoulder line across the inside face, working from the end. Using a marking knife and mitre square, mark the mitre on each edge between the gauge line and outer corner.

Set the gauge to the width of the lap and mark the rebate. Mark the end from the outside face and mark the rebate depth line from the end (1). Saw out the rebate waste and trim the surface with a shoulder plane.

Begin marking out the pins by first gauging a line parallel with each edge from the shoulder line to the lap. Set the line not more than 6mm ($\frac{1}{4}$in) from the edge (2).

Set out the width and positions of the pins on the end between the gauged lines. Make a card dovetail template and hold it against the lap face to keep it true.

Square the lines down to the shoulder line, then mark the waste.

Saw and chisel out the waste between the pins as for a lapped dovetail. The saw can cut into the lap slightly (3). Saw off the mitre waste.

Set the work upright and pare most of the waste from the lap mitre with a chisel (4). Finish the mitre with a shoulder plane. Back up the edge with a mitred block to help guide the plane.

Marking and cutting the tails
Follow the procedure given for marking out the pin member up to and including cutting the rebate.

Lay the tail member on the bench, inside face up. Place the pin member on the end with its inside face level with the gauge line. Mark off the shape of the pins with a scriber (5). Square the lines onto the end and mark the waste.

Saw off the mitre waste (6). Then saw down the sides of the tails and chop out the waste between the tails and between the end tails and mitre shoulder (7). Pare and plane the lap mitre in the same way as the pin member to complete the joint. Try the joint for fit before gluing.

1 Set out the lines

2 Gauge the ends of the pins

5 Mark the tails from the pins

3 Saw the sides of the pins

6 Saw off the mitre waste

4 Pare the mitre waste

7 Chop out the waste

Double-lapped dovetail joint

Mitred dovetail joint

BEVELLED DOVETAIL JOINT

The bevelled dovetail is used to make a rigid joint in the sloping sides of a frame which meet at a compound angle. It is not an easy joint to make as it is difficult to visualize, the setting out is complicated and all the edges of the parts are angled, requiring careful cutting. The wood must be the same thickness and has to be cut oversize in length and width. It is necessary to make an elevation drawing from which to calculate the true shape of the parts before the joint can be marked out.

Making a drawing

Begin by drawing the side elevation of the frame joint as it would appear when complete. Show the thickness of the wood and add broken lines representing its initial width and length. Draw its plan immediately below the side elevation.

However, neither drawing will give a true view as the parts seen from these angles are foreshortened. To get the true view project the side to lie flat (1). Start by setting a pair of compasses on point A. Strike an arc from point A¹ to the base line at B. Strike a second arc from point A². Set the compass point on A³ and swing an arc to meet a vertical line at C. Draw a line through C parallel with the base line. Join up points BD and draw

a line parallel to it from A, which will give a true section of the side.

Drop a vertical line from A to E on the plan. Drop a line from B to F on a line extended from the outer edge of the plan. Similarly, drop a line from C¹ to G and from D to H. Join G to H with a solid line which represents the inside of the end. Join E to F with a broken line to represent the outside edge. The angle X is the true angle of the end.

To find the true bevel angle, draw a line at right angles to line EF at I. Draw a second line parallel to it and set away from it by the thickness of the wood to point J. Run a line through IJ. The angle Y is the true bevel angle.

1 Construct an elevation and true-view drawing of the joint

Bevelled dovetail joint

244

Marking and cutting the ends

Cut the parts to length and width as shown by the broken lines on the side elevation. Set an adjustable bevel to the end angle X (2). Mark the angle on the inside face of the wood from the corner (3). Saw the ends to the angle (4). Set a second bevel to the end angle Y. Mark the angle on the edges from the outer face side (5). Join up the edge marks to give a guide line for planing the end bevel. In fact, the bevel should be checked with the adjustable bevel held at right angles to the edge as planing progresses to give the true bevel (6). Set the wood in the vice with the end horizontal and carefully plane the end bevel on each part.

2 Set bevel to the end angle

3 Mark the angle

4 Saw the end angle

5 Mark angle Y on the edges

6 Hold bevel at right angles

Marking and cutting the joint

Set out the tails on the face side of the tail member. First mark the thickness of the wood on both faces of both parts, taken from the bevelled ends (7). Join the lines on each edge of the tail members.

With the adjustable bevel set to the end angle X, mark a line from the inside bottom corner on the end of the tail member. Make a mark 6mm ($\frac{1}{4}$in) down from the top edge and up from the bottom mark. Set out the size and spacing of the tails between these marks. Then set a card dovetail template against a try square and mark out the dovetails on the outside face (8).

Mark the slope of the dovetail ends on the bevelled end of the tail member. Use the bevel set to the end angle X. Hold the stock of the bevel square to the end face (9), as it was flat when set from the drawing.

Use the try square and dovetail template to mark the dovetail on the inside face. Mark the waste.

Cut the tails carefully, following the marked angles. Place the work at an angle in the vice to set each cutting line vertical (10).

Mark the cut dovetails on the end of the pin member. Apply chalk to the end to help make clear scriber lines. Lay the tail member on the end with the edges and inner shoulders flush and mark round the tails.

Using the bevel set to the end angle X, mark parallel lines down from each dovetail to the shoulder (11). Mark the waste, then saw and chisel it out carefully, following the angled lines.

You can plane the bevel on the long edges before or after gluing up. Use the bevel set to the end angle X to check the bevel, whichever way you choose. The sloping sides can present problems when gluing up. If you tap the joints home with a hammer, use a block to protect the work.

7 Mark the thickness of the wood

8 Using a card template, mark the tails

9 Hold the stock square to the end face

10 Set cutting lines vertical

11 Mark pin cutting lines

● **Clamping the joint**
To clamp the joint use webbing cramps, or glue wedge-shaped blocks to the surface and use sash cramps. Place thick paper between the block and the surface, so you can remove the block without damaging the wood.

BOARD JOINTS

Plywood, blockboard, laminboard, chipboard and medium-density fibreboard (MDF) are all used for carcass construction. Man-made boards are more stable than panels of solid wood, but on the whole they do not have its long-grain strength. The means of joining these boards varies according to their composition. Most joints used for solid-wood carcass construction can be used. Framing joints, such as mortise and tenon, halvings and bridle joints, are unsuitable for joining man-made boards.

JOINT GUIDE

The chart shows the typical range of man-made boards and the carcass joints suitable for a particular material. The first column indicates the strength of each joint in each material. The second column shows the best ways of making the joints. The third column indicates the relative difficulty in terms of hand-cutting and machine-cutting.

Treat solid-core laminated boards, such as blockboard and laminboard, like solid wood when selecting a joint for a particular application. A dovetail, for example, would be cut in the end grain only, not the side grain.

Dovetails are more difficult to cut in these materials because of the changing grain direction of the board's structure. Make coarse, even-sized tails and pins (machine-cut dovetails are preferable). For dovetail-jointed cabinets that are to be veneered, use lapped joints. The mitred variety is best, as it will not show the joint's construction through the veneer if the wood shrinks or swells.

Man-made boards which are ready-finished with a decorative veneer must be mitre-jointed if the core material is not to show on the face. The alternative is to use a corner lipping, which makes an attractive decorative feature.

TYPICAL CARCASS JOINTS

Corner joint

'T' joint

Edge-to-edge joint

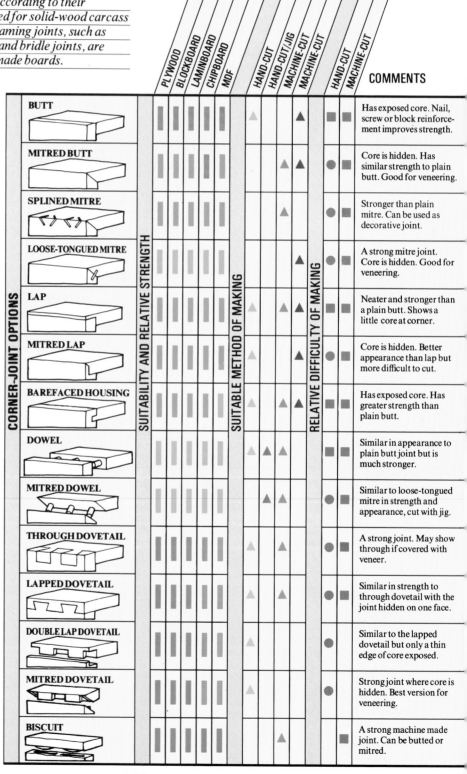

CORNER-JOINT OPTIONS	SUITABILITY AND RELATIVE STRENGTH	SUITABLE METHOD OF MAKING	RELATIVE DIFFICULTY OF MAKING	COMMENTS
BUTT				Has exposed core. Nail, screw or block reinforcement improves strength.
MITRED BUTT				Core is hidden. Has similar strength to plain butt. Good for veneering.
SPLINED MITRE				Stronger than plain mitre. Can be used as decorative joint.
LOOSE-TONGUED MITRE				A strong mitre joint. Core is hidden. Good for veneering.
LAP				Neater and stronger than a plain butt. Shows a little core at corner.
MITRED LAP				Core is hidden. Better appearance than lap but more difficult to cut.
BAREFACED HOUSING				Has exposed core. Has greater strength than plain butt.
DOWEL				Similar in appearance to plain butt joint but is much stronger.
MITRED DOWEL				Similar to loose-tongued mitre in strength and appearance, cut with jig.
THROUGH DOVETAIL				A strong joint. May show through if covered with veneer.
LAPPED DOVETAIL				Similar in strength to through dovetail with the joint hidden on one face.
DOUBLE LAP DOVETAIL				Similar to the lapped dovetail but only a thin edge of core exposed.
MITRED DOVETAIL				Strong joint where core is hidden. Best version for veneering.
BISCUIT				A strong machine made joint. Can be butted or mitred.

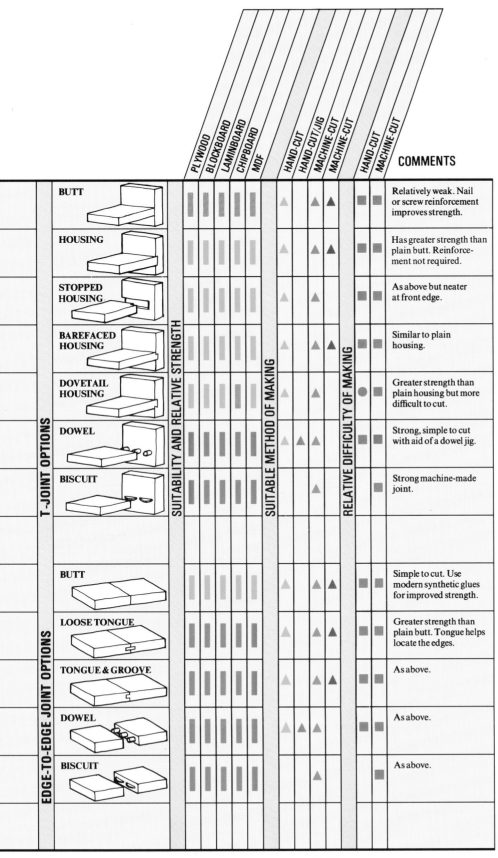

Column headers (angled): PLYWOOD · BLOCKBOARD · LAMINBOARD · CHIPBOARD · MDF · HAND-CUT · HAND-CUT/JIG · MACHINE-CUT · MACHINE-CUT · HAND-CUT · MACHINE-CUT · COMMENTS

Vertical axis labels: SUITABILITY AND RELATIVE STRENGTH · SUITABLE METHOD OF MAKING · RELATIVE DIFFICULTY OF MAKING

T-JOINT OPTIONS

Joint	Comments
BUTT	Relatively weak. Nail or screw reinforcement improves strength.
HOUSING	Has greater strength than plain butt. Reinforcement not required.
STOPPED HOUSING	As above but neater at front edge.
BAREFACED HOUSING	Similar to plain housing.
DOVETAIL HOUSING	Greater strength than plain housing but more difficult to cut.
DOWEL	Strong, simple to cut with aid of a dowel jig.
BISCUIT	Strong machine-made joint.

EDGE-TO-EDGE JOINT OPTIONS

Joint	Comments
BUTT	Simple to cut. Use modern synthetic glues for improved strength.
LOOSE TONGUE	Greater strength than plain butt. Tongue helps locate the edges.
TONGUE & GROOVE	As above.
DOWEL	As above.
BISCUIT	As above.

KEY TO CHART

Suitability and relative strength

▌	Excellent
▌	Good
▌	Fair
▌	Poor
▌	Unsuitable

Suitable method of making

▲	Hand-cut (Using handtools)
▲	Hand-cut/jig (Using handtools with jigs)
▲	Machine-cut (Using hand-held power tools)*
▲	Machine-cut (Using machine tools)*

Jigs may also be used

Relative difficulty of making

●	Difficult
■	Simple

USING A CORNER LIPPING

For pre-veneered chipboard a lipping can be used to make a corner joint which also masks the core. The grain of the lipping is set at right angles to the face veneer of the board and forms a feature. The lipping can be left square or you can shape it. You can also use contrasting wood.

Shapes for corner lippings

Square

Full-round

Chamfered

Beaded

Bevelled

Part-round

Joints for corner lippings

Butt-joint the lipping or, for improved strength, make a tongue and groove joint. Use a loose-tongued joint or cut the groove in the edge of the board and the tongue in the lipping. Whichever way you decide, stop the tongue and the groove so they do not show on the edge **(1)**.

A stronger joint suitable for plinths or carcass construction can be made using a thicker lipping. Cut a barefaced tongue on the board and a matching goove in the lipping. The section can be shaped if required, as indicated by the broken line **(2)**.

1 Loose tongue and groove joint

2 Shape the lipping if required

TYPES OF LIPPING

The edges of man-made boards must be finished with a lipping to cover the core material. You can use either long-grain or cross-grain veneer or a more substantial solid-wood lipping of matching or contrasting timber. Lippings can be applied before or after surface veneering. In the case of pre-veneered boards you have no choice but to lip the edge last.

Applying lippings

The simplest edging to apply is the pre-glued veneer type which is ironed onto the edge. These edge lippings are primarily sold for finishing veneered chipboard panels and are available in a limited range of matching veneer.

For a more substantial edging, and one which can be shaped, cut thick lippings from matching solid wood. Butt-joint the lipping to the edge, or tongue and groove it for greater strength.

Mitre the corners of thick lippings to improve the finished appearance. This is particularly necessary if the edge is moulded.

When gluing up a long lipping, use a stiff batten between the lipping and the cramp heads to help spread the clamping forces over the full length of the work.

When planing glued-on edge lippings to width, take care not to touch the surface veneer, particularly when working across the direction of the grain. Finish the edge with a sanding block.

Deep lippings will substantially stiffen the boards for use as shelves or worktops. Set the full thickness of the board into a rebate cut in the lipping.

Deep lipping stiffens board

WORKING MAN-MADE BOARDS

Cutting by machine

Man-made boards are best cut to finished dimensions with clean-cutting high-speed machine tools. Use a universal saw blade with tungsten-carbide tipped teeth if cutting a lot of board. The teeth of the saw blade should pierce the board from the face side. When using a hand-held power saw have the panel face down; and for a table saw, face up. Run the board across the saw relatively quickly. If using a band saw, run the saw fast but feed the board slowly.

Cutting by hand

For hand-sawing use a 10 to 12 PPI panel saw. A tenon saw can also be used for smaller work. To prevent break-out of the surface, make all cutting lines with a knife to sever the fibres or laminate. Also, hold the saw at a shallow angle. Support the board close to the cutting line. Lay it face side up over the bench; or if it is a stout timber board, support it on trestles.

If cutting a large board, climb onto it to allow you to reach the cutting line comfortably. Have an assistant support the offcut if it is unmanageable. Otherwise, set up some means of support so it does not break away before you finish the cut.

Planing the edges

Plane the edges as you would for solid wood, but treat each edge as though it were end grain. You should therefore plane from both ends towards the middle to prevent break-out of the core or surface veneers. Be prepared to sharpen the blade regularly during the course of planing.

Have assistant support offcut

Plane edges from both ends

Use support boards

Lippings
1 Long-grain veneer
2 Cross-grain veneer
3 Lipped after veneering
4 Lipped before veneering
5 Butt-jointed
6 Tongued lipping
7 Grooved lipping
8 Mitred lipping

CHAPTER EIGHT

BENDING *Curved furniture*

frames are difficult to make and extremely curved forms cut from straight sections of wood require complex joinery if weak short grain and costly wastage are to be avoided. However, by employing dry or wet bending techniques you can produce elaborate curvilinear shapes economically and, since the grain runs with the curve rather than across it, the resulting frame will be stronger. Dry bending requires wood cut into thin sections, but thicker sections can be bent if the wood is soaked or steamed. The café and rocking chairs made by Michael Thonet are classic examples of steam-bent furniture; and in the 1930s laminated furniture WOOD *became high style, following the development of mass-produced veneers. Both steam-bending and laminating can be done in the home workshop, and both techniques are still used commercially for making reproduction furniture and by craftsmen-designers.*

KERFING

A stiff section of wood can be dry-bent by kerfing the inside face. Kerfs are the grooves formed by a saw; and if a series of equally spaced sawcuts is made partway through the wood, it can be bent where its thickness is reduced. The technique is mainly used for curved work which shows only one face, such as 'bullnose steps' in stairs. It can be used in cabinet-making to make plinths that have radiused corners.

CUTTING THE KERFS

The width of the kerf is determined by the saw used. A fine saw will give a narrow cut, a coarse one a wide cut. The width of the cuts and their spacing have a direct bearing on the radius of the bend (see opposite). You need more finer-cut kerfs for a given radius than you do coarse kerfs. Closely spaced kerfs give a smoother contour to the bend. However, the face is usually slightly faceted and it is necessary to sand down the bend to a smooth curve.

Using a power saw

The most efficient way to cut kerfs across a board is to use a radial-arm power saw. Power-saw blades are thicker than handsaws and produce a wider kerf. You will therefore need fewer cuts for a given radius. Once set, the radial-arm saw will make square equal-depth cuts across the board. All you need concentrate on is the spacing of the cuts. Either do this by eye, using a mark on the back fence to align each cut, or fit a stop tab on which to locate each sawcut.

Radial-arm saw
A radial-arm saw will cut wide kerfs across the board.

Cutting by hand

For hand sawing use either a crosscut saw or a tenon saw. First, mark the cutting lines on the wood. Then set a marking gauge to about a quarter of the thickness of the wood and gauge each edge from the face side. Mark and square the cut lines across the back face of the board. Make the cuts using a bench hook to steady the work. For wide boards clamp the work to the bench, setting a guide batten on each line to be cut.

Use a guide batten on wide boards

MAKING THE BEND

Gluing the bend

Try the bend against your plan elevation. Either hold the curve or pull it into shape using a web cramp. If the curve is satisfactory, open the kerfs, apply glue to each and reclamp. As only the corners of the sawcuts meet for gluing, it will not be particularly strong. If the work is likely to be stressed in use, apply reinforcement in the form of glued canvas or veneer around the inside face. Set the grain of the veneer to follow that of the wood and clamp it in the curve with shaped blocks until the glue is set.

Apply glue and clamp the bend

Adjusting the bend

If the bend is not tight enough, run a triangular file through each sawcut and check again. Remove the same amount from each cut.
  If the bend is too tight, insert a piece of paper or card into each cut.

Relieve edges to adjust bend

Duo-faced bends

It is possible to produce kerfed bends with a smooth face on both sides by laminating two kerfed boards back to back. Cut the boards in the normal way, but glue them together using formers where necessary to support the inside curve.

Glue kerfed boards back to back

Laminated kerfed bends

Kerfed bends are usually made with the kerfs cut across the grain. Bends at the end of a section of wood can be made by cutting kerfs with the grain and inserting strips of veneer into them to make a laminated bend.
  A sufficient waste allowance must be made at the end to accommodate the shortening of the outside 'tongues'. Cut a series of equally spaced kerfs on a band saw. The thinner the tongues, the easier they will bend.
  Glue oversized strips of veneer into the kerfs. You may have to double them up to increase their thickness to fill the kerfs. Clamp the bend around a former. When set, saw the stepped end square and plane the veneers flush with the sides.

Insert veneers with the grain following the bend

CALCULATING THE KERF SPACING

Draw a full-size plan of the bend to determine the radius and length. Calculate the length mathematically, or measure it directly from the drawing by stepping off or bending a rule.

When a piece of timber is bent, material on the outside of the bend will tend to stretch while that on the inside is compressed. Somewhere in between will be the neutral line. For greater accuracy, use this line in calculations; as kerfing brings it near the outside face of the member, it is probably sufficient to use this face as a datum.

When kerfing a bend it is desirable to remove exactly the right amount of wood, as the curve is likely to be more even than if excess material is removed. This is because when the sides of each cut touch, the degree of bending must be the same at each cut (**1**).

To determine spacing of the kerfs required to produce the bend, saw almost through the thickness of the board at the point from which the bend will spring, leaving at least 3mm ($\frac{1}{8}$in) of wood. From this cut, measure and mark the length of the radius on the edge. Clamp the end of the board firmly to the bench, then lift the free end of the board until the saw-cut closes and bending stops. Wedge the board in this position. At the radius mark, measure the gap between the underside of the board and the bench top. The distance between the two faces gives the spacing of the sawcuts (**2**).

Draw a full-size plan
Use the drawing to determine length of bent section.

1 The sides of each cut must touch

2 Calculating the spacing
At the radius mark, measure the gap between the board and bench.

STEAM BENDING

Steamed wood can be bent into relatively tight curves. The steam softens the wood fibres sufficiently to allow them to bend and compress as the wood is bent around a shaped former. It may take considerable force to bend the wood, but it can be done in a home workshop using basic equipment. You will need to make a former, support strap and steam chest. Bending wood is not an exact science. There are many variables, and trial and error is sometimes the only way to achieve satisfactory results.

Bending wood
Thinly cut wood will take a bend without pre-treatment. The radius to which it can be bent will depend on the thickness and natural stiffness of the wood. Thin unrestrained 'free-bent' wood will form a ring when both ends are pulled together. For tighter bends, the wood must be steamed and held around a former to 'set' the wood to the required shape. When thicker wood is to be bent, it is necessary to restrain the outer fibres of the wood to prevent them from splitting out. The method described here is for bending a relatively thick section of wood.

Preparing the wood
Select straight-grained timber, free of knots and shakes, for bending. Any flaw in the wood is a potential weakness, and you should expect to have some failures. There are dozens of woods that can be steam-bent, many of them hardwoods. You will find a short list of the most suitable ones on the following page.

Well-seasoned wood can be bent, but newly cut green timber is easier. Wood that is air-seasoned tends to bend better than kiln-dried wood. You can soak the wood for a few hours prior to steaming if it is too dry and proves difficult to work.

Depending on the nature of the work, either prepare the wood to finished size before bending it or reduce it to size with a saw, drawknife or spokeshave after bending. The latter method is often used in making Windsor chairs. Smooth-finished

wood is less likely to promote splitting and will make final finishing easier. Prepared green wood will shrink to a greater degree than seasoned wood; and if turned to a round section prior to bending, will tend to become oval when it dries. Whatever the size or shape of the section, cut the wood about 100mm (4in) over-length. Any end splitting or compression damage from the strap can be cut away after the wood has been bent.

To calculate the length, make a full-size drawing of the shape. Measure the outside of the shape to establish the right length to cut. This will ensure the outer fibres are not stretched, leading to tension fractures. The softened inner fibres will compress sufficiently to take up the smaller inner curve.

Measure outside curve

1 Good bend
This bend in beech shows no signs of distress.

2 Poor bend
This bend in kauvula has suffered from compression failure.

Making a strap

The key to bending tight curves successfully is to use a flexible metal backing strap. Make the strap from mild steel 2mm ($\frac{1}{16}$in) thick and at least as wide as the wood to be bent. This will suit most work you are likely to tackle. To avoid possible chemical stains use plated or stainless steel strapping, or protect the wood with polyethylene sheeting.

Fit end stops to the strap to restrain the ends of the wood, preventing it from stretching and splitting on the outside of the curve. The end stops must be strong enough to resist the considerable pressure put on them and of sufficient size to support the whole end of the wood. You can make them from thick metal angle or hardwood, though hardwood blocks are usually the easiest to make. To give a good bearing on the strap, make the end blocks about 225mm (9in) long. Drill 9mm ($\frac{3}{8}$in) holes about 150mm (6in) apart along the centre line of each block. Mark and drill the strap to take the end-stop bolts. Set the distance between the stops to the length of the work, including the waste. Provide extra leverage by attaching stout lengths of timber to the back face of the strap, using long end-stop bolts.

HARDWOOD END STOP

FLEXIBLE METAL STRAP

END-STOP BOLTS

Metal angle end stop
As an alternative to wood you can use an offcut of thick metal angle.

HARDWOOD LEVER

LENGTH OF WOOD TO BE BENT

Flexible backing strap
Make the strap at least as wide as the wood to be bent.

Making a former

The steamed wood is bent around a former, which sets the shape and supports the inner fibres. The former must be strong – it needs to be at least as wide as the wood to be bent and must provide some means of locating the cramps used to hold the work.

You can construct the former from thick sections of wood mounted on a base of man-made board, or use layers of plywood glued together. Because bent wood tends to straighten when it is released from a former, it will be necessary to modify the shape of the former to allow for straightening. Use trial and error in order to establish the required modification.

Solid-wood former
Glue and screw shaped solid-wood blocks to a baseboard.

Laminated former
Glue plywood layers together and cut to shape.

Box-construction former
Glue and screw a shaped plywood panel to a stout frame.

CRAMP HOLES

SELECTED WOODS FOR STEAM BENDING

- ASH
  Fraxinus excelsior
  Fraxinus americana

- BEECH
  Fagus grandifolia
  Fagus sylvatica

- BIRCH
  Betula pendula
  Betula alleghaniensis

- ELM
  Ulmus americana
  Ulmus procera
  Ulmus hollandica
  Ulmus thomasii

- HICKORY
  Carya spp.

- OAK
  Quercus rubra
  Quercus petraea

- WALNUT
  Juglans nigra
  Juglans regia

- YEW
  Taxus baccata

Making a steam chest

Make a steam chest from exterior-grade plywood, or use plastic or metal piping. Plywood allows you to make a simple glued and screwed chest to your exact requirements. This type of chest is best if you plan to steam batches of wood. A chest made from plastic or metal pipe limits your choice to available sizes, but it is adequate for small work.

Cut a length of pipe to suit the size of your work. A 1m (3ft 3in) length is a useful size which can contain whole pieces or take longer pieces which only need part of their length to be bent. Make removable push-fit end plugs from exterior-grade plywood. Drill a hole in one end plug for the steam feed pipe and plane the bottom edge of the other flat to provide a vent and a drainage hole. Make special open-ended plugs for long pieces to pass through. Fit wooden bridging pieces inside the pipe, to support the wood off the bottom.

Insulate the pipe with thick plastic foam or wooden battens held in place with wire ties. Set the pipe at a slight angle on support brackets to allow the condensation to run out. Provide a receptacle for the drained water.

You can generate the steam using a small electrically heated proprietary boiler, or make your own using a 20 or 25 litre (5 gallon) drum fitted with a removable cap or plug. Fit one end of a short rubber hose to a spigot soldered into the drum, and plug the other end into the end plug of the steam chest. Use a portable gas burner or an electric hotplate for heating the water.

Half fill the drum and heat the water to 100°C (212°F) to produce a continuous supply of steam. As a rough guide, leave the wood to steam for one hour for every 25mm (1in) of thickness. Prolonged steaming does not necessarily improve pliability and can lead to breakdown of the wood's structure.

Bending the wood

You have only a few minutes to work the wood into a bent shape before it begins to cool and set. Prepare your work area before you begin. Have sufficient cramps on hand and enlist the help of a friend when bending thick material.

Shut down the steam generator. Remove the wood from the steam chest and place it in the pre-set and pre-warmed strap. Set the assembly on the former. Clamp the centre, placing waste-wood blocks between the cramp and strap. Pull the wood round the former and fix it securely in place with a series of cramps.

Allow the wood to set for at least 15 minutes before transferring and reclamping it to a similarly shaped drying jig. Alternatively, leave it on the former. Either way, leave it to dry for anything from one day to one week.

Plywood steam chest
Paint all surfaces with exterior-grade varnish.

300mm (12in)

300mm (12in)

LENGTH AS REQUIRED

WOODEN BATTENS

WIRE TIES

END PLUG

OPEN-ENDED PLUG

STEAM FEED PIPE

STEAM GENERATOR

BRIDGING PIECE

END PLUG

PIPE

SUPPORT BRACKETS

HEATER

DRAINED-WATER RECEPTACLE

Basic steam chest
Plastic or metal pipe can be used for a small steam chest.

Clamp centre and pull wood around former

Clamp the wood securely until dry

LAMINATED BENDING

When cut into thin sections, wood is flexible and can be bent dry. In the laminating process used for shaping wood, thin layers of veneer or cut strips are bent round a former and glued together to form a solid shape. Unlike laminated plywood sheet, which has the grain direction alternating with each veneer, in shaped laminating work the grain of each laminate follows the same direction. A laminated component can therefore be bent into a tighter curve than a steamed-wood component of comparable dimensions and is more reliable. The layered edges are a strong feature of laminates – however, if the face of a laminated component is cut to a taper, the glue lines can look unsightly.

FREE-FORM BENDING

Free-form compound curves are difficult to visualize and draw, so – instead of making a former first – bend one strip of wood and twist it into the desired shape, then build the former around it to create an interesting and pleasing shape. Experiment with the technique for yourself. The end result will be determined not only by the flexibility of the strip but also by your own skill and imagination.

The basic technique

First, sketch out your idea and cut strips of wood that will suit the size of your design. Next, start to build the former by making a baseboard with a stout post fixed at each end. Clamp the end of the strip to one post, then bend it to shape and clamp the other end to the other post.

Cut and fix triangulated intermediate posts to the baseboard to support the strip at the required angles. Mark the line of the strip on the posts and remove it.

The key to successful free-form bending is to have sufficient cramps to hold the work. A length of bicycle inner tube (with the valve cut away) bound round the work makes a handy and efficient cramp.

Apply resin glue to the strips of laminate and bind them together. Clamp the lamination to the former-posts, carefully bending it to follow the marked line.

When set, shape and finish the curved component, using spokeshaves, knives, files, scrapers and abrasives as appropriate.

Free-form bend
Clamp the lamination to the posts.

Preparing the wood

Laminations for frame members such as chair or table legs can be made from strips of thin commercially cut veneer, or you can cut thicker strips from solid wood of the required width. The grain pattern will be more consistent if you cut the laminates yourself from solid wood.

As a general rule, select straight-grained timber that is free of knots and shakes, though a decorative veneer of random grain can be used for face laminates.

Air-dried wood is preferable to kiln-dried wood, as it is not so brittle and will therefore bend more readily. For tight bends or relatively thick laminates, pre-bend the wood prior to gluing by wetting it and setting it in the former until dry.

Cut veneer strips in the direction of the grain using a knife and straightedge. Choose quarter-sawn boards from which to cut strips of solid wood. This will ensure the growth rings run across the width of the strips, which makes them more amenable to bending. Mark the face or the end with a V-shaped reference line to enable you to realign the grain when the strips are glued together **(1)**.

The thinner the veneer or cut strip, the tighter it can be bent. Bends made with thin sections are also less likely to spring back. However, if you are cutting your own strips it is more economical to make them as thick as possible, as wood is wasted with every saw-cut. Cut a strip and test its bendability.

You can cut the wood on a band saw or table saw. When using a band saw, pass the planed edge of the board through the saw to remove a strip slightly thicker than required. Plane the sawn edge of the board and then cut a second strip. Repeat the process to produce the required number of strips. Run the strips through a thicknesser.

A table saw may be used to cut strips entirely, but it can be hazardous. Make sure there is not a wide gap between the blade and the table insert, if fitted. As the cut strips are flexible, it is helpful to have an assistant receive the cut pieces in order to prevent them being snatched and broken or, worse, thrown back at you. If cutting a number of very thin strips, make a guide batten fitted with an end stop to push the workpiece along the fence **(2)**.

1 Mark V-shaped reference line

SELECTING WOOD

Virtually any wood can be bent using the laminating process, providing it is thin enough. However, some woods are naturally more pliable than others. A short list of popular woods that bend well would include:

- ● ASH
  Fraxinus excelsior
  Fraxinus americana

- ● BEECH
  Fagus grandifolia
  Fagus sylvatica

- ● BIRCH
  Betula pendula
  Betula alleghaniensis

- ● ELM
  Ulmus americana
  Ulmus procera
  Ulmus hollandica
  Ulmus thomasii

- ● HICKORY
  Carya spp.

- ● OAK
  Quercus rubra
  Quercus petraea

- ● WALNUT
  Juglans nigra
  Juglans regia

2 Make a guide batten to push the workpiece along the fence

FORMERS

A former is used to hold the glued laminates to the desired shape until the glue sets. You can make a single male former or two-part matched male and female formers. The best type to use will depend on the degree of bend and the size and number of components.

Making a male former

Male formers are the simplest to make and are suitable for most curved shapes. They are the best type for large bends where the size of two-part formers would be excessive.

Make the former from thick solid wood, or glue up layers of particle board. The profiled face must be wider and longer than the wood to be bent. Take the shape from a full-size drawing, then mark it out on the face of the block and cut it on a band saw. The clamping force must be applied at right angles to the face of the former, as far as possible. Cut the back of the former to follow the contour of the face, or cut it to the approximate shape (1).

The number of cramps you will need to hold the work will depend on the degree of bend and the pliability of the wood. Use as many as is practicable to apply even pressure. To help avoid local indentations in the top laminate, cover it with a strip of waxed hardboard or spare laminate. Use softwood blocks under the cramp heads to distribute the load (2).

Particle-board former

Solid-wood former

1 Cut back of former to follow shape

BACKING STRIP LAMINATED STRIPS
SOFTWOOD BLOCK
FORMER

2 Use blocks under the cramp heads

Male and female formers

The construction of matched two-part formers for making frame members or wide panels is more demanding, since even pressure must be applied along the moulding. To apply adequate pressure, use a number of individual cramps or a veneer press, if you have access to one.

If cramps are used, some provision must be made in the design of the male former to accommodate them. Either make the male former from blocks of thick solid wood, or drill holes in a slab made from man-made board (1). Design the formers to use the minimum amount of material while applying even pressure to the greatest area of the lamination (2). This usually means setting the orientation of the bend at an angle different to the one shown on the drawing (3).

You cannot make two-part formers by simply cutting the material in two with a single contoured cut; two parallel cutting lines are required. Clamp the prepared strips or veneers together and measure the thickness to establish the exact spacing of the cutting lines. For compass-curved bends, simply mark the internal and external radii on the material for the former. For freehand or random bends, mark one contour line and set off the other from it using a pair of compasses. Make a series of closely spaced arcs with the radius equal to the thickness of the laminate (4), then draw the second line touching the peak of each arc. Cut each contour line carefully, using a band saw.

In most instances, male and female formers are comprised of two complete parts. Where the shape to be formed requires the male former to be undercut, it will be necessary to cut the female part into sections to facilitate assembly and removal of the laminates (5).

MALE FORMER
CRAMP HOLES
FEMALE FORMER

1 Drill holes in male former

2 Design formers to save material and apply even pressure

3 Set out shape on drawing

4 Mark off thickness of laminate

FEMALE SECTIONS
MALE FORMER

5 Make female former in sections

Making wide formers

Wide laminations, such as bowed door panels, would need a considerable amount of material to make solid male and female formers. To save material, make the formers with shaped ribs which are spaced out on a baseboard and faced with thin plywood (1).

First, cut a series of over-sized blanks from man-made board. The number you need will be determined by the size of the workpiece and the pressure required to shape it. The higher the pressure, the more ribs you will need to make.

Next, mark out the shape of the bend on the top piece, making an allowance for the thickness of the plywood facing (2). Temporarily pin the blanks together with the edges flush. Cut housings across them to receive spacer rails (3). Band-saw the stack to shape before pulling them apart. Glue the ribs to the spacer rails approximately 50mm (2in) to 100mm (4in) apart. Glue and screw each assembly on a baseboard (4). Pin and glue a 3mm ($\frac{1}{8}$in) plywood panel to the curved edges of the ribs (5). Seal and wax the surface of the formers to stop the work sticking, or line them with polyethylene sheeting. If you do not have a veneer press, clamp the formers between two or more stiff wooden beams (6).

1 Male and female formers for wide panels

2 Allow for plywood facing

3 Cut housings for spacer rails

4 Glue assembly to baseboard

5 Fix plywood to curved ribs

6 Clamping formers
Use cramps and stiff wooden beams to apply pressure if you do not have access to a veneer press.

GLUING AND CUTTING

When gluing laminates, lay them on a flat board covered with polyethylene sheeting. Use a urea-formaldehyde glue – since it sets slowly, which allows time to assemble the work in the former, and is less likely to creep than PVA glues.

Stack the laminates in the order in which they are to be glued. If decorative face veneers are to be used, place them on the top and bottom.

Apply an even coating of glue with a brush to the meeting faces of each veneer, then restack them in reverse order. Place the stacked laminates on or in the former(s) and clamp them together using even pressure. To exclude air and glue, start from the centre and work outwards. Strip laminates are liable to slip as the glue is squeezed out. Slacken the cramps slightly and tap the laminates into line, using a block of wood and hammer. When male and female formers are used for shaping wide laminates, bands of self-adhesive tape will help keep the laminates together. Leave the work to set for at least 12 hours.

Cutting to size
Before removing a wide lamination from a former, mark the position of the centre line on the edges. Draw a line between the marks to help you mark out the size of the panel. Cut the panel by hand, or use a band saw or table saw. If machine-cutting the work, as you feed the curved panel through the saw keep the point being cut in contact with the table. Finish the edges with a plane.

Mark the length of a narrow component from reference marks on the former. Trim the edges on a band saw, or plane them flush. Cut the component to length and finish the ends.

If you require a number of narrow components with the same curve, make one wide lamination and cut it into identical parts.

256

VENEERING

A sophisticated process requiring artistic skill as well as manual dexterity, veneering is known to have been practised by the ancient Egyptians. In Europe, veneered furniture reached its peak of inventiveness and elegance in the eighteenth century and in Victorian times gained popularity as a substitute for solid-wood furniture. Today, veneers are not only made from natural wood but also from plain-coloured paper foil or from foil printed to look like wood which may even have simulated pore indentations. However, the advantages of natural-wood veneer are not always appreciated. Some of

& MARQUETRY

the most attractive wood is produced as a result of abnormal or irregular growth, so would be prohibitively expensive in solid form and unsatisfactory because of its lack of stability. But bonded to modern man-made boards with modern adhesives, veneer provides an economic and stable material that stands up well to central heating and offers the aesthetic and tactile qualities of solid wood. In addition, reconstituted wood is now available in a variety of shapes and panels, all of which can be covered with veneer.

TOOLS FOR VENEERING

Veneer laying may require the relatively straight-forward application of a single veneer or complicated cutting and fitting of different veneers to make intricate patterns. The woodworker's basic tool kit will contain a number of tools used in veneer work – including measuring and marking tools, a fret saw, bench, block and shoulder planes, chisels, scrapers and sanding equipment. If you wish to concentrate on veneering, additional specialized tools will be required. Most of the tools you are likely to use are available from good tool stores or from veneer suppliers. You will also need to make some equipment, such as a scratch stock and a shooting board, and a simple cutting jig for parquetry work.

Sharpening a blade
Usually the point is the only part of a knife blade that becomes dull. To create a new point, hone the back edge only on an oilstone.

Rules and straightedges
In addition to a steel tape measure, you will find that a graduated metal 'safety ruler' 300mm (12in) long is handy since it can double as a straightedge for cutting small work. A safety ruler is designed to grip the work, to prevent slipping when used as a cutting guide, and is wide enough to keep your fingers clear of the knife. For cutting longer veneers, use a steel straightedge.

Cutting mat
Use plywood or other fine-surfaced man-made board for cutting on – or better still, particularly for fine knife-cutting work, use a special cutting mat. This is made of a self-sealing rubber-like compound which allows the point of the knife to penetrate its surface without causing permanent scoring or dulling the blade.

Veneer saw
A veneer saw can be used, with the aid of a straight-edge, to cut veneers of any thickness. It produces a square-edged cut for accurate butt-jointing of matched veneers and has a reversible double-edged blade with fine teeth that have no set.

Electric iron
An old domestic electric iron may be used to soften the animal glue applied to the groundwork and veneer, both for traditional hammer veneering and to activate heat-sensitive glue film.

Knives
Use a surgical scalpel or craft knife fitted with a pointed blade for cutting intricate shapes, and a stiffer curved-edge blade for cutting straight lines (particularly if extra pressure is required).

These blades are ground on both sides, producing a 'V' cut. If it is vital that the edge of the veneer is cut square, hold the knife at an angle away from the straightedge.

Veneer punches
Veneer punches are made in eight sizes and used to repair unsightly defects in veneer. Each punch has an irregularly shaped cutter which will make a hole in the defective veneer and will also cut an identical patch from matching veneer. A sprung ejector pushes out the cut patch from the tool.

Glue pot

Veneer-trimming tool

Metal veneer hammer

Wooden veneer hammer

Toothing plane

Veneer punches

Veneer pins

Veneer saw

Craft knife

Veneer-trimming tool
A trimming tool is used for removing the surplus veneer around the edges of a panel. One type consists of a short adjustable blade fitted into a wooden handle. The tool is simply run along the edge of the panel and cuts the veneer cleanly both with and across the grain.

Toothing plane
A toothing plane is used to 'key' the surface of the groundwork ready for gluing. It differs from a conventional wooden plane in having the blade set almost vertical. The blade has a finely grooved face with a bevel ground on the back, producing a series of teeth across the blade similar to those of a fine saw. The blade may be sharpened by honing the bevel.

Detail of toothing-plane blade

Glue pot
Traditional veneer laying uses hot animal glue which is prepared in a double or jacketed glue pot. The inner pot holds the glue and the outer pot the water, which is heated to keep the glue at working temperature and prevent it burning.

Originally glue pots were made of cast iron, but modern versions are usually made from aluminium. They are heated by any convenient heat source, such as a gas or electric ring.

Purpose-made thermostatically controlled electric glue pots are also available, but are more expensive.

To prepare pearl animal glue, quarter fill the inner pot with the beads and add an equal quantity of water. Leave the beads to soak, then half fill the outer jacket with water and heat the glue pot in it. Stir the glue to a smooth consistency, adding a little water to it if necessary. Do not let the glue boil or allow the heated water to run dry.

Veneer tape
Gummed paper tape 25mm (1in) wide is used to hold pieces of veneer together and prevents the joints of newly laid veneer opening up as a result of shrinkage. The tape is removed, after the glue has set, by wetting and scraping.

Veneer pins
Fine, short pins with large plastic heads are used to hold veneers temporarily while the joints are taped.

Veneer hammers
A veneer hammer is used for hand-laying veneers. The wooden type has a rounded brass-strip blade mounted in the edge of a hardwood head fitted with a handle. The metal type is more like a conventional hammer, but the head is designed for pressing blisters. Work the blade across the panel in a zigzag motion, using firm pressure to press the veneer down and exclude surplus glue and trapped air.

Cutting mat

Veneer tape

Scalpel

Metal safety ruler

GROUNDWORK

Veneer is always glued to a backing material called the 'ground' or 'groundwork'. The choice and preparation of the groundwork is fundamental to the quality of the work, as the veneer itself will not mask defects. An uneven surface will show, or 'telegraph', through the thin veneer and will become plainly obvious when the surface is polished.

Traditionally, solid pine and, for better-quality pieces, mahogany were used for the groundwork of veneered furniture. Today man-made boards are generally used as they are simpler to prepare and more reliable, though solid wood is still used for flat and curved veneer work.

PREPARING THE GROUNDWORK

Groundwork should provide a smooth even surface on which to lay the veneer. Solid wood is not ideal since it 'moves' with changes in humidity and requires careful preparation, particularly for wide panels. Man-made boards are stable materials and are manufactured in large sheets with flat sanded surfaces. Whichever type of material is used, it must be flat or smoothly shaped and free from dust.

Solid wood
When veneering solid-wood boards, lay the veneer with the grain so that the wood moves together. If only one side of a tangentially cut board is to be veneered, always veneer the heart side. These boards tend to cup – but if laid heartside up, the veneer will help pull them flat as the glue dries.

Where possible, use quarter-cut boards as these are more stable, with only slight shrinkage across the thickness. To maintain an even balance, veneer both sides of the board.

VENEER

HEART SIDE

Tangentially cut board
Lay the veneer on the heart side to counter the board's tendency to cup.

Man-made board
Most man-made boards are ready to use, apart from cutting to the required dimensions and (in the case of laminated boards) toothing and sizing the surface. Laminated boards may require the application of a cross-banding veneer if the grain does not run in the opposite direction to the veneer.

Repairing solid-wood defects
Where possible, select defect-free wood. Cut out unavoidable defects such as fine knots to receive diamond or round shaped plugs, which are cut with their grain following that of the wood. Make the plugs slightly thicker than the board, and level them with a plane after gluing.

Toothing the surface
To improve the adhesion of the glue, 'key' the surface of solid-wood or laminated-wood groundwork; either use a toothing plane, working diagonally from opposite sides, or drag a tenon saw across the surface. Blow away loose dust before sizing.

Sizing the surface
Sizing is used to seal the pores and control suction to make gluing easier and improve its performance. The rate of absorption varies, depending on the type of board used.

You can use either hot diluted animal glue (about one part glue to ten parts water) or cold synthetic wallpaper paste.

Apply the size evenly to the surfaces and coat the edges liberally. When thoroughly dry, sand the surface lightly to remove any nibs.

Diamond plug

Round plug

SHAPED GROUNDWORK

Since veneer is thin and flexible, it can be laid on curved surfaces and bent with or across its grain. The shaped groundwork can be formed either by laminating thick constructional veneers or by steam-bending solid wood. These techniques are described in the section on bending wood.

Solid wood
Small shallow-curved groundwork can be cut from solid blocks of wood on a band saw. The curved surfaces are planed smooth with a compass plane and spokeshaves, and the surface toothed ready for veneering. The offcuts can be faced with thick felt and used as cauls for laying the veneers.

Brick construction
Cutting curved shapes from solid wood of any reasonable size is wasteful, and short grain can make the component weak. Brick construction is a traditional method of making curved groundwork, such as a bowed drawer front. The wood fibres approximately follow the direction of the curve, thus overcoming the problem of weak grain.

The short 'bricks', cut from lengths of wood a little wider than the finished groundwork, are glued end to end to make curved layers or 'courses'. The joints in each course are staggered or 'bonded' as in conventional brickwork, so the joints in one course are reinforced by the bricks in the next.

Coopered construction
This method uses bevelled strips of wood glued edge to edge. It is sometimes used for bowed doors. The edges of the strips are planed to the required angle, then glued and clamped together in specially made jigs with shaped saddles to hold the curve. For lighter work you can use self-adhesive tape to bind the glued strips together. When set, the surfaces are smoothed with a compass plane and toothed, ready for cross-banding veneer laid with cauls.

Solid wood · WEAK SHORT GRAIN

Brick construction · THICK LIPPING · BRICK COURSE

Coopered construction

Use adhesive tape to clamp small panels

Make a clamping jig for large panels · CRAMP · SOFTENING STRIP · SADDLE · PIVOTING ARM · BEVELLED STRIPS

PREPARING VENEER

One of the joys of veneer is the opportunity it offers to use wood purely for its appearance, without the need to consider its structural properties. The veneer's natural decorative features of figure and colour revealed by the cutting process can be used at will, or the leaves can be cut and manipulated to create the pleasing patterns offered by matched veneer.

Handling veneer
Veneer is a fragile material and must be handled with care. Store veneers flat and, for matching purposes, keep them in the order they were supplied. When selecting veneers from a bundle, do not try to pull the lower veneers from the stack but lift off the upper veneers to reach them. Long veneers should be handled by two people.

Flattening veneer
You will often find that veneer needs flattening before it can be worked. If the veneer is slightly distorted, simply apply moisture by means of steam from a kettle, or light immersion in water or a wipe with a damp sponge, then press between sheets of chipboard until dry. Use cramps or heavy weights to apply pressure. Flatten veneer just before laying.

Buckled and brittle veneer will respond better if an adhesive is used in the damping process. You can use wallpaper paste or a weak solution of hot animal glue. Lightly brush on the paste or thinned glue to dampen the veneer, then press it between boards lined with thin polyethylene sheeting. Leave the veneer in the press for at least 24 hours. You can heat the boards to help speed up the process.

VENEER MATCHING

If your chosen veneer is narrower than the groundwork, you will need to join it. Joining veneer gives the opportunity to create decorative effects by the juxtaposition of the wood's natural features of figure and colour.

Slip matching
Slip matching is used to create a wide veneer from narrow ones. Consecutive veneers are slipped sideways and joined together without altering their grain direction.

This method is best used for striped veneers if the joint is not to be obvious. Should the stripes not be parallel to the jointing edges, the joint may have a poor match and will require trimming to true up the figure.

Book matching
Book matching is used for jointing two consecutive decorative veneers when the figure is biased to one side of the leaf.

The direction in which the leaves are turned depends on the position of the dominant figure. If it is on the left-hand side, turn the top leaf to the left as if you were opening a book (**1**). If the figure is on the right-hand side, then turn the top leaf to the right (**2**). The figure must be perfectly aligned to avoid a disjointed match of poor appearance.

1 Turn top veneer to left · **2 Turn top veneer to right**

Four-piece matching

This method takes the book-matching technique a stage further. Take four consecutive veneers and select a portion which places the focal point of the figure at the bottom.

Take the first pair of leaves and book-match the vertical edges. To get an accurate match, true the jointing edge of one leaf first. Lay the trued edge on the edge of the adjacent leaf and match the pattern, then cut the second leaf to match and tape the joint (1). Next, cut the horizontal jointing edge straight and square.

Book-match the vertical edges of the second pair as for the first, but reverse them along the horizontal edge so they are face down (2).

Now match the horizontal edges by laying the first pair on the second and cutting the veneer at the point where the figure matches. Tape the horizontal joint in readiness for laying.

Diamond matching

For diamond matching, use striped veneers. Lay four consecutive veneers together and true the two long edges. Cut both ends to 45 degrees, making the cuts parallel to each other (1). Open the top two veneers book-match fashion – but turn them along the top diagonal edge to form an inverted 'V', then tape the joint (2). Next, make a straight horizontal cut from corner to corner (3). Fit the triangular piece into the 'V' at the bottom to form a rectangle (4).

Now repeat the process with the second pair of veneers but first reverse them so they are face down, as for four-piece matching. Finally join the two rectangles along the centre (5).

Testing the match

To see how the grain pattern will repeat, hold a mirror perpendicular to the veneer and slide it over the surface. Draw a cutting line along the mirror at the best point, then cut the other veneers to match.

1 Book-match vertical edge

VERTICAL EDGE
HORIZONTAL EDGE
FIRST PAIR
SECOND PAIR
HORIZONTAL EDGE

2 Reverse and tape second pair

1 Cut ends to 45 degrees

2 Turn and tape diagonal edges

3 Cut from corner to corner

4 Fit triangular piece into 'V'

5 Join the two rectangles together

TONAL VARIATION

Veneers often appear lighter or darker when viewed from a particular direction – so a difference in tone is noticeable if consecutive veneers are laid in opposite directions.

If you chalk numbers and arrows on the top face of the veneers as you take them from the bundle, that will not only make it easier to identify grain direction but will also enable you to tell at a glance which is the better 'closed' face and which is the slightly coarser 'open' face. Wherever possible, the open face should be laid on the groundwork.

Jointing veneer

The meeting edges of the veneer must be cut straight. When you are matching two veneers, lay them together with the figure accurately aligned. Temporarily pin them to the cutting board and, holding them down with a straightedge set just inside the edge to be cut, cut through both veneers with a knife or veneer saw.

To check the fit, hold the two veneers together against the light. If any gaps show, 'shoot' the edges by running a finely set bench plane along the edges of the veneer held between two straight battens.

Taping the joint

Place the two edges together and apply 100mm (4in) lengths of veneer tape across the joint at about 150mm (6in) intervals, then run a length of tape along the joint. The tape will pull the joint together as it shrinks.

Run tape along the joint

261

CAUL VENEERING

In caul veneering a press is used to lay the veneer. Cauls are stiff boards, either flat or curved, between which the groundwork and veneer are pressed. Unlike hand-laying techniques, caul veneering requires extra work and materials, both for making cauls and the press. However, it is the best method for laying veneer made from taped-together pieces or weak veneers such as burrs or curls. It also offers the possibility of veneering both sides of the groundwork simultaneously. With caul veneering, larger curved surfaces are easier to handle as cold-setting glues allow time for 'laying up'.

MAKING A CAUL ASSEMBLY

The complexity of the caul assembly will depend on the size and shape of the work and the extent to which it will be used.

Flat cauls

For small or narrow work, make the cauls from stout lengths of wood and apply pressure to them with cramps placed along the centre line.

For veneering wide panels, make a simple press with cauls cut from man-made board at least 18mm ($\frac{3}{4}$in) thick and larger than the panel to be veneered.

To provide pressure across the cauls, cut at least three pairs of stiff cross-bearers from 75×50mm (3×2in) softwood. Plane a shallow convex curve across one narrow edge of each, in order to apply initial pressure at the centre of the cauls and force surplus glue and trapped air out to the edges. This compensates for the cramping forces, which can only be applied at the ends.

Use cramps to apply the pressure, or bolt the cross-bearers together with threaded rods fitted with nuts and washers.

With resin glues, to accelerate setting time, introduce an aluminium-sheet caul which can be independently heated. With animal glue, the hot cauls prevent premature gelling during pressing.

You will also need a softening pad of newspaper sheets and a sheet of polyethylene to overlay each veneer. The pad takes up any unevenness on the surface caused by the tape, and the polyethylene prevents the work sticking to it.

Clamping small work
Use cramps to apply pressure to stout wooden cauls.

CURVED CAULS

Curved panels can be caul-veneered using male and female formers, as in laminated bending. Or you can make a press similar to the ones used for flat work but with the cauls made from strips of wood and held by shaped cross-bearers.

Make a section drawing to calculate the curves to be cut in the cross-bearers. This should allow for the thickness of the caul material and the groundwork sandwiched between them.

You can make a permanent caul using the coopered groundwork method described earlier, but a flexible caul is more versatile.

Make a flexible caul from strips of wood about 12mm ($\frac{1}{2}$in) square and glue them to a sheet of canvas. Cut pairs of top and bottom cross-bearers to the required curvature; make sufficient to be able to space them about 150mm (6in) apart.

Lay the cauls between the cross-bearers with the canvas side facing upwards, and line them with an aluminium or hardboard caul to even out the surface.

Assemble the work in the manner described for flat work. Apply pressure by clamping a pair of stiff bearers along the centre line of the curve, then tighten the cross-bearers.

Using a sandbag

For small curved work you can press the veneer into place using a hot sandbag.

Make a flat bag and fill it with dry fine sand. Heat it and press it around or into the shaped work, as appropriate, then clamp it with a caul and cramps.

LAYING THE VENEER

As with any jointing process, you should prepare your work area so everything you require is to hand. You can lay the veneer one side at a time or both together. Lay the backing veneer first, if laying them separately.

Using a brush, evenly apply a cold-setting adhesive, such as PVA or urea-formaldehyde glue, to the groundwork only and let it become tacky. Do not apply glue to the veneer.

The sequence illustrated shows how to veneer both sides together. Fit the top cross-bearers, and clamp the cauls applying even pressure. This is best done by two people.

Leave the work to set for up to 12 hours. On release, trim away surplus veneer and stand the board on edge to allow even air circulation. Leave it to acclimatize for a few days, then plane and lip the edges to complete the panel.

Wide-caul assembly
Make a simple flat press.

Curved-caul assembly
Make shaped bearers and flexible cauls.

Laying the veneer
Sequence for veneering both sides of flat panel.

HAND VENEERING

The centuries-old method of laying veneers by hand with hot animal glue has many advantages. The glue can be softened with heat, even after the veneer has been in place for years, so mistakes can be rectified simply and damaged or blistered veneers easily repaired. However, raw glue must be melted to reduce it to the required consistency, and the laying technique requires practice. Modern glues are cleaner and simpler to use, although they are not quite so versatile. Whatever method you adopt, always prepare and size the groundwork. Otherwise, too much glue will be absorbed and the bond will be weak. Cut and prepare the veneer and, if necessary, join small leaves together. The methods described here assume the veneer is large enough to cover the groundwork in one piece.

HAMMER VENEERING

The secret of successful hammer veneering lies in keeping the glue at a working temperature. Heat pearl or liquid animal glue in a double or jacketed glue pot until it is about 49°C (120°F). The glue should be of a smooth, lump-free consistency that runs from the brush without separating into droplets. Work in a warm, dust-free atmosphere so that the glue does not cool quickly. Have a bowl of hot water and a sponge to hand, plus a veneer hammer and a domestic electric iron heated to the setting for silk.

Applying the glue

Brush a thin, even coat of glue onto the groundwork and veneer (1), then lay them aside until the glue is almost dry but still just tacky. Lay the veneer onto the groundwork so that it overlaps all round, then smooth it down with the flat of your hand (2).

Pressing the veneer

Dip the sponge in hot water and squeeze it almost dry, then dampen the surface of the veneer (3) to close its pores and prevent the iron sticking to it.

Run the heated iron over the surface (4), in order to melt the glue and draw it into the veneer. Without delay, take the veneer hammer and, starting near the centre, press the veneer onto the groundwork using a zigzag stroke towards the outer edges (5).

As air and melted glue are pressed out from beneath the veneer, increase the pressure using two hands on the hammer (6). Take care not to stretch the veneer by applying too much pressure across the grain. Work back towards the other end of the panel – but if the glue cools before you have finished, dampen and iron the veneer again, then repeat the process. Clean off the melted glue with a damp cloth before it sets.

Checking for blisters
Tap the surface with your fingernails to detect air bubbles. Treat any hollow-sounding areas by pressing the veneer again with the hot iron and veneer hammer. If necessary, slit it along the grain with a sharp knife to allow trapped air to escape.

1 Apply glue to groundwork and veneer

3 Dampen the surface of the veneer

5 Press with a veneer hammer

2 Smooth down the veneer

4 Heat glue with an iron

6 Apply more pressure with two hands

USING GLUE FILM

A paper-backed film of glue which becomes liquid only when heated with an iron is the modern equivalent of traditional animal glue. It can be reworked in a similar way, with a further application of heat, comes ready for use and takes less skill to apply. However, experience is required before using glue film to lay difficult veneers such as curls and burrs.

Applying the film
Using scissors, cut the glue film slightly larger than the groundwork. Place the film face down on the groundwork and lightly smooth it flat with a domestic iron heated to a medium setting. When the glue has cooled, peel off the backing (1).

Laying the veneer
Lay the veneer on the glued groundwork and place the paper backing on top to protect the veneer. Press with the heated iron, working slowly across the surface from the centre outwards. Follow behind with a veneer hammer (2) or a block of wood to keep the veneer pressed flat as the glue cools. Remove any blisters, as described in the section on hammer veneering, and trim off surplus veneer when the glue has set.

1 Peel off the paper backing

2 Press with iron and hammer

USING CONTACT GLUE

Specially developed contact glues enable you to veneer flat or curved surfaces without a press or special tools or heat. A solid lipping or some other form of edge protection is recommended, as veneer is more vulnerable to chipping with this type of adhesive. Do not use a contact glue for curls or burr veneers.

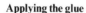

Trimming surplus veneer
When the glue has set, trim the edges of the panel, using a trimming tool, or turn it face down on a flat cutting board and use a sharp knife to trim surplus veneer flush with the groundwork. Trim cross grain by cutting from the corners towards the centre in order to avoid splitting the veneer.

Applying the glue
Using a brush or a scrap of thick veneer, apply a thin, even coat of glue to the veneer. Work diagonally from corner to corner, first in one direction then the other, making sure that you cover the surface thoroughly. Apply glue to the groundwork in the same way, then leave it to dry.

Laying the veneer
Lay a sheet of newsprint or brown paper over the groundwork, leaving a 50mm (2in) strip of dried glue exposed at one edge (1). Lay the veneer on top; and when it is aligned with the groundwork, press the veneer against the strip not covered by paper. Gradu-ally slide the paper out from between the veneer and groundwork, pressing the two glued surfaces together with a block of wood (2). Finally, rub over with the block to flatten the veneer, then trim off the surplus (see left), using a knife or veneer-trimming tool.

Dealing with blisters
Tap across the surface to locate any air pockets under the veneer. Slit along the veneer locally with a sharp knife and work some fresh glue into the blister; roll it down with a hardwood seam-roller, as used for wallpapering. Wipe glue from the surface of the veneer before it can set.

1 Leave strip of groundwork exposed

2 Slide paper from beneath veneer

REMOVING A FOREIGN BODY

If a speck of grit or coarse sawdust gets trapped beneath the veneer, no amount of pressure will remove it. Make a V-shaped incision in the area of the foreign body and peel back the flap of veneer so that you can remove the speck with the point of a knife. With animal glue or glue film, press the flap down using a warm iron and veneer hammer; with contact adhesive, apply a little fresh glue to the flap and groundwork.

Cut a V-shaped flap to remove foreign body

BANDINGS & INLAY MOTIFS

Bandings and inlays can transform a plain panel into an attractive piece of decorative woodwork in the traditional manner. Bandings are plain or patterned strips of veneer used to create decorative borders. You can make your own, but commercially produced bandings offer a wide choice and come ready to use.

Inlays are marquetry motifs used as decorative features; they are available in traditional, pictorial or floral patterns. Commercially made inlays are relatively simple to apply either to veneered or solid-wood surfaces. You can hand-lay individual motifs, but use cauls for veneer assemblies.

Veneering a bordered panel
Cut and lay the centre-panel veneer so that it stops short of the edges all round. Trim the veneer true to the edges with a cutting gauge set to the planned width of the cross-banding (1). Peel the waste and remove surplus glue (2). Soften animal glue with an iron, if necessary.

1 Trim veneer with cutting gauge

2 Peel the waste

3 Use edge of board as a guide

Cutting cross-bandings
Cut cross-bandings from the ends of consecutive veneers, using a cutting gauge. First, shoot the end of the veneer with a finely set plane; then cut the cross-bandings for the border slightly longer and wider than required. Use a straight-edged board to guide the gauge (3).

Hand-laying cross-bandings
The ends of the bandings can either be mitred before laying or cut *in situ* after they have been glued in place. The latter should guarantee a good fit.

Apply animal glue to the groundwork and both sides of the bandings. Press each in place, using either a veneer hammer or a cross-peen hammer. To cut the mitres *in situ,* align a straightedge with the inner and outer corners of the over-lapped bandings and cut through both layers carefully (4).

Remove the top waste, then lift the end of the border to extract the bottom piece. Press the mitred ends with the hammer. Cut the waste from the long edges and wipe away the surplus glue. Apply veneer tape to the joints and edges.

4 Overlap bandings and cut through both layers

Laying stringings and bandings
If you wish to include stringings or decorative bandings between the centre panel and the cross-banding, lay them as described above. Then lay the cross-banding the same way.

LINES AND BANDINGS

Commercially produced decorative inlay bandings are made in batches from selected woods. Always buy sufficient when you first order, as you may not be able to obtain an exact match at a later date. Not only will the wood be different but the size may vary, too.

Stringing lines
Stringings are fine strips of wood used to divide areas of veneer by providing light or dark lines between different types of veneer or where the grain direction changes. Ebony and boxwood were the traditional materials for stringings, but nowadays black dyed wood is used instead of ebony.

Bandings
Decorative bandings are made from side-grain sections of coloured woods glued together and sliced to produce strips approximately 1mm ($\frac{1}{32}$in) thick. They come ready-edged, with a choice of boxwood or black stringings, and are used to make ornamental borders.

Strips of veneer cut across the grain are known as cross-bandings and are used to make bordered panels. Make cross-bandings yourself, cutting them from the veneer used for the panel.

Stringing lines

Decorative bandings

265

Caul-laying bandings

You can use cauls to lay bandings after the centre panel veneer, or lay them together.

By laying the centre panel first and trimming it with a cutting gauge you can be sure it is centred and that the border will be even all round. You will need to take the veneered panel from the press and trim it before the resin adhesive has cured. Cut and mitre the bandings to fit. Apply adhesive to the groundwork border, then tape the veneers in position and return the panel to the press.

Alternatively, cut the centre-panel veneer and the banding to size, allowing extra at the border, and tape them together (1). Pencil centre lines across the length and width of the groundwork and the assembled veneer. Apply glue to the groundwork, carefully position the veneer and press it down by hand or with a seam-roller before placing it in the press.

Inlaying bandings

Bandings can be inlaid into the surface of solid wood, using a cutting gauge and scratch stock to cut the grooves.

Set the gauge to cut the width lines of the groove, working from the edge. Cut the groove with the scratch stock, but use a chisel at the corners. Make the depth of the recess slightly less than the thickness of the banding. Mitre the ends of the banding, then apply the glue and press it into place with a cross-peen hammer (2).

1 Cut and tape centre panel and banding

2 Press banding with cross-peen hammer

Surface laying
Motifs can be glued directly onto a solid-wood surface without inlaying them. To improve the appearance, gouge a groove around the edge to give a shadow break line.

INLAY MOTIFS

Inlay motifs are supplied with a protective paper backing. They are laid with the paper surface uppermost. Some are made to a finished size and shape, others have spare veneer surrounding the design for cutting to shape.

Insetting an inlay motif

You can inset the inlay into your veneer assembly before caul-veneering. Ideally, the inlay should be the same thickness as the veneer so as to maintain even pressure across the panel.

For a centred motif, mark centre lines on the veneer background and on the motif. Using a patch of double-sided tape, position the motif and carefully trace round it with a knife to cut the shape in the background veneer (1). If the motif has spare material surrounding it, mark the required shape on it and cut both layers together.

Tape the motif in position and then lay the complete assembly with cauls. When set, dampen the paper backing and scrape it off ready for sanding.

1 Cut the shape in background

Solid-wood inlay

Position the inlay on the surface and cut round it with a knife. Using chisels and gouges, cut the waste from the edges of the recess (2). Remove the remaining waste with a finely set hand router. Alternatively, use a power router first then trim the edges by hand. Make the depth of the recess slightly less than the thickness of the motif.

Glue the inlay into place and clamp it with a block of wood, with a layer of polyethylene sheeting or waxed paper placed between them.

2 Cut the edges of the recess

MARQUETRY

Since recorded history, applied decoration has been used to enhance artefacts beyond their functional needs. Wood veneer has long been used as a decorative medium, and the diversity of natural figure and colour has provided craftsmen with a rich 'palette' from which to cut and assemble decorative patterns and pictures known as marquetry. Craftsmen of the past keen to express their virtuosity developed marquetry techniques into a fine art and produced elaborate ornamentation based on natural forms. Although it involves skilful handiwork, marquetry is far from being a dying craft – indeed, it is still practised commercially for applied decoration in the form of inlay motifs and today flourishes in lively fashion in the hands of amateur marquetarians, who often produce work of great beauty as a hobby.

Marquetry work

Marquetry designs can be cut using a fret saw or a knife. The saw method is generally used for cutting intricate shapes in multiple layers of veneer; the knife method for single layers – when making marquetry pictures, for example.

It takes skill to cut the parts accurately and it is worth practising on pieces of scrap veneer before tackling a project. You can make your own design or, to begin with, buy a kit containing a pattern and all the material you need.

If you plan to make your own design, collect together a wide selection of veneers. It is not until the veneer is placed in context that you can really see if it has the right effect.

The success of the work lies not just in the skill of cutting and joining the pieces but also in the artistic interpretation of the chosen veneers.

SAW CUTTING

Commercially produced motifs are cut from packs of veneers on a 'marquetry donkey' – a specialist's tool on which the operator sits and works a reciprocating fret saw, while holding the veneer in a foot-operated clamp. Each pack is manipulated in the jaws with the left hand, while the operator works the saw horizontally with the other. The various shaped parts are assembled on a flat table and held together with a layer of gummed paper.

Fret-saw cutting

For the non-specialist, an electrically powered fret saw will make light work of cutting the veneer as well as being generally useful in the workshop.

Alternatively, the traditional hand-held fret saw and cutting table can be used. Cutting a number of layers accurately with a hand-held fret saw is difficult, but you can saw a design using two contrasting veneers relatively easily.

Cutting two veneers together

Select your veneers – one for the background and one for the inlay. In fact, this method produces two identical profiles which reverse the colours when assembled. Cut the pieces about 12mm (½in) larger than the proposed design. Tape them together between waste veneers as backing, set with their grain in the opposite direction (1).

Insert the blade through a small starting hole on a line near the centre and fix it in the saw. Holding the work firmly on the saw table, cut accurately round the line (2). Turn the work to present the line to the cutting edge, as required.

Assemble the cut pieces and fix them together with a sheet of gummed paper. Fill the sawcut with coloured stopping, rubbing it in from the back face, then wipe clean ready for laying when dry.

Transposing a design

You can choose a two-dimensional representation of any subject to serve as the basis for your design.

Make a line drawing from your source material. If the scale is not right, reproduce it using a scaled grid or a photocopier that will reduce or enlarge the size. The latter is particularly useful since, apart from altering the scale and producing repeat prints quickly, the design can be offset onto the wood to give a reverse image by hot-ironing the back of the photocopy.

The traditional method for reproducing a number of identical copies and reverse images used a spiked wheel to prick through all the lines of the original. Black bitumen powder was then pounced through the holes and fused to the paper by heating it.

Iron the back of a photocopy

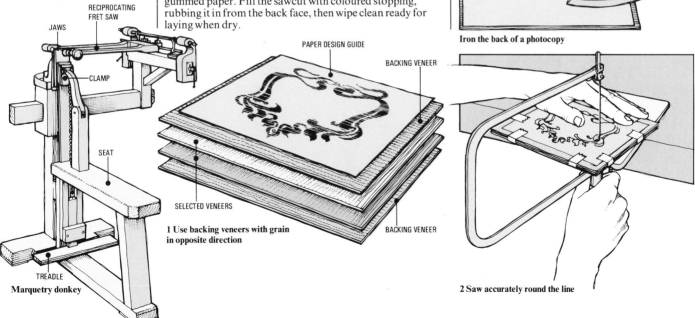

RECIPROCATING FRET SAW

JAWS

CLAMP

SEAT

TREADLE

Marquetry donkey

PAPER DESIGN GUIDE

BACKING VENEER

SELECTED VENEERS

BACKING VENEER

1 Use backing veneers with grain in opposite direction

2 Saw accurately round the line

MAKING A PICTURE

The art of making marquetry pictures is in using the natural features of the veneer to interpret the colour, texture and light and shade of the original reference.

Choosing a subject

Any subject – animals, plants, seascapes, landscapes etc. – can be created by marquetry.

Photographs make a good source of reference from which to trace a design, but choose one with bold areas rather than lots of fine detail.

Photographs show every subtlety of form and must be simplified for a marquetry design. The outline of the features can be simply traced around, but the subtle shading that gives it form has to be interpreted with artistic skill. Shadows will, by the nature of the technique, tend to be hard-edged; but with careful veneer selection and the use of shading techniques, graduated tones can be created to give three-dimensional effects.

Starting marquetry

The beginner is best advised to start with a marquetry kit in which the veneers have been selected and numbered to key in with a printed design guide. However, the chosen veneers will still need to be orientated to provide the right effect for the surfaces they are depicting and will need careful cutting.

The window method

Veneers for picture-making are cut individually and, because they are thin, can be readily cut with a sharp pointed knife.

The 'window method' enables the picture to be built-up in such a way that the interrelationship of the veneer pieces can be tried before cutting them.

The design is either marked on a background veneer or on a card 'waster'. One shape is cut out, then the veneer is placed behind the 'window aperture' and tested for colour and effect. It is then cut to an exact fit, using the window as a template. Successive windows are cut and fitted until the design is completed as a

1 Mark border lines and centre marks

2 Cut out one of the main elements

3 Use window as a template

4 Cut and tape veneer in position

5 Cut smaller parts using window method

6 Mitre ends of decorative border

single sheet for caul veneering to the groundwork.

Using the window method

Hinge the design along the top edge of the card waster with tape. Place a sheet of carbon paper under the design sheet (unless the designs are carbon-backed) and mark border lines and centring marks on the three edges (**1**).

Next, mark the main features of the design, leaving the smaller details until later. Cut out one of the main elements, following its contour precisely but allowing the edges to overlap the border (**2**).

Place the selected veneer behind the window and position it to give the best grain effect. Lightly tape it in position, then carefully score the veneer with the knife, using the window as a template (**3**). Remove the veneer and cut it to shape, then retape it into the aperture (**4**).

Cut the next window and repeat the process; but this time apply a film of PVA glue to the edge which meets the first veneer, then press it flat using a weighted board. Repeat this process until the main picture area is complete.

Turn the hinged design sheet back over the picture; re-mark the border lines and trace the smaller elements onto the veneer now in place. Repeat window-cutting procedure (**5**) to complete the picture.

Cut the picture from the waster border. Tape over-length decorative border strips around the four edges, and mitre the overlapping ends (**6**). Tape the mitres to complete the assembly ready for laying with cauls.

CLEANING UP MARQUETRY

Before marquetry can be given a finish, the surface must be prepared. Remember that veneer is very thin and must not be overworked.

First, any gummed tape must be removed. Dampen it with a sponge dipped in warm water, do not soak it. Use a wide chisel or scraper to scrape it off, then let the surface dry.

Clean up raised grain or surface unevenness with a scraper. Work with the grain of plain veneer, but for veneer assemblies with varied grain use the scraper diagonally.

Sand the surface lightly with progressively finer abrasive papers. Wrap the paper round a cork block, and sand with the grain as far as possible. Brush away all traces of dust, then wipe the surface with a tacky rag.

Use scraper diagonally on veneer assemblies

Shading veneer

The traditional method for producing three-dimensional shaded effects for shell, oval and fan inlay motifs is to scorch part of the veneer lightly by inserting it in hot sand. You can use this technique for marquetry pictures. The aim is to produce a subtle, natural-looking gradation of tone to achieve the desired effect. Practise on waste veneer, using trial and error to obtain the best tones.

Heat a bed of fine silver sand in a baking tray. Maintain an even temperature that will produce the required tonal range in not more than about 10 or 12 seconds. It is better to increase the heat rather than leave the veneer longer, as it will shrink if it is left in the sand too long.

Holding the veneer with tweezers, insert it into the sand. Count the number of seconds, determined by your sampling, and then remove it **(1)**.

You can use oversized pieces of veneer (which will allow you to make some adjustment of effect), using the window-cutting method. Alternatively, cut the pieces to finished shape and size, but be sure to shade them quickly in order to avoid shrinkage and distortion. You can dampen them and press them with a flat board after shading, if necessary.

For shading portions of veneer that are not at the edge, use a spoon to pour the hot sand onto the area that is to be toned down **(2)**.

Mask the veneer with gummed tape to produce 'hard-edged' shading, if required.

1 Remove after a few seconds

2 Pour hot sand from spoon

PARQUETRY

Parquetry uses symmetrically shaped pieces of veneer to make geometric patterns or motifs. The shapes are derived from basic geometry. Any number of designs can be created by cutting veneers of different type, colour or grain into square, rectangular, triangular, diamond or other polygonal shapes and joining them together.

Working out a design

The permutations of simple geometric forms offer a seemingly endless choice of patterns. You can experiment with pattern-making on graph or isometric-grid paper, using different-coloured pens or pencils to fill in the shapes of your design **(1)**.

Designs that form repetitive strips are easier to set out and to cut and assemble accurately. With motifs that have interlocking shapes, such as cubes and stars, you will need to assemble the parts individually.

1 Create designs on printed-grid paper

Preparing for work

As with any repetitive cutting work, a simple jig helps to keep the work true and consistent.

Make a jig from a piece of man-made board about 600mm (2ft) square. Screw a metal or hardwood fence about 6mm (¼in) thick to the surface of the board flush with one edge. Mark two setting-out lines at 90 degrees to it **(2)** and any other angles required by the design.

Cutting is done with a knife or veneer saw, always with a straightedge to guide them. To set the straightedge parallel to the fence, cut pairs of thin plywood spacer blocks to the required width. You will also need gummed tape to hold the pieces together.

2 Make cutting jig and mark with setting-out lines

STRAIGHTEDGE

SPACER BLOCKS

FENCE

BASEBOARD

SETTING-OUT LINES

MAKING A CHEQUERBOARD PATTERN

Perhaps the simplest and most widely known example is the chequerboard pattern of squares of alternating colours. The 'colour' may be achieved by using contrasting woods or, for subtle effect, the same wood but with contrasting grain direction in alternate squares. Generally, the best effects are produced using straight-grained or plain veneers.

Select your contrasting veneers and cut the length of each slightly longer than the proposed baseboard. Cut one edge of each veneer straight. Place this edge against the fence and cut the strips to the required width, using the spacer blocks to position the straightedge (1). Cut four of one colour and five of the other, it does not matter which. This is to keep the grain in the same direction when they are assembled. Number them to keep them in the order they were cut.

Carefully butt and tape alternate coloured strips together. Place the assembled panel on the cutting board with one side edge on the 90-degree setting-out line. Set the straightedge parallel with the fence, using small spacer blocks, and trim the ends square (2).

Remove the waste and push the cut edge against the fence. Cut the assembled veneer as before, producing strips of alternating squares.

Tape the cut edges together again, but first stagger alternate strips by one square (3). Cut off the projecting squares to leave the chequerboard square.

Complete the assembly by cutting and taping an inlay banding and cross-banding border all round, ready for laying with cauls.

1 Cut strips to width

2 Trim ends of strips

3 Stagger and tape strips

MAKING A CUBE PATTERN

The classic isometric-cube effect is produced by using 60-degree diamonds cut from three shades of wood and set together to form a hexagon.

To make a symmetrical repeat pattern, first cut the diamonds using the strip method but only taping them lightly.

Separate the diamonds and assemble the field of hexagons on a sheet of clear self-adhesive film laid sticky side up over your isometric grid paper.

Cover the assembly with gummed paper and press it between flat boards. When dry, peel off the film ready for laying.

Assemble diamonds over grid

STRIP VARIATIONS

Using the methods described above for the chequerboard design, you can create a variety of patterns. Cutting strips of different widths and offsetting the resulting squares or rectangles by half or whole units will produce alternatives.

If the squares are cut diagonally, strips of right-angle triangles are made which, when half-staggered, produce a zigzag pattern. If alternate strips are reversed and staggered, alternating coloured triangles will result.

Diamond patterns are produced by cutting strips at 60 degrees. First, cut parallel strips of contrasting veneer to the required width. Pin the first strip level with a 60-degree setting-out line marked on the board. Then tape the strips together, with the end corners butted against the fence. Trim off the 'toothed' ends, using the straightedge and spacer blocks. Remove the pins and push the cut edge against the fence.

Cut the assembly once more into strips, using the same spacer blocks. You will now have strips of 60-degree diamonds which, when staggered by one diamond and taped together, will produce an alternating repeat pattern.

By cutting this arrangement horizontally through the centre of the diamonds, strips of equilateral triangles are produced. You can then stagger or reverse these strips to create other patterns.

Make alternative square patterns

Or cut squares diagonally

Tape and cut strips to 60 degrees

Cut and stagger diamond strips

Cut and stagger or reverse diamonds to create other patterns

WOOD

Ever since early man discovered that a sharp instrument could be used to shape a piece of wood, carving has been employed to produce all manner of functional and decorative artefacts ranging from basic utensils to sacred icons. Today, with the development of woodworking machinery and man-made materials, carving has become largely a leisure activity. However, age-old techniques are still used commercially by practising carvers in restoring buildings and furniture and also for creating new pieces by traditional methods. Woodcarving goes beyond the utilitarian and offers the carver a means of self-expression that raises it to the level of art. In carving perhaps more than CARVING *in any other kind of woodwork the ability to execute a fine piece of work only comes with practice, though a natural eye for form is an undoubted advantage. Indeed, the shape and complexity of the work has no limitation other than the imagination of the carver. Specialized chisels, gouges and other handtools are therefore made to cope with the immense diversity of form.*

CARVING CHISELS & GOUGES

A standard range of carving chisels and gouges can include 18 different cutting-edge profiles, with a choice of up to five shapes of blade, and most of them are produced in a range of sizes from 2mm ($\frac{1}{16}$in) up to 50mm (2in). They can be purchased from good tool stores or from specialist mail-order suppliers, some of whom offer a worldwide service. Wood-carving tools are sold with the cutting edges ground but not sharpened. Unlike conventional wood-working chisels and gouges, woodcarving tools are generally bevelled on both sides of the cutting edge to facilitate cutting the wood at a variety of angles. The chisels have equal bevels ground on each side, and the gouges and parting tools have a larger bevel on the outside than on the inside. A good-quality sharpening stone and shaped slipstones are essential to maintain a keen edge on these tools. For the beginner only a few basic tools are necessary.

Fitting a handle
Many carving tools are supplied without handles, so you can fit a manufactured handle or one of your own. Drill a fine pilot hole down the centre of the handle. Set the blade in an engineer's vice fitted with soft jaws. Tap the handle partway onto the tang, then twist it free. Refit the handle and repeat the process until it is about 6mm ($\frac{1}{4}$in) from the shoulder of the blade. Check the alignment and tap the handle home.

Hold the blade in vice
Support the shoulder of the blade on the jaws.

Carving-tool handles
Hardwoods such as beech, boxwood or ash are used for handles. You can buy round handles with brass ferrules or traditional octagonal handles without ferrules. The flats of octagonal handles prevent small straight tools rolling off the bench.

12mm ($\frac{1}{2}$in) No 1 straight chisel
For general shaping, cutting straight lines and finishing.

12mm ($\frac{1}{2}$in) No 2 skew chisel
For finishing and undercutting details.

3mm ($\frac{1}{8}$in) No 3 straight gouge
For fine shaping work.

25mm (1in) No 9 straight gouge
For faster cutting or general shaping work.

8mm ($\frac{5}{16}$in) No 10 straight gouge
For cutting flutes and general shaping.

9mm ($\frac{3}{8}$in) No 14 curved gouge
For cutting hollows and curved details.

9mm ($\frac{3}{8}$in) No 21 spoon-bent chisel
For cutting and finishing acute recessed curves.

12mm ($\frac{1}{2}$in) No 27 spoon-bent gouge
For shaping tight curves and deeply recessed work.

9mm ($\frac{3}{8}$in) No 39 straight parting tool
For outlining separate areas, lettering and detail carving.

Octagonal ash handle

Round beech handle

SHAPES AND SIZES

Carving chisels and gouges are usually referred to by name and number. The names generally describe the shape of the blade and cutting edge – for example, a 'straight gouge' or 'spoon-bent chisel'. However, the profile of the cutting edge can vary too. So, to overcome the need for long descriptions and make identification easier, a system of numbers was adopted in the nineteenth century, indicating the profile of the cutting edge as well as the shape of the blade.

Chisels and gouges form the majority of carving tools and, although the numbering may vary slightly from one manufacturer to another, it usually starts with the straight-bladed versions of these tools – so No1 is a basic chisel, No2 is a skew chisel, No3 a shallow gouge and so on up to No11, which is a deep gouge. The higher the number, the deeper the curve or 'sweep', as it is called, of the gouge's cutting edge. All the sweeps are true radius curves except the 'veiner' (No11), which has straighter sides. The next set of numbers (12-20) represents the same sweeps but with a curved blade; the next set (21-32) the same sweeps but with a spoon-bent blade; and so on, each number representing a change in the cross-section shape of the cutting edge combined with the longitudinal shape of the blade. Each number is available in a range of sizes, so the width of the cutting edge should be specified in addition to the identification number when ordering.

Carving tools
The chart (right) shows the wide range of carving tools available. The red squares refer to the blade shapes illustrated opposite.

CUTTING PROFILES

- Chisel
- Skew chisel
- Gouge

RANGE OF SWEEPS

- Fluter
- Veiner
- Parting tool
- 60°
- 45°
- 90°
- Wing parting tool
- Veining tool
- Macaroni
- Fluteroni

SPECIALIZED TOOLS

Specialized tools
Special shaped tools are used for intricate or detailed carving whenever a particular tool makes the cut easier or a special shape of cut is required.

- Spoon-bent corner chisel (right-handed)
- Spoon-bent corner chisel (left-handed)
- Back-bent gouge
- Dog-leg chisel
- Fishtail gouge
- Wing parting tool
- Curved macaroni
- Spoon-bent fluteroni

Typical blade shapes
1 Straight
2 Curved
3 Spoon-bent
4 Back-bent
5 Fishtail

BLADE SHAPES / BLADE SIZES AVAILABLE (INCHES ABOVE, MM BELOW)

	STRAIGHT	CURVED	SPOON BENT	BACK BENT	FISHTAIL	1/16 (2)	1/8 (3)	3/16 (5)	1/4 (6)	5/16 (8)	3/8 (9)	7/16 (11)	1/2 (12)	5/8 (16)	3/4 (18)	7/8 (22)	1 (25)	1 1/4 (32)	1 1/2 (38)	2 (50)
CHISEL	1		21		61	•	•	•	•	•	•	•	•	•	•	•	•	•	•	•
SKEW CHISEL	2		22-3		62	•	•	•	•	•	•	•	•	•	•	•	•	•	•	
GOUGE	3	12	24	33	63	•	•	•	•	•	•	•	•	•	•	•	•	•	•	
	4	13	25	34	64	•	•	•	•	•	•	•	•	•	•	•	•	•	•	
	5	14	26	35	65	•	•	•	•	•	•	•	•	•	•	•	•	•	•	
	6	15	27	36	66	•	•	•	•	•	•	•	•	•	•	•	•	•	•	
	7	16	28	37	67	•	•	•	•	•	•	•	•	•	•	•	•	•	•	
	8	17	29	38	68	•	•	•	•	•	•	•	•	•	•	•	•	•	•	
	9	18	30		69	•	•	•	•	•	•	•	•	•	•	•	•	•	•	
FLUTER	10	19	31		70	•	•	•	•	•	•	•	•	•	•	•	•			
VEINER	11	20	32		71	•	•	•	•	•	•	•	•	•						
PARTING TOOL	39	40	43				•	•	•	•	•	•	•	•	•					
	41	42	44				•	•	•	•	•	•	•	•						
	45	46					•	•	•	•	•	•	•							
WING PARTING TOOL	47							•	•	•	•	•	•							
VEINING TOOL	48							•	•	•	•									
MACARONI	49	50						•	•	•	•	•	•	•						
FLUTERONI	51		52				•	•	•	•	•	•	•							

273

CARVER'S MALLET AND ADZES

In addition to a selection of carver's chisels and gouges, woodcarving uses a number of general woodworking tools, including handsaws, planes, spokeshaves, rasps and files. Machine tools such as a power drill, band saw and chain saw – the latter for roughing out larger work – are used, too. The specialized tools described below also form part of the wood-carver's basic kit.

Carver's mallet

A mallet is essential for driving chisels and gouges when cutting across the grain or working hard woods or large pieces.

The carver's mallet has a round head, made from solid or laminated beech or lignum vitae, with a turned ash or beech handle. The round head allows the chisel to be struck from practically any angle.

Carver's mallets are made in a variety of diameters, from 75mm (3in) up to 150mm (6in), and are sometimes specified by weight. A medium size and weight are adequate for most work. A large, heavy mallet is tiring to use for any length of time.

Adzes

Carver's or sculptor's adzes are short single-handed versions of the traditional two-handed carpenter's adze. Both chisel-head and gouge-head types are made. Adzes are designed for the quick removal of waste when roughing out the work. The gouge type is particularly useful for hollowing out wood for bowl-carving.

Punches
Carver's punches make indentations in the work and are used to produce crisp carving details or to create a pattern or textured effects. They are made of steel and are available in a wide range of decorative patterns.

Carver's mallet

Chisel-head adze

Gouge-head adze

Carver's punches

SHARPENING WOODCARVING TOOLS

The sight of curling woodshavings and the feel and sound of the cutting edge slicing effortlessly through wood are a joy for any woodcarver. Only razor-sharp woodcarving tools will give the right results, whereas blunt tools are hard work to use and produce poor results. Resharpen your tools as you work and at the first sign of a tool catching or tearing the wood give it a light honing, either by hand or using a buffing wheel, to keep the edge keen.

Sharpening new tools

New carving tools are generally supplied ground but not honed to a razor-sharp edge. Be prepared to spend some time sharpening carving tools, as they are honed on both sides of the cutting edge and need careful handling to maintain the shape. The sharpening stones required are described in the chapter on handtools.

Sharpening a chisel

The honing angle of a carving chisel, unlike that of an ordinary woodworking chisel, is the same as the bevel. The point where the bevel meets the full thickness of the blade is known as the 'heel'. This is usually honed down to produce a rounded bevel.

Start with the bevel flat on the lubricated stone and draw the chisel backwards, at the same time lowering the handle, then push the tool forward and lift the handle. Repeat this action on both sides until the bevel is smooth and well-rounded and a fine burr is produced on the cutting edge.

Remove the burr and polish the bevel to a razor-sharp edge by stropping the tool on a dressed leather strop (available from carving-tool suppliers).

Hone the bevel on both sides

Sharpening a V-tool

When you are sharpening a V-tool, it is important that the point where the two outside bevels meet is first rounded over to follow the inside shape.

Sharpen the bevels on the stone as you would a chisel, but work the 'point' as well. This can be done on a bench stone or by working a flat slipstone up and down the corner while rocking the stone from side to side.

Work the inner bevel with a triangular slip, used in a similar way to sharpening a gouge. Strop the inner and outer bevels to produce a razor-sharp edge.

Hone the point with a slipstone

274

WOODS FOR CARVING

Sharpening a gouge

Hold the gouge at right angles to the side of the stone, with the bevel flat on the surface. Stroke the tool back and forth along the stone while rolling it from edge to edge. Take care not to overrun the edge and round over the corners. If you introduce a rocking motion by lowering and lifting the handle, the heel of the bevel will also be ground into a curve.

Hone the inside bevel with a suitably shaped slipstone, working the stone with a rocking motion to produce a rounded bevel. The inner bevel is about a quarter to one-third the length of the outer bevel.

Strop the outside bevel with a rolling motion, and the inside bevel by pulling the blade along the edge of a folded strop. For wide gouges, hold the strop over a convenient edge to form the appropriate curve.

Roll the gouge from edge to edge

Hone inside bevel with slipstone

Wood for furniture-making is converted into regular sections and then joined together to make three-dimensional structures. Carving in the round, on the other hand, starts with an oversized piece of wood which is gradually cut away to reveal the desired form. Virtually any wood can be used for carving, its suitability being largely determined by the size and type of work as well as availability and ease of working. Wood for carving need not be new or 'dressed' stock. Old wood reclaimed from buildings, discarded furniture or driftwood found on a beach are all suitable and offer inspiration to the creative carver. Woodcarvers perhaps more than other woodworkers tend to hoard all manner of pieces of wood – for in their mind's eye every piece is a special carving waiting to be revealed.

As a general rule, fine-textured straight-grained woods such as lime and jelutong are easier to work than woods with coarse or interlocked grain. Generally, because of their close grain, hardwoods are chosen for carving in preference to softwoods. This makes them easier to work, both with and across the grain, without splintering. Some softwoods with a distinct difference in hardness between the earlywood and latewood of the growth rings, such as Douglas fir, can be difficult to cut cleanly across the grain.

Both the colour and the figure of the wood contribute to the quality of a carving. Choose a wood which is sympathetic to the subject matter. For example, select a light-coloured wood such as lime for a polar bear and a dark wood such as teak for a brown bear.

The grain of the wood can be used to advantage, but it can also spoil your work. For example, stripy woods with a pronounced figure can look effective on smooth-surfaced forms where the lines emphasize the contoured shape; when used for portrait carving, however, the strong lines can detract from subtle features.

Not all carvings are intended to have a natural finish. If you propose to paint the surface, you can use a cheaper or less attractive wood that is easy to work rather than one that has a fine appearance.

Using dry or wet wood

Newly cut or 'green' wood shrinks as it dries, as it contains a high percentage of moisture, and logs or large sections of wood shrink unevenly. As a result, the wood splits. Use well-seasoned wood whenever possible, you can then be sure your work will not be ruined by splitting. However, it is not always easy to find seasoned wood for large carvings.

If you have acquired a log or two from a recently felled tree, to facilitate more even seasoning roughly convert it into halves or quarters, depending on its size.

It is possible to use untreated wood in its green state rather than wait years for it to season, but you run the risk of the finished article splitting as the wood continues to dry. Thin-sectioned symmetrically shaped carvings are less likely to split. Thick carvings should be hollowed out, leaving a relatively thin wall of wood that will dry out evenly. An alternative is to treat the wood with PEG (see right). To guard against splitting, always work wet wood quickly and keep it covered with a sealed plastic bag while not being worked.

Peregrine falcon
The smooth finished plumage is given character by the stripy figure of the wood.

The fool
Lime is a good wood to carve and can be worked to produce fine details and thin sections.

Using PEG

You can confidently carve green wood treated with polyethylene glycol (PEG) stabilizing agent without fear of splitting. PEG 1000 is a water-soluble wax material which diffuses into the wood's structure, rendering it 'fully-seasoned' in about three to six weeks. It is available in kits from specialist wood suppliers.

HOLDING THE WORK

Woodcarving employs very sharp tools which are either pushed or driven through the wood. It is therefore essential for accurate and safe work that the wood is held firmly. The best method for holding the work depends on the size and shape of the wood being carved. You can use specially manufactured holding devices or standard woodworking cramps, and in some cases you can make your own.

The workbench

You can work carvings on a traditional woodworking bench or a special carver's stand. The choice will depend on the type of carving you propose to do.

The bench or stand must provide a secure and solid surface that is comfortable to work at. For carving in the round the base of the work should either be about 100mm (4in) below your elbow or level with it.

With some chip-carving techniques the carving is worked on the seated carver's lap, the carver's hands being the only holding device used. But ultimately the best way to hold the work is the way that feels most comfortable to you.

Pivoting clamp

It is useful when carving in the round to be able to alter the angle of the work quickly. A special wood-carving clamp allows the work to be set at virtually any angle and securely locked into position. The pivoting head can be fitted with different-sized face-plates to suit the size of the work.

Engineer's vice

A metalworking vice can be employed for woodcarving, using 'soft jaws' since metal jaws will mark the wood unless the work has a waste area that can be gripped in the vice. You will find that a metalworking vice designed to swivel on its base is the most versatile.

Bench holdfast

A bench holdfast is useful for holding flat work securely on the bench. Always use a softening block of waste wood between the cramp head and the work.

Engineer's vice

Pivoting clamp

A woodworking bench provides good support for flat work

For incised and relief carving a standard woodworking bench will often give you the best base, as you will be able to bear down on the work. Its large work surface provides good support for larger flat work, such as a mirror frame, and various holding devices can be fitted to the top.

Holding the work

Generally, a standard woodworking bench vice is unsuitable for carving. It can serve, however, to hold a sash cramp which is in turn used to hold the work. This arrangement can be used successfully for carving a cabriole leg or similarly shaped work.

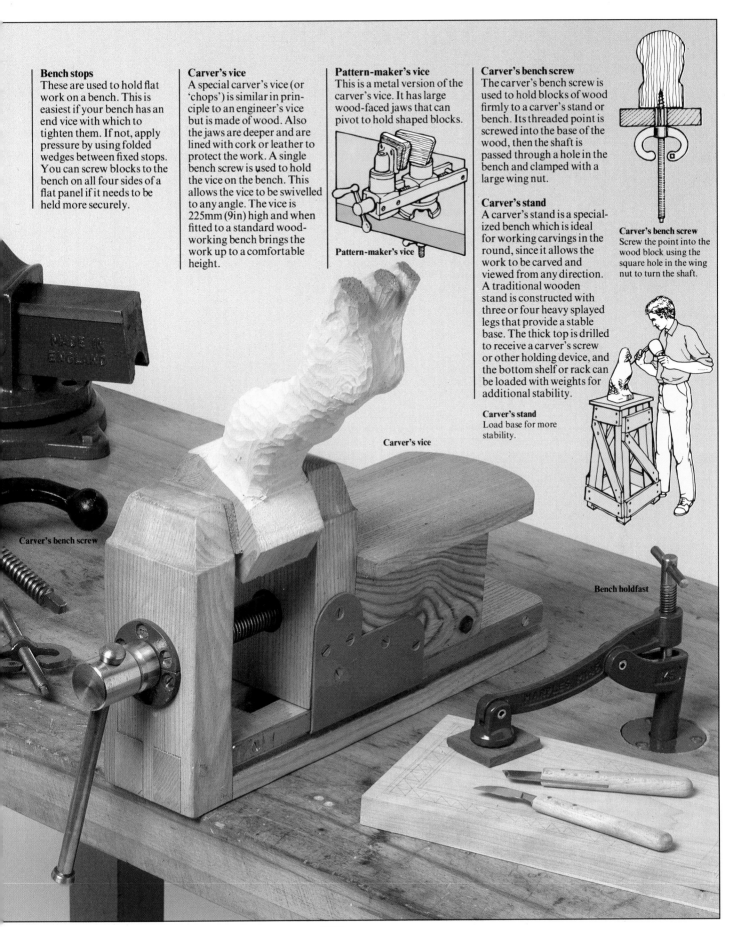

Bench stops
These are used to hold flat work on a bench. This is easiest if your bench has an end vice with which to tighten them. If not, apply pressure by using folded wedges between fixed stops. You can screw blocks to the bench on all four sides of a flat panel if it needs to be held more securely.

Carver's vice
A special carver's vice (or 'chops') is similar in principle to an engineer's vice but is made of wood. Also the jaws are deeper and are lined with cork or leather to protect the work. A single bench screw is used to hold the vice on the bench. This allows the vice to be swivelled to any angle. The vice is 225mm (9in) high and when fitted to a standard wood-working bench brings the work up to a comfortable height.

Pattern-maker's vice
This is a metal version of the carver's vice. It has large wood-faced jaws that can pivot to hold shaped blocks.

Pattern-maker's vice

Carver's bench screw
The carver's bench screw is used to hold blocks of wood firmly to a carver's stand or bench. Its threaded point is screwed into the base of the wood, then the shaft is passed through a hole in the bench and clamped with a large wing nut.

Carver's stand
A carver's stand is a specialized bench which is ideal for working carvings in the round, since it allows the work to be carved and viewed from any direction. A traditional wooden stand is constructed with three or four heavy splayed legs that provide a stable base. The thick top is drilled to receive a carver's screw or other holding device, and the bottom shelf or rack can be loaded with weights for additional stability.

Carver's bench screw
Screw the point into the wood block using the square hole in the wing nut to turn the shaft.

Carver's stand
Load base for more stability.

Carver's vice

Carver's bench screw

Bench holdfast

MAKING WOOD CARVINGS

The principal forms of woodcarving are relief carving and carving in the round. A relief carving is intended to be viewed from one side and so is nearly always carved from a flat board or relatively thin stock. The thickness of the wood and the degree to which the background is cut away determine whether a piece of work is classified as low-relief or high-relief carving.

The technique is used for embellishing furniture and wall panels, and for creating non-functional works of art. A carving in the round is fully three-dimensional and is meant to be seen from all sides. It gives the carver complete freedom of expression and is perhaps the most challenging kind of carving since it requires a well-developed or intuitive sense of form.

HOLDING THE TOOLS

For both relief carving and carving in the round the techniques for working the tools are the same. Carving is a craft that draws upon natural skills. Coordination between hand and eye, a sense of proportion, the interpretation of materials and texture and a feel for natural line all contribute to make a fine carving. Holding the tools properly is the first step. The way carving chisels and gouges are handled depends on the type and size of the project, the hardness of the wood and the type of cut being made.

Paring cuts

Paring cuts are made with both hands on the tool. Generally, the handle is held in the hand used for writing. However, you should learn to work the tools with either hand, as it is often easier to change hands rather than turn the wood round.

Assuming you are right-handed, hold the handle in your right hand with your forefinger along or in line with the blade. The end of the handle will automatically fall on the centre of your palm, giving you good control. The left hand rests on the wood and is used to provide resistance to the thrust from the right hand. It also helps guide the blade. The amount of resistance applied to the blade controls the speed of the cut.

For a heavy cut, place the forefinger of your right hand on top of the blade and grip the blade in the fist of your left hand (**1**). For lighter cuts, pinch the blade between your left forefinger and thumb, with the hand placed above or below (**2**).

When making vertical cuts, grip the handle in your fist and place your thumb on the top. Guide and control the blade with the thumb and forefinger of the left hand, the side of which is planted firmly on the surface of the work (**3**).

1 Grip blade for heavy cut

2 Pinch blade for light cut

3 Guide and control blade

Using a mallet

When carving with a mallet, assuming you are right-handed, the chisel or gouge is held in the left hand and the right hand is used to drive the mallet.

Grip the lower two-thirds of the chisel or gouge handle with the top face of the blade in the same plane as the front of your folded hand (**4**). In this way you can change the angle of the cut by rotating your wrist without changing your grip.

Use the mallet to apply short sharp blows to the tool. With practice you will sense the correct angle to set the cutting edge and will be able to judge how much force is needed to cut the wood away efficiently.

Reading the grain

Woodcarving differs from other methods of cutting wood in that the slicing cuts are generally made across the grain. This is particularly the case when using a gouge for roughing out the shape. Providing the tool is razor-sharp, a controlled clean cut is possible and the relatively deep cut won't tear into the wood, which can easily happen when working with the grain.

Invariably the wood is cut from all angles at some point in the work. Study the grain and make the cuts in the direction which is least likely to tear the fibres. The quality of the cut will be your best guide.

A gouged cut made diagonally across the fibres will produce a groove which is clean-cut on one side and a rougher cut on the other, where it runs against the grain (**5**).

Similarly, where the fibres run at an angle to the surface of the wood, whether a smooth or rough cut will result depends on the direction of the cut (**6**).

Wild or irregular grain can be difficult to work, since it follows no particular pattern. Take only shallow cuts, to minimize tearing the wood, and keep your tools razor-sharp.

5 Diagonal cut

6 Vary cut according to grain

MAKING STUDY DRAWINGS

Most woodcarving work is representational, although often stylized rather than naturalistic. However, if it is to resemble its subject closely, a carving must be well-observed – and a stylized carving must look 'right'.

To achieve an understanding of the way something looks takes practice and is best achieved by making drawings. These need not be used as subjects in themselves but will help you to see how surfaces, textures and forms relate in the world around.

With this knowledge, you will find it easier to visualize how the shapes should look when you come to make a carving. Also, by making numerous sketches you will develop the drawing skills that are fundamental to setting out a carving in the first instance.

4 Grip lower part of handle

RELIEF CARVING

Relief carving uses the play of light and shade to express form. The greater the degree of relief, the more contrasting and dramatic are the effects. Relief carving makes a good introduction to woodcarving as it employs most of the carving tools and the work is somewhat easier to visualize. Moreover, it is economic in the use of material and the wood can be worked on a conventional bench without the aid of specialized holding equipment.

Setting out the design
The first step is to make an accurate full-size working drawing of your proposed carving. The example used here is an ornamental letter which includes both geometric and naturalistic forms. It also makes an interesting exercise. If you are working from a reference which is not the right size, scale it up or down using the grid method (see right) or a photocopying machine that can enlarge and reduce. Tape the design to the wood and, using carbon paper, trace it onto the surface. Mark the depth of the relief on the edge of the wood, using a marking gauge set to 18mm ($\frac{3}{4}$in).

Relief carving of ornamental letter

Cutting the background
Start by cutting around the design with a parting tool or deep gouge. Make the cut about 3mm ($\frac{1}{8}$in) from the line, taking note of the grain direction (**1**). Next, remove the waste down to about 2mm ($\frac{1}{16}$in) from the ground line. Use a No8 or No9 gouge about 18mm ($\frac{3}{4}$in) wide and work across the grain (**2**).

'Setting in' follows the rough grounding work. Using a chisel, or gouges of appropriate curvature, trim the edges of the design vertically (**3**). Do not cut too deep or the cuts will show after you have finished the ground area.

Finish the grounding work with a wide shallow gouge such as a 25mm (1in) No3, then use a spoon-bent gouge for the centre of the letter (**4**). You can either leave the subtle tool marks or level the surface further with a chisel, as you prefer. Now repeat this procedure to lower the level of the letter's face by 9mm ($\frac{3}{8}$in), leaving the foliage standing proud.

Using a scaled grid
Draw vertical and horizontal grid lines, say 6mm ($\frac{1}{4}$in) apart, on a tracing of your design reference. Also draw a 24mm (1in) grid on plain paper. Following the lines of your original design carefully, draw in the shape on the larger grid, using the lines of the two grids to help you draw it to scale. This will give you a four times enlargement, but you can make grids (and therefore the scale) any size suitable for your project.

Draw grid over design

1 Cut groove around design

4 Use spoon-bent gouge in centre

2 Remove waste with gouge

5 Round over the inner area

3 Trim vertical edges of design

6 Shape leaves with sweeping cuts

Modelling
The foliage and the letter's face can now be modelled. Draw in the border lines around the edges of the letter. Cut a shallow V-groove around the inside of the borders. Round over the inner area with a chisel (**5**). You can smooth it with an inverted gouge that fits the curve; otherwise use abrasive paper, but only after completing the main carving.

'Bosting in' or roughly cutting the shape of the leaves now follows. Start with a gouge and use a spoon-bent gouge for tight curves.

Set in the tips of the curled leaves. Form and smooth the contoured shapes of the leaves with long sweeping cuts (**6**), then use a parting tool to detail the veins. Undercut the curled leaf tips to make them appear thin at the edges.

Add the decorative lines on the letter and borders, using a parting tool. Punch or drill the spot detail before cutting the broken decorative lines.

CARVING IN THE ROUND

This type of work represents a challenge to the carver, as it requires an appreciation of aesthetics in addition to well-developed craft skills. The subject matter can be naturalistic or abstract, the concept being dictated by the carver and sometimes by the *natural features of the wood. Carvings which are deeply undercut or pierced, leaving thin weak sections, can be difficult for the beginner. Simple solid shapes are easier to execute successfully while you are developing your techniques.*

Setting out the work

For some, carving in the round is a matter of selecting and setting up a block of wood and cutting into it, the shape of the carving evolving as the wood is cut away following an imaginary outline. However, this can be a hit-and-miss process. Until you are an experienced carver it is better to prepare an accurate drawing and mark guide lines on the block before you start.

A carving of a clenched hand is shown here as a typical example. Hands make an interesting subject for carving in the round. You can study your own as you work and try more complex poses as you progress.

Prepare an actual-size side and front view of your intended carving. A rear view and plan are also helpful. You can base the drawings on your own reference photographs, ideally taken from four sides. Photographs reproduce the effects of perspective, so those parts furthest from the camera will be smaller and you will have to adjust any foreshortening in your drawings. Use the grid method to enlarge the image as required.

Using carbon paper, transfer the side and front views to adjacent sides of a block of prepared wood that will just contain the shape (1). Some extra material on the height is desirable, as it will give you something to hold in a vice.

Initial shaping

The bulk of the waste can be carved away, but it is quicker to use either a handsaw or a machine saw first. With a handsaw, make a series of straight cuts down to the outline, working from each face (2). Chop away the waste with a chisel, leaving a roughly shaped block with square corners. Alternatively, cut around the marked profiles with a band saw. Cut the side view first, then tape or temporarily nail the waste offcuts back in position, using fine nails or pins (3). This keeps the block square and retains the line for cutting the front view. Make sure any nails are driven into waste material only and are kept clear of the sawcut.

Cut around the front-view outline. The roughly shaped block is now ready for carving. If they will be of help, draw in other guide lines that fall within the rough shape.

Rough shaping

With the wood held firmly on your bench start to rough in the shape by cutting away the square corners, using a gouge and mallet and working across the grain (4).

Using a shallow gouge, shape the planes formed by the folded fingers. Cut into the block where the fingers meet the palm and the hollow of the forefinger and thumb (5). Look at the shape from all sides as you work.

1 Mark out shape on adjacent sides

2 Make a series of cuts with a handsaw

3 Or remove waste with a band saw

4 Start to rough in the shape

MOUNTING CARVINGS

Carvings in the round can be carved with an integral base or mounted on a separate one, as appropriate.

Consider the shape and size of the base carefully. An attractive mounting will enhance the appearance of the carving. The mount can be made from a contrasting wood or another material, such as marble. Screw the base to the carving, or glue it using dowel pegs.

This carving of a jester is jauntily poised on a polyhedral base of onyx.

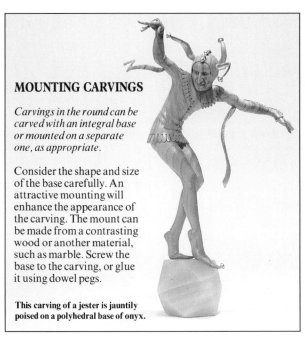

Chip carving is an old technique used for decorating furniture and woodware. It is based on a series of simple cuts that are combined to produce a variety of incised geometric patterns. The cuts can be made with chisels and gouges, but most chip carvers use knives designed for the purpose.

CHIP-CARVING TOOLS

A good chip-carving knife has a short stiff blade with a well-shaped handle that fits comfortably in the palm of the hand.

Chip-carving knives are made with various blade shapes. It is not necessary to have a wide range, as you can make most cuts with only two types – the cutting knife and stab knife.

The cutting knife usually has a straight cutting edge and is used for removing wood chips, while the stab knife has a sharpened skewed end which is stabbed into the wood to make short cuts and decorative patterns. The stab knife is not used to remove wood.

Start with these two knives and only try other types if you find your cutting technique is not producing the required clean cuts. In addition to the knives, you will need a rule, a sharp Grade B pencil, a pair of compasses and a try square for setting out your designs.

Sharpening knives
Clean crisply incised shapes are the essence of good chip carving. No matter how well you have set your design out or followed the line, if the cuts are not sharp the end result is bound to look rough – so keep your knives razor-sharp.

First, hone the cutting knife on a medium-grade stone. Hold the knife blade at right angles to the stone, with the side face at an angle of not more than 10 degrees to the surface.

Rub the blade back and forth, keeping the full length of the cutting edge in contact with the stone. Turn the blade over and treat the other side the same way. Repeat the process on a fine stone, then rub the blade on a dressed leather strop.

Sharpen a stab knife in the same way, but hold it at 30 degrees to the stone.

Straight cutting knife

Stab knife

Honing blade
Hold knife at right angles to the stone.

Modelling

Form the knuckle shapes and rounded fingers by paring the wood with a gouge and chisel. Then refine the shapes of the fingers and thumb, and set in the details of the finger lines, folds of flesh and fingernails **(6)**. Small chisels and gouges will be needed here. The degree to which you smooth the shape is a matter of choice. You can either leave the tool marks or smooth the surface using rifflers and fine abrasive paper. Finish the wood with a clear sealer and apply a wax polish.

5 Shape the planes of the hand

6 Refine the shape of the carving

Marking out

Chip carving is generally based on geometric shapes, although free-form chip carving is also done.

You can set out your design on paper and then transfer it to the surface of the work, or mark it out directly.

Draw accurate fine guide lines, as many of the lines will remain after the carving is completed. These can be removed with a pencil eraser. If you try to sand them away you will lose the crisp edge of your carving.

Holding the knives

You can use the cutting knife to cut into the work vertically or hold it at an angle to make a sloping cut. A faceted chip cut is made by holding the knife at a constant 45 degree angle.

There are three basic cuts with the cutting knife. The first two are made with a pulling action and the third is pushed away from you. Use your thumb as a guide to steady your hand as a fulcrum when making curved cuts. It also gives you a means of sensing the depth of your cut.

Hold the stab knife vertically and push it into the surface to make short straight cuts or wedge-shaped indentations.

Hold cutting knife at constant angle — Vertical cut — Angled cut (pulled) — Angled cut (pushed) — Stab knife cut

Equilateral-triangle border — Right-angle-triangle border

1 Mark out guide lines

2 Cut towards base line

3 Slice out chip

4 Pull blade out to surface

5 Repeat with a push cut

6 Finally cut along base line

MAKING BORDERS

Borders are a common feature of chip-carved work and are typically based on equilateral or right-angle triangles.

To make an equilateral-triangle border design, first mark out the guide lines (1). Hold the cutting knife on one side line, with its point on the apex. Press the point straight down into the wood to a depth of about 3mm (⅛in). Pull the knife towards you so the point rises out to the surface at the marked base line (2). Repeat the cut on the other side. Slice out the chip with the blade held at a shallow angle and following the base line (3). Repeat this chip cut to make various border patterns.

To make faceted right-angle-triangle border patterns, first mark a series of squares and draw in the diagonals. Hold the knife at an angle to the surface, with the point on the apex of the triangle. Push the blade into the wood and pull it along the line and out to the surface (4). Repeat this cut on alternate squares. Turn the work round and make the same cut in the adjacent squares, but this time pushing the knife away from you (5).

Now revert back to the first cutting action and cut along the base line (6), always remembering to hold the knife at the same angle so the cuts meet exactly on the centre of the chip cut.

CUTTING BORDER LINES

Incised lines are used to define the edges of border patterns. Carve a border line by making two cuts to form a 'V'.

Your first cut should slope away from the design. Pull the blade through the wood and follow the line accurately by looking just ahead of the blade. Turn the work round and make a similar cut to remove the waste.

Make two sloping cuts

Border line

Equilateral-triangle borders — Equilateral-triangle borders (facet cut)

Right-angle-triangle borders — Right-angle-triangle borders (facet cut)

Vary cuts to make different border patterns

FINISHING

Enhancing the beauty of timber with polish, lacquer, varnish or oil is one of the most pleasurable aspects of woodworking. Similarly, a great deal of satisfaction can be obtained from staining or colouring wood. Finishing also has a practical purpose – to protect the wood and keep it free from marks. You therefore need to consider how a piece will be used, as well as how it will look, when selecting a finish. If, for example, it is likely to be subjected to hard wear, choose a varnish or lacquer rather than French polish, which is more vulnerable and so better suited to display items where protection is less vital. Another important consideration is the texture of the wood. For smooth-textured hardwoods, such as mahogany and walnut,

WOOD

French polish gives the finest finish. Open-grain timbers such as oak, on the other hand, look better with an oil or wax finish that penetrates the grain without forming a thick surface coating. For the best results, whichever finish you choose, always work in a warm, clean and well-lit environment.

PREPARING THE SURFACE

Wood must be smooth, clean and free from blemishes before you apply a surface finish. Paint may cover minor imperfections, but a clear finish will exaggerate every defect including fine scratches across the grain. Preparing the surface is the first essential stage of finishing timber.

FILLING HOLES AND CRACKS

When selecting timber you should reject poor-quality materials exhibiting cracks, holes and dead knots, but occasionally it is necessary to accept a less-than-perfect sample, especially when buying wood that is rare or temporarily in short supply. Even when you have chosen carefully, cracks can open up at a later stage and must be dealt with before you apply a finish.

Shellac sticks

Wax sticks

Cellulose filler

Stopper

- **Removing patches of glue**
  When gluing joints, always wash away excess adhesive from the surface using a cloth dampened with hot water. If you let the glue set, it seals the wood and will show as pale patches after staining or polishing. Use a cabinet scraper to remove any spots of hardened glue before finishing.

- **Applying knotting**
  Resinous knots will 'bleed' through paintwork, leaving dark stains on the surface. Before you apply a primer, pick off any hardened resin, then paint the knots with two coats of knotting (shellac-based sealer).

Stopper
A proprietary stopper is a stiff paste made to fill small holes and cracks before applying a clear or opaque finish. Although stoppers are made in a range of colours resembling various common species of wood, at best you can only expect a close match and the match will hardly ever be perfect. However, you can adjust the colour of the stopper with a drop of wood stain – but as stoppers are either water-based or oil-based, make sure you always use a similarly constituted stain.

Cellulose filler
If you are planning to apply an opaque paint finish, you can fill blemishes with ordinary decorator's cellulose filler mixed to a stiff paste with water, using it like a stopper.

Shellac sticks
Sticks of solidified shellac are ideal for repairing a crack or small knot holes before applying any type of finish. They are made in several woodlike colours.

Wax sticks
Filling sticks of carnauba wax mixed with resins and colouring pigments are used to disguise small worm holes and hairline cracks in timber. It is advisable to use them only for work which is to be wax-polished, as most finishes will not dry over a wax-filled hole. Special wax crayons are made for retouching scratches in polished surfaces.

Using stopper
Press stopper into the blemish with a small flexible filling knife, as used by decorators, or the tip of an old chisel. When the stopper has set hard, sand it flush with the surface of the wood. If the colour match isn't satisfactory, touch in the stopper with minute quantities of artist's oil paint, using a fine paintbrush. Let the paint dry thoroughly before applying a surface finish.

Melting a shellac stick
Using the tip of a warm soldering iron, melt the shellac, allowing it to drip onto the blemish. While the shellac is still soft, dip the tip of a chisel in water and use it to press the shellac into the crack or knot. When the shellac is cool and hard, pare it flush with a chisel then sand it with very fine abrasive paper.

Melt shellac with a soldering iron

Filling with a wax stick
Sand the surface of the wood and seal it with shellac before filling with wax. Use a warmed knife blade to soften the wax and to press it into cracks or small holes. As the wax hardens, scrape it flush with the knife, then burnish it with the back of a piece of sandpaper.

RAISING A DENT

If you accidentally dent a workpiece, lay a damp cloth over the blemish and apply the tip of a heated soldering iron. The heat generates steam, which causes the wood fibres to swell locally, lifting the dented section flush with the surrounding surface. Allow the wood to dry before sanding.

SAFETY WITH SURFACE FINISHES

When finishing wood, take the following precautions to safeguard health and safety.

- Most of the materials used to finish wood are flammable, so store them in a separate building away from your workshop and your house.
- Keep finishes and thinners locked away from children. If a child should swallow any, do not attempt to make it vomit but seek medical advice immediately.
- Oily rags are a fire risk. They should be opened flat and allowed to dry outdoors before you throw them away.
- Install a fire blanket and an extinguisher.
- Don't smoke while applying finishes.
- Inhaling solvent fumes can be very unpleasant, if not actually harmful. Follow manufacturer's instructions with regard to toxicity, and wear a face mask or respirator if you experience any discomfort.
- Provide adequate ventilation and don't spray finishes unless you have proper extraction facilities.
- Wear protective gloves when applying wood stains.
- Wear barrier cream to protect your hands, and use a skin cleanser to remove paint or other finishes before washing with soap and hot water. Do not use paint thinners to clean your hands.
- If you splash a finish in your eyes, flush them with water and contact a doctor or hospital casualty department for advice.

SANDING TIMBER

Power sanders relieve a woodworker of the chore of smoothing large flat areas – but for best-quality work, give the wood at least one final light sanding by hand.

Abrasive papers

A variety of abrasive materials glued to paper backing sheets are used to smooth timber and hardened surface finishes. All these abrasives are known collectively as sandpaper, though this term was originally used to describe glasspaper only.

Glasspaper is pale yellow in colour. It wears quickly and, although not really suitable for fine woodwork, is a cheap option for sanding softwoods. It is also known as flintpaper.

Garnet paper is made from a reddish-brown natural mineral that forms hard particles with sharp cutting edges. Garnet paper is a good-quality abrasive both for softwoods and hardwoods.

Aluminium-oxide paper is even harder than garnet paper. It is produced in standard-size sheets for handwork and is also used widely as an abrasive for power tools. Aluminium-oxide papers are available in different colours. This type of abrasive is especially good for sanding dense hardwoods.

Silicon-carbide paper varies from dark grey to black. It is made from a synthetic material and is used mainly for finishing metals or, with water as a lubricant, for smoothing paintwork between coats. Often referred to as 'wet-and-dry paper', it is used without a lubricant for sanding hardwoods. A pale-grey silicon-carbide paper dusted with zinc-oxide powder that acts as a dry lubricant is preferable for rubbing down French polish, which would be spoilt by using water as a lubricant.

Grading sandpaper

Sandpapers are graded according to abrasive-particle size and are roughly classified as having very coarse, coarse, medium, fine or very fine grit. They are also graded by number (typically from 600 to 50 or, using another system, from 9/0 to 1) – the higher the number, the finer the grit. Use progressively finer grits, so that each grade removes the scratches left by the previous paper. As a guide, coarse to fine grades are suitable for general work and very fine grades for cutting back surface finishes.

In addition, there are closed-coat or open-coat types of sandpaper. Closed-coat papers have particles grouped closely together for fast sanding, whereas open-coat abrasives have large gaps between the particles, which clog less readily, and so are better for resinous softwoods.

Sandpaper grades		
Very coarse	50	1
	60	$\frac{1}{2}$
Coarse	80	0
	100	2/0
Medium	120	3/0
	150	4/0
	180	5/0
Fine	220	6/0
	240	7/0
	280	8/0
Very fine	320	9/0
	360	—
	400	—
	500	—
	600	—

Sanding by hand

Tear sheets of abrasive paper into convenient strips over the edge of a bench. Wrap a strip around a cork sanding block and use it to smooth a flat workpiece, always working with the grain (1). Take care not to round over sharp corners inadvertently when you approach an edge – but if you want to remove the arris (the sharp 'line' where two surfaces meet), sand a chamfer deliberately, using the same block (2). Wrap sandpaper around a shaped block when you are sanding mouldings (3).

Lay aside sanding blocks and use your fingertips to apply pressure to sandpaper when smoothing curved surfaces or for very light sanding (4). When sandpaper becomes clogged with wood dust, tap it against the workbench to clear the abrasive particles.

When the surface appears to be as smooth as possible, in order to raise the grain dampen the wood with a wet rag and leave it to dry. A final light sanding will then remove the fine fibres, leaving a perfect finish. Last of all, remove the wood dust with a cloth dampened with white spirit, or use a proprietary 'tack rag' (a cloth impregnated with resin).

Sanding end grain

Rub your finger along the surface of end grain before sanding. It will feel rougher in one direction and relatively smooth in another. Sand in the smoother direction for a superior finish.

1 Sanding flat work

2 Removing an arris

3 Sanding a moulding

4 Use fingertip pressure for light sanding

● **Storing sandpaper**
Wrap sheets of sandpaper in plastic to keep them dry while being stored.

Abrasive papers
1 Glasspaper
2 Garnet paper
3 Aluminium-oxide paper
4 Silicon-carbide paper
5 Self-lubricating silicon-carbide paper

Always fill the pores of coarse-textured open-grain timbers such as mahogany, walnut, oak and ash with a grain filler before applying a glossy finish. If you omit this process, a pitted uneven finish will result.

The best method is to apply successive coats of varnish, rubbing down in between, until the pores are filled. Colour-matching of filler to wood is then not needed. However, this is a laborious process, so most woodworkers prefer to use a proprietary grain filler sold as a thin paste coloured to match a variety of timbers. Choose a filler slightly darker than your wood, since filler dries to a lighter tone and you can always adjust its colour by adding a compatible wood stain to the paste.

Rub the filler onto the wood with circular strokes, using a coarse cloth to remove any excess filler, and let it harden overnight before sanding very lightly with a fine-grade paper in the direction of the grain.

Filling stained wood
If you fill the wood after staining, the dried filler can only be sanded very lightly or you will change its colour – and if you stain after filling, uneven absorption may result in patchiness. The safest way is to seal the stained wood with a coat of the intended clear finish, then once it is dry fill the grain. This way, the sealer coat will protect the colour when you sand the filler.

Using sanding sealer
In place of grain filler, use a commercial sanding sealer when preparing fine-textured woods or man-made boards for finishing. Brush the sealer on and sand it when dry with a fine-grade paper. Seal again and rub down the dried surface with 0000 grade (extra-fine) wire wool. Some varnishes may not adhere satisfactorily when applied over sanding sealer.

Fill the grain of coarse-textured wood

BLEACHING AND STAINING

In most cases a woodworker will apply a clear finish directly to a sanded workpiece, but occasionally it may be necessary to bleach discoloured wood before polishing or varnishing. Conversely, you might want to enhance the colour of an unusually dull piece of timber with a light coat of stain or use stain to blend poorly matched samples of the same species of wood.

BLEACHING WOOD

Two-part commercial wood bleaches remove the colour from timber by chemical action. Having applied the bleach itself, it is necessary to use a neutralizer to arrest the process. Not all timbers bleach successfully. Chestnut or rosewood, for example, do not respond favourably to bleach, whereas oak or birch react well. Always test a sample of the wood before attempting to bleach your workpiece. Wood bleach is a potent chemical – so follow the manufacturer's recommendations with care. Wear protective gloves, goggles, old clothes and an apron whenever you handle the chemicals.

Apply an even coat of bleach to the wood, using a clean white rag or an old bristle or nylon brush. Keep checking on the reaction for up to 20 minutes and, as soon as the required tone is achieved, wash the surface with the neutralizer. After about four hours, wash the wood again with clean water, leave it to dry and then sand it smooth.

Wood stains
1 Coloured water-based stain on sycamore
2 Walnut water-based stain on beech
3 Light-oak spirit-based stain on beech
4 Red-mahogany oil-based stain on beech

Bleached utile

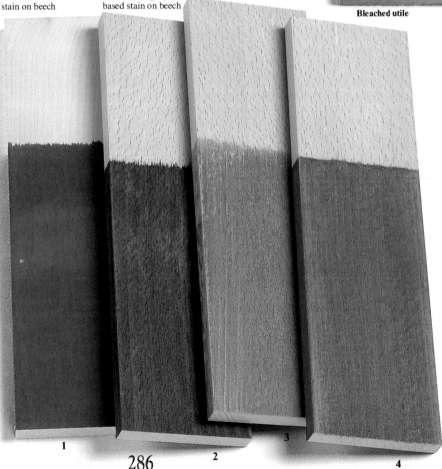

1   2   3   4

WOOD STAINS

Wood must be perfectly clean, grease-free and sanded smooth in the direction of the grain before you apply wood stain. After using a powered orbital sander, sand by hand to remove the swirls of fine cross-grain scratches left on the wood. Unless you wet the wood first and sand it smooth, a water-based stain will raise the grain, leaving a rough surface after it dries.

TYPES OF STAIN

Ready-mixed wood stains are available in an enormous range of colours from most DIY stockists or hardware shops, but dry powdered pigments that you have to mix for yourself usually have to be bought from a specialist supplier. Ready-mixed stains are very convenient, but many professionals recognize the advantages of being able to mix the exact colours they want using dry pigments.

Water-based stain
Water-based stains flow and penetrate well and, because they are relatively slow to dry, it is easy to get an even distribution of colour. You can even shade water stains when they are on the wood, using a damp rag to remove colour. Once it is dry, any wood finish may be applied over a water stain. You can buy ready-mixed stain or dry water-soluble aniline powder. To make your stain, mix about 30g (1oz) of the powder in 1.25 litres (1 quart) of warm water. Let the stain cool before applying it.

Spirit-based stain
Spirit-based stains are not popular with amateur woodworkers because, being dissolved in methylated spirit, they dry very fast and skilful application is required to avoid overlaps and hard edges showing when the stain dries. For this reason, spirit-based stains are often sprayed on. This type of stain will not raise the grain of the wood. Buy it ready-mixed or in powder form to be mixed with spirit, using the same proportions recommended for a water stain. Adding a little shellac (French polish) makes it easier to brush on spirit stain and helps bind the pigment.

A spirit-based stain may 'bleed' through a subsequent coat of French polish or brushed-on cellulose lacquer, but a sprayed lacquer finish will not be affected in the same way.

Oil-based stain
Oil-based stains evaporate reasonably quickly, but there is usually plenty of time to achieve a satisfactory result. These stains, based on white spirit and oil-based solvent naptha, will not raise the grain. Oil-based stains will be redissolved by the white-spirit content of polyurethane varnish and wax polish. Seal the stained surface with one coat of shellac sanding sealer before applying varnish and two coats before applying wax. Oil stains are only available ready-mixed.

APPLYING WOOD STAIN

You can apply stain to a flat area of wood with a good-quality paintbrush or a paint pad. Spread the stain liberally and evenly; work with the grain and blend wet edges as quickly as possible. As soon as you have applied a coat of water stain, wipe the wet surface with a soft dry cloth to distribute the colour evenly and absorb excess stain.

You may prefer to apply stain with a ball of clean rag – especially if you have to colour a vertical panel, since it is easier to control runs. Using a rag is also the only really practical way to stain turned components. Wearing protective gloves, saturate the rag in stain, then squeeze it out to avoid dripping spots of colour on the wood. Drips and runs may show through the finished coat of stain unless you can blend them before they begin to dry.

MAKING A TEST STRIP

Each species of timber absorbs stain differently, affecting the colour of the stain as it dries. The type of finish you use to overlay the stain also has an effect on its colour and tone.

Before you stain a workpiece, make a test strip, using a scrap of the same wood. Paint the test strip with one coat of stain and allow it to dry; then paint the strip with a second coat, but leave a small section of the first application exposed for comparison. Two coats of stain are normally sufficient, but for the purposes of the test make three or even four applications and leave them to dry thoroughly. Paint a band of clear finish along one half of the test strip to see how it affects each coat of stain.

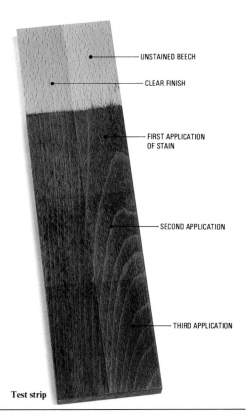

UNSTAINED BEECH

CLEAR FINISH

FIRST APPLICATION OF STAIN

SECOND APPLICATION

THIRD APPLICATION

Test strip

FUMING TIMBER

Exposure to ammonia fumes chemically colours woods that contain tannic acid. Oak – the most popular wood for fuming – turns a golden honey colour to a medium-dark brown, depending on the length of exposure. Mahogany, chestnut and walnut can also be coloured with ammonia.

You can obtain a strong ammonia solution (27 to 30 per cent) from a retail pharmacy, but may have to buy a minimum of about 2 litres (3½ pints). Alternatively, you can use ordinary household ammonia, though expect the process to be slower. Ammonia irritates the eyes, nose and throat – so build a fume cupboard either outside or in a well-ventilated room and wear goggles plus a face mask or respirator when handling the chemical.

Making a fume cupboard
To construct a makeshift fume cupboard, make a scrap-wood framework to enclose the workpiece then drape the frame with black plastic sheeting to create an airtight tent. Seal all seams and joints with adhesive tape. Don't use transparent plastic, as daylight can affect the colour change.

Place several saucers containing ammonia solution inside the tent along with the workpiece. Do not include metal fittings or exposed screws, since they will stain the wood.

Leave the tent sealed for about 24 hours to obtain a medium-dark colour. Check from time to time if you want a lighter tone. Even when you remove the workpiece, the reaction will continue for a while and the wood will darken still further.

PLASTIC COVER

FRAMEWORK

AMMONIA

WORKPIECE

Home-made fume cupboard

FRENCH POLISH

French polish, the most celebrated wood finish of Victorian times, is still very popular today. The polish is made by dissolving shellac, a secretion of the lac insect, in industrial alcohol. It can be burnished to an almost glasslike texture that belies its vulnerability to scratching and its susceptibility to alcohol and water, which etch the surface leaving white stains. Despite these obvious disadvantages, French polish is such an attractive finish that many woodworkers are prepared to put in hours of practice in order to master the technique.

French polishes
1 Unfinished mahogany
2 Mahogany finished with button polish
3 Mahogany finished with garnet polish
4 White polish on sycamore

TYPES OF FRENCH POLISH

You can make your own French polish by dissolving shellac flakes in methylated spirit, but it is far more convenient to buy the polish in ready-made liquid form.

Button polish
Button polish, which is golden brown in colour, is made from the highest grade of shellac. It takes its name from the way the shellac is left to cool in 50mm (2in) diameter discs resembling buttons. Thin enough to be translucent, they can be viewed against the light to ensure the shellac is pure. Button polish is now more commonly sold in flake form.

Standard French polish
Made from the less pure flake shellac, standard French polish is nevertheless free from impurities in every practical sense. It is a rich medium-brown colour.

Garnet polish
This is a dark red-brown French polish used for mahogany and similarly coloured timbers.

White polish
Made from bleached shellac, white polish is used for pale-coloured woods.

Transparent polish
Transparent polish is made by removing the natural wax suspended in bleached shellac. It is used when additional colour would spoil the appearance of an especially pale wood.

Coloured polishes
Coloured polishes contain red, black or green stain. Black polish is used primarily for finishing pianos, red and green polishes for adjusting the colour of timber. Green polish, for example, will reduce the intensity of a raw-red mahogany, giving it an older-looking patina. Red polish will have the opposite effect, adding richness to a brown-coloured wood. The colour of any shellac polish can be altered by the addition of a drop of spirit-based wood stain.

BRUSHING FRENCH POLISH

Traditional French polishing demands skill and practice before you can achieve perfect results. Consequently, many woodworkers prefer to brush slightly thinned shellac onto the wood then rub down between coats rather than apply the polish in the traditional manner.

Better still, you can use a French polish containing a special additive that slows down the drying process, allowing enough time for brush marks to flow out of the polish after it has been painted onto the surface.

The technique for applying special brushing polish is easy to master. Use a soft brush to apply an even coat, then after 15 to 20 minutes rub down lightly with self-lubricating silicon-carbide paper and apply a second coat. Having applied a third coat in the same way, rub it down with 0000 grade wire wool dipped in wax polish, then after five minutes burnish with a soft cloth.

Applying brushing French polish
Use a soft brush to apply an even coat of this special brushing polish.

Rubbing down with wire wool
Rub the final coat lightly in the direction of the grain.

TRADITIONAL FRENCH POLISHING

Traditionally, French polish is applied, thin layer upon layer, using a ball of cotton wool wrapped in a white linen rag to make a soft pad known as a 'rubber'.

Making a rubber

Upholsterer's skin wadding is the best material for making a rubber, but ordinary cotton wool will do almost as well. Take a handful of the material, squeeze it roughly egg-shaped and place it in the centre of a 225 to 300mm (9 to 12in) square of linen (1). Fold the fabric over the cotton wool (2), then turn in the edges (3), gathering the loose material in the palm of your hand (4). Smooth out any wrinkles across the sole of the pad.

1 Place ball of wadding on a square of linen

2 Fold one corner

3 Turn in the edges

4 Hold in the palm of your hand

Charging a rubber

Unfold the linen square then, holding the rubber in the palm of your hand, pour shellac polish onto the pad until it is fully charged but not absolutely saturated. Fold the rubber again, as described left, and press it against a scrap board to squeeze out the polish and distribute it evenly across the sole. Use your fingertip to apply a drop of linseed oil to the sole to act as a lubricant.

Applying the polish

To apply French polish to a flat surface, first make over-lapping circular strokes with the rubber, gradually covering the whole panel with shellac (1). Then go over the surface again, this time using figure-of-eight strokes (2). Varying the stroke ensures an even coverage. Finish with straight overlapping strokes parallel to the grain (3).

Very little pressure is required with a freshly charged rubber, but gradually increase the pressure as the work proceeds. Always keep the rubber on the move, sweeping it on and off the surface at the beginning and end of each complete coverage. If you stop with the rubber in contact with the work it will stick and scar the polish, in which case you must let it harden thoroughly before rubbing it down with very fine self-lubricating silicon-carbide paper. Recharge your rubber with polish as necessary and add another spot of linseed oil when the rubber starts to drag.

Assuming the first application is free from blemishes, leave it to dry for about half an hour then repeat the process. Build up four or five coats in this way, then leave the shellac to harden overnight. Keep your rubber in a screw-top glass jar while you allow the polish to dry.

Next day, sand out any runs, dust particles or rubber marks with silicon-carbide paper before applying another four to five coats of polish. Judge for yourself when you have built up a protective body of polish with the required depth of colour, but 10 to 20 coats will be sufficient.

Polishing mouldings and carvings

Panels with large shallow mouldings can be polished with a rubber, but use a soft brush to apply slightly thinned shellac to deep mouldings or carvings. A squirrel-hair brush from a specialist supplier is ideal, but you can make do with an ordinary good-quality paintbrush. Apply the polish relatively quickly and evenly, but not too quickly or it will run. When the shellac has hardened, spirit off with a rubber as described below, but only burnish lightly or you will remove too much polish from high points.

Spiriting-off

The linseed-oil lubricant leaves streaks in the surface of the polish. Remove the streaks and burnish the polish to a gloss finish using a rubber practically empty of shellac but with a few drops of methylated spirit on the sole. Apply the rubber to the polished surface using straight parallel strokes only, gliding on and off the panel at the beginning and end of each stroke. Recharge with more methylated spirit as soon as the rubber begins to drag. Leave the work for a couple of minutes to see if the streaking disappears. If it doesn't, spirit off again until you have achieved the required finish. After half an hour, burnish the surface with a dry soft duster, then leave the work for at least a week to harden completely.

Creating a satin finish

If you don't care for a high-gloss finish, matt the fully hardened surface by rubbing it lightly with a ball of 0000 grade wire wool dipped in soft wax polish. Use straight, parallel, overlapping strokes until the surface is matted evenly, then burnish it to an attractive satin sheen with a soft cloth, adding a little more wax polish if necessary.

Charge the rubber with shellac

1 Cover the panel with circular strokes

2 Continue with figure-of-eight strokes

3 Finish with straight parallel strokes

LACQUER, VARNISH AND PAINT

Lacquer, varnish and paint are grouped together here for two main reasons. Firstly, manufacturers rarely distinguish between lacquer and varnish. Secondly, *these finishes are applied in similar ways, either by brush or spray gun. Furthermore, certain paints are in effect clear varnishes with additional pigments.*

Lacquers, varnishes and paint
1 Cellulose lacquer on sycamore
2 Clear catalysed lacquer on pine
3 Black catalysed lacquer
4 Clear polyurethane varnish on utile
5 Tinted polyurethane varnish on oak
6 Solvent-based paint on pine

Nitrocellulose lacquer

This has been a popular industrial wood finish for decades, primarily because it dries extremely quickly. There are special brushing varieties, but lacquer normally has to be sprayed on to achieve the desired result. Lacquer dries by solvent evaporation, leaving a surface layer that is partly redissolved by the next application – a process that eventually results in one integral coat of lacquer.

Nitrocellulose lacquer is practically water-clear and will hardly change the colour of the wood to which it is applied. It forms a hard finish that is resistant to heat and moisture.

Catalysed lacquers

A catalysed lacquer cures by chemical action – the lacquer won't set without the introduction of a hardener. With pre-catalysed lacquers, the catalyst and lacquer are mixed by the manufacturer, although setting does not occur until the finish is exposed to air. An acid-catalysed lacquer is supplied as two separate components for the woodworker to mix just before applying it to the work. Catalysed lacquers are very transparent – they are also exceptionally hard-wearing and stain-resistant. Both gloss and matt lacquers are available, and you can buy opaque black and white acid-catalysed lacquers as well as the more familiar clear variety. All catalysed lacquers can be diluted with special thinners for spraying and some are formulated for brushing on.

Varnishes

Synthetic resins such as polyurethane are used to make modern wood varnishes that are heat-resistant, waterproof and extremely hard-wearing. Although most varnishes can be used straight from the can, some are supplied with a catalyst that is added just before the varnish is applied. These two-part varnishes are so resistant to abrasion that they are used for finishing wooden floors, but they have a relatively short pot life and adhesion between coats is not always satisfactory. They also give off unpleasant fumes.

Exterior-grade varnishes are made to be weather-resistant – and 'yacht varnish', which will withstand exposure to salt water, is especially suitable for coastal climates.

There are clear varnishes that dry to a matt, semi-matt or gloss finish, and tinted varnishes are available for colouring wood. As a tinted varnish does not penetrate the wood like a true stain, there is always the possibility of colour loss due to localized wear. As a safeguard, apply one or two additional coats of clear varnish to preserve the colour. Tinted varnish is useful for adjusting the colour of a workpiece that has already been varnished. You can apply varnish with a paintbrush or dilute it with thinner for spraying.

Paint

Solvent-based paints for wood are made from solid pigments suspended in a synthetic resin, such as alkyd, vinyl, acrylic, urea or polyurethane, mixed with oil. Certain additives alter the quality of the paint to make it glossy, matt, semi-matt, fast-drying and so on. Most solvent-based paints have a liquid consistency, but you can also buy thixotropic (nondrip) paints that are jelly-like in the can and flow only when agitated by brushing them onto a surface.

Paints with specific properties are used in sequence to build up a hard-wearing protective coating. A primer is used first, to seal the bare timber and prevent absorption of subsequent coats. It is followed by one or two applications of a heavily pigmented undercoat to obliterate the primer and build up a body of paint. The final top coat provides a wipe-clean surface of the required colour and texture.

Opaque paints are intended for finishing cheap hardwood as well as softwood and man-made boards. Resin-based paints can be applied by brush and all but thixotropic paints can be sprayed. Water-based paints such as emulsion will raise the grain if used to finish wood.

1

3

2

4

5

6

UNFINISHED WOOD

PRIMER

UNDERCOAT

TOP COAT

CLEANING PAINTBRUSHES

When you have finished work, brush out excess paint, varnish or lacquer on newspaper in order to clean the bristles. Flex the brush in the finish-maker's recommended thinner (white spirit for most paints and varnishes), then wash the dirty thinner from the bristles with hot soapy water and rinse them. Shape the bristles with your fingers while they are still wet. When dry, wrap the bristles in soft paper and slip an elastic band around the ferrule of the brush to secure the wrapping.

APPLYING FINISHES BY BRUSH

Spraying produces the most professional-looking finish, but it is expensive to build and equip a spray booth that complies with health and safety recommendations. Consequently, applying clear finishes and paints with a brush is the only viable option for many amateur woodworkers. However, provided you use well-maintained good-quality brushes and exercise care and patience, you can achieve more than satisfactory results employing ordinary workshop facilities. Buy a range of brushes – say 12, 25 and 50mm (½, 1 and 2in) wide – for general work, and a 100mm (4in) brush for coating large flat surfaces.

Brushing cellulose lacquer

It requires a certain amount of experience to apply a brushing lacquer without leaving brush marks or ridges that are difficult to rub down. First, using a soft cloth or a brush, apply lacquer thinned by 50 per cent to act as a sealer coat. Load a soft brush with full-strength lacquer and, holding the bristles at a shallow angle to the horizontal surface, lay the finish onto the surface with long straight strokes. Don't attempt to brush it out like varnish, and avoid going back over the same area twice. Quickly pick up wet edges with fresh lacquer and allow the brush marks to flow out by themselves. Build up two or three coats of lacquer, rubbing down with very fine silicon-carbide paper in between. Each coat usually takes about an hour to dry – but check the manufacturer's instructions. If you are unhappy with the appearance of the final coat, flatten it with abrasive paper again and apply a proprietary burnishing cream with a soft cloth to buff the finish.

Some experienced woodworkers prefer to use a 'pull-over solution' made from one part cellulose thinner mixed with three parts white spirit to put the final shine on nitrocellulose lacquer. This is not an easy technique to perfect and you must take care to avoid stripping the surface by applying too much solution. Having flattened the lacquer with silicon-carbide paper, moisten a cloth pad with pull-over solution and apply it to the surface, using overlapping circular strokes followed by straight ones in the direction of the grain, as when applying French polish.

Applying acid-catalysed lacquer

Chemical composition and balance is crucial to the curing of acid-catalysed lacquer, so it is essential to follow the manufacturer's recommendations for mixing the components and preparing the surface of the wood. Clean the wood well, since the presence of grease or wax, for example, can delay curing for days.

Mix just enough lacquer for your needs, and don't return the residue to the original container or the entire contents will become unusable.

The specific method of application may differ from product to product, but as a rule you can brush a liberal coat of lacquer onto the wood, spreading it with straight parallel strokes along the grain. There is no need to brush it out like varnish – just leave the film to settle naturally. When you are coating a large area, work relatively quickly to blend wet edges before the lacquer starts to set. This will probably take between 10 and 15 minutes. Apply a second coat about two hours later and, having rubbed it down lightly with very fine silicon-carbide paper to remove dust particles, add a third coat two hours after that. For perfect adhesion between coats, try to apply all three in the same day.

If you want a mirror finish, leave gloss lacquer to harden for 24 hours, then buff it with a burnishing cream on a soft cloth. For a semi-matt finish, rub the gloss lacquer with 0000 grade wire wool dipped in wax polish then buff with a duster.

Applying varnish

When finishing bare timber with clear or tinted varnish, first apply a sealer coat thinned by 10 to 20 per cent with white spirit. Use a soft cloth pad to rub it into the wood in the direction of the grain, or brush on the sealer coat where a pad would be inconvenient. Apply the second coat by brush not less than six hours later – and if more than 24 hours have elapsed between coats, key the surface of gloss varnish with a very fine silicon-carbide paper. Remove the wood dust, using a cloth dampened with white spirit, before brushing on the varnish. For a hard-wearing surface, apply a third coat in the same way.

To load a brush with varnish, dip only the first third of the bristles into the finish and touch it off on the inside of the container to remove excess liquid. Do not drag the bristles across the rim of the can as that promotes bubbles in the varnish – which, if transferred to the work, may end up set in the surface coating.

Paint the varnish onto the wood, brushing it in different directions to spread the finish evenly and blend each new coat with the wet edges of the previous application. Finally, 'lay off' with light strokes in the direction of the grain. Don't brush back over a coat of varnish once it has begun to set or you will leave permanent brush marks. If this should happen, leave the finish to harden overnight then rub out the brush marks and any other blemishes with silicon-carbide paper lubricated with water.

If dust particles settle on your final gloss surface, either rub down and varnish again or modify the finish with wire wool and wax. Dip 0000 grade wire wool in wax polish and burnish the surface in the direction of the grain. Buff the treated surface with a duster to raise an attractive soft sheen free from obvious imperfections.

Apply a sealer coat of varnish with a cloth pad

Applying paint

Most solvent-based paints are applied like varnish, brushing them out to provide an even cover, then laying off with parallel strokes of the brush. However, there is no need to brush out thixotropic paints – instead, apply a fairly liberal coat of paint, brushing with virtually parallel strokes only, and leave the brush marks to flow out naturally.

Allow enough time for each coat of paint to dry according to the manufacturer's instructions, then rub down with a very fine silicon-carbide paper and wipe the surface clean with a rag. Leave the final top coat to dry overnight in a dust-free environment before handling the workpiece again.

AVOIDING RUNS IN PAINT OR VARNISH

If you neglect to brush out a liberal coat of normal solvent-based paint or varnish on a vertical surface, it will sag to form a heavy ridge similar in appearance to a draped curtain. Prevent 'curtaining' by applying an even coat, then lay off with upward brush strokes (1).

1 Laying off

Teardrop runs are caused by flexing a loaded brush against a moulding or the corner of a panel. Always apply paint along mouldings – never across them – and pay particular attention to brushing out in both directions from corners where two mouldings meet (2).

2 Brush out from corners

When painting up to the edge of a panel, brush outwards away from the centre (3). If you brush back against the arris you will scrape paint off the bristles, leaving it to run down.

3 Brush towards edge

SPRAYING WOOD FINISHES

Once you have mastered the basic techniques you can finish a workpiece with a perfectly even coat of varnish, paint or lacquer, using a spray gun and compressor. When these volatile finishes are distributed as a fine mist in the air, they form a potentially explosive environment and constitute a serious health hazard. You should therefore either spray woodwork outside or, preferably, build a spray booth equipped with an efficient extractor. However, check with your local authority that you are permitted to spray in your locality and that you will not be contravening any fire or safety regulations.

SPRAYING EQUIPMENT

Paint-spraying equipment mixes pressurized air with a liquid finish and deposits it in the form of very fine particles on the surface of the work.

HORN · AIR CAP
FLUID TIP
HORN
AIR-FLOW SCREW
FLUID-OUTPUT SCREW
GRACO MODEL 700
TRIGGER
HANDGRIP
AIR-ADJUSTMENT VALVE
AIR-SUPPLY HOSE
FINISH CONTAINER

Spray gun

Spray gun and compressor

An electrically powered compressor pressurizes filtered air and delivers it via a flexible hose to a spray gun. Squeezing the gun's trigger opens an air-inlet valve, allowing air to flow through the gun and exit through the fluid tip – a small hole in the centre of the air cap – where it is mixed with paint or a clear finish siphoned from a sealed container that is usually mounted below the gun. Some of the pressurized air is diverted to horns on either side of the fluid tip, where it emerges through tiny holes causing the spray to spread out like a fan. Air flow and fluid output are modified by turning valve screws on the back of the spray gun. Some guns are made with an additional air-adjustment valve at the base of the handgrip for finer tuning.

Cleaning a spray gun

When you have finished spraying, empty the finish container and add clean thinner. Operate the gun until perfectly clear thinner emerges, then release the air pressure, dismantle the air cap and clean the components with a rag dampened in solvent. Use a wooden toothpick to clear a paint blockage in the cap.

Use a toothpick to clear a blockage

Building a spray booth

The only safe way to spray indoors is to construct a fully enclosed booth that will isolate this activity from the rest of the workshop. Install a powerful extractor fan on an outside wall to remove noxious solvent fumes. However, these fumes create such a flammable atmosphere that even a sparking electric motor can cause them to ignite – so obtain an extractor with an explosion-proof motor from a specialist supplier and fit a paint filter in front of the fan to collect the overspray. You will also need explosion-proof lamps that can be switched on or off from outside. Check with your supplier that your compressor is safe to use inside the booth, or install it outside with a connection for the hose fitted to the booth wall. Ideally, include a water trap at this point to prevent moisture in the pressurized air condensing in the hose and spoiling the work. To hold small workpieces, make a turntable, using a disc of chipboard screwed to an old swivel-chair base, and stand it in front of the filtered extractor. Support larger pieces on trestles.

THINNING PAINT, VARNISH OR LACQUER

All finishes, most of which are sold in a brushable consistency, must be diluted with the appropriate thinner to render them fluid enough to be sprayed. Check manufacturer's recommendations for the type of thinner to use and the ideal ratio of thinner to finish.

Having measured out and mixed the components, use the following rough rule of thumb to test the consistency of the finish. Stir the finish with a wooden stick, then lift it out and watch how the finish runs from the tip. When the finish runs in a steady continuous stream it is about right for spraying. A slow interrupted stream indicates an over-thick consistency that will not spray efficiently. It is not so easy with this method to tell when a finish is too fluid, but a short burst of diluted finish sprayed onto a vertical practice board will give you a clue – if it runs almost at once, it is too thin.

For a more accurate gauge of consistency, obtain a viscosity cup from the spray-equipment manufacturer. Fill the cup, which is similar to a funnel, with thinned finish and time how long it takes to empty. Adjust the consistency until the time corresponds with the recommended figure.

Use a viscosity cup to test the consistency of a finish

BASIC SPRAYING TECHNIQUES

If you have never sprayed finishes before, it is best to practise on a piece of scrap board before spraying a workpiece.

Spraying a vertical panel

To spray a vertical panel, hold the gun approximately 200mm (8in) away from the surface, with the air horns turned horizontally to create a vertical fan-shaped spray pattern. Point the gun directly at the work and keep it moving on a path parallel to the surface throughout one pass **(1)**. Avoid swinging the gun in an arc **(2)** or the finish will be applied thinly at each end of the pass. Squeeze the trigger just before each pass, and don't release it until the spray pattern is clear of the work at the other end **(3)**. Aim the centre of the spray pattern at the edge of the panel. On the return pass, overlap the previous application by about 50 per cent **(4)** and continue with overlapping passes until you have covered the panel with finish.

1 Move a spray gun on a path parallel to the work

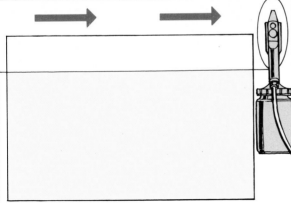

2 Swinging the gun produces uneven coverage

3 Start and finish clear of the work

4 Overlap previous application on the return pass

Spraying a horizontal panel

To spray a horizontal panel, such as a table top, spray the edges first, then work in parallel bands, aiming the gun at about 45 degrees to the surface. Work away from you, overlapping each pass as you do so.

Spraying legs and rails

Aim the gun at a corner to spray two sides of a leg or rail simultaneously. Spray from the opposite side of the leg to coat the remaining surfaces.

Spray enclosed surfaces in sequence

Spraying inside a cabinet or drawer

When you spray the inside of a cabinet or drawer, be systematic and concentrate on spraying each surface in turn to achieve even coverage. Spray the underside of the top panel first, followed by one side, always using overlapping vertical passes. Continue across the back of the cabinet or drawer in the same way. Then spray the other side, and last of all the bottom surface. Spray the outside after finishing the interior.

MODIFYING THE FINISH

A spray finish may be perfectly satisfactory without further attention, but you can improve or modify the surface texture in a number of ways.

To obtain a glossy finish, after allowing 24 hours for hardening, rub down with very fine silicon-carbide paper to flatten runs and remove specks of dust – then buff the resulting surface to a high gloss, using burnishing cream on a soft cloth.

To produce a satin finish, after the 24-hour hardening period, rub the surface with 0000 grade wire wool dipped in wax then polish with a duster. Alternatively, use powdered pumice mixed to a paste with a little liquid paraffin or water, rubbing it on with a hard felt block. Once you have achieved a satisfactory finish, wipe the slurry off the surface with a cloth pad. A similar treatment using rottenstone – an even finer abrasive powder – will polish the finish.

OIL AND WAX

Oil and wax polish are among the easiest wood finishes to apply, no experience being necessary in order to achieve first-rate results. Unlike varnishes and lacquers that coat the surface, oil penetrates the wood without leaving a film that holds brush marks or other blemishes – and provided you use a fast-drying variety, it does not form a sticky surface to attract dust particles. Wax is used as a finish in its own right and also as a dressing over varnish and lacquer.

WOOD-FINISHING OILS

Oil is traditionally used to treat naturally oily timbers such as teak and afrormosia, which tend to reject the majority of finishes. But it is equally suitable for other hardwoods – and even for softwoods, which it endows with a rich amber colour. Oil's water-resistant properties are particularly advantageous for exterior woodwork. Moreover, a subsequent application nourishes oiled timber suffering from the effects of exposure to the sun. However, it is not suitable as a finish for the interior of drawers or cupboards, where it could stain the contents.

● **Restoring an oil finish**
If the surface becomes scratched or stained, you can easily renovate it – simply by applying a dash of fresh oil.

Oil and wax polishes
1 Danish oil on iroko
2 Clear wax on oak
3 Antique wax on oak

Linseed oil
Raw linseed oil is suitable for small objects only. It can take up to three days to dry, by which time it may be covered with fluff and dust. Boiled linseed oil is marginally better since it dries after 24 hours, but neither oil forms a hard durable finish.

Danish and teak oils
Tung oil and other vegetable oils usually form the basis of a number of commercially prepared finishes known variously as Danish or teak oils. Driers are incorporated in these oils to shorten the time between applications to about six hours. Heat, alcohol and water may temporarily leave white stains on the surface, but they disappear quickly. More permanent blemishes can be effaced with a wipe of fresh oil.

Salad-bowl oil
Most wood-finishing oils contain toxic materials. However, you can buy non-toxic 'salad-bowl oil' for wooden counter tops, chopping blocks and other objects, such as bowls and spoons, that come into contact with food. Or, if you prefer, use olive oil, or other edible oils, instead.

Tung oil
Pure tung oil, also known as China wood oil, is the most durable oil finish. It shrugs off water and is resistant to heat and alcohol. It takes 24 hours to dry, but careful rubbing down with very fine silicon-carbide paper between coats will produce a superb finish. Apply five or six coats in all.

WAX POLISHES

In the past woodworkers made wax polish by dissolving a mixture of beeswax and hard carnauba wax in turpentine. These raw materials are still available, but there are so many excellent ready-made preparations on the market that most woodworkers do not find it necessary to make their own.

Wax polish makes for an attractive mellow finish that seems to improve with age. It is produced in a range of colours, from practically transparent polish for pale woods to deep brown 'antique polishes' that create the impression of an aged patina and will disguise scratches in a ready-polished surface.

Silicones are added to some polishes to make them easier to buff, but if they penetrate the timber they are difficult to remove and will repel practically any other finish should the workpiece ever have to be restored.

Liquid or cream polish
Liquid or cream polishes are fluid enough to be brushed onto the wood. Two or three applications are required to build up a protective body of polish.

Paste polish
A paste polish, made to a slightly thicker consistency, is ideal for application with a pad of very fine wire wool or lint-free rag. On hardening, it can be buffed with a clean soft duster to an impressive lustre.

Woodturning wax stick
A stick of wax, hard enough to be used as a friction polish, is rubbed against a workpiece spinning on a woodturning lathe.

APPLYING OIL

Apply a generous coat of Danish or teak oil to a clean well-prepared surface with a cloth pad or paintbrush. Leave it to soak into the wood for a few minutes, then wipe over the surface with a clean rag to absorb excess oil. Six hours later apply a second coat and leave it to dry overnight.

Next day apply one more coat, and buff it with a duster to create a sheen.

It takes longer to finish a surface with pure tung oil. After the initial coating, applied liberally with a brush and rubbed over as already described, apply several thinner coats to allow the oil to dry between applications. If dust particles adhere to the surface during the 24-hour drying period, rub it down lightly with very fine abrasive paper in the direction of the grain.

APPLYING WAX

Although you can apply wax polish directly to bare timber, it is an advantage to seal the surface first with a varnish or, for superior-quality work or oil-stained timber, with two coats of shellac sanding sealer or white French polish. Sealing prevents the initial coat of wax being absorbed too deeply into the grain, especially when you are using a liquid wax polish. It also prevents dirt sinking through the wax and permeating the wood over a period of time.

Having flattened the sealer coats with very fine silicon-carbide paper, if you are using a liquid wax polish apply the first liberal coat of wax with a brush or use a soft cloth pad to rub it into the wood with circular strokes first and then straight ones in line with the grain. One hour later, buff up the wax and apply a thin coat with the pad in the direction of the grain only. Add a third coat, if needed, similarly and buff it as before. Leave the wax to harden for several hours, then burnish the surface vigorously with a clean soft duster.

If you decide to use a paste wax polish, apply it with a pad of 0000 grade wire wool, rubbing with the grain only, and bring it to a shine with a soft cloth.

OTHER

From time to time most woodworkers find themselves using materials other than timber, either for practical reasons or to enrich the appearance of a workpiece. Ready-made or purpose-made metal fittings can be found in every workshop and metal inlays are used to decorate chair backs, box lids and gunstocks. For pastry-making, nothing compares with a cool marble slab set into a kitchen worktop or dresser. Despite improvements in plastics, glass is still the best material for picture-framing and for china cabinets or display cases; and glass or marble table tops are attractive and easy to clean. Leather makes an ideal writing surface for desks and bureaux; it can also be used to line presentation cases or jewellery boxes or as

MATERIALS

a handsome facing for cabinet or drawer fronts. It is well worth learning the basic skills of cutting, shaping and fitting these materials, or at least enough about them to brief a specialist supplier or craftsman when expert services are needed.

METAL

Metal ornamentation and inlays make a pleasing contrast to the softer and more muted tones of wood. Metalworking skills also enable you to design and *make your own fittings or adapt ready-made ones to suit your own requirements, thus adding a satisfying touch of originality to your work.*

Support work on a notched sawing peg

Metalworking tools
1 Hacksaw
2 Needle files
3 Piercing saw
4 Metalworking files
5 Engineer's square
6 Dividers
7 Universal snips
8 Straight snips
9 Curved snips
10 Steel rule
11 Scriber

METALWORKING TOOLS

Most metals can be worked by hand with a basic selection of metalworking tools.

For inlays and for inscription plates and other decorative fittings, jeweller's tools are most appropriate.

For heavier work, such as support brackets and frame members, a hacksaw and universal snips are needed plus a range of larger files, both fine-cut and coarse-cut, in flat, half-round and round profiles. For cutting thick metal sections, bars and tubes, use a 300mm (1ft) hacksaw frame with either a medium-tooth or fine-tooth blade. Having hardened teeth fused to a flexible-steel back, bi-metal hacksaw blades last much longer and are less likely to shatter than ordinary carbon-steel blades.

For decorative fretwork, such as keyholes and fancy escutcheons, a jeweller's piercing saw and an assortment of needle files of various shapes are essential. When cutting with a piercing saw, support the work on a sawing peg and cut on the downstroke only.

For marking out you will need a scriber to score the surface of the metal, and dividers for scribing arcs and circles. An engineer's steel square is ideal for checking and marking right angles. Use a steel rule for setting out and measuring dimensions.

For cutting flat sheets two smaller pairs of snips are useful – one flat-bladed for cutting straight lines and external curves, and the other with curved blades for cutting internal curves.

A bench-mounted electric grinder is a worthwhile investment. One side of the grinder can be used to drive abrasive grinding and sharpening stones; the other side has a tapered mandrel or spindle so mops and buffing wheels can be interchanged quickly.

METALWORKING BENCH

If possible, install a separate bench for metalwork. This avoids metal particles straying onto wooden workpieces. It also keeps blowlamps, or other heat sources, and flying sparks away from sawdust and shavings. Ideally, the top of the bench should be covered with galvanized-steel sheeting. As well as the sawing peg and electric grinder, bolt a medium-sized engineer's vice rigidly to the bench and a drill press for drilling precise vertical holes. Even if you already have a drill press for woodwork, a vertical power-drill stand for metalwork only will help confine oil and swarf (metal shavings) to a limited area.

JOINING METAL

Metals can be joined either by gluing, soldering, brazing or welding, depending on the strength of joint required.

Gluing
Generally, gluing is only used for attaching decorative metals and small fittings, although modern adhesives form an extremely strong bond. Glued metal-to-metal joints are useful for mock-ups and also for temporarily holding items together prior to final fixing. Structural joints should be brazed or welded.

Soldering
Stainless steel, brass and copper can all be joined by soft soldering or by brazing. For soft soldering on brass and copper you will need one or two 150W electric soldering irons for soldering sheet up to 1.5mm ($\frac{1}{16}$in) and one of 40W for thin-gauge sheet, strip or wire. Heavier-gauge sheet can be soft-soldered using a fine-jet gas blowlamp – a small portable lamp which uses replaceable gas cylinders is ideal. Soft solders, which are alloys of lead and tin, have a low melting point. Do not try to make edge-to-edge joints when soft-soldering, but form overlaps or interlocking seam joints.

Make sure that the surfaces to be joined are perfectly clean and free from grease. In all forms of soldering a flux is used to keep the surfaces clean during the soldering process and prevent them from oxidizing.

For most brass and copper fittings, use a paste flux with either bar or wire solder. Avoid the flux-cored type of wire solder, as used for electrical connections, since it tends to be soft and therefore weak.

Keep the tip of the iron clean and, before using it, tin the tip when hot by fluxing it lightly and running a thin coat of solder over it.

Soldering a joint
To form a joint, wipe flux along the joint lines and bring the heat source close to it. Heat the surface with the tip of the iron or flame. Allow the heat to build up until the solder starts to flow. Do not overheat the surface or burn the flux, otherwise the metal may distort or the solder will not flow properly. Neither will the solder flow if the surfaces are not hot enough, but will remain as small globules along the joint.

To avoid overheating with a blowlamp, apply the flame away from the joint and let the metal conduct the heat to it.

Allow the joint to cool gradually (do not cool it with water or you will weaken it), then clean off any excess flux.

Brazing and welding
Although soft soldering is easily performed in the home workshop, it is generally better to have brazing and welding done professionally. Moreover, garages and small engineering firms are often willing to do small brazing or welding jobs.

However, with the availability of small inexpensive metal inert-gas (MIG) welders, which weld aluminium and stainless steels as well as other metals, it is now feasible to make small metal fittings in the home workshop.

Adhesives
Metals can be bonded to non-porous surfaces (including other metals and glass) using cyanoacrylate, epoxy-resin or rubber-based contact adhesives.

METALS

Gold and silver
Traditionally gold and silver have been used as inlays to decorate cabinets, often combined with exotic materials such as tortoiseshell and mother-of-pearl.

Gold alloys, in the form of 9 carat wire or sheets, can be used for inlay work – but because of its cost, gold is more commonly used as thin foil.

Silver is easier to work than gold alloy and is available in a wider range of sheet and wire thicknesses. Since silver is cheaper than gold, thin sheet is often used rather than foil.

Pure gold and silver can only be purchased through authorized bullion agents.

Brass
Brass is usually available in small quantities from engineering suppliers as sheet, rod, tube and strip as well as other sections such as angle and bar. Another good source of supply is model-engineering shops, which often stock brass (and other metals) in a wide range of profile and sheet thicknesses cut in short lengths and sizes.

Carbon steel
Mild or medium carbon steels (the higher the carbon content, the harder the steel) are available from steel stockholders in the form of tube, bar and plate (sheet). Most will supply small orders or sell offcuts for making your own frames, brackets and other fittings.

Mild steel is easy to work with handtools, but difficult to solder. Structural joints are generally brazed or welded, though for concealed work nuts and bolts or rivets may be used. Carbon steels (other than stainless) rust unless they are painted or plated.

Stainless steel
Stainless steel is available as sheet, tube and angle from metal or boatbuilding-material stockists. Most varieties are easy to work and will retain a good surface finish. Though not easy to join, stainless steel can be glued, soldered, brazed or welded.

Aluminium
DIY outlets and builder's and metal merchants sell aluminium in a vast variety of sections. It is an easy metal to work, but difficult to solder and soft varieties clog the teeth of files and hacksaws. To prevent clogging, coat the blade with white spirit, turps or talc. Finished surfaces need to be protected with a clear metal varnish or a professionally applied treatment such as anodizing.

Copper
Copper is available in sheet, tube, rod and strip form from metal merchants and model-engineering shops. It is easy to work and join. Polished copper surfaces dull quickly.

LAYING METAL INLAYS

Decorative metal inlays may take the form of strips, bands, circles, ovals, or other regular or irregular shapes.

To recess a metal inlay into the surface of the wood (or 'ground'), use a power router guided either by its fence for straight grooves or by a trammel bar for circles. Other shapes can be cut freehand or with a template. The groundwork must be perfectly flat, particularly when laying thin foil. For most recessing, use a straight two-flute plunge cutter that has a 6mm ($\frac{1}{4}$in) shank and a diameter of not less than 9mm ($\frac{3}{8}$in). For intricate figures or thin strips, use a finer cutter.

Square up the corners of the recess by removing the waste with a sharp chisel and check that the inlay lies fractionally below the surface of the wood by laying the edge of a metal rule or straightedge across it.

Metal inlays are glued to the groundwork with an epoxy-resin adhesive. Apply a thin layer of glue to the metal and press it into the recess. Cover the work with thin polyethylene sheeting, then – to ensure that the inlay lies flush with the surface – either clamp a flat block over the inlaid area or place the work in a veneer press.

FINISHING METAL

Various skilled techniques can be used to enhance the appearance of metal, including planishing, sandblasting, chasing and embossing.

Scratch-brushing
One technique that does not involve special skills or equipment is scratch-brushing. This produces a satin texture by using a rotating stainless-steel brush (or progressively finer brushes) fitted to the spindle of a bench grinder. The coarseness and speed of the brushes determine the depth of finish.

Polishing
Always wear a face mask when polishing metal, since the fine metal dust raised can be dangerous when breathed in.

If possible, metal inlays and fittings should be polished before fitting, using brushes and mops fitted to the mandrel of a bench grinder.

Start by removing scratches and marks, using a stiff brush coated with Tripoli (an abrasive polish available from jewellers and craft-material suppliers).

Next, buff the metal to a high sheen using soft buffing mops, first with Tripoli and then with jeweller's rouge or a suitable metal polish.

If you have to polish inlays or fittings *in situ,* use small brushes or mops held in the chuck of a flexible drive fitted to a bench-mounted power drill or electric motor. Before polishing, protect the surrounding wood with a thin coat of clear sealer and cover with masking tape to avoid staining.

● **Bonding metal to wood**
When gluing metal to timber, seal the wood first with thinned varnish or diluted PVA glue. To allow for shrinkage and expansion, use a flexible contact adhesive when bonding metal to a wide wood surface.

CUTTING LUBRICANTS

Most metals are easier to cut if you use a lubricant, not only to prevent the blade or drill binding but to act as a coolant and prevent swarf clogging the teeth.

Steels: Use a little general-purpose oil.
Aluminium: Use white spirit, turps or talc.
Copper: Use light machine oil, white spirit or talc to stop the teeth clogging.
Brass: Work dry.

Polishing metal inlays or fittings
A miniature mop held in a powered flexible drive is ideal for polishing inlays or fittings *in situ.*

Applied finishes
Cellulose-based or polyurethane-based paints and lacquers, used with compatible undercoats and primers, are most suitable for finishing metal. They can be brushed or sprayed on, though spraying generally produces better results more quickly and easily. Car-paint touch-up aerosols offer an economical method of spraying metal fittings. Small DIY spray guns and compressors also give good results.

When brushing or spraying paint, always work in a dust-free atmosphere – and never spray indoors except in a spray booth (see chapter on finishing wood). Make sure that the surface is perfectly clean and grease-free. If better adhesion is needed, score the surface of the metal lightly with wire wool or fine wet-and-dry paper. Allow each coat of paint to dry thoroughly and rub down with wet-and-dry paper between coats.

GLASS

There are three categories of glass: transparent (including polished plate, drawn sheet and float glass), translucent (comprising patterned, frosted and rough-cast glass) and special (for example, toughened, laminated, antique, non-reflective and solar-control glass). Most glass is now produced by the float method, since drawn glass tends to be uneven in thickness, which creates some distortion in vision and reflection. Plate, drawn and float glass are available in various qualities.

● **Safe design**
Glass shelves should be designed so that the glass is supported over the greatest practicable area.

● **Retaining glass**
Where shelves or table tops overhang a support rail or bracket, use clips, screws or other fastenings to retain the glass.

Steel-wheel glass cutter

HANDLING GLASS SAFELY

● Wear leather gloves and take care when handling or disposing of broken glass or glass dust.
● Wear goggles and leather gloves when cutting glass, plus a mask when grinding.

Drawn sheet glass
Drawn sheet glass is designated OQ (ordinary quality) for general glazing purposes; SQ (selected quality) for better-quality work; and SSQ (special selected quality) for high-grade work, picture framing and cabinetwork. Drawn sheet is normally available in thicknesses of 3 to 6mm ($\frac{1}{8}$ to $\frac{1}{4}$in).

Float glass
Float glass has similar designations: GG (general glazing); SG (selected glazing) for superior work, bevelling and mirrors; and SO (silvering quality) for high-class mirrors and for display cabinets and screens. Float glass is generally available in thicknesses of 3 to 25mm ($\frac{1}{8}$ to 1in).

Antique glass
Antique glass is still available from specialist sources and is handmade by traditional methods to retain the characteristics of old glass, such as variations in thickness and colour, and defects such as flaws and air bubbles.
   Opal glass is now generally referred to as antique glass but tends to be more regular in thickness, the colour appearing as faintly translucent to opaque.

Non-reflective glass
This type of glass is mainly used for framing pictures and notice boards. Both sides of the glass are very slightly textured, but when positioned close to an object appear transparent.
   In picture frames, the gap between the glass and the picture should not exceed the thickness of the mount. For other purposes, a gap of not more than 20mm ($\frac{3}{4}$in) is acceptable.

Annealed glass
Thick float glass is often annealed (heated to relieve internal stresses) in order to make it less fragile and more workable. However, under impact it breaks into large jagged fragments.

Toughened glass
Toughened glass is annealed glass that has been further heat-treated to introduce a deliberate stress pattern, making it four to five times stronger. When broken, toughened glass disintegrates into small squares or dice. It is expensive to have a small amount or a single piece toughened, although larger glass merchants can arrange for it to be done.

Laminated glass
Laminated glass is much stronger than ordinary glass. It is produced by sandwiching a clear plastic film between two sheets of glass. If it is shattered, the film holds the fragments together, possibly saving items standing on it and also reducing risk of injury. As a result, it can be used for load-bearing plinths, bases or shelves.

Where to buy glass
Most types of glass are available from larger glass merchants, who also offer cutting, bevelling and mirroring services and can often arrange for special treatments and decorative finishes.

Drilling glass
Glass can be drilled using a special spearpoint bit running at low speed in a power or hand drill. Mark the centre of the hole with the tip of the bit and build a well of putty around the spot filled with white spirit, turpentine or paraffin to cool the bit.

Cutting glass
Glass over 4mm ($\frac{5}{32}$in) thick is best cut or drilled by a glass merchant. But if you prefer to do it yourself, use a diamond-impregnated disc driven by a small cordless angle grinder fitted with a coolant dispenser – which can also be used for grinding edges and trimming corners.
   Most flatsheet glass up to 4mm ($\frac{5}{32}$in) thick can be cut easily with a steel-wheel or diamond cutter. Lay the glass on a padded surface, such as a piece of blanket or carpet, spread over a flat work surface. Clean all grease from the surface with white spirit, turpentine or paraffin – a greasy surface will not cut evenly.

1 Draw a cutter towards you

   Mark each end of the cut line on the edges of the glass with a felt-tip pen and align a T-square or wooden straightedge between them. Holding the cutter firmly between your middle finger and forefinger, with your thumb supporting the back, draw the cutter along the line with a gentle even pressure **(1)**. Take care not to chip the edge of the glass at the end of the cut.

2 Press on each side of line

   Wearing leather gloves and goggles or safety spectacles, lay the glass on a piece of thin board with one of its edges aligned with the cut, leaving one side unsupported. To snap the glass press down firmly with one hand on each side of the scored line **(2)**.
   If any jagged pieces of glass are left along the edge, nibble them off using the correct-width notch on the side of the cutter **(3)** or a pair of pincers. Narrow strips can be broken off the sheet after scoring by holding the glass on each side of the line at one end and snapping along the line **(4)**.

3 Clean up any jagged edges

4 Snap a strip off a sheet

Grinding and polishing

On unframed panels, such as table tops and shelves, glass edges must be ground smooth for safety. They can be ground and polished to one of several standard profiles, including flat, bevelled, bullnose, mitred, full-round and half-round.

Edge-grinding is best left to the glass merchant, but you can polish the edges yourself using various grades of wet-and-dry paper down to 600 grit, followed by metal polish or a fine cutting compound as used for repolishing car paintwork.

 Flat edge   **Bevelled edge**   **Bullnose edge**

Mitred edge **Half-round edge** **Full-round edge**

Joining glass

Both butt and lap joints can be formed between glass panels using modern adhesives, such as epoxy resin, silicon mastics or cyanoacrylates. The latter can be used to form virtually invisible joints if the two surfaces are finished so they mate perfectly. Mitred joints are best ground by a glass merchant.

Butt joint **Lap joint** **Mitred joint**

Selecting glass

For small panes in cabinet doors, picture frames and vertical panels up to 300 × 300mm (1 × 1ft), select either 2mm or 3mm glass.

For cabinet doors and vertical panels up to 750 × 375mm (2ft 6in × 1ft 3in), select 4mm glass.

The safe loading for glass shelves is given in the table below, which is based on the formula:

$$\frac{2}{3} \times \frac{\text{width (front to back)}}{\text{span between supports}}$$
$$\times \text{thickness of glass}^2$$
$$= \text{max. load in kilograms.}$$

However, the shelf width from front to back should not be less than 150mm (6in) nor greater than a span to width ratio of 7 to 1. For example, the span of a shelf 150mm wide should not exceed 1.05m.

For general storage, shelves should be designed to withstand loads of up to 15 or 20kg.

Supported table tops

Where the edge of a glass top is fully supported along each edge, the recommended maximum size is:

6mm glass: 500 × 500mm (1ft 8in × 1ft 8in) or 0.25sq m (2.78sq ft).

10mm glass: 875 × 875mm (2ft 11in × 2ft 11in) or 0.77sq m (8.50sq ft).

12mm glass: 1070 × 1070mm (3ft 6in × 3ft 6in) or 1.14sq m (12.25sq ft).

The glass top should be held in the table underframe by a rebate or with clips.

Overhanging table tops

If the glass overhangs the supporting underframe, it must be held in place by fastenings or by dowels that pass through the glass to prevent it being pushed off. Metal bolts or dowels should be cushioned with flexible washers (nylon, rubber etc).

As a general guide, use 12mm ($\frac{1}{2}$in) glass and do not allow the overhang to exceed 500mm (1ft 8in) all round.

Span	Width	6mm	10mm
500mm	150mm	7kg	20kg
500mm	200mm	9kg	26kg
500mm	300mm	14kg	40kg
750mm	150mm	4kg	13kg
750mm	200mm	6kg	17kg
750mm	300mm	9kg	26kg
1000mm	150mm	3kg	10kg
1000mm	200mm	4kg	13kg
1000mm	300mm	7kg	20kg

MARBLE

Marble is prized for its rich and varied appearance, but it also has its practical uses. As a durable hygienic surface resistant to stains and scratches, it is suitable for use as a cutting or pastry slab inset into a dresser or a kitchen worktop.

Types of marble

Marbles range in colouring from Italian pure whites and creams to the Belgian greys and blacks. Other colours include Green Tinos from Greece; beige and browns from Portugal, Sicily and France; yellow/gold from Iran, Spain and Yugoslavia; and reds to pinks from Italy, Greece, Scandinavia and Portugal.

Some limestones that are not true marbles, such as Travertine (UK), also produce a good natural polish.

Cutting and working marble

Machining marble involves the use of expensive cutters and is best left to a skilled mason. Despite its hardness, marble is worked in a similar way to wood. In fact, standard woodworking machinery is often used (in particular band saws, circular saws and routers) with the blades replaced by diamond-impregnated cutters, bands and discs.

Holes up to 16mm ($\frac{5}{8}$in) may be drilled using tipped masonry drills at a cutting speed around 900rpm. Larger holes can be drilled using tipped core drills.

All cutting is performed with water continuously directed onto the tool as a coolant. Wire wool is then used to polish the marble. Wire wool is also used with specially prepared poultices to take out the unsightly surface stains associated with old marble that has been subjected to damp conditions.

Buying marble

The best sources of supply are marble importers or stone merchants, since both are used to small orders.

When ordering, always give exact measurements, and for shaped work supply an accurate template with the top face clearly marked.

Show also the position and detailing of any decorative machining or carving that you require.

Marble is generally available in thicknesses from 7mm ($\frac{5}{16}$in) to 50mm (2in). However, it can be cut to any thickness you want if ordered specially. Most types are supplied in slabs up to 3.5 × 1.7m (11ft 6in × 5ft 6in), although the most common standard size is 600 × 300mm (2 × 1ft).

Fixings and adhesives

Make sure the frame or base is perfectly square, level and rigid to avoid the slab bending or twisting when fastened down. Successful repairs can be made using an epoxy adhesive.

1 Wooden button

Table tops are sometimes screwed to the underframe using bolts or screws with decorative screw caps to conceal the heads. To make a hidden fixing, brass bolts can be set into blind holes drilled in the underside of the slab, using a two-part epoxy glue to secure them. In either case, allow for movement of the timber frame by fastening into buttons (1) or into slotted angle brackets (2).

2 Metal bracket

Where the slab is set flush into a worktop or frame, brass edge dowels can be used to locate the slab (3).

Marble can be glued to marble and to most other materials using an epoxy adhesive. However, for gluing to a timber surface a flexible rubber-based adhesive must be used.

3 Brass edge dowel

LEATHER

Leather is primarily used by furniture-makers in three ways – as a furnishing fabric, as a facing material for writing tables and bureaux, and as a structural material stretched across a frame for various forms of seating.

Buying leather

Traditionally most leather is sold by the square foot and by thickness. However, some suppliers are now switching to metric units. Alternatively, it may be described by weight – a piece 300mm (1ft) square and 0.4mm ($\frac{1}{64}$in) thick, for example, weighs approximately 25g (1oz).

Furniture hide, a specially dressed and softened natural cowhide, is used for upholstery. Usable hide from a full-grown cow covers about 4.5 to 5.5sq m (50 to 60sq ft).

For desk and table tops, skiver leather (sheepskin) is generally preferred. This is thinner and easier to lay than cowhide but is much smaller – the maximum rectangle obtainable being about 840 × 600mm (2ft 9in × 2ft). For larger table tops it is necessary to join two pieces of hide (they are usually supplied taped together ready for laying).

Small pieces of leather are often available from craft-material shops or suppliers, and it is sometimes possible to buy offcuts from leather-clothing manufacturers. Skivers cut to order for desk tops and other purposes can be obtained from suppliers of materials for cabinet-making and furniture restoring. Skivers are available in several colours and also in 'antique' finishes.

Ordering skivers

When ordering a skiver it is important to give the exact dimensions of the recess in which it is to be laid. Note all dimensions and angles, and preferably provide an accurate template with the top face clearly marked. A template is essential if you plan to cover a curved or shaped surface, and can be used to indicate the preferred position of any decorative tooling. A professional cutter will allow for a trimming margin and may make slight adjustments to the position of tooling to disguise imperfections or add lines of tooling to hide joins.

TOOLING

Inlaid-leather desk tops are often decorated with gold tooling, the gold being imprinted into an embossed pattern.

You can buy embossing punches and rollers from craft shops. However, for the best results have leather professionally tooled.

Typical tooling patterns

LAYING A LEATHER SKIVER SURFACE

Skiver leather is often used for writing slopes, desks and bureaux, and as a decorative feature on coffee or wine tables. It is also sometimes used to line cabinets or presentation boxes and as a decorative facing for cabinet or drawer fronts.

Traditionally, leather writing surfaces and panel facings were applied using thin animal glue or a cold-water paste. However, diluted PVA glue (four parts glue to one part water) is now more commonly used.

You can inset the leather into a desk top by creating a recess for it using a power router (1) or frame it with solid-wood lippings (2). Alternatively, a cushioned effect can be obtained by cutting a radiused V-groove around the perimeter of the writing area (3), pressing and gluing the edge of the leather into the groove.

When fitting a tooled skiver, before trimming make sure that it is accurately aligned within the recess (allowing for equal margins outside the tooling pattern). First trim one long edge using a craft knife and, having covered the surface of the wood with PVA glue, gently press the trimmed edge into the recess (4).

Rub down the skiver with a clean folded felt pad – working along to each end, then across the centre to the opposite edge (5), and last of all to the sides and corners. Gently smooth out any wrinkles or bubbles, without stretching the leather, until a taut flat surface is obtained.

The three remaining edges can now be trimmed. Either use a straightedge as a guide or mark the cut lines on the leather by carefully indenting along the edges of the recess with the corner of a wooden ruler (6). Then cut to fit (7), avoiding scraping or cutting into the surrounding wood. While the glue is drying, check periodically for blisters and rub down any that appear.

PACKING SHEET KEEPS ROUTER LEVEL

1 Routing a recess for a skiver

2 Cover the edge with a lipping

3 Run a skiver into a V-groove

4 Press trimmed edge into recess

5 Rub outwards towards edges

6 Mark uncut edges with a ruler

7 Cut edges to fit recess

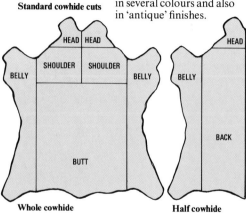

Standard cowhide cuts

HEAD HEAD

SHOULDER SHOULDER

BELLY BELLY

BUTT

Whole cowhide

HEAD

BELLY

BACK

Half cowhide

FIXINGS

The following pages provide a guide to the fixings and fittings that eventually find their way into just about every home workshop. Screws and nails are needed so regularly, for DIY purposes as well as woodworking projects, that it makes sense to maintain a permanent stock of useful sizes and gauges. Fittings such as handles, locks and good-quality hinges, on the other hand, are often relatively expensive, so it is best to buy them as need arises. Joining with adhesive is without doubt the most common method of construction used in woodworking and, given the specialized properties of many modern glues, you will probably find yourself accumulating a range of different types. However, not all glues have a long shelf life.

& FITTINGS

As a result, an almost full can of adhesive which you have had in store for some time may prove to be unusable when you need it again. So, although it may seem cheaper to buy glue in bulk, you may find that bulk buying is not truly economical unless you are planning numerous projects.

WOODWORKING ADHESIVES

For centuries glue has been used to join wood to wood without the need for mechanical reinforcement. But if you examine old furniture you will discover that these early glues had distinct disadvantages – notably a tendency to break down due to the presence of moisture, allowing the joints to become slack. Today woodworkers are able to select from a range of excellent adhesives with different properties, such as resistance to heat or moisture, slow drying, long pot life or fast setting, most of them capable of forming a bond so tough that the glue line is stronger than the surrounding wood fibres.

Animal glues
The traditional woodworker's glue is still made using animal skins and bone to provide the protein that gives this type of glue its adhesive quality. Animal glue was once the staple woodworking adhesive but today it is rarely used except for hand-laid veneers, where its thermoplastic quality is especially advantageous.

Animal glue is usually supplied in the form of 'pearls' or fine granules, ready for dissolving in water in a jacketed glue pot heated either by electricity or on a gas ring or stove. A slower-setting animal glue is also available, which has a jelly-like consistency and is liquified in the same kind of pot or by standing the glue container in hot water before application.

Animal glues are non-toxic. They form a hard glue line that can be planed and sanded, and they can be resoftened with the application of heat or moisture – a boon for the furniture restorer, though their susceptibility to heat and moisture sometimes leads to structural failure.

Hot-melt glues
Hot-melt glue is sold in the form of cylindrical sticks for application using a special-purpose electrically heated 'gun'. This type of adhesive is convenient to use and sets within seconds, which makes it ideal for constructing mock-ups and jigs. Different sticks are available for gluing materials other than wood.

Hot-melt glue is also made in thin sheets for veneering. The glue is laid between the veneer and groundwork then activated by a heated domestic iron.

Jacketed glue pot

Pearl glue

PVA adhesives
Polyvinyl-acetate (PVA) 'white glue' is one of the cheapest and most convenient woodworking adhesives on the market. It is a ready-made emulsion of PVA suspended in water that sets when the water evaporates or is absorbed into the wood.

An excellent general-purpose non-toxic wood glue, it has an almost indefinite shelf life so long as it is kept in reasonably warm conditions. The tough semi-flexible glue line can creep, though usually only when a joint is subjected to stress over a prolonged period. Standard white glue is not water-resistant, but there is a fully waterproof exterior-grade version.

A slightly thicker yellow aliphatic-resin PVA glue dries to a less resilient glue line that is resistant to heat and moisture. Unlike white glue, it sands well without clogging abrasive paper. You can also buy PVA glues modified to increase gap-filling capacity or to give a slower setting rate for large-scale assemblies.

Urea-formaldehyde adhesives
Urea-formaldehyde glue is an excellent water-resistant gap-filling adhesive that cures by chemical reaction. It can be obtained in a powdered form which, once it has been mixed with water, is applied to both mating surfaces.

Some urea-formaldehyde glues are made to be used in conjunction with a separate liquid catalyst or 'hardener' The hardener is applied to one half of the joint and the powdered glue mixed with water is spread onto the other. Clamp the work once the joint is closed.

Wear protective gloves and spectacles when handling the uncured materials, and work in a well-ventilated workshop.

Resorcinol-resin glues
Similar in many ways to urea-formaldehyde adhesive, resorcinol-resin glue is completely waterproof and weather-resistant. It is a two-part glue comprising a resin and a separate hardener. Some manufacturers supply both the resin and hardener as liquids; other glues are supplied with one component in powdered form. In each case, the resin and hardener are mixed together before applying the glue to both surfaces of the joint. The cured adhesive forms a reddish-brown glue line that may be noticeable on pale-coloured timbers. Setting time is accelerated by hot weather and the adhesive may not cure at all at temperatures much below 15°C (60°F). When handling the uncured glue, wear hand and eye protection and ventilate the workshop.

Hot-melt-glue gun
Squeezing the trigger melts the glue and drives it out of the nozzle.

USING ADHESIVE

Contact adhesives
A contact adhesive is spread as a thin layer on both mating surfaces. After the glue has set, the two components are brought together and the bond is instant. Modified versions allow the positions of the components to be adjusted until pressure is applied with a block of wood or a roller, causing the glue to bond. This type of adhesive is used extensively for gluing melamine laminates to kitchen worktops, but soft thixotropic (gel-like) versions are also used for applying wood veneers. Solvent-based contact glues set quickly, but they are extremely flammable and emit unpleasant fumes. Use them in a well-ventilated workshop only. Water-based contact adhesives are safer but take longer to dry.

Spread contact glue thinly

Epoxy-resin adhesives
Epoxy adhesive is a synthetic two-part glue consisting of a resin and hardener, normally mixed in equal proportions just before application. The most common form of epoxy glue – sold in tubes – is a general-purpose adhesive for joining diverse materials. As it is relatively thick, it is not really suitable for woodwork except for rub-jointing. However, liquid versions of the adhesive are made for gluing wood. Epoxy glues cure by chemical reaction to form a very strong, insoluble, transparent glue line. Standard epoxy adhesive sets hard in a few hours, but fast-setting glues are also available. Wipe uncured glue from the surface of a workpiece, using a cloth dampened with methylated spirit. Epoxy glues may irritate sensitive skin.

A well-prepared joint is essential if glue is to be effective. The joining surfaces must be clean, grease-free, flat and smooth. Roughing them to provide a better 'key' is not recommended for wood joints.

Moisture content
The moisture content of the wood can affect the quality of a joint. If it is more than about 20 per cent, for example, some glues may never set satisfactorily; and if it is less than 5 per cent, the glue may be absorbed too quickly and the bond will be poor.

Applying adhesives
Unless the manufacturer's instructions suggest otherwise, it is best to spread glue evenly but not too thickly onto both surfaces of a joint. This is especially important for joints like a mortise and tenon – where most of the adhesive can be scraped from the tenon as it is inserted, so that the joint is starved of glue.

Some two-part resin-and-hardener glues are applied differently. The resin is spread onto one half of the joint, and the hardener applied to the other. Reaction does not begin until the joint is closed, providing plenty of time to assemble large or complicated workpieces.

Clamping joints
Most joints have to be clamped while the glue sets. This brings the joining surfaces in close contact and squeezes excess glue from the joint. Wipe glue from around the assembled joint with a damp cloth before it sets. A few minutes later, return to the assembly to check whether hydraulic pressure within the joint has forced out more glue. If it has, give the cramp screws an extra turn and wipe away the excess glue.

Rub-jointing
A close-fitting butt joint will often bond satisfactorily under atmospheric pressure, without clamping. This is achieved by wetting both surfaces with glue, then rubbing them together to squeeze glue and air out of the joint while aligning the components. This is known as a rubbed joint.

Applying glue to a mortise
Unless adhesive is applied to a mortise the whole joint can be starved of glue.

Clamping glued joints
Most glued joints must be clamped while the adhesive sets.

Making a rubbed joint
Rubbing two glued components together achieves a close-fitting butt joint without the use of cramps.

APPLICATORS
Unless an adhesive is sold with a specific applicator, spread glue with a brush, flat stick or roller. When mixing adhesive, always follow the manufacturer's recommendations.

Glue brush
A wire bridle stiffens the bristles of a glue brush. It is removed when the bristles wear down.

Glue syringe
Use a plastic syringe to apply an exact amount of woodworking adhesive when you need to glue inaccessible joints.

WOODSCREWS

Woodscrews are primarily used for joining wood to wood, the clamping force they provide creating an extremely strong joint that is easily dismantled. They are also used for attaching fittings such as hinges, locks and handles. Most general-purpose woodscrews are made of steel, which is sometimes case-hardened for extra strength. Brass screws are more decorative and stainless-steel screws have a high resistance to corrosion even outdoors. Both brass and stainless-steel screws can be used to fix acidic woods such as oak that are stained by ordinary steel fixings. Steel screws are sherardized (coated with zinc) to prevent corrosion, and chrome plating and black japanning are used as decorative coatings.

How screws are measured

SCREW SIZES

The specified length of a screw corresponds to the part of it that actually enters the wood. A countersunk screw, for example, is measured from end to end, whereas a round-head screw is measured from its point to the underside of the head. This measurement can be anything from 6 to 150mm (¼ to 6in). Select a screw that is about three times as long as the thickness of the piece of wood or board it is to secure. Even if a screw is not long enough to burst through the back of a workpiece, it will deform the wood fibres, creating a noticeable bulge in the timber, unless you make sure the point stops at least 3mm (⅛in) short of the surface.

Screws are also specified by their nominal diameter or 'gauge'. This is never described using a precise measurement. Instead, screw gauges are specified by numbers from 0 to 20 – the higher the number, the larger the screw. A No5 screw, for example, is about 3mm (⅛in) in diameter and a No14 screw is about 6mm (¼in). For a strong fixing, select the largest possible gauge, though the nominal diameter of the screw should never exceed one tenth of the width of wood into which it is to be inserted. The table of woodscrew sizes below shows the lengths commonly available in the various gauges.

Conventional woodscrews

About 60 per cent of the overall length of a conventional woodscrew is threaded. This spiral thread bites into the wood as the screw is turned, pulling it into the timber. The plain cylindrical shank of a woodscrew acts like a dowel peg and is surmounted by a wider head that holds the workpiece or attachment in place.

Conventional woodscrew THREADS SHANK HEAD

Twin-threaded screws

A newer generation of woodscrews is made with coarse twin threads that provide a strong fixing even in chipboard or MDF. Compared with a conventional screw, more of the overall length is threaded and the shank is much narrower so there is less risk of splitting the wood. The steep pitch of the threads enables the screw to be driven quickly.

Twin-threaded screw THREAD SHANK HEAD

Choosing the length of a screw
A screw should be three times as long as the thickness of the wood it is to secure.

NOT LESS THAN 3mm

Pilot holes
To prevent the wood splitting, drill a pilot hole in the work to guide a screw. Use a drill bit that is slightly narrower than the width of the screw thread.

WOODSCREW SIZES

LENGTH		GAUGE NUMBER														
METRIC	**IMPERIAL**																
6mm	¼in	0	1	2													
9mm	⅜in		1	2	3			6		8							
12mm	½in			2	3	4	5	6	7	8							
16mm	⅝in				3	4	5	6	7	8		10					
18mm	¾in				3	4	5	6	7	8	9	10	12				
22mm	⅞in					4		6	7	8							
25mm	1in				3	4	5	6	7	8	9	10	12	14			
32mm	1¼in					4	5	6	7	8	9	10	12	14			
38mm	1½in					4		6	7	8	9	10	12	14	16		
44mm	1¾in							6	7	8	9	10	12	14	16		
50mm	2in							6	7	8	9	10	12	14	16	18	20
57mm	2¼in							6		8		10	12	14			
63mm	2½in							6		8	9	10	12	14	16		
70mm	2¾in									8		10	12	14			
75mm	3in							6		8		10	12	14	16	18	20
89mm	3½in									8		10	12	14	16		
100mm	4in									8		10	12	14	16	18	20
112mm	4½in											10	12	14			20
125mm	5in											10	12	14	16		
150mm	6in												12	14	16		

SCREW SLOTS

Screw slots (the recesses cut in screw heads) are designed to accommodate the tip of a particular type of screwdriver.

Slotted screw
Has a single groove machined across the head for a straight-tipped screwdriver.

Cross-head screw
Has intersecting slots designed to accept the tip of a matching screwdriver.

Clutch-head screw
A 'thief-proof' screw, used for fixing locks or securing valuable objects. Inserted with an ordinary straight-tipped screwdriver, but the tip rides out when the driver is turned anticlockwise.

Slotted screw **Cross-head screw** **Clutch-head screw**

SCREW HEADS

Both conventional and twin-threaded screws are made with a choice of heads.

Countersink head
A flat-topped head, which lies flush with the surface of the work. It fits into a tapered recess.

Raised head
Fits into a similar recess, but has a slightly domed top. Often used if the fixing will be exposed.

Round head
Normally used to fix flat sheet material to wood. Has an appreciably domed top, but a flat underside.

Countersink head **Raised head** **Round head**

SCREW CUPS AND COVERS

Many woodworkers regard exposed screw heads as unsightly, but there are several types of fitting that conceal screw heads or enhance their appearance.

Recessed screw cup
A durable brass collar for demountable countersunk screws. Lies flush with the surface of the wood.

Surface-mounted screw cup
Made from pressed brass. Provides a raised collar for countersunk or raised-head screws. Ideal for softwood, since it increases the bearing area beneath the screw head.

Domed cover
A plastic 'dome' that snaps over the rim of a matching screw cup to hide the head of a woodscrew.

Cross-head cover
A moulded plastic cover with spigot on the underside that provides a tight friction fit in screw slots.

Mirror-screw cover
A chromed brass dome with a threaded spigot that screws into the top of special countersunk screws designed to hold mirror glass.

Screw cups and covers
1 Recessed screw cup
2 Surface-mounted screw cup
3 Domed cover
4 Cross-head cover
5 Mirror-screw cover

NAILS

A wide variety of nails are made for the building industry but woodworkers generally use only a limited range, mainly for constructing mock-ups and nailing man-made boards. Specialized tacks and nails are required for attaching upholstery to wooden underframes. The sizes given below are those most commonly available.

Round wire nail
A strong fixing used for rough carpentry and for constructing mock-ups.
Finish: Bright steel.
Size: 25 to 150mm (1 to 6in).

Oval wire nail
A general-purpose nail with an oval-section shank which is designed to reduce the risk of splitting wood. Its head can be punched below the surface.
Finish: Bright steel.
Size: 25 to 150mm (1 to 6in).

Lost-head nail
A finishing nail that has a narrow shank. Used in making large butt joints and mitres. The head is punched below the surface.
Finish: Bright steel.
Size: 40 to 100mm ($1\frac{1}{2}$ to 4in).

Panel pin
Used for securing thin plywood or hardboard and for fixing small joints.
Finish: Bright steel.
Size: 12 to 50mm ($\frac{1}{2}$ to 2in).

Corrugated fastener
This fixing is used when making mitres and butt joints for rough framing. Placed across the joint line, the fastener is driven flush with the surface of the wood.
Finish: Bright steel.
Size: 6 to 22mm ($\frac{1}{4}$ to $\frac{7}{8}$in) deep.

Timber connector
Spiked metal plate used for securing framework joints. The plate is placed across the joint line and the spikes are driven or pressed into the wood.
Finish: Galvanized steel.
Size: 25 × 125mm (1 × 5in) to 175 × 350mm (7 × 14in).

Cut tack
This nail is designed for attaching fabric to an upholstered underframe. Its sharp point is pushed into the wood ready for driving. The wide head grips the fabric.
Finish: Blued steel.
Size: 12 to 30mm ($\frac{1}{2}$ to $1\frac{1}{4}$in).

Upholstery nail
A decorative fixing for upholstery fabric or braid.
Finish: Brass, chrome or bronze.
Size: 12mm ($\frac{1}{2}$in).

Gimp pin
These small tacks are for the 'invisible' fixing of upholstery braid.
Finish: Various colours to match braid.
Size: 9 and 13mm ($\frac{3}{8}$ and $\frac{1}{2}$in).

Corrugated fastener
Drive this fastener across a joint.

Timber connector
This fixing makes a strong butt joint.

Nails and fixings
1 Panel pins
2 Round wire nail
3 Oval wire nail
4 Lost-head nail
5 Corrugated fastener
6 Timber connector
7 Cut tacks
8 Upholstery nail
9 Gimp pins

HINGES

Well-made hinges for cabinet doors and fall flaps are relatively expensive, but cheap hardware with slack knuckles, shallow screw recesses and insubstantial leaves can be troublesome and may ruin the appearance of an otherwise handsome piece.

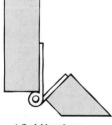

Piano hinge
A piano hinge, made in continuous 2m (6ft 6in) lengths, is used where an especially strong fitting is required. The hinge is cut to fit the workpiece.

A flush hinge is not recessed into the wood.

Butt hinge
The solid brass butt hinge is the traditional cabinet-maker's hinge. Broad-suite butt hinges – which have relatively wide leaves – are suitable for wardrobes and large cupboards. Narrow-suite hinges are used for small cabinets and boxes. Butt hinges can be used to hang inset and lay-on doors.

Lift-off hinge
Lift-off hinges are used when it is necessary on occasion to be able to remove a hinged component such as a dressing-table side mirror. A good hinge is made of solid brass, usually with a steel pin. Left-hand and right-hand versions are made.

Flush hinge
A flush hinge is used for the same purposes as a butt hinge but for lightweight doors only. This type of hinge is easy to fit as it does not have to be recessed into the wood.

Concealed cabinet hinge
Lay-on kitchen-cupboard doors are usually hung using modern concealed hinges, since these fittings are capable of adjustment so that a row of doors can be aligned accurately. Most concealed hinges have a circular boss, which fits into a hole drilled in the door, and a baseplate that screws to the cabinet. These hinges are designed to allow a door to be opened without colliding with another door butted next to it. Spring-loaded versions keep the door closed.

CABINET

DOOR

DOOR CLOSED

DOOR OPEN

Concealed cabinet hinge in use

Soss invisible hinge
Used in the same situations as a cylinder hinge but for heavier-weight doors.

Cylinder hinge
This hinge allows a door to be opened a full 180 degrees, so is especially suitable for bifold or concertina doors. It can also be used for hanging normal inset or lay-on doors. Fitted into holes drilled in the wood, cylinder hinges are invisible when the door is closed.

Cylinder-hinged bifold doors

Cranked hinge
The cranked hinge is used for fine cabinetwork with lay-on doors. The door can be swung through an arc of 180 degrees.

DOOR CLOSED

DOOR OPEN

Cranked hinge in use

Flush-fitting flap hinge
This type of adjustable hinge allows a lay-on fall flap to lie flush when open.

FLAP

Flap closed

FLAP

Flap lies flush when open

Backflap hinge
With its wide leaves recessed into the wood, the traditional solid-brass backflap hinge is used for attaching bureau fall flaps.

FLAP

Bureau flap closed

FLAP

Bureau flap open

Centre hinge
Recessed into the edge of a door, lid or fall flap, this type of hinge is practically invisible when closed.

Centre-hinged door closed

Centre-hinged door open

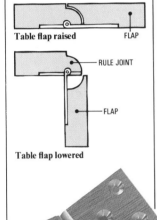

Table hinge

This is a version of the backflap hinge specially designed for mounting fold-down table flaps made with a rule joint. The hinge's longest leaf is screwed to the table flap.

Table flap raised   FLAP

RULE JOINT

FLAP

Table flap lowered

Counter hinge

A counter hinge is used for a double-thickness table top that opens up to twice its size. It is also used for fall flaps. Its dovetail-shape leaves resist the shear forces imposed on the screws.

Table top folded

Table top opened up

FITTING A BUTT HINGE

The leaves of a butt hinge can be recessed into the door and cabinet equally, with exactly half of its knuckle protruding from the face of the door.

Alternatively, the hinge can be offset so that the front edge of the cabinet's side panel appears as an unbroken line.

Lay-on doors can be hung either way.

The hinge is usually placed at a distance equal to its own length from the top or bottom edge of the door; if the door is framed, it is aligned with the edge of the rail.

CABINET   DOOR

Butt hinge recessed equally

CABINET   DOOR

Offset butt hinge

CABINET   DOOR

Butt-hinged lay-on door

Having marked the position of the hinge and the depth of the recess with a try square and marking gauge, make sawcuts across the waste (**1**). Chop along the back edge of the recess with a chisel and mallet before paring out the waste (**2**). Fit each hinge and insert the screws.

1 Make sawcuts across the waste

2 Pare out waste with a chisel

MAKING A KNUCKLE JOINT

The pivoting wooden brackets that support the folding flaps of a Pembroke table can be attached to the table's underframe with deep butt hinges, but they are not as strong as the integral wooden hinges known as 'knuckle joints'.

Marking out the joints

Using a cutting gauge set to the thickness of the wood, mark a line parallel with the end of each half of the joint on all four faces. Draw diagonals on the edges (**1**). Place the point of a compass where the diagonals cross and draw a circle with a diameter equal to the thickness of the work (**2**). To mark the knuckle chamfers, use a try square to draw lines that pass through the points where the circumference of each of the circles bisects the diagonals (**3**). Square these lines all round the work.

Pivoting wooden bracket

CHAMFER   HOLE FOR PIVOT ROD

KNUCKLES

Knuckle joint

Cutting the joint

Saw down the chamfer lines across each side of the work-pieces to meet the marked circles, then cut out the waste on the knuckle side of the kerfs (**4**). Clamp a 45-degree guide block across the work and shoulder-plane each chamfer (**5**).

Form the rounded knuckle ends with a rasp and file, then smooth them with a shaped sanding block. Divide each piece of wood into five equal parts and use a marking gauge to scribe lines around both knuckle ends (**6**). Mark the waste between the knuckles to leave three on one end and two on the other. Cut down each line on the waste side with a dovetail saw, then remove the waste with a coping saw. Shape the concave shoulders by scoop-ing out the wood between the knuckles with a chisel held bevel downwards. If possible, trim the knuckle ends with an in-cannel gouge (**7**); then clean them up with a file until you achieve a tight friction fit.

Assemble the joint and clamp the workpieces between battens to align them, then use a drill press to bore a hole through the knuckle centres to match the diameter of a steel or brass pivot rod (**8**). Tap the rod into the hole and file it flush.

1 Draw diagonals   **2 Draw circles on edges**

3 Mark knuckle chamfers   **4 Cut out the waste**

5 Plane each chamfer   **6 Mark out knuckle ends**

7 Trim knuckle ends   **8 Drill hole for rod**

KNOCK-DOWN FITTINGS

When making large-scale constructions, especially those that have to be assembled on site, you will usually find it expedient to use components or sub-assemblies joined with mechanical fixings rather than adhesive. These 'knock-down' fittings are also convenient when you want to build a workpiece that can *be dismantled at some future date for transportation. In general, knock-down fittings are designed for use with square-cut butt joints and require precisely bored holes for accurate positioning. As a result, they are most popular with woodworkers who are equipped with power tools or machinery.*

Chipboard insert
It is impossible to make a really strong fixing in the edge of chipboard using ordinary woodscrews. Threaded nylon inserts, pushed into pre-drilled holes, expand as wood-screws are driven into them to make a secure fixing.

Screw connector
Special coarse-threaded screw connectors are used to join man-made boards without the aid of inserts. The connector is driven into a pilot hole with a conventional cross-head screw-driver. The connector will form its own countersink except in hard melamine-faced boards.

Screw socket
Threaded metal sockets provide a means of bolting together solid-wood components or man-made boards. The socket is driven into a drilled hole with a screwdriver until it is either flush with or just below the surface. A machine screw fits the threaded hole in the centre of the socket.

Tee nut and bolt
The tee nut is a simple if somewhat crude fixing for joining wooden framing. Identical holes are bored through each component and the nut is tapped into one of them. The matching threaded bolt pulls the nut still further into the wood as it is tightened.

Chipboard insert

Screw connector

Screw socket

Tee nut

Block joint
This knock-down fitting consisting of two inter-connecting plastic blocks is used to join panels at right angles. With one block screwed to each component, a clamping bolt or tapered metal plate pulls the two blocks together.

Cam fitting
For a relatively neat panel fixing, use a cam fitting with a cranked nylon peg that is plugged into the edge of one component and fits into a circular boss recessed in the other. Turning a cross-head screw operates a cam in the boss, locking the components together.

Panel connector
Panel connectors are used to bolt worktops edge to edge. To fit a connector, drill a stopped hole in the underside of each panel and cut a narrow channel, link-ing the two holes, to accom-modate the connecting bolt. Turning the hexagonal nut with a spanner pulls the worktops together, and wooden locating dowels in their edges help alignment.

Cabinet connector
A cabinet connector is a neat bolt for linking adjoin-ing cupboards, kitchen cabinets or other built-in furniture. The ribbed 'nut' remains stationary while the threaded bolt is turned with a screwdriver.

Assembled block joint

Disassembled cam fitting

Panel connector

Cabinet connector

LOCKS AND CATCHES

CABINET
BOLT
DOOR

Small finely made locks are fitted to furniture and boxes. However, they do not provide total security – merely some degree of privacy, since most furniture locks can be forced. For everyday storage, a simple catch avoids the inconvenience of having to use a key.

CABINET
RECESSED LOCK
DRAWER/DOOR

INNER DOOR
OUTER DOOR

Door bolt
On a twin-door cupboard, one door is often fitted with a pair of neat surface-mounted or flush bolts and the other with a lock or catch.

Taper connector

The taper connector is a crude but effective concealed fixing for hanging wall cupboards or large-frame constructions. Since the two parts of the connector are dovetail-shaped as well as tapered, sliding one part into the other locks them securely together.

Disassembled taper connector

Bolt and barrel nut

This fixing is so strong and positive that it is used to join table and chair frames. The bolt passes through the upright or leg into the end of the rail, where it meets a threaded hole in the barrel nut. Wooden locating-dowels in the end grain keep the rail aligned correctly as the bolt is tightened up with an Allen key.

LEG
RAIL
BOLT
NUT

Bolt and barrel nut

Corner plates

Metal corner plates are used to join table rails at each corner. Flanges on each side of the plate locate in narrow grooves cut into the rails, and woodscrews hold the assembly firmly together. A hanger bolt screwed into the chamfered inner corner of the table leg passes through the hole in the plate and is tightened with a wing nut, pulling the leg against the square-cut shoulders of the rails.

LEG
RAIL
RAIL
PLATE
HANGER BOLT
WING NUT

Corner plate

Shrinkage plates

These right-angle plates are designed for attaching a solid-wood table top to its underframe while allowing for the natural shrinkage of the timber. Each plate is screwed to the inside of a rail flush with its top edge. A round-head woodscrew is driven into the top through whichever slot in the plate runs across the grain.

TABLE TOP
RAIL

Shrinkage plate

Cabinet lock

The traditional cabinet lock is used to secure drawers and cupboards. A surface-mounted lock is screwed directly to the inside of a lay-on door or drawer. When either is inset it is possible to fit a neater recessed lock that lies flush with the surface of the wood. A similar lock for boxes with lift-up lids has a striker plate with hooked pins that are engaged by the lock mechanism. Cabinet locks are often made with two keyholes at right angles to each other so they can be mounted horizontally or vertically. Left-hand and right-hand versions are available.

LOCK
STRIKER FLAP PLATE

Fall-flap lock

The fall-flap cylinder lock is designed to lie perfectly flush with the inside surface of a fold-down bureau or counter flap. The key, which can only be removed when the flap is closed, is pushed in and turned to operate a spring-loaded bolt.

Sliding-door lock

A special cylinder lock is required to secure overlapping sliding doors. The lock, which is fitted to the outer door, is operated by a push button that sends a bolt into a socket recessed in the inner door. A turn of a key withdraws the bolt.

Escutcheons

An escutcheon is a small decorative metal plate used to surround a keyhole cut in timber. Most escutcheons are pinned to the surface, but there are also small unobtrusive recessed versions.

Magnetic catch

Small encased magnets are screwed to the inside of a carcass side panel or located in a hole drilled in its edge. The magnet attracts a flat metal striker plate fixed to the cupboard door.

Ball catch

This catch comprises a spring-loaded steel ball trapped in a cylindrical brass case that is inserted in the edge of a cupboard door. When the door is closed the ball springs into a recess in a metal striker plate screwed to the carcass.

Magnetic touch latch

A cupboard fitted with a touch latch doesn't need a handle. Pressure on the door operates a spring that pushes the door open.

Magnetic catch

CABINET
CATCH
DOOR

CABINET
DOOR
CATCH

Ball catch

Surface-mounted ball catch

CABINET
TOUCH LATCH
DOOR

Magnetic touch latch

STAYS AND HANDLES

A stay is a mechanism designed primarily to support a fall-flap in a horizontal position, taking the strain off the hinges. However, stays are also used to stop a hinged door opening more than 90 degrees and to support chest lids or high-level lift-up doors.

Handles are essentially functional pieces of hardware, but they have always been used as decorative features to enhance the appearance of drawers and cabinets. Select an appropriate size and shape to suit the style and scale of your workpiece.

Cabinet handle
The classic cabinet handle is suspended from two pivots, one at each end. It is available in a variety of forms, including the distinctive swan-neck handle and the stronger and even more decorative plate handle.

Drop handle
A single teardrop-shaped or decorative finger grip is suspended from the centre of a drop handle. A drop handle is often fitted in the centre of a small drawer.

Ring pull
This is similar in construction to a drop handle, but the ring hangs from the top of a backing plate.

Door or drawer knob
Traditional rounded door or drawer knobs are made in wood, metal and ceramic in a variety of sizes to suit furniture ranging from wardrobes to collector's cabinets. The method of attachment may be a screw projecting from the back of the knob or, alternatively, an ordinary woodscrew or a machine screw passed through the cabinet front into the knob.

Flush handle
A pivoted ring or D-shaped handle lies flush with a thick solid-brass backing plate, which is recessed into the drawer front and fixed with countersunk woodscrews.

Drawer pull
One-piece cupped drawer pulls were originally used on military chests. They serve as strong screw-fixed handles for cupboards and chests of drawers.

D-handle
These slim metal, plastic or wooden handles suit simple modern-style furniture. They are invariably made with threaded inserts for machine-screw attachment.

Sliding-door handle
Circular or rectangular recessed finger grips are made for gluing into overlapping sliding doors.

Joint stay

Sliding stay

Friction stay

Door stay

Lift-up door stay

Fall-flap stays
The simplest fall-flap stay is screw-fixed at both ends and has a riveted joint approximately halfway along the arm that breaks to allow the stay to fold back into the cabinet. A better-quality version slides silently on a bar fixed either horizontally or vertically on the inside of the cabinet. A friction stay controls the movement of the flap so that it falls slowly and smoothly under its own weight. A small turnscrew regulates the amount of friction and consequently the rate at which the flap falls.

Door stay
A door stay prevents a cupboard door being ripped off its hinges or opened too far by restricting its swing to a maximum of 90 degrees. A rigid metal arm, screwed to the door, slides through a pivoting nylon fixing attached to the cabinet.

Lift-up-door stays
Stays for lift-up doors or lids lock automatically when the door or lid is raised, and are released for closure by lifting it slightly before allowing it to fall. Friction stays that prevent doors or lids slamming shut are also available.

Handles
1 Swan-neck cabinet handle
2 Plate handle
3 Ring pull
4 Drop handles
5 Drawer pull
6 Knobs
7 Flush handle
8 D-handles
9 Sliding-door handle

GLOSSARY OF TERMS

A

Air drying
A method for seasoning timber that permits covered stacks of sawn wood to dry naturally in the open air.

Alloy
A mixture of two or more metals to create a composition with specific properties.

Animal glue
A protein-based wood glue made from animal skins and bone.

Anthropometry
The comparative study of the dimensions of the human body.

Arc
Part of an unbroken curved line as drawn by a compass.

Arris
The sharp edge where two surfaces meet at an angle.

Axis
The imaginary line about which an object such as a chair rail is symmetrical.

B

Backing grade
The category of cheaper veneers that are glued to the back of a board in order to balance better-quality veneers glued to the front face.

Banding
A plain or patterned strip of veneer used to make decorative borders.

Barefaced
The description of a joint that has one shoulder only.

Batten
A strip of wood.

Bead
A rounded convex shape turned on a lathe. *or* A fine moulded strip of wood, also known as beading.

Bevel
A surface that meets another at an angle other than a right angle. *or* To cut such surfaces. *See also* chamfer.

Bifold door
A type of sliding door made from two hinged panels that fold as the door is slid sideways.

Blank
A piece of wood roughly cut to size ready for turning on a lathe.

Bleed
A process whereby a substance such as natural wood resin permeates and stains the surface of a subsequent coating.

Blister
A small raised area of veneer resulting from insufficient glue at that point.

Blockboard
A man-made building board with a core of approximately square-section solid-wood strips sandwiched between thin plywood sheets. *See also* laminboard.

Bore
To drill a hole.

Bosting in
Carving roughly to shape.

Bowed
Twisted.

Bruise
To make a dent in timber by striking it with a hard object such as a hammer.

Burl
See burr

Burr
A warty growth on the trunk of a tree. When sliced it produces speckled burr veneer.
or An extremely thin strip of metal left along the cutting edge of a blade after honing or grinding.

Button
A wooden device screwed to the underside of a table top in order to fix it to an underframe.

C

Cabinet-maker
A manufacturer of good-quality furniture.

Cabriole leg
A furniture leg developed in the 18th century that is made with an upper convex curve that descends, tapering, to a concave curve.

Calibrated
Marked out with one or more scales of measurement.

Carpenter
A woodworker but not necessarily one who specializes in fine work.

Case-hardened
A term used to describe unevenly seasoned timber with a moisture content that varies throughout its thickness.

Catalyst
A substance that stimulates or increases the rate of a chemical reaction.

GLOSSARY OF TERMS

Cauls
Sheets of wood or metal used to press veneer onto groundwork.

Chamfer
A 45-degree bevel along the edge of a piece of wood or board. *or* To cut such bevels.

Chattering
The noise caused by a work-piece vibrating.

Checks
Splits in timber caused by uneven seasoning. *See also* knife checks.

Chipboard
A mat of small particles of wood and glue compressed into a flat building board.

Claw
A split hammer peen used to grip a nail by its head and lever it out of a piece of wood.

Clear timber
Good-quality wood that is free from defects.

Closed-coat
A term used to describe sand-paper that has abrasive par-ticles packed closely together.

Coarse-textured
See open grain.

Collet
A tapered sleeve made in two or more segments that grips the shaft of a cutter.

Comb-grain
Another term for quarter-sawn.

Compound mitre
A mitre that is angled in two planes.

Concave
Curving inwards.

Contact glue
An adhesive that bonds to itself without the aid of cramps when two previously glued surfaces are brought together.

Convex
Curving outwards.

Core
The central layer of plies, particles or wooden strips in a man-made board.

Counterbore
To cut a hole that permits the head of a bolt or screw to lie below the surface of a piece of wood. *or* The hole itself.

Cove
A concave moulding along the edge of a workpiece. *or* Another term for hollow.

Crest rail
The top rail forming part of the back rest of a chair.

Cross-banding
Strips of veneer cut across the grain and used as decorative borders.

Crosscutting
Sawing across the grain.

Cross grain
Grain that deviates from the main axis of a workpiece or tree.

Crotch figure
Another term for curl figure.

Crown-cut
A term used to describe veneer that has been tangentially sliced from a log, producing oval or curved grain patterns.

Cup
To bend as a result of shrink-age – specifically across the width of a piece of wood.

Cure
To set as a result of chemical reaction.

Curl figure
The grain pattern on wood that has been cut from that part of a tree where a branch joins the main stem or trunk.

Curly figure
See curly grain.

Curly grain
Wood grain exhibiting an irregular wavy pattern.

Curtaining
An undulating ridge of sagging paintwork resembling the shape of a draped curtain.

D

Dimension stock
Prepared timber cut to standard sizes.

Double insulated
A power tool with a non-conductive plastic casing that protects the user from electric shock is said to be double insulated.

Dressed stock
Another term for dimension stock.

Dust panel
A horizontally mounted panel that protects the contents of a drawer from the dust created by the drawer above rubbing on its runners.

E

Earlywood
That part of a tree's annual growth rings that is laid down in the early part of the growing season.

Edge-grain
Another term for quarter-sawn.

End grain
The surface of wood exposed after cutting across the fibres.

Ergonomics
The study of the relationship between the average human body (especially that of a worker or machine operative) and its environment.

Escutcheon
The metal lining of a keyhole or a protective plate that surrounds it.

F

Face edge
The surface planed square to the face side and from which other dimensions and angles are measured.

Face quality
A term used to describe better-quality veneers that are used to cover the visible surfaces of a workpiece.

Face side
The flat planed surface from which all other dimensions and angles are measured.

Feed
To push a workpiece in a con-trolled manner towards a moving blade or cutter.

Fence
An adjustable guide to keep the cutting edge of a tool a set distance from the edge of a workpiece.

Ferrule
A metal collar that reinforces the wood where the tang of a chisel or other handtool enters the handle.

Fibreboards
A range of building boards made from reconstituted wood fibres.

Fielded panel
A solid-wood panel with edges bevelled to fit grooves in a frame.

Figure
Another term for grain pattern.

Fillet
A narrow strip of timber.

Flat-grain
Another term for plain-sawn.

Flat-sawn
Another term for plain-sawn.

Flat sliced
A term used to describe a narrow sheet of veneer that has been cut from part of a log with a knife.

Flitches
Pieces of wood sawn from a log for slicing into veneers. *or* The bundle of sliced veneers.

Flute
A rounded concave groove.

Flux
A substance used to clean the surfaces of metal prior to soldering.

Fox wedging
A jointing procedure where wooden wedges are used to spread a tenon in a stopped mortise.

Front elevation
A scale drawing showing the front view of a workpiece.

G

Grain
The general direction or arrangement of the fibrous materials of wood.

Gravity guard
A blade or cutter guard that is raised by the passage of the work, then drops back under its own weight.

Green wood
Newly cut timber that has not been seasoned.

Groove
A long narrow channel cut in the direction of the grain. *or* To cut such channels.

Groundwork
The backing material to which veneer is glued.

Gullet
The space between saw teeth.

H

Hardwood
Wood cut from broadleaved, mostly deciduous, trees which belong to the botanical group Angiospermae.

Haunch
The shortened part of a tenon that prevents it twisting out of line with the upright member at a corner of a frame.

Heartwood
The mature wood that forms the spine of a tree.

Hollow-ground
A term used to describe circular-saw blades that are reduced in thickness towards their centres.

Hollows
Concave shapes turned on a lathe.

Hone
To produce the final cutting edge on a blade or cutter by rubbing it on or with an abrasive stone.

GLOSSARY OF TERMS

Horn
Excess waste wood left on a workpiece to support the end of a mortise while the joint is being cut. The horn is sawn off after the joint is assembled.

Housing
A groove cut across the grain.

I

In-cannel
A term used to describe a gouge with a bevel ground on the inside of the blade.

Infeed
A term used to describe that part of a machine's worktable that is in front of the blade or cutter.

Inlay
To insert pieces of wood or metal into prepared recesses so that the material lies flush with the surrounding surfaces. *or* The piece of material itself.

In wind
See winding

Isometric drawing
A scale drawing with its main axes equally inclined, but giving an impression of perspective.

J

Jig
A device used to hold a workpiece or tool so that an operation can be repeated accurately.

Joiner
A woodworker who specializes in the construction of building components such as windows, doors and stairs.

K

Kerf
The slot cut by a saw.

Kickback
The action of a workpiece being thrown towards a machinist by a moving blade or cutter. *or* The action of a power tool when it jumps backwards as a result of its blade or cutter jamming.

Kicker
A strip of wood fixed above a drawer's side to prevent it tipping upwards as the drawer is withdrawn.

Kiln drying
A method for seasoning timber using a mixture of hot air and steam.

Knife checks
Splits across veneer caused by poorly adjusted veneer-slicing equipment.

Knock-down fittings
Mechanical devices for joining components, especially those that may have to be dismantled at a future date.

Knotting
A shellac-based sealer used to coat resinous knots that would stain subsequent finishes.

Knuckle
The cylindrical part of a hinge to which the leaves are attached and through which the pin passes.

L

Laminate
A component made from thin strips of wood glued together. *or* To glue strips together to form a component.

Laminboard
A man-made building board with a core of narrow strips of wood glued together and sandwiched between thin plywood sheets. *See also* blockboard.

Latewood
That part of a tree's annual growth ring that is laid down in the latter part of the growing season.

Laying off
The action of finishing an application of paint or varnish using upward brush strokes.

Lipping
A protective strip of solid wood applied to the edge of a man-made-board panel or table top.

Long grain
Grain that is aligned with the main axis of a workpiece. *See also* short grain.

Lopers
Rails that are pulled from a cabinet in order to support a fall flap.

M

Marquetry
The process of laying relatively small pieces of veneer to make decorative patterns or pictures. *See also* parquetry.

Mitre
A joint formed between two pieces of wood by cutting bevels of equal angles (usually 45 degrees) at the ends of both pieces. *or* To cut the joint.

Mock-up
A temporary construction made from scrap materials in order to test a design.

Modesty board
A deep rail fixed between the two end frames of a desk. Its original purpose was to conceal the legs of a seated female.

Mortise
A rectangular recess cut in timber to receive a matching tongue or tenon.

Muntin
The central vertical member of a frame-and-panel door. *or* A grooved strip of wood that divides and supports the two sections of a wide drawer bottom.

O

Offcut
Waste wood cut from a workpiece.

Open-coat
A term used to describe sandpaper that has widely spaced abrasive particles.

Open grain
A term used to describe ring-porous wood with large pores. Also known as coarse-textured.

Out-cannel
A term used to describe a gouge with a bevel ground on the outside of the blade.

Outfeed
A term used to describe that part of a machine's worktable that is behind the blade or cutter.

Oxidize
To form a layer of metal oxide as in rusting.

P

Pare
To remove fine shavings with a chisel.

Parquetry
A similar process to marquetry but using veneers cut into geometric shapes to make decorative patterns.

Particle boards
Building boards made from small chips or flakes of wood bonded together with glue under pressure.

Patina
The colour and texture that a material such as wood or metal acquires as a result of a natural aging process.

Pawls
Pivoted pointed levers designed to grip a workpiece as soon as it is thrown back by a moving blade or cutter.

PEG
Polyethylene glycol – a stabilizing agent used in place of conventional seasoning processes to treat green timber.

Photosynthesis
A natural process that takes place when energy in the form of light is absorbed by chlorophyll, producing the nutrients on which plants live.

Pilaster
A shallow rectangular column of wood attached to the face of a cabinet.

Pilot hole
A small-diameter hole drilled prior to the insertion of a woodscrew to act as a guide for its thread.

Plain-sawn
A term used to describe a piece of wood with growth rings that meet the faces of the board at angles of less than 45 degrees. *See also* rift-sawn.

Plan A scale drawing showing the top view of a workpiece.

Plan elevation
Another term for plan.

Plywood
A building board made by bonding a number of wood veneers together under pressure.

Pocket-screw
To bore a hole at an angle through the inside face of a rail in order to insert a top-fixing screw.

Pull-over solution
A mixture of thinners used to partially dissolve a recently applied wood finish in order to shine it.

Pumice
A light volcanic rock that is ground to a fine abrasive powder and used to modify the texture of a wood finish.

Push stick
A notched batten used to feed a workpiece into a blade or cutter.

Q

Quarter-sawn
A term used to describe a piece of wood with growth rings at not less than 45 degrees to the faces of the board. *See also* rift-sawn.

GLOSSARY OF TERMS

R

Rack
To distort a frame or carcass by applying sideways pressure.

Ratchet
A device that permits motion in one direction only.

Rebate
A stepped recess along the edge of a workpiece, usually as part of a joint. *or* To cut such recesses.

Relief carving
A type of carving where the background is cut away leaving a motif projecting from the surrounding area.

Rift-sawn
A term used to describe a piece of wood with growth rings that meet the faces of the board at angles of more than 30 degrees but at less than 60 degrees.

Ripsawing
Cutting parallel to the grain.

Rotary-cut
A term used to describe a continuous sheet of veneer peeled from a log by turning it against a stationary knife.

Rottenstone
An abrasive powder similar to pumice but ground even finer.

Rubber
A padded cloth used to apply polish, stain or varnish.

Runners
Strips of wood that support a drawer and upon which it slides.

S

Sapwood
New wood surrounding the denser heartwood.

Sawing peg
A notched plate of metal or wood that is clamped or screwed to a bench so that the notch overhangs the edge. It is used to support work being cut with a piercing saw or fret saw.

Scribe
To mark with a pointed tool. *or* To mark and shape the edge of a workpiece so that it will fit exactly against another surface such as a wall or ceiling.

Seasoning
Reducing the moisture content of timber.

Secret haunch
Another term for sloping haunch.

Section
A scale drawing that shows a view of a workpiece as if it had been cut through.

Set
To bend saw teeth to the right and left of the blade in order to cut a kerf wider than the blade itself.

Setting in
The fine shaping of carved work.

Shank
The cylindrical shaft of a screw or nail. *or* The shaft of a drill or cutter.

Shear force
The force applied to a structure by a transverse load.

Shellac
A secretion of the lac insect used to manufacture French polish.

Sherardized
Coated with zinc.

Shoe
The adjustable jaw of a G-cramp.

Shoot
To plane accurately using a finely set plane.

Short grain
A term used to describe where the general direction of wood fibres lies across a narrow section of timber.

Shoulder
The squared end of a workpiece on one or both sides of a tenon or tongue.

Side elevation
A scale drawing showing the side view of a workpiece.

Skiver
Thin leather prepared for gluing to a desk or table top.

Slash-sawn
Another term for plain-sawn.

Sloping haunch
A tenon haunch cut at an angle so that it is invisible when the joint is assembled.

Softening
Pieces of scrap wood used to protect workpieces from metal vice or cramp jaws.

Softwood
Wood cut from coniferous trees which belong to the botanical group Gymnospermae.

Splitting out
When a cutter or drill breaks through the bottom or back of a workpiece.

Springwood
Another term for earlywood.

Stile
A vertical side member of a frame-and-panel door.

Stop
A strip of wood against which a drawer front or door comes to rest when it is closed.

Stopped mortise
A mortise that does not pass right through a piece of wood.

Straight grain
Grain that aligns with the main axis of a workpiece or tree.

Striker plate
The metal plate against which a latch or lock comes to rest.

Stringing
Fine strips of wood used to divide areas of veneer.

Strop
To produce a razor-sharp cutting edge by rubbing it on a strip of leather. *or* The strip of leather itself.

Stub mortise
Another term for stopped mortise.

Stub tenon
A short tenon that does not pass right through a piece of wood.

Summerwood
Another term for latewood.

Sweep
A term used to describe the curved section of a carving gouge.

Swing
The maximum diameter of a workpiece that can be turned over a lathe bed.

T

Tack rag
A cloth impregnated with resin for picking up loose dust. Also known as a tacky rag.

Tang
The pointed end of a chisel or file that is driven into the handle.

Tangentially cut
Another term for plain-sawn.

Template
A cut-out pattern to help shape a workpiece accurately.

Tenon
A projecting tongue on the end of a piece of wood which fits in a corresponding mortise.

Thermoplastic
A term used to describe a material that can be resoftened with heat.

Thermosetting
A term used to describe a material that cannot be resoftened with heat once it has set hard.

Thinner
A substance used to reduce the consistency of paint, varnish or polish.

Thixotropic
A property of some paints which have a jelly-like consistency until stirred or applied, at which point they become liquified.

Throat
The clearance between a blade of a machine such as a fret saw and its frame. *or* The outlet for shavings above the mouth in a plane's sole.

Tongue
The projecting ridge cut along the edge of a board which fits into a corresponding groove in another board. *or* A plywood strip that fits in grooves cut in two boards to be joined.

Tusk tenon
A wedged through tenon used to join floor joists. An additional stub tenon (the tusk) below the through tenon provides extra support.

V

Veneer
A thin slice of wood used as a surface covering on a less expensive material such as a man-made board.

Vertical grain
Another term for quarter-sawn.

Viscosity
The extent to which a fluid resists the tendency to flow.

W

Waney edge
The natural wavy edge of a plank. It may still be covered by tree bark.

Wavy grain
A term used to describe the even wave-like grain pattern on wood cut from a tree with an undulating cell structure.

Wild grain
Irregular grain that changes direction, making it difficult to work.

Winding
A warped or twisted board is said to be winding or in wind.

Y

Yacht varnish
An exterior-grade varnish especially suitable for coastal climates.

INDEX

315